D1266239

CATEGORIES AND PROCESSES
IN LANGUAGE ACQUISITION

Categories and Processes in Language Acquisition

Edited by

Yonata Levy
Izchak M. Schlesinger
Hebrew University of Jerusalem

Martin D. S. Braine
New York University

LEA LAWRENCE ERLBAUM ASSOCIATES, PUBLISHERS
1988   Hillsdale, New Jersey   Hove and London

Lawrence Erlbaum Associates, Inc., Publishers
365 Broadway
Hillsdale, New Jersey 07642

Library of Congress Cataloging-in-Publication Data

Categories and processes in language acquisition.

  Includes bibliographies and indexes.
  1. Language acquisition.   I. Levy, Yonata.
II. Schlesinger, I. M.   III. Braine, Martin D. S.
P118.C38   1988   401'.9   88-3991
ISBN 0-8058-0151-0

Printed in the United States of America
10 9 8 7 6 5 4 3 2 1

Contents

7. Learning Syntax and Meanings Through Optimization and Distributional Analysis

J. Gerard Wolff

8. Modeling the Acquisition of Linguistic Structure

Martin D. S. Braine

Preface

During the academic year 1982–1983 a study group met at the Institute for Advanced Studies at the Hebrew University of Jerusalem to discuss problems in native language acquisition. In spite of divergent theoretical orientations, we found we had enough in common to interact fruitfully. Some of the contributors decided to put together a volume that would capture part of this interaction and would be devoted to certain central issues in the theory of language acquisition. Gerard Wolff was invited to contribute a chapter so as to provide for a more rounded presentation.

We take this opportunity to express our gratitude to the Institute, its Director at the time, Professor A. Dvoretsky, and the entire staff, who did their utmost to make our stay at the Institute pleasurable and productive. We are grateful for the Institute's financial support for some of the editorial work on this volume. Partial support was also given by the Institute for Human Development, the Hebrew University of Jerusalem, which is highly appreciated.

We are indebted to Moshe Anisfeld and to Mazal Cohen, who gave generously of their time to advise us on some important matters.

Y. L.
I. M. S.
M. D. S. B.

Introduction

Martin D. S. Braine
New York University

Understanding how a child acquires his or her native tongue is one of the major unsolved mysteries of Psychology, notwithstanding the fact that it has been the target of a huge amount of attention for 25 years. Quantities of facts about language development—facts that tell small but pertinent stories—have been discovered, and the well of interesting new data has certainly not run dry. However, it has turned out that the knowledge we have gained constrains our theories only a little. In trying to explain the mystery we permit ourselves a wondrous variety of theoretical ideas[1]—wondrous, that is, if one views the scientific spectacle like the visitor to an art gallery, intrigued by the phantasmagoria of systems that can be constructed around the developmental detail; discouraging, rather, if one is a participant researcher seeking the one picture that represents the reality.

However, there has certainly been progress, in theory as well as in description. Both the researcher in the business and any dispassionate onlooker who has stayed watching for a quarter century would undoubtedly attest that we understand enormously more than we did when we started. It is probably not possible to leap out of our heritage of gradual cumulative work to nearly complete understanding in one great jump. One who did so would probably not be recognized as having succeeded. For some of us share the tastes of some art gallery visitors who like to behold complexity, and would undoubtedly play the role of the Ptolemeians who disagreed with Copernicus and Galileo for data-driven reasons. In any case, this book continues the cumulative heritage and presents some new

[1]Anderson (1983), Berwick (1985), Bruner (1983), MacWhinney (1978), Pinker (1984), Snow (1979), and Wexler and Culicover (1980) illustrate the variety.

1

facts—significant facts we believe—blended with much analysis and theory, the whole weighted on the theory side, but for the most part theory that stays in touch with what has been discovered about the development of language.

The book grew out of work done by the participants of a language-acquisition research group that spent the year 1982–83 at the Institute for Advanced Studies of the Hebrew University of Jerusalem. Most of the chapters started off as papers delivered and discussed that year at the Institute. All have been extensively developed and revised since their origins.

As our discussions and interchanges progressed that year, we found that, despite our many differences, we nevertheless shared a number of important concerns and perspectives—on topics, on methods, and on how language acquisition is to be explained. These commonalities gave the group a certain unity and together they distinguish the volume from other works on language development.

First of all, a cross-linguistic perspective fell comfortably together with an interest in Hebrew as a data source. Cross-linguistic comparisons of development can reveal what is common to children and to language learning environments, and inform about the child's learning mechanism by uncovering the variety of structures children are able to acquire. Because of the location, there were people in the research group who worked on Hebrew, there was a psychologically sophisticated audience that understood it, and others who found this an occasion to become interested or to put to some purpose their interest in this language and the general problems it raises. Hebrew is the source of the data discussed in half the chapters, and several chapters compare and integrate information about the development of Hebrew and English. As I describe later, Hebrew has a number of properties that provide for interesting contrasts with English, and thus bring out resources for language learning that children have that would not be apparent from observing English alone. An important case in point is the demonstrably great early sensitivity to shared phonological properties of words, documented especially in Levy's chapter, which would not be expected from the literature on the acquisition of English. Clearly, as Levy points out, even very young children are sensitive to morphophonological patterns in the input that play no obvious role in communicating the intended message.

A second commonality is a belief in the usefulness of focusing, at this stage in our ability to explain language learning, on elementary rather than complex syntax—on how children get into language, on word class phenomena, and on the acquisition of relational categories. (For want of a better term, I use the label "relational category" to refer both to categories like "subject," "object," "adverbial phrase," and the like, and also to caselike or thematic categories like "actor" [or "agent"], "patient," "experiencer," "instrument," etc.) Together, relational categories and word classes are the two crucial types of linguistic category to be found in simple sentences. Indeed, a theory that accounts for both word class phenomena and relational categories would amount to a nearly complete acquisition model for simple declarative and imperative sentences (or, more technically, sentences without embedded S-nodes). Thus, a theory that explains elementary syntax explains most of the development of the early years (pronunciation apart), whereas an explanation of some facet of complex late-developing syntax must remain highly speculative in the absence of an understanding of earlier developments.

The third and final commonality is a metatheoretical perspective that I shall call "methodological empiricism." This is in contrast both with nativism and with naive empiricism (the belief that the innate contribution to language acquisition is small). Thus, like the nativist, the methodological empiricist recognizes that in constructing a model of language learning, if the model is to acquire anything at all one has to take some mechanisms and concepts as primitive, i.e., as available to the child at the outset of learning and not explained by the model. However, methodological empiricism takes such primitives as a challenge to further analysis instead of being content to postulate them as innate. Thus, the perspective consists in the belief that the developmental psycholinguist should not be satisfied merely to postulate innate concepts and abilities, but has the scientific responsibility to analyse their components and mechanisms. Anything that a psycholinguist might want to take as innate has a long and complex developmental history. It may have a starting point in genes, but genes are merely complicated biochemicals; the causal chain that begins with genes and ends with some feature of language two or more years later must ultimately be unraveled by some combination of sciences. It is the responsibility of developmental psychologists to perform their share of this analysis—to do whatever cognitive and behavioral analyses are necessary so that the definition of what is innate is put in a form that successor sciences (for instance, embryology, developmental neuropsychology) can handle. Thus, an innateness claim is viewed as involving a promissory note—a promise that someone in one's discipline will carry out the necessary analysis. This inevitably results in a reluctance to postulate innate primitives for which the promissory note seems likely to be difficult to redeem.

This perspective dictates a preference for primitives that take the form of mechanisms, and a reluctance to postulate innate concepts. Learning mechanisms, perhaps of more than one kind, must be built into the infant's maturing nervous system—there is no way that developmental psychology can evade that assumption. But we see no reason to assume that such mechanisms are simple, and in particular, no reason to believe that they are confined to the uncomplicated associative learning devices assumed by the classical empiricist philosophers. Innate concepts, however, are problematic unless they are perceptual, motoric, or affective categories that it is reasonable to suppose are given by innate sensory, motor, or affective processing systems. The problem for the language-acquisition theorist is, of course, that there is no way of explaining language learning without taking some concepts as primitives—concepts, moreover, that are unlikely to be reducible to perceptual or motor categories, and which we cannot now see a way of accounting for as the output of learning mechanisms. Thus, the language-acquisition theorist has no option but to accept some conceptual primitives; he or she can only seek to minimize their number and their complexity. For the methodological empiricist, a crucial theoretical question is to determine what the minimum set of conceptual primitives is whose availability to the child enables the acquisition of linguistic structure. These define our promissory notes, the concepts that require a reductive analysis.

In saying that the contributors shared this perspective, I certainly do not mean to imply that all would subscribe to everything I have just said. Nevertheless, the perspective is manifest in the chapters in a variety of ways. It is manifest in the emphasis on pragmatics in the chapter of Ninio and Snow. It is manifest in the emphasis on the child's use of morphophonologically marked categories in some papers, especially that of Levy. Such categories are among those that are least problematic for an empiricist because of their close relation to articulatory and auditory systems, and evidence for their early role in syntax acquisition is congenial to an empiricist perspective. This perspective also motivates the concern with mechanisms of distributional learning that are the main focus of Wolff's paper and mine, and somewhat less directly the focus of other papers, e.g., those of Maratsos and Schlesinger. Among these papers, Wolff's takes perhaps the most extreme empiricist position: He postulates no problematic concepts as primitives at all, only mechanisms and sensory categories. (However, it seems to me that in the aspects of linguistic structure where conceptual primitives are most needed his theory tends to be most sketchy.) In general, the conceptual primitives we find ourselves unable to avoid are the complementary notions of predicate and argument, and some basis for thematic or caselike categories. The predicate-argument distinction is discussed at some length in my chapter, and is assumed as primitive in several others. Elsewhere (Braine, 1987) I argue that it is the only conceptual primitive needed to explain word classes. With respect to thematic or caselike categories, it is the main burden of Schlesinger's paper to propose an analysis of how such categories might be acquired; however, his proposal must still postulate some sort of "similarity space" as primitive, which would define the dimensions along which his mechanism of "semantic assimilation" takes place. His proposal could thus be regarded as a first step in a developmental analysis of caselike categories.

As the title indicates, the book is about the acquisition of linguistic categories, and about the child's learning processes. The categories of concern are those that are manifest in structure, i.e., other than simply as word meanings. The book begins with a chapter on the earliest nonlexical categories for which there is evidence. Then there are several chapters on word classes and the acquisition of relational categories, followed by papers that discuss models of the child's learning mechanism. Finally, there is an integrative concluding chapter by two of the editors.

In the first chapter, Ninio and Snow investigate the kinds of categories manifest at the late one-word stage and in the first word combinations. Citing data from both Hebrew and English, they elegantly show that many gambits at the one-word stage express particular speech acts, and likewise that much of the simple syntax of early word combinations reflects the speech act performed by the utterance. In both cases, they argue, prior work has overlooked the reflection of the speech act, and in fact, when it has been noted, it has been misinterpreted as semantic rather than pragmatic.

A highly salient feature of natural languages is that they have word classes—nouns and verbs, and often also, subclasses of these like genders, declensions, and conjugations. The next group of papers addresses developmental issues that arise from this fact. Word class phenomena are an essential part of the structure of the simplest kinds of sentences spoken by adults, making such phenomena a key problem for students of language acquisition. For although a satisfactory acquisition theory must account for much much more than the acquisition of word classes, nevertheless a failure to explicate word class phenomena is a failure to get past one of the early hurdles in the model-building stakes. And the lack of an agreed theory of word classes says how little we understand the deeper problems of language acquisition.

Although all languages have Noun and Verb, at least as syntactic categories, languages vary enormously in *how* they have word classes. Moreover, Hebrew, which is the focus of two of the chapters that discuss word classes, differs sharply from English and other studied languages in ways that can provide interesting contrastive data for the acquisition theorist. For example, one way that languages differ is in the extent to which the main word classes are subdivided into marked subclasses like genders, declensions, and conjugations. Unlike English, but like Indo-European languages such as French and Spanish, Hebrew has gender subclasses of nouns; it also has verb subclasses (*binyanim*) that bear some resemblance to the conjugations of languages like Latin and Russian, but which also differ from these in interesting ways that are discussed by Berman and Levy.

Another and perhaps more basic dimension of difference among languages with respect to word classes is that languages vary in the extent to which words are marked in the lexicon for their class, and in the extent to which one can know the class of a word from hearing the surface (pronounced) form of it in isolation. In these respects, Chinese is close to one extreme and Hebrew to the other, with English in between. Thus, in English, there are a number of words (e.g., *hit*, *dream*) that can appear as either noun or verb in sentences; in Chinese, more words can so appear; in Hebrew, no word can. For most English words one cannot tell from the pronunciation of the word in isolation to which part of speech it belongs. In Chinese this same property is even more salient because it is true of a higher fraction of its words than of English words. But in Hebrew, a word's pronunciation almost always betrays its part of speech category. On the other hand, in this same dimension, Hebrew has a formal property that may be more like Chinese than English. That is, as the basic building blocks of its vocabulary, Hebrew has root morphemes that do not belong to any particular part of speech. However, quite unlike Chinese, these morphemes are discontinuous triads of consonants that are totally unpronounceable in isolation, and the "meaning" these roots have is never concisely definable in words. For instance, a meaning that has something to do with telling a story is associated with the triad *s-p/f-r;* the triad is not pronounceable in isolation, but it appears in the nouns *sipur* 'story' and *sefer* 'book', in the verb *lesaper* 'tell', and in the adjective *sifruti* 'literary'. Even if they did not know any of these words, a Hebrew speaker could know from their form that *sipur* and *sefer* had to be nouns, *lesaper* a verb, and *sifruti* an adjective.

In this group of papers Maratsos sets the stage with a succinct and very readable summary of the basic problem of accounting for acquisition of word classes, and of his present views on it (cf. Maratsos, 1982; Maratsos & Chalkley, 1980). He explains why he is sceptical that notional categories (e.g., actions as the basis of verbs, things of nouns) play a role, and he argues that young children must be assumed to be quite sensitive to the formal kinds of regularities that mark word classes, whose nature he sketches.

Berman's chapter is a detailed review of the acquisition of word class distinctions with a focus on the conceptual sequence in which children confront the different kinds of structural problems posed by word classes, and on the kinds of solutions they come up with. Her review summarizes much data of her own and others on the development of word class phenomena in Hebrew, and compares this with available information for English and several other languages. She finds that as children acquire a language there is a regular succession in the kinds of features that they notice and the kinds of structures they internalize. She shows that this succession conforms to a descriptive model previously found to fit the acquisition of other aspects of syntax than word classes.

Levy is also concerned with the development of Hebrew noun and verb morphology, especially at early stages of development. Her purpose is to redress an imbalance in the conclusions in much current literature about the aspects of language to which young children are sensitive. A common view is that in the early stages of syntactic development children attend primarily to meaning communicated, i.e., to semantic and pragmatic aspects of language and to the lexical and syntactic devices (primarily morpheme order) used to express the meaning. This view is no doubt due largely to the disproportionate representation of English in available data; however, a frequent theoretical emphasis that equates learning language and learning to communicate may also play a role. Against this view, the Hebrew data summarized by Levy show that at surprisingly early stages of development children can and do register formal morphophonological patterns that play little or no role in communicating meaning. Thus, the early

English data tell an incomplete story: children attend to all salient patterns, not just to those most relevant to meaning.

Ninio's theoretical analysis is concerned with both word classes and relational categories in early child language. She discusses whether young children can be credited with abstract categories of these sorts, and suggests that the question itself is ill-defined because of unclarities in the transfer of concepts from linguistics to developmental psychology. Her own analysis leads her to a lexicalist position according to which much of syntax acquisition consists in learning the argument (NP) configurations associated with particular predicate terms (e.g., verbs). She ultimately proposes that the abstractness of formal categories is a by-product of hierarchical structure, i.e., of learning to use predicate-argument configurations as predicates or as arguments.

The last three papers (prior to the concluding chapter) directly address the mechanism of learning—the acquisition process itself. Schlesinger's paper provides a possible process by which relational categories might be acquired. Various writers (e.g., Schlesinger, 1971, and Braine & Wells, 1978, among others) have largely taken it for granted that caselike or thematic notions are cognitively available to the child prior to language, and used to organize the perception of events into actors, things acted upon, instruments, used, etc. In recent years, however, Schlesinger (1979) has put forth evidence and arguments, some of which he summarizes here, to show that this assumption is too simple: Such categories shade into each other—there is no sharp conceptual boundary, for instance, between Agent and Experiencer, between Agent and Instrument, and between Instrument and Comitative—and different languages place boundaries at different points on these continua. Thus, to a substantial extent such categories must be learned, or at least considerably refined, in the course of the child's contact with the language. One cannot, therefore, regard syntax learning as involving the acquisition of a mapping of such categories on to sentence positions without also providing some account of the formation of the categories themselves. Schlesinger's chapter proposes a process, semantic assimilation, to account for such categories, a process that could perhaps be extended to account for still broader relational categories like "subject."

Wolff's chapter argues for a language acquisition theory that is an outgrowth of his work developing a computer program that can segment continuous text into word units, and acquire phrase structure grammars. It incorporates procedures that find and generalize productive patterns in the text and that correct overgeneralizations; it may mimic some of the processes used by children in acquiring their language. The theory is precise where it has been programmed, less precise in its extensions. Wolff argues that the theory accords well with evidence, and that the same kind of mechanism could account for the acquisition of nonlinguistic cognitive structures as well as language. It thus comes out against the idea that there is a fundamental difference between language and other kinds of cognitive structure. An underlying idea is that human learning mechanisms have evolved in the direction of building structures that code linguistic and nonlinguistic objects and events in a form that is optimally efficient taking into account their frequency.

My own contribution is also an inquiry into the nature of the learning mechanism used by children in acquiring their language. It begins with a critique of a model recently developed in studies of language learnability (Wexler & Culicover, 1980) and argues that it does not offer a useful starting point for theorizing about how syntactic rules are acquired. I then pose a number of questions whose answers indicate requirements that a plausible mechanism must satisfy, and go on to argue that a certain kind of learning mechanism, called a "sieve memory", provides a natural and plausible way to satisfy these requirements. This type of mechanism causes features of the input to be registered in a memory in which rule consolidation is a function of frequency of registration, and in which rarely repeated features tend to be forgotten. I elaborate how such a mechanism provides solutions to some wellknown problems that face language acquisition models, and end by suggesting an experimental methodology for testing and improving models of the child's learning processes.

The final overview chapter concentrates on the problem of the nature and developmental origin of linguistic categories, on which all the chapters have something to say. It discusses their differences and shared assumptions in relation to the range of opinion in the field. An important dimension of difference among theories, to be resolved in future work, lies in their conception of how sensitive young children are to properties of morphophonemic form and how readily they use such properties to form categories.

REFERENCES

Anderson, J. R. (1983). *The architecture of cognition.* Cambridge, MA: Harvard University Press.
Berwick, R. C. (1985). *The acquisition of syntactic knowledge.* Cambridge, MA: MIT Press.
Braine, M. D. S. (1987). What is learned in acquiring word classes—A step toward an acquisition theory. In B. MacWhinney (Ed.), *Mechanisms of language acquisition.* Hillsdale, NJ: Lawrence Erlbaum Associates.
Braine, M. D. S., & Wells, R. (1978). Case-like categories in children: The actor and its subcategories. *Cognitive Psychology, 10,* 100–122.
Bruner, J. S. (1983). *Child's talk: Learning to use language.* New York: W. W. Norton.
MacWhinney, B. (1978). The acquisition of morphophonology. *Monographs of the Society for Research in Child Development, 43* (Nos. 1–2, Serial No. 174).
Maratsos, M. P. (1982). The child's construction of grammatical categories. In L. R. Gleitman & E. Wanner (Eds.), *Language acquisition: The state of the art.* Cambridge, MA: Harvard University Press.
Maratsos, M. P., & Chalkley, M. A. The internal language of children's syntax: The ontogenesis and representation of syntactic categories. In K. Nelson (Ed.), *Children's language* (Vol. 2). New York: Gardner Press.

Pinker. S. (1984). *Language learnability and language development.* Cambridge, MA: Harvard University Press.

Schlesinger, I. M. (1971). Production of utterances and language acquisition. In D. I. Slobin (Ed.), *The ontogenesis of grammar: A theoretical symposium.* New York: Academic Press.

Schlesinger, I. M. (1979). Cognitive and linguistic structures: The case of the instrument. *Journal of Linguistics, 15,* 307–324.

Snow, C. E. (1979). The role of social interaction in language acquisition. In W. A. Collins (Ed.), *Minnesota Symposia on Child Psychology,* (Vol. 12). Hillsdale, NJ: Lawrence Erlbaum Associates.

Wexler, K., & Culicover, P. W. (1980). *Formal principles of language acquisition.* Cambridge, MA: MIT Press.

1 Language Acquisition Through Language Use: The Functional Sources of Children's Early Utterances

Anat Ninio
Hebrew University

Catherine E. Snow
Harvard University

The fact that language is a means of communication enjoys a rather curious position in contemporary theories of language acquisition. On the one hand, most students of the field would agree that children typically use language for communicative purposes, that linguistic input to children consists of speech addressed to them to accomplish social purposes in the course of interaction, and even that such social-linguistic interaction is prerequisite to normal language acquisition. However, for the majority of developmental psycholinguistics, these facts are completely irrelevant to their theories about the process of language acquisition. Although these researchers might well agree with our view that language acquisition is made possible only by virtue of the social interaction surrounding linguistic input, nonetheless, they would maintain that the child is acquiring a language system independent of communication. The irrelevancy of the communicative nature of language to most theories of language acquisition is a consequence of the generally held beliefs concerning the nature of the relationship between language and its uses.

The often repeated argument goes as follows: Language is a set of rules for assigning meaning to words, and for combining words and other elementary units (morphemes) into meaningful (and well-formed) sentences. Since, in principle, every sentence can be used for any communicative purpose whatsoever, meaning and use are completely independent.[1] Meaning is assigned by linguistic

---

[1]In the adult linguistic systems a particular function (e.g., request information) can be performed with a variety of grammatical forms (imperative: Tell me your name; interrogative: What is your name?; declarative: I don't believe I know your name). Conversely, a particular form (e.g., the interrogative) can be used to perform a myriad of functions (Request information: How old are you? Request action: Can you hand me that book? Greet: How are you? Inform: Did you know that the Celtics won the Eastern Playoffs? Warn: What do you think will happen to you if you don't get to bed immediately? Threaten: Do you want me to call the police? Insult: What kind of an idiot are you? etc.).

rules, but appropriate use is determined by social convention and limited only by user ingenuity. Language use, therefore, is an extralinguistic phenomenon. And, because what children have to acquire is the use-independent linguistic system, facts about language use, whether in the input or the output, are in principle not pertinent to the question of how language *itself* is acquired (cf. Bloom, 1983).

It could be questioned whether this picture of language as a closed system of rules and readings in which meaning is exclusively propositional in nature is the correct view of the adult language system (cf. Alston, 1963; Austin, 1962; Vendler, 1972, Wittgenstein, 1953). However, we avoid in this paper the highly vexed topic of the relationship between adult syntactic and pragmatic systems. We do wish to argue, though, that neither the linguistic interactions that children participate in, nor the language forms they are exposed to and process, are characterized by this extreme, adult-level independence of form and function.

It has been reported repeatedly that the language addressed to young children constitutes a limited subset of the full adult system. Vocabulary (Broen, 1972; Drach, 1969; Phillips, 1970; Remick, 1976), grammatical constructions (Broen, 1972; Sachs, Brown, & Salerno, 1976; Snow, 1972), case relations (Retherford, Schwartz, & Chapman, 1981; Snow, 1977), and illocutionary act types (Ninio, 1983) have a restricted range in input. In addition, there appears to be a basic set of vocabulary items, sentence types, case relations, and illocutionary acts which is commonly used by people addressing young children (Broen, 1972; Thomas, 1979; Snow, 1977; Ninio, 1983).

The most important characteristic of input language, however, from the point of view of the present discussion, is that it exhibits a higher than usual degree of form-function correspondence. Shatz (1977) found that, for various speech acts such as requests for actions and requests for information, a single prototypical sentence-frame accounted for the majority of maternal utterances with the relevant intent, and that the sentence frames were different for different speech acts. Similar observations have been made by Ninio and Bruner (1978) and Broen (1972).

In general, then, the language addressed to young children does not seem to have the characteristics of a use-independent system of morphemes and of rules for their combination. Rather, it seems to be a limited set of discrete subsystems, each of which is a means for the linguistic realization of some communicative function. Moreover, the existence of form-function correspondence in this system implies that the formal (lexical, morphological, syntactic) features of utterances in input language explicitly mark the communicative function of the utterances. This, in turn, implies that the communicative intent underlying the utterances is recoverable from the surface of the utterances.

If this is a correct description of input language, it raises the serious possibility that the production system constructed by young children on the basis of this type of input relates communicative intent directly to a formal linguistic expression. That is, it could be argued that during the early stages of language acquisition, children's linguistic productions can be adequately explained, and a number of aspects of these productions, their relations to input language and their ontological status for the child better explained, by positing a functional system as the generative source of the utterances, rather than an autonomous syntactic system (see also Ninio, 1983; and Snow, 1979). The exact nature of the functional production model we propose is explicated later, after we present the evidence that has driven us to positing communicative intent as the basic category generating children's early utterances.

The communicative intents for which children seek forms of expression might emerge in primitive form from their own needs and cognitions (e.g., requests for food, notice of novel objects) or might emerge from long-established interpersonal routines (e.g., maternal requests for labels, maternal markers of completion). Whatever the source of the child's communicative intent, she or he must find in the input language, or in the history of interaction with the adult, some way of expressing it effectively. Our production model would predict (and much evidence confirms) that only *one* means of expression is typically found and mapped onto the communicative intent, at least during the early stages of language acquisition. Thus, although a complete explanation for the relationship of pragmatic to syntactic systems (which we do not aspire to offer) will have to account for the acquisition of the knowledge required to produce and comprehend multiple bidirectional mappings, the task we have set ourselves is somewhat simpler: to present a production model that explains children's early utterances, taking into account the kind of language they hear and comprehend, the interactions they engage in, and the social-cognitive competence they can be demonstrated independently of language to possess.

Hypothesizing a production system like this presumes that children make use of knowledge about the purpose, goal, and structure of social interaction, in order to recognize others' communicative intents and to map their own intents onto others' forms of expression. Such a presumption is not, however, unparsimonious; children can be demonstrated to possess this sort of knowledge before the onset of language (see for example, Eckerman & Stein, 1982).

The hypothesized, pragmatic-based production system is very close in spirit to Schlesinger's (cf. 1971, 1977, 1982) semantically based production model. As in Schlesinger's model, grammatical rules in early child language are seen as directly tied to the contents the child intends to express, i.e., as realization rules for communicative intents. The difference between the two models is one of emphasis on the semantic versus pragmatic component of the communicative intent. In Schlesinger's model, the generative substratum of speech is defined primarily in terms of semantic categories such as agent, action, location, etc. Such categories are purported to be applicable wherever the propositional content of the intended utterance can be seen as expressing the relevant semantic relations. Formally, Schlesinger accords a prominent position to the pragmatic intent of the utterance as well. Since different speech acts (e.g., statements, questions, or requests), although their propositional content might be seen as expressing the same semantic relations, typically have different surface structures, Schlesinger maintains that the realization rules of the same semantic relations will be different for different speech acts. He posits a specific element in the semantic deep structure which marks the illocutionary force of the intended utterance and which has a superior status over semantic elements as it is responsible for triggering an appropriate set of realization rules, different for each kind of speech act, regardless of the identity of the semantic relation expressed. In Schlesinger's (1982) words, "the child must therefore learn which *sets* of rules go with the making of statements, which with the asking of questions, and so on" (p. 253, italics in the original). In fact, although Schlesinger offers this theoretical solution for the problem of meaning-function-form relationship, he does not elaborate on it further.

Although Schlesinger's model can accommodate the need for different rules to express different pragmatic forces, it does so by assuming that semantic categories and semantic relations are identical across pragmatic categories. In our pragmatic-based model, the semantic categories themselves are considered to be function-specific rather than identical across different speech acts. Clearly, the choice between a pragmatic-based and a semantic-based model is an empirical one. Which can better explain the regularities in children's productions? If children treat semantic categories like actor identically across a variety of pragmatic forces, then a semantic-based account is indeed more parsimonious. If, on the other hand, children treat categories that in adult semantic analyses are equivalent differently in different speech acts, then the pragmatic model better accounts for regularities. We believe the data presented below on children's one-word speech support the pragmatic model, at least for this stage of development.

In addition, there are purely theoretical reasons for preferring a pragmatic-based account. In the first place, much of what is said cannot be described at all by the semantic categories developed for the description of the propositional content of assertions, such as the content of agreements, rejections, greetings, attention directives, markings and acknowledgements of all sorts. In the second place, a given propositional content and associated set of semantic relations are quite dissimilar in different speech acts. For instance, the relation of agent to action in assertions is in fact the relation of listener to desired action in requests. Not only the grammar of expressing these relations is different but the semantics, too: The "agent" of a requested action is exclusively the addressee of the utterance and not any possible actor. This has important consequences for the grammar of requests, e.g., that the "agent" term can usually be elided, whereas in an assertion the "agent" term is nondeletable.

Although in theory Schlesinger's pragmatic amendment of his semantic production model generates adequate predictions of child language to account for function-related regularities, in reality semantically oriented authors, including Schlesinger himself, neglect in their writings this aspect of speech production and derive their explanations of children's productions from the semantic intent only. The present chapter attempts to remedy this neglect of the pragmatic sources of early speech. The hypothesized, pragmatics-based production system obviates the need to attribute to the child knowledge of abstract semantic categories before she or he acquires rules for expression of pragmatic categories. We see this as a major advantage, because it predicts that the child will discover a set of regularities which is quite clear in the input—the mapping of form to pragmatic force—earlier than a set of regularities as unpredictably mapped as the expression of semantic or syntactic relationships. Furthermore, the discovery of semantic and syntactic mappings within pragmatic categories is much easier, since they *are* quite predictably expressed within, even if not across, pragmatic category boundaries. Lastly, if it can be demonstrated that children in the early stages of language operate with a pragmatics-based production system, then a serious shortcoming of present descriptions of child language would be remedied: that they tend to ignore the communicative functions of speech, even though it is uncontested that communicative intent is decoded by children, and that it is an inseparable part of the meanings they express in their own utterances.

EVIDENCE IN SUPPORT OF A PRAGMATIC "DEEP STRUCTURE"

In this section we briefly review published analyses of one-word and early combinatorial speech, most of which have advocated semantic (or, occasionally, syntactic) analyses of child utterances, to demonstrate that a functional analysis better accounts for the data.

One Word Speech

Children's early one-word utterances are acquired for specific, unitary functions, and can only with difficulty be seen as expressing semantic relations or parts thereof. Even the advocates of semantic case-type analyses of one-word speech admit that the earliest one-word utterances are purely functional, and use a classification system for later utterances which is a hodge-podge of semantic and functional categories. Consider Greenfield and Smith's (1976) proposal, for instance: The first categories they identify as emerging in one-word speech are Performative (e.g., *brm-brm* while pushing a car); Performative object (*dada* while looking at daddy), and Volition (*nana* while crawling to forbidden bookcase). (See Greenfield & Smith, 1976, for definitions of their categories performative object and volition.) All of these are clearly functional, to the extent that they go beyond the simple association. More important, however, in the categories Greenfield and Smith label as if they capture semantic relations, all the examples given point to the existence of more basic functional categories such as *request, direct attention, or state intent to act,* whereas the semantic categories they identify are both abstruse and impossible to map onto any categories in an adult grammar. For example, most of the utterances classified by Greenfield and Smith (1976) as "objects associated with another object or location" were clearly demands to be given the object mentioned, for instance, Nicky's reaching toward the kitchen counter, whining and saying "apple" or Matthew's holding up an empty glass, whining and saying "milk" (pp. 143–146).   Although the context, the children's behavior and the lexicalization rule were identical with those of utterances Greenfield and Smith categorized as "volitional object," this identity was ignored as a result of the insistence on semantic rather than functional categorization. Examination of other examples offered by Greenfield and Smith suggests that the class of utterances they label "agents" could as easily be categorized as "direct attention to non-present object/event," and that their class "indicative object" emerges from a very small set of highly-constrained naming routines.

Indeed, Greenfield and Smith in their notations concerning the categories they established and in the examples they give reveal the confusion between a functional and a semantic basis in their thinking, e.g., "The Action or State word *up* is part of a more complicated structure involving both demand and description of action" (p. 114); "Nicky uses *down* when he wants someone else to pick him up or put him down. Here, *down* describes the Action or State of a Dative . . ." (p. 114). Among utterances classified as "object associated with another object or location" we find the following: "Matthew says *[f]ishy,* then goes to get his fish-book, which he brings to his mother. One striking feature of this example is the use of a word to signal an intention requiring sustained action for its realization" (p. 145). Many more examples are given in their Table 23 (pp. 116–117) of requests or statements of intent to act which Greenfield and Smith classify as instances of Action or State of Agent, i.e., semantically, but which they discuss in the text in terms of their function.

Nelson (1973) gives lists of the first 50 different words acquired by 8 children. Inspection of the contents of the lists makes very clear how embedded in use the acquisition of these words probably was. Many are pure performatives like *bye-bye, whoosh, thank you,* and *crash* or the names of important people, used typically as request or as greeting forms. Many are request or rejection forms. Most striking, however, are the common nouns included in the lists, many of which are typically words taught in the context of book-reading or of oft-repeated games such as body-part routines, while another larger group consists of names of objects typically requested by children (e.g., *bottle, juice, pacifier, blanket, cookie*). A similar conclusion might be reached by inspecting Benedict's (1979) list of the first 'action words' comprehended and produced by 8 children. Unfortunately, neither Nelson nor Benedict present the data on use that would confirm our predictions.

EARLY COMBINATORIAL SPEECH

Subsequent to the one-word stage, the evidence for children's ability to express semantic relations, using general semantic categories like agent, action, patient, location, etc. might be presumed to be much stronger. However, recent work from a number of researchers has challenged the notion that the semantic categories necessary for describing early combinatorial speech are either general or universal (see Bowerman, 1973, 1975; Braine, 1976; Ingram, 1979; Maratsos & Chalkley, 1980). Huttenlocher, Smiley, and Charney (1983) analyze limitations on children's uses of verbs as related to semantic action categories (own vs. observed actions, characteristic actions vs. change verbs), but their findings could also be explained by appealing to the different pragmatic functions associated with the use of the various verb types. Braine offered data to suggest that children who appear to be using general patterns may instead be relying on rather narrow semantic categories (e.g., "ingesting action + ingested" rather than "action + patient") and that certain categories such as patient need not be postulated at all, for instance in cases where only one form [*it*] is used to express patient. Careful inspection of the utterances from the "pronominal" children identified by Bloom, Lightbown, and Hood (1975) suggests that certain of the semantic categories coded for these children have a similarly limited membership, e.g., agents and possessors (p. 19). Goldfield (1982) analyzed data from Heather, a girl who would have been classified as pronominal by Bloom et al., and found that Heather's possessor category consists of *my,* her agent category of *I,* and her patient category of *it.* Under these circumstances, it obviously is operating at too high a level of abstraction either to label the child as pronominal or to give the child credit for semantic categories.

Evidence against the existence of general semantic categories in the base structure of children's early utterances comes, not just from limited membership in any category, but also from limited application of some rules. For example, Bowerman's subject Eva used *more, no more, again,* and *all gone* as one word utterances, but when she started producing utterances of the form *more + X,* she did not also produce combinations with the other words, e.g., *no more + X* or *again + X* (Bowerman, 1976). It seems that the semantic similarity between 'more' and 'again', 'no more', and 'all gone' apparent to adults was not a factor in Eva's system.

We would argue that Eva's failure to generalize the *more + X* pattern to produce *again + X, no more + X,* and *all gone + X* reflects the fact that each of these expressions was used by her in functionally different ways; their function was, at the stage of her acquisition being studied, the basic fact that governed the constructions into which such forms could enter. Though the absence of *again + X, no more + X,* and *all gone + X* is surprising to those who assume that semantic similarity governs the application of newly acquired rules, we would predict no generalization from patterns involving 'more' to patterns involving 'again', since these expressions are learned as the realizations of different interactive functions.

The existence of a functional basis for distinguishing children's categories is implicitly acknowledged in much of the work that purports to be about semantic categories (just as was the case for one-word speech; see discussion of Greenfield & Smith above). Bloom (1970), for example, in one of the most consistently nonfunctional analyses so far offered of children's early speech, distinguished nonetheless among three types of negatives (nonexistence, rejection, denial) on purely functional grounds. Similarly, Braine's (1976) limited scope formulae include some of a basically semantic and others of a basically functional character, e.g., his identification of a class of "requesting expressions" in the subject David's corpus. Braine (1976) specifically rejects the position we advocate:

> While some of the children's positional patterns are specific to one of these purposes . . . many patterns can be used for more than one purpose, just like single-word utterances. Thus, *more x* may either request or comment on recurrence; similarly, locatives and action-action forms can sometimes request as well as describe. Thus, the data indicate that a particular aspect of meaning, namely, the purpose for which a child uses an utterance, may or may not be part of the semantic representation of a pattern. (pp. 61–62)

Despite this disclaimer, Braine's own analysis identifies certain categories on the basis of the children's purpose in speaking.

Braine's data offer some clear examples of similar semantic relations being expressed by different surface patterns according to the utterance's function. Kendall during Stage II had two different patterns for locative combinations with "there" as an element. She used "*there + X*" primarily for drawing attention to an object, and "*X + there*" for true locative statements (see Braine, 1976, pp. 18–19). Jonathan made the same differentiation (p. 38; see p. 87 for Braine's discussion of this finding).

Outline of a Pragmatic Theory of Child Language

A pragmatic theory of speech production posits that the starting point for communicative speech is that a speaker has an intention to carry out some social-communicative act by verbal means. The act which speaker intends to perform is an overtly communicative act; that is, speaker intends to be interpreted by hearer as performing that act, and moreover, speaker intends hearer to recognize the overtly communicative nature of his act (cf. Grice, 1957; Searle, 1969, 1975; Strawson, 1964).

The speaker's *communicative intent* forms the communicative "deep structure" of the utterance he utters in order to carry out his intention. The communicative intent is a cognitive plan which contains all that a speaker overtly intends to communicate. Successful communication consists of hearer's correct identification of the meanings speaker intended to communicate; that is, of hearer's reconstruction of the communicative intent underlying the produced utterance.

The next step in the speech production process is the selection of a subset of the communicative intent for verbal encoding. It is the rule rather than the exception in natural discourse for utterances to be less than fully explicit. For instance, most utterances are not marked for illocutionary force (Searle, 1975; Streeck, 1980). Succinctness is a social norm as well as a conversational maxim (Grice, 1975). Because full encoding of the communicative intent is seldom necessary for successful communication to take place, speakers are motivated to be laconic. In full-blown adult communication, the selective-encoding process is governed by anticipatory decoding (Rommetveit, 1974); that is, speakers intent to enable the hearer to reconstruct the full message from what is uttered.[2] In other words, the selection of a subset of the communicative deep structure for eventual verbal encoding is governed, in adults, by a set of *selection rules* which specify those elements of the communicative intent which it is minimally necessary to encode in order to assume full comprehension of the whole message. The resultant cognitive plan is the to-be-encoded communicative intent. This is then realized in a surface form according to a grammar, which contains a set of *realization rules* determining the lexical, morphological, and syntactic encoding of the communicative intent.

It is proposed here that young children's speech production is also governed by a set of selection rules which selectively reduce the communicative "deep structure" of their utterances. The reason for the reduction in the children's production probably includes a limitation on the complexity of the utterances they are able to realize in a surface form. Nevertheless, their selection of elements to encode is also rule-governed and shaped at least partly by anticipatory decoding. Here we are at odds with Greenfield and Smith's (1976) suggestions that children select for encoding that element which is maximally informative for themselves rather than for the listener (pp. 184–198). Greenfield and Smith's own data strongly support an interpretation on the lines proposed here and not at all their own noncommunicative selection hypothesis. For example, in order to explain why children encode the object in demands but encode the negative force in rejections, they need to say that in a demand situation there is a greater uncertainty of the object *for the child* than there is in a rejection situation, which

---

[2]Herrmann (1982) discusses a superficially similar model of speech production in which selective restriction of the utterance's propositional base is thought of as taking place. However, in Herrmann's model the starting point of the production of utterances is not what is intended to be communicated but rather "all that the speaker has perceived, recollected, imagined, inferred, presumed, planned, etc. in connection with the process of speaking" (p. 25). It is easy to reject the claim that the speaker intends the addressee to reconstruct all these; and Herrmann's examples of such reconstructions are singularly unconvincing (see for instance pp. 41–43).

is absurd, whereas the difference in uncertainty is obviously true *for the listener*. It might be true that young children have not perfectly mastered the task of anticipatory decoding, but there is no basis for assuming that they choose what to say with a complete disregard for their listeners.

The strong version of this theory would claim that in the case of young children the rules of grammar are nothing but realization rules directly tying elements of the communicative intent to surface forms. By this version, the *to-be-encoded communicative intent* is the generative substratum of the surface form the child chooses. A communication-independent grammar is then thought to emerge as a later development, by a process of reorganization of the whole linguistic system and the gradual achievement of an abstract and autonomous grammatical component. Similar ideas have been advocated by Bowerman (cf. 1978) and Berman (in press).

Applying this model of speech production to children's one-word utterances allows one to credit children with a richly specified social-cognitive communicative intent, and at the same time not to postulate a linguistic deep structure which is more complex than the surface structure. To wit, the actual surface string expresses the complete linguistic deep structure, without necessitating a reduction transformation that would delete elements of it (cf. Bloom, 1970; Bowerman, 1973) or without a special "lexical-insertion process" by which a word is inserted into an inappropriately high node in the rule system (cf. Braine, 1974). Rather, the linguistic deep structure is already the output of a prior selective process which determines which elements of the total communicative intent are to be verbally encoded.

An analysis of children's early utterances in terms of their intended communicative intent should reveal the nature of the encoding and realization rules which constitute their linguistic system. In the following, data from four 18-month-old Hebrew-speaking children (Sivan, Roni, Adi, and Rafi) are used to illustrate this method of analysis. These children were videotaped at their homes with their mother or father in a 30-minute free interaction period. Within a week of the videotaping session, detailed explanations of the interaction were obtained from the parents while they were watching the tapes. Subsequently, the children's utterances were coded for their communicative intent. A more detailed description of the explanation-eliciting procedure and of the coding system is to be found in Ninio and Wheeler, 1983).

A conservative approach to coding the function expressed by children's utterances would rely on adult word semantics as the basis. Thus, for example, 'mummy' in a request would be identified as encoding 'addressee'. We have chosen a somewhat more controversial approach based on our assumption that forms are acquired and initially used in a functionally specific way. Thus, we assume that 'mummy' in a request encodes the requestive force as well as the addressee. Such an analysis would be strongly supported by the occurrence of overgeneralization errors, for example, 'mummy' used as a request to daddy.

The data so far analyzed for the children discussed here do not provide such instances, but we predict their occurrence and, in fact, such overgeneralizations have been noted in other corpora, such as that of Snow's son Nathaniel, who used 'more' as a request for newly requested as well as recurrently requested objects (see Snow, 1988).

In deciding which element or elements of the intended communicative act were encoded by a particular utterance, distributional evidence about the child's use of the relevant expression was taken into account. For example, various expressions were considered to encode the illocutionary force of a request if they were consistently and exclusively used in directive contexts. This procedure is illustrated in the first communicative act presented here: the act of requesting the cessation of an ongoing joint activity. Two of the four children produced utterances with such a communicative intent. These are given below, with an English translation and some contextual comments.

Sivan:	*day.*	("enough.")	Said to request ending of ballplaying.
	day.	("enough.")	Said to request ending of cleaning up.
	ima.	("mummy.")	Said to request ending of mother's swinging her in the air.
Rafi:	*day.*	("enough.")	Said to request ending of game of rolling a tin back and forth.

The *selection* rule for requests to end an ongoing activity is *either* to encode *the force of the request to end something* or to encode *the force of a request addressed to Mother* (for Sivan). Although a purely formal analysis of the children's utterances would suggest that they are encoding solely the concept of continuation or the addressee, a distributional analysis of the utterances supports our contention that the requestive force is being encoded as well. *Day* ("enough") was used exclusively in requestive contexts by both children. The same is true for *ima* as used by Sivan: All 52 'mummy's produced by her were requests of one kind or another. Similar findings on the use of 'mother' as a request form were made by Greenfield and Smith (1976, pp. 91–94), among others.

The *realization* rules were:

a. for requests to end an activity: the word *day* ("enough")

b. for requests to Mummy to do something: the word *ima* ("mummy")

"Enough" does not encode the identity of the activity which speaker wants to end, nor of the person addressed with the request. "Mummy' does not encode the activity to be ended either, nor does it encode what is specifically requested, i.e., that something will be ended. However, it does encode the identity of the person addressed as well as the requestive force of the act. Figure 1.1 illustrates the proposed three-tier organization of this speech act in the children studied.

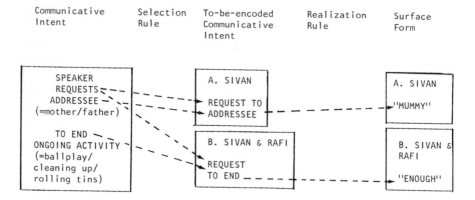

Communicative Intent	Selection Rule	To-be-encoded Communicative Intent	Realization Rule	Surface Form

FIG. 1.1. Production rules for a communicative act.

Similar selective encoding rules were found in the case of requests to continue a recursive activity at the completion of a cycle of the activity.

Sivan:	*ima* ("mummy")	Said to request being fed another olive by mother.
	ima ("mummy")	Said to request more telephone-play from mother.
Roni:	*od* ("more")	Said to request to be played more music by mother.
Adi:	*od* ("more")	Said to request another piece of a form-board to place it.
Rafi:	*ani* ("me")	Said to request another bout of being bounced on father's knee.
	ani ("me")	Said to request another bout of being swung by father.
	ani nadned ("me swing")	Said to request another bout of being swung by father.
	od ("more")	Said to request another bout of being swung by father.

The *selection rules* and *realization rules* for requesting a continuation of a recursive activity for each of the children are presented in Table 1.1.

All four children produced some spontaneously emitted (i.e., nonelicited) statements discussing a concrete object, a picture, or a person which was at that moment at the focus of joint attention with their parent. All of Sivan's and Adi's utterances are given below, along with a representative sample of Roni's and Rafi's.

Sivan: *ze* ("this")   Said while pointing at a picture of
                                a house previously discussed by
                                her mother.
Roni: *shaon* ("watch")   Said while looking at, pointing at,
                                or showing the object, etc., dis-
                                cussed.
      telefon ("telephone")   "
      kadur ("ball")   "
      dolly ("dolly")   "
      doda ("woman")   "
      tapuax ("apple")   "
      eyn ("no one")   Said on there being no one on the
                                phone.
Adi: *buba* ("doll")   Said during picture-book reading.
     meruba ("square")   Said in discussion of a piece of
                                form-board prior to placing it.
Rafi: *sefer* ("book")   Said when father showed book.
      shaon ("watch")   Said when father showed watch.
      sukariya ("candy")   Said when father showed candy.
      kapit ("teaspoon")   Said during picture-book reading.
      tzipor ("bird")   Said during picture-book reading.
      kadur ("ball")   Said during picture-book reading.
      oto ("car")   Said during picture-book reading.
      sus ("horse")   Said during picture-book reading.

TABLE 1.1
Rules for Requesting Continuation of a Recursive Activity

Selection Rules	Realization Rules
Sivan – encode the force of an unspecified request and its addressee	for request addressed to mother <u>ima</u> (mummy)
Roni – encode the force of a request to continue Adi some activity	for a request to continue ■ <u>od</u> (more)
Rafi – encode the force of a request to continue some activity	for a request to continue <u>od</u> (more) or <u>ani</u> (me)
– encode the activity to be continued	for activity to be continued: realize name of activity (e.ge., <u>nadned</u>, swing)
–encode both elements above and their relationship	word order: request element + activity element

The *selection* rule for statements discussing a joint focus of attention is, for all four children, to *encode verbally the object, etc., at joint focus of attention.*
The *realization rule* for objects etc. at joint focus of attention is:

for Sivan, a pronoun (*ze*—"this")
for Roni, Adi and Rafi: a noun naming the object or person.

That is, the same element in the "deep structure" is realized differently by Sivan and by the other children.

In the case of this communicative act, no meaning-element other than the focus of attention is ever encoded, e.g., neither the force of the act, nor the speaker, nor the addressee.

Interestingly, the selection and realization rules were exactly the same in the case of a very different speech act: answers to a where-question by which speaker requests hearer to direct her attention to the focus named. In all the quoted cases, the children actually pointed out the requested object, accompanying the gesture with the reported utterance.

Sivan:	*ze* ("this")	Answering the question, *"Efo ha-sab-on?"* ("Where is the soap?")
	ayin ("eye")	Answering the question, *"Efo ayin shel ha-dubi?"* ("Where is the eye of the teddy?")
Roni:	*eynayim* ("eyes")	Answering the question, *"Efo ha-eynayim shel Roni?"* ("Where are the eyes of Roni?")
Adi:	*ze* ("this")	Answering the question, *"Efo lavan?"* ("Where's the white one?")
	ze ("this")	Answering the question, *"Efo ha-af?"* ("Where's the nose?")
	yarok ("green")	Answering the question, *"Efo yarok?"* ("Where's the green one?")

As in discussions of a joint focus of attention, these young children encode in answers to where-questions the *object* which is under consideration. (By contrast, adults and older children invariably encode in the same circumstances the *location* of the object, as in "Here," or both the location and the object, as in "Here's his nose.") The realization-rules are the same as for discussions of a joint focus of attention: realize a pronoun or a noun naming the object.

As the last example, we shall take affirmative answers to yes–no questions used to request clarification of the child's previous utterance; to suggest a new activity; to offer help; or to suggest continuation of a recursive activity. The affirmative answers to these four different kinds of speech acts are grouped together because the children's encoding and realization rules were identical.

The element encoded was the affirmative force of the act; its realization consisted, in most cases, of the repetition of the key word (i.e., a stressed content word on final or prefinal position) in the question.[3] To make the process easier to follow, the questions are presented to the left of the children's answers.

Roni:	*Rotza lalala?*	*Lalala*	("Want lalala (music)?" "Lalala.")
	Od?	*Od.*	("More?" "More.")
	Eyn?	*Eyn.*	("No one?" "No one.")
	Dolly rotz pita?	*Pita.*	("Dolly wants pita?" "Pita.")
	Bakbuk?	*Bakbuk.*	("Bottle?" "Bottle.")
	Rotza tapuax?	*Tapuax*	("Want an apple?" "Apple.")
	Rotza ledaber im Miri ba-tele-fon?	*Miri.*	("Want to talk with Miri on the phone?" "Miri.")
	Eyn Miri?	*Miri.*	("No Miri?" "Miri.")
	Rotza she-ani avi lax xatixat pita?	*Pita.*	("Want me to bring you a piece of pita?" "Pita.")
	Rotza she-ani exapes lax oto?	*Oto.*	("Want me to look for it for you?" "It.")
Rafi:	*Rotze nadned?*	*Nadned.*	("Want 'swing'?" "Swing.")
	Od?	*Od.*	("More?" "More.")
Sivan:	*Ah, at rotza zeitim?*	*Ken.*	("Ah, you want olives?" "Yes.")
	Day?	*Day.*	("Enough?" "Enough.")
	Rotza bexazera et ha-sakit?	*Ima.*	("Want the paperbag back?" "Mummy.")
	Rotza lehistakel bo?	*Ze.*	("Want to look at it?" "This.")

---

[3]It has been pointed out to us that the children's responses in these examples may be just echoing the last word of the adult utterance, and not performing the speech act of answering affirmatively. However, the attribution of communicative intent here has been based on the existence of other behavioral cues, for example, Roni assuming the posture she used for listening to music after answering 'lalala'. Furthermore, the repetition of the last word of the adult utterance is highly specific to certain intents and not at all general in these corpora.

Furthermore, it is minimally controversial to claim that the affirmative force of the act is being encoded by these utterances, since repetition is one of the legitimate means by which adult speakers confirm others' interpretation of their unclear utterances. Strictly speaking, affirmation is carried out by the act of repetition itself, and it is irrelevant for uptake which component or components of the utterance are repeated.

Roni and Rafi realize the affirmative force of their utterances by repeating the key word in the yes–no question. The effect of this strategy is the production of utterances which replicate spontaneous requests of the same children. For example, Rafi spontaneously demands the setting up of a game of "swinging" by uttering "swing" (*nadned*), and he uses the same form to affirm that he indeed wishes to play this game when his father suggests it. Roni, in response to her mother's multiword object offers, picks out for repetition the word referring to the proffered object in her mother's utterance. She is quite adept at identifying this word even if it is a pronoun, as in the case of *oto,* which is "it" in the accusative, a form she would probably not produce spontaneously at this age.

Sivan uses three different selection and realization strategies. The first consists of encoding and realizing the affirmative force of her utterance by the conventional "yes" (*ken*). The second is a repetition of the adult question, which incidentally is also a repetition of Sivan's previous spontaneous request to end an activity ("enough" = *day*). The third is an encoding of the fact that she wants the proffered objects, realized in two different generalized request forms, "mummy" (*ima*) and "this" (*ze*). We might say that in general these children agree by requesting anew that which they are offered; and that they confirm by stating anew that which they are asked to confirm. Thus, affirmative answers are governed at this age by a superordinate encoding rule: affirm by generating a new utterance without ellipsis which expresses anew that which has already been uttered. The specific encoding rules depend on what is affirmed: if it is a description, as in *eyn* ("none") the encoding rules are the same as for a statement; if it is the child's wanting some object or activity, the encoding rules are the same as for the relevant request.

As we have demonstrated, the communicative analysis of children's early utterances reveal a lawfulness which is not evident unless the pragmatic nature of the deep structure of these utterances is recognized. For instance, Roni's affirmative answers which follow the same encoding and realization rules would, on a semantic analysis, be classified all differently, e.g., as "object of volition," "modifier of whole event," "dative object," "nonpresent person associated with another object," and so forth. A pragmatic analysis puts all these utterances in the same category, that of an affirmative answer, and thus makes possible the discovery of their shared laws of production.

Conclusion

We have attempted to demonstrate that a communicative, speech-act based analysis of children's early utterances is preferable to an analysis in which syntactic or semantic categories are taken as primary. Our demonstration was based on the following evidence:

1. That children's earliest words express specific communicative functions.
2. That semantic classifications of children's later one word and multiword

language productions fail to account for a significant proportion of the utterances, which even semantically inclined researchers have therefore ended up assigning to functional categories by default.

3. That a semantically based theory cannot account for basic facts about language development such as the failure of newly acquired rules to generalize across a semantic category, whereas a functionally based theory would predict these facts.

4. That a pragmatically based theory requires only that the child understand initially the parameters of his own and others' individual communicative acts, a claim which squares well with a large body of evidence concerning children's precocious social understanding.

5. That a pragmatically based analysis of children's productions reveals a lawfulness which a semantic-based theory obscures, both in the nature of children's productions and in the relationship between child and adult forms (this latter point has not been dwelt upon in this paper, but see Ninio, 1985).

We have presented an outline of a pragmatic theory of language production; the essentials of this theory, which differentiate it from a semantically based theory, are that the deepest level of representation specifies the communicative intent primarily and semantic content secondarily. Thus, within this theory a given semantic class can easily be realized differently for different speech acts, as is most often the case in child language and not infrequently the case in adult language. It is incumbent on this model, as on any serious attempt to provide a theory of language acquisition, to answer questions about how the model accounts for changes in the child's knowledge with development, and how the model can be fleshed out to account for the adult's language system. Such a presentation is beyond the scope of this paper, but is nonetheless a task that cannot be shirked.

A theory such as the one presented here requires a usable speech-act theory as a place to start in describing pragmatic deep structure (see Ninio, 1986). Speech act theories have suffered from linguists' preoccupation with descriptive, propositional language as the standard for language production. Although assertions need to be accounted for by any linguistic theory, taking them as the model for language use ignores a good proportion of adult language behavior, and more seriously, greatly distorts our understanding of language development. Neither in the input language nor in children's productions are assertions typical; they are, on the contrary, relatively infrequent (cf. Folger & Chapman, 1978), more characteristic of the later than of the earliest stages, and largely limited to particular situations, such as naming games and book reading, with young children. It is not surprising, then, that a theory which starts from assertions, and which derives its descriptive categories from the semantics of assertions only, fails to account satisfactorily for children's linguistic knowledge. Language needs to be understood in terms of the way it is used, and a satisfactory theory of language acquisition will account for children's learning the linguistic system by explaining how they learn to use the system.

ACKNOWLEDGMENT

The research described in this paper was supported by Grant No. 2467/81 from the United States-Israel Binational Science Foundation (BSF), Jerusalem, Israel, to A. Ninio and C. Eckerman.

REFERENCES

Alston, W. P. (1963). Meaning and use. *Philosophical Quarterly, 13,* 107–124.

Austin, J. L. (1962). *How to do things with words.* New York: Oxford University Press.

Benedict, H. (1979). Early lexical development: Comprehension and production. *Journal of Child Language, 6,* 183–200.

Berman, R. (1983). *From non-analysis to productivity: Interim schemata in child language* (Working Paper No. 31). Tel-Aviv: Unit for Human Development and Education, Tel-Aviv University.

Bloom, L. (1970). *Language development: Form and function in emerging grammars.* Cambridge, MA: MIT Press.

Bloom, L. (1983). Of continuity and discontinuity, and the magic of language development. In R. M. Golinkoff (Ed.), *The transition from prelinguistic to linguistic communication.* Hillsdale, NJ: Lawrence Erlbaum Associates.

Bloom, L., Lightbown, P., & Hood, L. (1975). Structure and variation in child language. *Monographs of the Society for Research in Child Development, 40*(2, Serial No. 160).

Bowerman, M. (1973). *Early syntactic development: A cross-linguistic study with special reference to Finnish.* Cambridge, England: Cambridge University Press.

Bowerman, M. (1975). Commentary. In L. Bloom, P. Lightbown, & L. Hood, Structure and variation in child language. *Monographs of the Society for Research in Child Development, 40*(2, Serial No. 160), 80–90.

Bowerman, M. (1976). Semantic factors in the acquisition of rules for word use and sentence construction. In D. Morehead & A. Morehead (Eds.), *Directions in normal and deficient child language.* Baltimore, MD: University Park Press.

Bowerman, M. (1978). Semantic and syntactic development: A review of what, when, and how in language acquisition. In R. Schiefelbusch (Ed.), *Bases of language intervention.* Baltimore: University Park Press.

Braine, M. D. S. (1974). Length constraints, reduction rules, and holophrastic processes in children's word combinations. *Journal of Verbal Learning and Verbal Behavior, 13,* 448–456.

Brain, M. D. S. (1976). Children's first word combinations. *Monographs of the Society for Research in Child Development, 41*(1, Serial No. 164).

Broen, P. (1972). The verbal environment of the language-learning child. *Monograph of American Speech and Hearing Association,* No. 17.

Drach, K. (1969). The language of the patient: A pilot study. *Working paper 14,* Language-Behavior Research Laboratory, University of California, Berkeley.

Eckerman, C. O., & Stein, M. R. (1982). The toddler's emerging interactive skills. In K. H. Rubin & H. S. Ross (Eds.), *Peer relationships and social skills in childhood* (pp. 41–71). New York: Springer-Verlag.

Folger, J. P., & Chapman, R. S. (1978). A pragmatic analysis of spontaneous imitations. *Journal of Child Language, 5,* 25–38.

Goldfield, B. A. (1982, October). *Intra-individual variation: Patterns of nominal and pronominal combinations.* Paper presented at the Seventh Annual Boston University Conference on Language Development.

Greenfield, P. M., & Smith, J. H. (1976). *The structure of communication in early language development.* New York: Academic Press.

Grice, H. P. (1957). Meaning. *Philosophical Review, 66,* 337–388.

Grice, H. P. (1975). Logic and conversation. In P. Cole & S. L. Morgan (Eds.), *Syntax and semantics: Speech acts* (Vol. 3). New York: Academic Press.

Herrmann, T. (1982). *Speech and situation.* Berlin: Springer.

Huttenlocher, J., Smiley, P., & Charney, R. (1983). Emergence of action categories in the child: Evidence from verb meanings. *Psychological Review, 90,* 72–93.

Ingram, D. (1979). Stages in the development of one-word utterances: Transition to semantic relations. In P. L. French (Ed.), *The development of meaning* (pp. 256–281). Hirushima: Bunka Hyoron Publishing Company.

Maratsos, M. P., & Chalkley, M. A. (1980). The internal language of children's syntax: The ontogenesis and representation of syntactic categories. In K. Nelson (Ed.), *Children's language* (Vol. 2). New York: Gardner Press.

Nelson, K. (1973). Structure and strategy in learning to talk. *Monograph of the Society for Research in Child Development, 38*(1–2 Serial No. 149).

Ninio, A. (1983, May). *A pragmatic approach to early language acquisition.* Paper presented at the Study Group on Crosscultural and Crosslinguistic Aspects of Native Language Acquisition. The Institute for Advanced Studies, Jerusalem.

Ninio, A. (1985). The meaning of children's first words: Evidence from the input. *Journal of Pragmatics, 9,* 527–546.

Ninio, A. (1986). The illocutionary aspect of utterances. *Discourse Processes, 9,* 127–147.

Ninio, A., & Bruner, J. S. (1978). The achievement and antecedents of labelling. *Journal of Child Language, 5,* 1–15.

Ninio, A., & Wheeler, P. (1983). Functions of speech in mother-infant interaction. In C. Garvey, R. Golinkoff, & L. Feagans (Eds.), *The Development of communicative competence.* Norwood, NJ: Albex.

Phillips, J. (1970). *Formal characteristics of speech which mothers address to their young children.* Unpublished doctoral dissertation, Johns Hopkins University.

Remick, H. (1976). Maternal speech to children during language acquisition. In W. von Raffler-Engel & Y. Lebrun (Eds.), *Baby talk and infant speech.* Lisse, Netherlands: Swets and Zeitlinger.

Retherford, K., Schwartz, B., & Chapman, R. (1981). Semantic roles in mother and child speech: Who tunes into whom? *Journal of Child Language, 8,* 583–608.

Rommetveit, R. (1974). *On message structure.* London: Wiley.

Sachs, J., Brown, R., & Salerno, R. A. (1976). Adults' speech to children. In W. von Raffler-Engel & Y. Lebrun (Eds.), *Baby talk and infant speech.* Lisse, Netherlands: Swets and Zeitlinger.

Schlesinger, I. M. (1971). The production of utterances and language acquisition. In D. I. Slobin (Ed.), *The ontogenesis of grammar: A theoretical symposium.* New York: Academic Press.

Schlesinger, I. M. (1977). *Production and comprehension of utterances.* Hillsdale, NJ: Lawrence Erlbaum Associates.

Schlesinger, I. M. (1982). *Steps to language.* Hillsdale, NJ: Lawrence Erlbaum Associates.

Searle, J. R. (1969). *Speech acts.* Cambridge, England: Cambridge University Press.

Searle, J. R. (1975). A taxonomy of illocutionary acts. In K. Gunderson (Ed.), *Minnesota Studies on the Philosophy of Science* (Vol. 7, pp. 344–369). Minneapolis: University of Minnesota Press.

Shatz, M. (1977, March). *How to do things by asking: form-function relations in mothers' questions to children*. Paper presented at the biennial meeting of the Society for Research in Child Development, New Orleans.

Snow, C. E. (1972). Mothers' speech to children learning language. *Child Development, 43*, 549–565.

Snow, C. E. (1977). Mothers' speech research: From input to interaction. In C. E. Snow & C. Ferguson (Eds.), *Talking to children*. Cambridge, England: Cambridge University Press.

Snow, C. E. (1979). The role of social interaction in language acquisition. In A. Collins (Ed.), *Children's language and communication: Proceedings of the 1977 Minnesota Symposium on Child Development*. Hillsdale, NJ: Lawrence Erlbaum Associates.

Snow, C. E. (1988). The last word: Questions about the emergence of words. In M. Smith & J. Locke (Eds.), *The emergent lexicon*. New York: Academic Press.

Strawson, P. F. (1964). Intention and convention in speech acts. *Philosophical Review*, LXXIII, 439–460.

Streeck, J. (1980). Speech acts in interaction: a critique of Searle. *Discourse Processes, 3*, 133–154.

Thomas, E. K. (1979, October). *It's all routine: A redefinition of routines as a central factor in language acquisition*. Paper presented at the Fourth Annual Boston University Conference on Language Development.

Vendler, Z. (1972). *Res cogitans*. Ithaca: Cornell University Press.

Wittgenstein, L. (1953). *Philosophical investigations*. Oxford: Blackwell.

2 The Acquisition of Formal Word Classes

Michael Maratsos
University of Minnesota

1. THE PROBLEM OF FORM CLASSES

The form classes are the major lexical categories of a language such as verb, noun, adjective, and preposition in English. At a superficial level, their nature is easily appreciated: Every speaker of a language (at least with a little education) can say whether a term is a verb or a noun, or may know things such as that one adds *-ed* to verbs to make their past forms (e.g., *kick—kicked*).

What is important is that they are central to the productivity of grammar. The members of a form class share many grammatical properties. So if a speaker knows a term has one or more of these properties, he can infer that it has the others as well. For example, let us take one of the most famous psycholinguistic tests, the Berko test. In the test, a speaker is given a single use of a nonsense word, a word he or she has never heard. He or she might hear, for example, *John glins dogs a lot.* From this single use of *glin,* the speaker can predict a potentially infinite set of utterances in which *glin* might be used—*why does John glin dogs?, to glin dogs is nice, Mary was glinned by most people who knew her, the glinning of dogs by John was excessive, to glin tables is ridiculous.* All this and more follows from exposure to just one use. Once the speaker hears just one grammatical use of a new word which suffices to identify its membership in a category, he can refer to the whole system of other rules involving that category.

The question is, however, how does a child break into this system of general rules? An adult knows a verb when he or she hears one. But presumably a child initially simply hears initial uses of individual words in meaningful sequences. The child has to analyze what words as semantically different from each other as *belong, kick, like, exist,* and *seem* have in common, such that they form a category useful for stating grammatical regularities.

Most everyone is taught at some point that verbs are words that denote actions; adjectives are words that denote stable states or qualities; and nouns denote persons and places and things. Statistically, there is something to this. The object and person words of a language are generally in the same grammatical category (which is then called nouns). Languages which have a grammatical distinction between verbs and adjectives put most actional words in the verb class, and stative terms with the adjectives. If this were consistently so, we might analyze the child's acquisition as follows: The child hears action terms taking various grammatical uses such as *-ed* past tense (*pushed, melted*), forms of *do* (*I don't sing, he doesn't eat*) in front, and so on, and notes that the terms which act in these grammatical ways all share the property of denoting an action. Thus, the semantic analysis of the term would be the key to analyzing how it works on grammar. This would occur similarly for adjectives, nouns, and prepositions (locative words).

The difficulty is, however, that the semantics of the categories are by no means this consistent. Words denoting emotion may be found in all the major categories. *Like, hate, enjoy* are verbs: *fond, sad, glad* are adjectives; *sadness, joy, hatred* are nouns. Many adjectives even seem more actional than many verbs—e.g., compare the adjectives *snoopy, helpful, quick,* to the verbs *like, belong,* and *exist.* Or it may be hard to see any meaningful difference at all between some verbs and adjectives: *John likes dogs—John is fond of dogs,* or *John liked it that Mary came—John is glad (of it) that Mary came.*

People still disagree over this, but it seems unlikely that the differences between nouns, verbs, adjectives, and prepositions can really be captured successfully by reference to the meaning of their members. But then the question is, what do members of each category have in common that unites them to each other, and differentiates them from members of other categories? No one can say exactly what the best answer for this is for the adult, nor exactly how the child comes to this answer. But over the past years, I, with others, have been developing some lines of reasoning and analysis of the available empirical data that point to the essentially circular nature of such categories: Form classes are devised for the purpose of stating generalizations about grammatical combinations of terms; yet their defining properties are, in fact, these combinatorial properties. Much of this has been put down at great (sometimes perhaps interminable) length in papers like Maratsos (1979), Maratsos, Kuczaj, Fox, and Chalkley (1979), Maratsos and Chalkley (1980), and Maratsos (1982), along with a briefer discussion in Maratsos (1983). So here I will just outline some of the ideas in a relatively brief form.

Perhaps the best way of seeing the problem is to think of it as a problem of prediction: How can we predict whether a particular word is likely to enter into a particular grammatical combination, such as *-ed* tensing. Let us do without the term verb altogether, since we are trying to explain what it is, rather than presuppose it. Instead, let us use something neutral like X to stand for the fact that there is some group of terms which takes some grammatical operation; or since we will be referring to more than one operation, use a subscripted X_i, X_j, and so on, for each operation. One such well-known grammatical operation in English is the addition of -ed to a term to denote past occurrence of the relation the word refers to, e.g., *like–liked, kick–kicked, belong–belonged.* We know this operation becomes productive for children, since they produce well-known, and somewhat appropriate errors, like *breaked* and *runned.* The question then is, what is it about a term that predicts it can take -ed to denote pastness? Why do children attach -ed to some words, but not (it turns out) to others?

Of course, all the terms that denote pastness in this fashion denote some kind of relation or property that can occur in the past. Perhaps X_i + -ed = 'past (X_i)' for any X_i that denotes a relation of any kind. Unfortunately, many terms also denote relations which can be spoken of in the past but do not do this by adding -ed. We cannot say *he happied,*[1] or *the boy inned the house,* though being happy or being in a house all can be thought of as taking place in the past (*he was happy, he was in the house.* Thus, while all the terms that take -ed past denote some kind of relation or property, this is still too broad. It also takes in all the relation or property terms that do not take -ed.

Probably most of the terms that take -ed past denote some kind of actional relation, e.g., *kick, push, concentrate* (construing actionality broadly). But this is still wrong. *Snoopy, helpful, fast, quick* are all fairly actional terms, but do not take -ed (*helpfuled, *snoopied*). Furthermore, many terms that do take -ed are not highly actional. These include *like, belong, exist, think* (in the sense 'I think so'). In fact, linguists of the 1960s (Fillmore, 1968; Lakoff, 1965) noted how the verb and adjective categories each have actional and nonactional members. So actionality or nonactionality are better predictors than simply noting that a term denotes a relation, but they are still inadequate.

Apparently it is very difficult to predict what kind of relation term (or predicate, as relational terms are commonly called) will take -ed past tense on the basis of the meanings of the terms *per se.* This is just the point already noted above. Suppose we shift from the meanings of the terms themselves to another tack: looking at related grammatical uses of terms. In English, again, there are terms that take -ed to denote past references, for which we might write:

$$X_i + \textit{-ed} = \text{'past of } X_i\text{'}$$

There are also some other characteristic tensing and negation operations of English relational terms. For example, there are predicates that denote present

---

[1]* is used here to mean unacceptable utterance.

tense after a third person singular subject by adding -s, e.g., *he likes it, he kicks chairs*. There are terms that denote nonoccurrence by use of a form of preceding *do*, e.g., *he didn't belong there, it doesn't fit*. Let us write these down:

$NP + X_i + -ed$ = 'past of X_i'

$NP + X_j + -s$ = 'present of X_j'
3Ps

$NP + don't + X_k$ = 'present, past negation of X_k'
doesn't
didn't

And so on. Now it turns out that a very good predictor of whether a term can take -*ed* tensing is whether it takes -*s* to denote present tense. Thus: *he likes it—he liked it, it belongs here—it belonged here*, or **he fonds of it—*he fonded of it, *he snoopies—*he snoopied*. Of course, if we ask what predicts whether a term takes -*s* present tense, a good answer is that it is likely to if it takes -*ed* past tensing. Similarly, whether or not a term takes preceding *do*-forms is a g-od predictor of whether it takes -*ed* past tense, or -*s* present tense. But again, a good predictor of taking preceding *do*-forms is taking -*s* present tense, or -*ed* past tense.

But such a system is, of course, circular. These verb operations predict each other, but it is hard to find something outside the system of operations, such as actionality, that predicts as well. This is why such categories are often called formal or structural categories—they are defined by use in the system itself.

How can this circle be broken into? The logical route involves lexical memorization and cross-correlation. The child must individually memorize that various individual predicates take -*ed* past tensing, various individual predicates take -*s* tensing, various individual predicates take preceding *do*-forms. (There are many other characteristic operations as well.) Over time the information must build up in long-term memory that there is a tendency for the same terms that take -*ed* past tensing to take -*s* tensing, to take preceding *do*-forms, and so on. This system of cross-implicational uses must form the basis for a process of category formation which operates when some groups of words share enough structural properties to justify forming a category. Once the category is formed, its shared distinctive properties then indicate membership in the category. Thus, first verbs are defined by taking various properties X_i, X_j, X_k, . . . If one hears a new predicate in some use, say X_j, one knows it is a verb, and so will take X_i, X_k, and so on. Similarly, adjectives are predicates which share another set of correlated grammatical operations. For example, verbs typically employ *do*-forms or inflections to mark tense. Adjectives typically employ some form of preceding *be*, e.g., *he (is, was, isn't, wasn't) happy*, rather than **he happies, *he happied, *she doesn't happy, *he didn't happy*. Another important characteristic of adjectives is that they can appear before noun arguments in noun phrase arguments as modifiers in unmarked form, e.g., *a happy man, a snoopy person.* Verbs can do this, but must always be marked somehow, e.g., *a sleeping dog, a pushed over chair.*

Of course, this is not the only way of breaking into a system defined on combinations. Another way, implicit or relatively explicit in many proposals (see Schlesinger, this volume), is the transformation of an early, more semantic-based category such as action predicate into the more formal verb category, by a process something like the following, in idealized form: A fairly large structural category is formed early, such as action. In fact, there is evidence for some kind of action category playing an early part in children's rules such as actor–action (Bloom, 1970; Bowerman, 1973; Braine, 1976; Brown, 1973; Schlesinger, 1971). Over time, the child learns that many of these take operations such as *-ed* tensing and use of preceding *do*-forms. These properties come to characterize the category as well. With more time, the child hears nonactional terms such as *want, belong,* and *like* taking the same grammatical operations. These terms are absorbed into the major predicate category, the basis of which thus slowly shifts towards a more formal or structural basis.

There are both similarities and differences among these two kinds of accounts. The first similarity is that in the end, the child internally decides that the combinatorial properties are the important defining properties for categories if we grant the points made previously about the very great semantic overlap among the formal categories. Second, such an account must still depend on a great deal of lexical tabulation. The account presupposes that the child tabulate which grammatical operations are becoming characteristic of the slowly changing originally semantic-based category. There is, however, the major difference that in the purely combinatorial account, the category is built up from a tabulation of individual uses per se. The second account builds on an implicit (and not unreasonable) intuition that it is easier to gradually transform a naturally given initial large category to a more formal one, instead.

I do not think that the available theoretical considerations and empirical data allow a firm decision among these (and other) possible accounts. But I think there are some interesting developmental data. First are data from the development of the English verb system, partly from work of mine with collaborators, and partly from the work of others (not necessarily intended for this problem). We can see from this work that there is in fact very little empirical support for the idealized picture of action category turning into the verb category that has been commonly proposed (e.g., Bates & MacWhinney, 1982; de Villiers, 1980). Second, less directly, there are data from noun gender systems in German, Russian, Polish, and other languages. These categories must have a purely structural basis, yet children do learn such systems in the early preschool years, with surprising skill and without instruction. Let me turn first to the acquisitional work from English.

2. THE EVOLUTION OF THE VERB CLASS IN ENGLISH

It is surprising how little knowledge we have of the empirical development of the operations characteristic of categories such as verb. Perhaps this is so because as Braine (1976) has noted many investigators have presupposed, or easily read into their data, the adult categories such as verb and adjective. Here, I review briefly two aspects of the data. First, when can we with some security say that the child has acquired a categorial system rather like that of the adult's? Second, what does acquisition look like before that point?

There is a difference between being able to positively say a development has occurred, vs. claiming it could not have occurred earlier, and it is only the first I intend here. For the class of verbs, what is wanted is some evidence that the child indeed uses something like the adult category in a productive fashion; that furthermore, the basis for such productivity is a category not defined upon a semantic basis such as actionality. Presently, the best evidence for when this has taken place lies in the patterns and inflectional uses in general, and -ed over-regularizations in particular (Cazden, 1968; Maratsos, 1983; Maratsos et al., 1979). The most famous phenomenon of this sort in English—and deservedly so—is the use of past tense -ed. Initially, children's uses of -ed past tense are all accurate. They may say *melted* or *dropped,* but not, as they later do, **runned* and **breaked* (Cazden, 1968; Ervin, 1964). It is actually fairly late that over-regularizations of -ed appear and become common, around Brown's MLU stages IV and V (Maratsos et al., 1979). When this happens, the range of use is surprisingly appropriate. Past tense -ed is not just used on actional verbs such as *break* and *run,* but also in nonactional verbs like *think (I thoughted we had cinnamon toast)* and *know* (I knowed it). There is furthermore evidence for the nonactional verbs that children understand.

These data do not, however, say anything about whether children might evolve the verb category out of the earlier action term category. They only show that by Stages IV or V children have devised something like this adult verb category. It is not impossible that the verb category does grow out of the earlier appearing action term category. But the kind of clear developmental picture that some writers (e.g., Bates & MacWhinney, 1982; de Villiers, 1980) predict to go along with this does not in fact occur.

First, it is common belief, I think, that all of children's early verbs are in fact action terms, and that all early action terms are verbs. Neither of these beliefs are correct. Terms like *away, up, down, back,* and *bye-bye* are observed in actor–action sequences like *spider away* in the earliest grammars (Bloom, Lightbown, & Hood, 1975; Bowerman, 1976). Judging from examples in Bellugi (1967) and Braine (1976), nonactional verbs like *need, want, know, like,* and *sleep* are found early in children's corpora as well, from Stages I or II onwards.

All this, however, is just a matter of vocabulary learning. It simply says which words called verbs in adult vocabulary are present early on and which are not. We can ask the developmental questions more pointedly by seeing how semantic properties such as actionality are linked to the emergence of various grammatical operations distinctive of the verb category. These, as already noted, are operations such as *-ed* tensing, use of *do*-forms in front, present tense with *-s*, use of auxiliaries, and so on. In fact, those who favor the idea that verb as a category grows out of the earlier action term category generally make an hypothesis (Bates & MacWhinney, 1982; probably de Villiers, 1980; Slobin, 1981). This hypothesis is that the operations characteristic of verbs will emerge first on the "best" or prototypical action terms, then spread outwards to other terms depending on how they resemble the semantically best terms.

It is not exactly clear what the "best" actions are, though one can see guesses in the literature. For example, *-ed* past tense tends to come in earliest on terms that denote some change of state or achievement, such as *touch* or *melt*. De Villiers (1980) notes this, and holds that such terms constitute the prototypical verbs. Slobin (1981) on the other hand thinks terms that refer to a very specific action of an animate agent, carried out with some particular body part, perhaps involving transfer, are the semantically most prototypical actions. In any case, the hypothesis is empirically false. What it claims, to recapitulate, is that verb uses initially cluster onto some central category of the actional verbs, then gradually radiate outwards to the less actional terms. The actual developmental picture is quite different. For example, one grammatical property distinctive of verbs (though not shared by all of them), is taking a transitive object. Early transitive uses include transitive actional verbs such as *give* and *make*. But corpora and examples in Braine (1976) and Bellugi (1967) also show fairly early uses of transitive objects with terms like *see, want, need,* and *like*. Or suppose we look at uses such as taking preceding *don't* and *can't* (I don't like it, he can't go). Bellugi (1967) looked at the development of negation in Adam, Eve, and Sarah. First, her records show that *don't* and *can't* are mostly used on different terms to begin with. They do not begin by use with a common core of verbs. Second, her examples show uses with nonactional predicates like *need, want, know,* and *like*. So these early verb operations are not even restricted to the action class when they begin to appear in Stages II and III. Much less do they appear first with a prototypical action "core." Bloom, Lifter, and Hafitz (1980) have made the most detailed investigation of the semantics of the verbs on which the inflections past tense *-ed*, progressive *-ing*, and present tense *-s* first appear. As noted already, they find that *-ed* past mostly occurs first on terms which refer to some change of state or achievement. Progressive *-ing* appears on actional terms as well, but mostly on ones denoting actions that go on for a while, a set mostly different from the ones that initially take *-ed*. Present tense *-s* appears initially on a few nonactional locative predicates. These include *fit* (*it fits here*) and *go* (*it goes here* to mean 'it belongs here'). In fact, Brown (1973) remarks in passing that he did not find the same verbs taking progressive *-ing* and present tense *-s* until around Stage V. As we have seen, this is when the data from the over-regularizations of -*ed* past indicate that the formation of an adult verb category has certainly taken place.

The problem here is not whether an action category plays some role in earlier or later grammar. There is every reason to believe that it does, in major constituent rules like actor+action, action+location, and so on. The question is whether the developmental data show obvious signs that the action category (or some prototypical core of it) serves as the organizational basis for the emerging structural verb category. I think the earlier summary shows that this is not true in any way that makes itself obvious in the empirical data. In fact, there is good reason in each of the above developments to think that these individual operations are being tabulated as applying individually to various predicate terms. Bellugi (1967) comes to essentially this conclusion in dealing with the occurrence of *don't* and *can't*. That is, she decided on the basis of the match between parental speech and children's speech that the children were memorizing individually which predicates take *don't* or *can't* as as negators, rather than applying them productively. It is well known that the initial uses of -*ed* past tense are probably memorized (Cazden, 1968; Ervin, 1964). Most investigators think that the initial uses of progressive -*ing* are memorized as well (Brown, 1973; Kuczaj, 1978a, 1978b; Maratsos & Chalkley, 1980). The initial uses of present tense -*s* are probably also memorized.

Thus, it is hard to find any evidence that the earlier action category or some core of it acts as an important developmental organizer for important verb operations as they emerge. Finally, suppose we look at the transition into Stages IV and V. Suppose children nevertheless had been organizing the encoding of many verb operations around the central semantic properties of action vs. nonaction. We might expect that as terms like *snoopy* and *helpful* were acquired—terms which have some clear actional meaning—there would be a tendency for the child to treat them like the other action terms because of their shared meaning. So errors like *I don't snoopy* or *he helpfuled* should occur, at least until the child could complete the transition from an action-based to a more structurally defined verb category. Similarly, the child would have trouble treating nonactional terms like *want, like, think,* and *know* in the same way as actional terms such as *melt* or *go* until this transition is made. But the absence of errors with adjectives, and the treatment of nonactional verbs like other verbs, all point to no such transition occurring.

Overall, what we know really does not sharply match what we could expect if the verb category emerges from the chrysalis of the earlier action predicate category. Proponents of this point of view (such as Schlesinger, in this volume) need, I think, to find more imposing data to support the idea than its general plausibility. It would be useful to know more about what is going on with verbs and adjectives in Stages III–V. But right now, the data do not look nearly like what we would expect if the central action predicate category serves as a strong early organizer for later developments.[2]

At this point, I must say that I agree with Braine's position (this volume) that the picture may be simpler for nouns for many reasons. In fact, the use of the predicate-argument distinction that he suggests (see also, Maratsos & Chalkley, 1980) probably provides important additional information to the child as well. There are probably many important additional assumptions or changes in the ideas sketched above, that would be necessary to give a successful outline of the development of the verb category. But presently it seems reasonable to guess that the child progresses to the verb category by a remarkably direct and accurate structural route that does not involve action predicates as a developmental intermediate.

3. NOUN GENDER CATEGORIES

In the end, arguments about the nature and development of the major form classes have to stand on their own. But recent studies on noun gender categories do provide a kind of corroborating evidence. For these studies show that children can and do form highly formal categories in the preschool years, sometimes probably by the age of 3, which is around when the evidence for the emergence of a formal category such as verb becomes strongest, in English at least (it may emerge earlier in more highly inflected languages, in which there is more evidence for it for the child, of course). These studies include data from German, Polish, Russian, French, Hebrew, and other languages (Karmiloff-Smith, 1979;

---

[2]These arguments do not prove that the early action category could not somehow grow into the later verb category. Some ways around them are discussed in Maratsos (1982), for example. But the fact remains that the positive evidence for the action category growing into the verb category is very slim. As outlined here, the actual empirical sequences do not resemble the hypothetical ones expected by a number of authors at all. The idea has a great deal of intuitive appeal, and better grounds than have been discussed here and elsewhere for being reasonable. So if such evidence turns up, that would be of real importance. As of now, it is generally not available.

Finally, even if it does, there remains the problem that somehow, children avoid pushing actionality as an explanation too hard just where it would not do. This is in fact only one of a number of cases in which semantic properties and structural categories almost overlap, and in which children who use these same semantic properties for some domains of grammar, somehow do not seem to overuse them incorrectly accounting for some other domains. That is, actionality is used appropriately to formulate early rules of major sentence structure, but not overused in attempting to account for verb operations. This is only one of a number of cases where children's ability to apportion analytic properties appropriately is basically mysterious. Some attempts are made to deal with the particular problems of acctionality and verb properties in Maratsos and Chalkley (1980). But for reasons which would take too long to discuss here, these attempts are almost certainly inadequate to the problem. So the problem remains.

Levy, 1983; MacWhinney, 1978; Maratsos, 1981; Maratsos & Chalkley, 1980; Mills, 1986; Smoczyńska, 1986), and a summary of very much of the work would require more space than is reasonable here (see Maratsos, 1983, for a general summary, other sources cited above for more detailed writing). Instead, I describe briefly here one of the grammatical systems, one that is paradigmatic in many ways, the German noun gender system. The German noun gender system, like that of Russian or Polish, exists as a kind of triple wrinkle in the system of case marking. Both gender and case marking are realized through differences in the forms of determiners (English articles, demonstratives), pronouns, and pre-nominal adjectives. For example, where the English speaker uses simply *the* whether saying *the fork, the spoon,* or *the knife is here,* the German speaker must say, respectively, *der Loffel (spoon), die Gabel* (fork), *or* das Messer (knife) ist hier. Where the English speaker can use simply the pronoun *it* to say of any of these that *it is blue,* the German speaker would have to say *er, sie,* or *es ist blau for the spoon, fork, and knife, respectively.*

Furthermore, English has just a rudimentary case system (nominative, genitive, objective) for the pronouns and determiners (*he, his, him; she, her(s), her; they, their(s), them*). German has four cases, nominative, accusative, genitive and dative, which in combination with gender class determine the choice of determiner or pronoun. Thus, for the masculine gender noun *spoon,* the following uses are typical: Nominative case: *Der Loffel ist hier. Er ist hier* ('it is here'). Accusative case: *Er diskutiert den Loffel. Er diskutiert ihn* ('He discussed the spoon. He discussed it'). Dative: *Er spricht von dem Loffel. Er spricht von ihm* ('He is speaking about the spoon. He is speaking about it'). For a feminine noun such as fork, the same contexts require the uses *Die Gabel ist hier. Sie ist hier* (nominative): *Er diskutiert die Gabel. Er diskutiert sie; Er spricht von der Gabel. Er spricht von ihr.* The grammatical paradigm for just the definite determiners (equivalent in meaning to 'the') and definite pronouns (equivalent in meaning to 'it' for inanimates) is printed below in the singular:

| | Masculine | | Feminine | | Neuter | |
	Pron.	Det.	Pron.	Det.	Pron.	Det.
Nominative	er	der	sie	die	es	das
Accusative	ihn	den	sie	die	es	das
Genitive	seiner	des	ihrer	der	seiner	des
Dative	ihm	dem	ihr	der	ihm	dem

As is well known, there is virtually no semantic basis for the noun gender distinctions. For example, the words for fork, knife and spoon are, respectively, feminine, neuter, and masculine, which does not even follow the appropriate Freudian symbolism. It is true that for a small number of truly sexed nouns ('boy', 'man', 'woman', a few others) the meaning does predict grammatical use. The truly masculine nouns are in the masculine set, most of the feminine nouns (except that for 'young girl') are in the feminine set, a situation similar to that found in Russian and Polish as well. But the best available evidence for gender systems in general, and for German in particular, is that children do not begin by analyzing the few nouns for which semantic correlates predict grammatical usage, then spreading this somehow to the arbitrary cases. For example. suppose children are shown a new type of person or animal which is clearly masculine or feminine, but which is referred to by a conflicting grammatical determiner. They apparently produce other combinations with the noun on the basis of its grammatical gender, rather than its conceptual gender (Bohm & Levelt, 1979). What is available from naturalistic observations of German, Russian, Polish, and Hebrew (see Maratsos, 1983, for a summary) also indicated that children do not begin by analysis of the small set of truly sexed nouns. Instead, they seem directly to analyze on the formal basis.

What is this formal basis? It is in principle much like that discussed earlier for verbs: the combinations in which individual terms can appear to predict each other. That is, a noun which takes *der* as determiner in the nominative takes *den* in the accusative, *des* in the genitive, and *dem* in the dative. This comprises part of the masculine gender system. A noun which takes *die* in the nominative, takes *die, der,* and *der* in the accusative, dative and genitive, respectively. And so on. (Because the cases themselves are not always straightforwardly defined, it is remarkable that children can analyze the total system at all.) Similarly, nouns which take *der* as nominative definite determiner, take *ihn* as accusative pronoun, nouns which take *das* as nominative definite determiner, take *es* as accusative pronoun, and so on. Such a system must begin with memorization of numbers of related uses for individual nouns, before the overall pattern of cross-correlations can be analyzed.

Again, it would be good to have more data than we do on the development of such remarkably complex systems. Children apparently have mastered much of it by the age of 3 or so in German (MacWhinney, 1978; Walters, 1975), and the basically similar Polish (Smoczyńska, 1986) and Russian (Maratsos & Chalkley, 1980) systems. There are some disagreements over the amount of error found, and this seems to be partly dependent on the language as well. In the Russian system, the one with the most exceptions, errors seem to be very common during the third year (see summaries in Slobin, 1973). But in Polish, much like Russian but with fewer irregularities, Smoczyńska (1986) reports a brief period of error early in the third year and then early mastery. Mills (1986) indicates some errors in tasks involving experimental elicitations, with a tendency to overuse the feminine. But remarkably enough, Walters (1975) reports from naturalistic studies that gender errors are very rare in determiner use.

On the whole, errors in noun gender learning seem to be more common than form class errors, and if this is so, this is an important difference which requires an explanation. But at the same time, the data from these systems indicate that even by the age of 3, children can delve through these very complicated and potentially confusing data to come up with the core properties of how related uses of terms predict each other. At the center of things, there is much similarity between saying that terms that take -*ed* in the past take preceding *don't, doesn't, can't,* and so on as negators, and saying that terms which take *der* as preceding determiner in the nominative, take *den* as determiner in the accusative, *ihn* as pronoun, and so on. At the heart of both noun gender systems and form class systems is the fact that the categories are structurally defined: what their members have in common most pointedly are sets of related uses, rather than sets of semantic properties. The noun gender systems are far clearer cases of this than the form class categories. The fact that the noun gender systems can be learned by age 3 makes it more plausible that similar mechanisms apply in the evolution of structurally defined categories such as verb and adjective as well. In fact, there is something else. It is clear that the noun gender distinctions, unlike case distinctions, have little communicative value. Yet they do crop up in languages, and children can learn them. It is hard to see how this could be so unless they tap a generalized capacity for this kind of analysis that is fairly automatically brought to bear upon linguistic problems by children. It is most plausible to think of their widespread occurrence as being parasitic upon analyses that are so readily abailable (as a type) that they can be diverted as well to the task of learning otherwise difficult and certainly unmotivated gender distinctions. So analysis of categories in terms of combinations shared by groups of terms is likely to be a very basic ability children bring to language learning.

4. GENERAL SUMMARY

In summary, our argument is that the major form class categories appear to have important semantic cores, but in the end appear to take central definition from the structural properties shared by their members. We have seen that children apparently can be shown to have constructed such systems in English by Stages IV or V (perhaps even earlier for nouns, as Braine's arguments suggest), without actionality having much earlier potency as an organizer for the relevant operations. The available evidence indicates that children can construct such systems for noun gender categories by about the age of 3 or so. In all the domains of evidence, it would be useful to have more evidence on important periods, or subsystems. These include the development of the English system of the use of *be,* which, as Braine argues in this volume, is probably central to the verb-adjective distinction, or the German prononimal system, which probably begins to appear earlier than the determiner system but which has received little study. It is also the case that sheer cross-correlation of all extant combinations carried out exhaustively would require peculiarly large storage space. It is thus very likely that there are factors making some properties more likely to play analytic roles. For example, in the case of predicates, our examples have concentrated heavily upon tensing morphemes—verbs are tensed in different ways from adjectives, such as being marked directly. This is in fact a common characteristic of many languages besides English that have a verb-adjective distinction. This is natural if a central aspect of the relations denoted by predicates is their place in a temporal framework, which is marked by tense (Maratsos, 1983). Perhaps most important would be more work, both theoretical and empirical, elucidating the relation of the semantic cores of form class categories and other categories (such as case categories in many languages) to their emergence as structural categories. I have summarized here evidence that we should not take for granted that there is a strong developmental and analytic relation. Also the point remains that however structural categories are eventually evolved, structural properties per se must be potent as defining, as opposed to simply symptomatic characteristics of the category (see Maratsos, 1981, for this distinction). But perhaps it is unlikely that semantic properties consistently fail to play a role of some kind (see Braine's discussion of the predicate-argument relation in this volume, for example), and elucidating the degree to which this is or is not so thus persists as a central developmental question.

ACKNOWLEDGMENT

This paper was written while the author was a fellow at the Institute for Advanced Studies at the Hebrew University of Jerusalem in 1982–1983, whose support during this time is gratefully acknowledged.

REFERENCES

Bates, E., & MacWhinney, B. (1982). A functionalist approach to grammatical development. In H. E. Wanner & L. Gleitman (Eds.), *Language acquisition: The state of the art.* Cambridge, England: Cambridge University Press.

Bellugi, U. (1967). *The acquisition of negation.* Unpublished doctoral dissertation, Harvard University.

Bloom, L. (1970). *Language development: Form and function in emerging grammars.* Cambridge, MA: MIT Press.

Bloom, L., Lifter, K., & Hafitz, J. (1980). Semantics of verbs and the development of verb inflection in child language. *Language, 56,* 386–412.

Bloom, L., Lightbown, P., & Hood, L. (1975). Structure and variation in child language. *Monographs of the Society for Research in Child Development, 40,* (Serial No. 160).

Bohm, K., & Levelt, W. J. M. (1979, June). *Children's use and awareness of natural and syntactic gender.* Paper presented at the conference on Linguistic awareness and learning to read. Victoria, British Columbia.

Bowerman, M. (1973). *Early syntactic development: A cross-linguistic study with special reference to Finnish* Cambridge, England: Cambridge University Press.

Bowerman, M. (1976). Semantic factors in the acquisition of rules for word use and sentence construction. In D. M. Morehead and A. E. Morehead (Eds.), *Normal and deficient child language*. Baltimore, MD: University Park Press.

Braine, M. D. S. (1976). Children's first word combinations. *Monographs of the Society for Research in Child Development, 41*.

Brown, R. (1973). *A first language: The early stages*. New York: The Free Press.

Cazden, C. (1968). The acquisition of noun and verb inflections. *Child Development, 39*, 433–438.

de Villiers, J. G. (1980). The process of rule learning in children: A new look. In K. Nelson (Ed.), *Children's Language, Vol. 2*. New York: Gardner Press.

Ervin, S. M. (1964). Imitation and structural change in children's language. In E. H. Lenneberg (Ed.), *New directions in the study of language*. Cambridge, MA: MIT Press.

Fillmore, C. J. (1968). The case for case. In E. Bach & R. T. Harms (Eds.), *Universals in linguistic theory*. New York: Holt, Rinehart, and Winston.

Karmiloff-Smith, A. (1979). *A functional approach to child language*. Cambridge: The University Press.

Kuczaj, S. A., II. (1978a). Children's judgments of grammatical and ungrammatical irregular past tense verbs. *Child Development, 49*, 319–326.

Kuczaj, S. A., II. (1978b). Why do children fail to overgeneralize the progressive inflection? *Journal of Child Language, 5*, 167–171.

Lakoff, G. (1965). *On the nature of syntactic irregularity*, Report NSF-16, Harvard University Computation Laboratory.

Levy, Y. (1983). It's frogs all the way down. *Cognition, 15*, 75–93.

MacWhinney, B. (1978). The acquisition of morphology. *Monographs of the Society for Research in Child Development, 43*.

Maratsos, M. P. (1979). How to get from words to sentences. In D. Aronson & R. J. Rieber (Eds.), *Psycholinguistic research: Implications and applications*. Hillsdale, NJ: Lawrence Erlbaum Associates.

Maratsos, M. P. (1981). Problems in categorial evolution: Can formal categories arise from semantic ones? In W. Deutsch (Ed.), *The child's construction of language*. New York: Academic Press.

Maratsos, M. P. (1982). The child's construction of grammatical categories. In H. E. Wanner & L. Gleitman (Eds.), *Language Acquisition: The state of the art*. Cambridge: The University Press.

Maratsos, M. P. (1983). Some current issues in the study of language acquisition. In P. Mussen (Ed.), *The Handbook of Child Psychology*, (Vol. 3). New York: Wiley.

Maratsos, M. P., & Chalkley, M. A. (1980). The internal language of children's syntax: The ontogenesis and representation of syntactic categories. In K. Nelson (Ed.), *Children's Language, Vol. 2*. New York: Gardner Press.

Maratsos, M. P., Kuczaj, S. A., II., Fox, D. E. C., & Chalkley, M. A. (1979). Some empirical studies in the acquisition of transformational relations. In W. A. Collins (Ed.), *The Minnesota Symposium on Child Psychology (Vol. 12)*. Hillsdale, NJ: Lawrence Erlbaum Associates.

Mills, A. (1986). The acquisition of German. In D. Slobin (Ed.), The *crosslinguistic study of language acquisition* (Vol. 1). Hillsdale, NJ: Lawrence Erlbaum Associates.

Schlesinger, I. M. (1971). Production of utterances and language acquisition. In D. I. Slobin (Ed.), *The ontogenesis of grammar*. New York: Academic Press.

Slobin, D. I. (1981). The origin of grammatical encoding of events. In W. Deutsch (Ed.), *The child's construction of language*, New York: Academic Press.

Smoczyńska, M. (1986). The acquisition of Polish. In D. I. Slobin (Ed.), The *cross-linguistic study of language acquisition* (Vol. 1). Hillsdale, NJ: Lawrence Erlbaum Associates.

Walters, S. (1975). *Zur Entwicklung Morphologischer Strukturen bei Kindern*. Diplomarbeit. Heidelberg.

3 Word Class Distinctions in Developing Grammars

Ruth A. Berman
Tel-Aviv University

INTRODUCTION

The way in which word-class distinctions evolve in children's emergent grammars is of interest from several points of view. It is an issue which touches on very general concerns for language acquisition, such as whether the knowledge in question is innate or learned, and what developmental route it follows. It is relevant to current conflicts concerning how children break into the linguistic system: Whether by initial attention to distributional factors in the co-occurrence of grammatical categories and/or by reliance on semantic factors as determinants of lexical class membership; whether by relating primarily to formal and/or to pragmatic cues, or to a combination of both, as the basis for distinctions operative in the endstate grammar—as has been argued from varying points of view, both in their contributions to this volume and elsewhere, by Braine, Levy, Maratsos, Ninio, and Schlesinger, among others. And this question intersects in important ways with the relationship between linguistic universals and the particular ways in which these are realized in the lexical and morpho-syntactic categories specified by specific languages and types of languages.

The present study attempts to address a few of these issues, along the following lines. It starts by focusing on linguistic theory and description as a source of hypotheses for children's development of word-class distinctions in learning their native tongue. I suggest that such knowledge may initially be triggered by children's experience with the most typical, least marked, or universal exemplars of the different categories, ones which manifest a confluence of semantic, morphological, and syntactic properties that set them apart from members of other word-class categories (Section 1). I then outline a model of language acquisition, evolved in studying rather different issues, in order to argue that the learning of word-class distinctions involves a lengthy developmental process. For while the underpinnings of some broad distinction between nouns and verbs can be identified very early on, the refinement of these distinctions to include new properties, subclasses, and exceptions will continue well beyond the early years (Section 2). Evidence for these claims is provided by considering the way verbs are learned compared with nouns and adjectives in children's acquisition of Hebrew as a native tongue (Section 3). The chapter ends by considering how typological or language-particular features of the target language may affect the child's task in acquiring word-class distinctions in a given language (Section 4).

1. VERBS, NOUNS, AND ADJECTIVES IN LINGUISTIC DESCRIPTION

Discussion of word-class distinctions typically devolves upon the three major lexical categories of N, V, A. The focus, here, too, will be on nouns, verbs, and adjectives as open-class items or contentives. These function as part of the patterns of **lexicalization,** in the sense of the way in which relatively autonomous lexical contents become realized in the shape of words that divide up semantic space in a given language (Talmy, 1985). In this, as in other respects, they contrast with closed-class items or functors—pronouns, articles, conjunctions, etc.—as relational terms which are bound up with the pattern of **grammaticization** of a language (Givon, 1979). Thus, function words in one language may take the form of bound affixes or clitics in another, whereas content words will tend to retain a relatively independent status in different languages. Besides, grammatical formatives are such that any addition or change in their class membership leads to a systematic reorganization of the class as a whole. They are typically high-frequency items and, since they are few in number and occur in nonextendable, closed sets, are presumably learned as belonging to that set and as contrasting with other members of it. For instance, a child will come to recognize that *I* shares certain features with *we* and others with *me,* and that these contrast in specific ways with *he, they,* and *him* as well as with *myself* or *himself.* (For relevant analyses concerning the learning of **paradigms,** see Pinker [1984].) One hypothesis, then, might be that there will be important differences of principle in the nature of the knowledge which children acquire in distinguishing between the major lexical classes in their language and in learning about the class-membership of grammatical formatives—whether function words or affixes. As noted, however, in the present context we disregard the learning of closed-class items or functors, in order to focus on the major lexical classes of N, V, and A.

All languages make a major class distinction between something like noun and verb, although there is no total overlap of membership from one language to another (Anderson, 1985; Hopper & Thompson, 1984). And many, but not all languages also possess a distinct class of modifying terms corresponding to what we know as adjectives (Dixon, 1977; Thompson, 1986). In classical grammars, a distinction is made between the class of terms known as *rhema,* corresponding basically to verbs, and the class of *onoma* or **substantives,** which includes nouns and adjectives (Robins, 1966). Such traditional classifications are based largely on morphological criteria. In Hebrew, for instance, Ns and As are alike in that they are inflected for number, gender, and definiteness, but not for person or tense; and in Latin and Greek, case-marking is assigned to N and A, but not to V. Contemporary analyses, by contrast, tend to treat V and A together, under the joint category of **predicate.** Thus, the following pairs of V/A expressions share both syntactic and semantic similarities: *like/be fond of, dislike/be averse to,* and so do inchoative pairs like *tire/get tired, age/grow old.* Both sets of claims represent N and V as most clearly distinct, with A lying somewhere between them, sharing properties of both. In developmental terms, we can thus hypothesize that the N/V distinction will have priority over acquisition of A as a distinct class of elements.

This basic distinction between two major classes has been characterized from different perspectives. Thus Braine (1987) and Keenan (1979) analyze it in terms of an underlying logical distinction between predicates and arguments; Givon (1984) relates to the distinction in **phenomenological** terms, suggesting that experiences which remain "relatively *stable* over time" will across languages tend to take the form of nouns, whereas those "denoting *rapid changes* in the state of the universe" are more likely to be lexicalized as verbs (pp. 51–52); while Hopper & Thompson (1984) provide a discourse-based orientation to the distinction as universal categories which serve for lexicalization of the canonic discourse functions of "discourse-manipulable participant" and "reported events" respectively. There seems good reason to agree with Braine (1987) in taking the distinction between predicate and argument phrases as a primitive notion, available from the outset of the language learning process. We thus assume that the basic word-class distinctions are rooted in the more primitive linguistic universal of a predicate/argument distinction, in both ontogeny and phylogeny—in children's developing grammars, on the one hand, and in evolution of the relevant categories in language history, on the other. This, then, is innate knowledge which the child brings to bear on acquiring word-class distinctions in a given target language. Beyond this, we argue that children utilize a variety of input cues in establishing the relevant distinctions: morpho-syntactic forms and distributional co-occurrences, lexico-semantic content, and discourse functions.

Consider, first, the relation between the major lexical categories themselves. Since A is more marginal across and within languages, it may be less functional in the early phases of language acquisition. Moreover, N and V are also themselves not of equal status. Semantically, predicates are less autonomous than arguments. As relational terms, their interpretation depends on the argument(s) with which they are associated. Thus, **intransitive verbs** are interpreted by reference to their subject nouns: compare the verb *is working* in association with NP subjects such as *that man, the horse, our car, my watch,* on the one hand, or *the system, our new project,* on the other; **transitive verbs** are interpreted in terms of their object nouns: compare the verb *play* when it occurs with NPs like *tennis, chess, the piano,* on the one hand, or with expressions like *a role, the fool* or *havoc,* on the other; and **adjectives** are interpreted relative to the noun arguments to which they are assigned: Compare the sense of *fresh* when used to modify nouns like *eggs, air, complexion* as against ones like *starts, ideas,* and *talk* respectively (Keenan, 1979). This relationality of verbs and adjectives compared with nominal arguments will affect the task faced by children in distinguishing the categories in question. Nouns may have a privileged status in acquisition, since they constitute the constants with which V and A will be associated as functions. And there is evidence that nouns do in fact have priority. This has been demonstrated by crosslinguistic data from very early child language by Gentner (1982a), who explains it as deriving from a quite general cognitively motivated distinction (Gentner, 1982b); it is shown to hold for the vocabulary development of 2- to 3-year-olds in a variety of studies reviewed by Clark (1983, pp. 799–801); while research shows that preschoolers consistently perceive nouns as being represented in written strings long before they do so for either verbs or function words (Ferreiro, 1978), and that on a variety of segmentation tasks children under the age of 6 will attend primarily to nouns (Holden & McGinitie, 1972, Tolchinsky-Landsmann, 1986).

Another source of hypotheses concerning how children learn word-class distinctions derives from research into the role of **typicality** in categorization (Rosch, 1977; Rosch & Mervis, 1975) as well as in semantic development (Keil, 1986; Mulford, 1979). The semantics of word-class membership can be characterized as a continuum from the best exemplars or most prototypical instances to cases which bear only a vague or remote family resemblance to other members of the class. From this point of view, both across languages and within a given language, the most "noun-like" nouns refer to individuals—that is, to concrete objects such as *toy* and *book* or animate creatures such as *frog* and *baby;* by comparison, nouns which specify attributive states, events, or actions are less typically nounlike, and closer to predicates (e.g., state-terms such as *tiredness, creativity,* events like *accident, journey,* or actions like *denial, provocation.*) Typical verbs denote dynamic physical actions where objects have things done or happen to them—e.g., *kick, push* and *fall, break* respectively—or where creatures perform actions—*walk, cry*—and so on; terms which refer to internal states or experiences—e.g., *hunger, ache*—are less good instances of the class of verbs. And the most prototypical adjectives denote perceptual attributes of size, shape, temperature, color, or appearance—e.g., *big, round, cold, brown, ugly* as compared with, say, verb-like participials—e.g., *upset, interesting*—or noun-derived forms like *childish, dramatic.*

Across languages, the extremes of these continua, those which constitute the clearest cases, will typically divide up into N or V and, where the language has this option, also A. Their status as lexical primes will be reflected by a confluence of morpho-syntactic and semantic properties.[1] In morphological terms, such words will tend to be structurally unmotivated, and are typically monomorphemic or at least monolexemic. For instance, count nouns are better exemplars of nouns than abstract or mass nouns—they can take plural morphology and semantically they refer to individuals; action verbs are good exemplars of their word-class—they take durative as well as perfective inflections in English, and they are semantically furthest from states or objects; and verb-related adjectives like Hebrew *agol* 'round' or *atsuv* 'sad', which semantically express basic perceptual attributes, are also more adjective-like in their syntactic patterning than are denominals like *moderni* 'modern' or *ta'asiyati* 'industrial' (Attias, 1981). These prototypical, best exemplars also enjoy a privileged status in development. They constitute the bulk of the early repertoire of nouns, verbs, and adjectives which are used by children.[2] And category-typicality plays a critical role in how children sort out the grammar of word-class membership in their language.

Finally, in crosslinguistic terms, languages obviously differ in whether and how they specify categories such as causative or inchoative for predicates, duality or gender for nouns. They also vary in how they distinguish between different word-classes: syntactically through co-occurrence and word-order patternings; by morphological devices of affixation; by prosodic features of stress or syllabicity (cf. English noun-verb pairs such as *transfer, record*); or by various combinations of these devices. Yet across languages, certain grammatical categories will typically be associated with either the noun-argument or the verb-predicate system. Thus, verbs are commonly marked for tense/mood/aspect and for person and number agreement with their subject; nouns, in contrast, are commonly marked for number, for gender or some other type of classifier, as well as for case, sometimes also for deixis (Bybee, 1985). Clearly, within a given language, such patternings are not a matter of all-or-nothing: Rather, there are "best exemplar" instances morphologically, syntactically, and semantically. Again, these instances are likely to form the basis for initial word-class categorizations made by children learning a given language. Moreover, for any given type of language, some kinds of marking will be more pervasive and typical than others, leading children to pay special attention to the formal features most characteristic of their particular native tongue.

---

[1]Prototypical or best instances of other linguistic constructs, too, will manifest a confluence of relative properties rather than a limited set of criterial features. This has been demonstrated in crosslinguistic characterizations of such notions as grammatical subject (Keenan, 1976) or the **word** as a lexical prime (Anderson, 1985).

[2]It could be claimed, of course, that such early selections simply mirror the input to which children are exposed. But the very fact that certain items prevail both in the speech addressed to young children and in that which they use themselves provides good evidence for their having a highly favored status. For further discussion along these lines, see Berman (1986a, pp. 200–201), and also de Villiers (1980, 1983), Slobin (1987).

As initial hypotheses, then, I assume that children come to the task of language acquisition equipped with a universally motivated distinction between predicates as relations and arguments as constants, and that this will predispose them to seek out N/V contrasts in their mother tongue. When they first start using items belonging to these categories in the endstate grammar, however, children will not associate them with any particular structural category or class.[3] Secondly, those items, structures, and properties which are most universal and least marked across languages, as well as within the particular language being learned, will enjoy a privileged status in acquisition. Thus, for instance, the N/V distinction is assumed to take priority over the N/A or V/A distinction, since adjectives constitute an intermediate class from this perspective, and this fact has developmental consequences (noted in Section 2). The claim that best exemplars may play a special role in acquisition is by no means confined to semantics, but refers to a confluence of semantic content, morphophonological shape, and syntactic distribution which together make some items distinctively Verbs, Nouns, or Adjectives in the language being learned. Relatedly, in initially cracking the system, of word-class distinctions as well as other facets of the linguistic system, children employ multiple routes to endstate knowledge: Some cues will be discourse-based, others morpho-syntactic, some will be governed by factors of lexical co-occurrences, others by the semantics of a given word or class of words. Finally, the least marked, most universal and most typical forms are not only among the earliest to occur in children's input and output language, they also constitute the initial basis of content needed to trigger structure-dependent, rule-bound acquisition of the grammar. Next, we consider the route taken by children in proceeding from their early item-based use of words as individual items to a category-based use of words as members of particular word-class sets.

2. FROM WORDS TO WORD-CLASSES AND BEYOND IN ACQUISITION

This section attempts to characterize learning of word-classes on the basis of a model of language development which I have described in detail elsewhere (Berman, 1985b, 1986b, 1986c), and which seems pertinent to the process of

---

[3]There is much evidence that at the initial, one-word stage of language production, children do not use these units in a way that corresponds to their word-class membership in the adult language (Berman, 1978a; Dromi, 1987, and references there). Nor do children necessarily treat the items which they use in their early word-combinations as belonging to either N, V, or any other lexical class or category. Consider, for instance, two-word strings like those produced by my daughter at age 1;11—all with the initial "verb" *rotsa* 'want+Fem' followed by such "nouns" as (her pronunciations of) the Hebrew words *zalav* 'milk', *gezer* 'carrots', on the one hand, or *ambatya* 'bath', *bayit* 'home', on the other, as well as by such "verbs" as *lishon* 'sleep', *le'exol* 'eat' and other, closed-class items like *po* 'here', or *gam* 'also, too'.

acquiring word-class distinctions.[4] Language learning is construed as proceeding via three main phases, roughly characterizable as pregrammatical, structure-bound, and discourse-oriented respectively—where the term "developmental phase" is compatible with the sense specified by Karmiloff-Smith (1983, 1986), as distinct from an across-the-board Piagetian-type "stage." A critical distinction is drawn between early, pregrammatical language acquisition, when children acquire, and combine, **words as items** as against subsequent, structure-dependent learning, when children apply linguistic rules not only to linear strings of items, but also to abstract grammatical **structures and categories** such as, for instance, word-class sets. From this point of view, language acquisition can be seen as proceeding along a succession of five steps, one leading into and following from the other, as follows:

(1) PREGRAMMATICAL:
  a. **Rote-learning**—item-based acquisition is manifested in the use of formally unanalyzed units or chunks;
  b. **Initial modifications**—formal alternations apply to a small number of highly familiar, good exemplars;
STRUCTURE-BOUND:
  c. **Interim schemata**—transitional or bridge strategies take the form of productive, but nonnormative rules;
  d. **Grammaticization**—structure-bound rules are those of the endstate grammar:
DISCOURSE-ORIENTED:
  e. **Convention and variety**—grammatical rules are deployed with appropriate, discourse-sensitive lexical restrictions, stylistic alternations, usage conventions, register distinctions, etc.

In construing the process in such terms, note that these phases are not strictly age-related across different kinds of linguistic knowledge. Language production at the one-word phase and during the period of initial word-combinations is largely "agrammatical." Yet a child may be well into mastery of the grammar of one particular subsystem (plural markings on nouns, for instance, as discussed by Levy, this volume) while still far from rule-bound knowledge in another area (genitive constructions and noun compounding, for example, Berman, 1987). The intermediate period of grammar acquisition, then, may be quite long drawn-out, and continue into the school years. Moreover, while some parts of the grammar may already be quite fully established and integrated within a phase-three level of discourse-sensitive usage by around age 4 or 5, others may be deployed and alternated appropriately only as late as puberty.

---

[4]The model in question has been shown to apply to findings from research into the acquisition of different facets of Hebrew as a native tongue—morphophonology, inflectional systems, word-formation processes, word-order patterning, syntactic constructions, and narrative discourse (Berman 1985b, 1986a).

Next, we trace the progress from initial item-based used of words at what we term step-a on through full command of relevant word class distinctions in the mother-tongue at the postgrammatical step-e.

a. The child starts out with a rote use of **words,** as linguistic primes, where "a word" is definable roughly as a sequence that disallows internal interruption by pauses or by other words. Children's initial "units of acquisition" (Peters, 1983) clearly do not correspond exactly to the words of endstate adult lexicons. Nor do the subclasses of elements they use correspond in a one-to-one fashion with adult word-class categories. Compare, for instance, use of the word for *door* to indicate a general notion of opening or removal in early child language in English (Griffiths & Atkinson, 1978) as well as in Hebrew (Berman, 1978a). Yet something like "a word" clearly pays an important role in early acquisition: It constitutes the basis for form-meaning connections; for phonological manipulations; and for subsequent grammatical combinations across items and modifications within items (Gleitman & Wanner, 1982).

b. Next, once children start to manipulate words structurally (e.g., by adding plural inflections to nouns, or using a verb in both present and past-tense forms), they will also first relate in some broad, general way to different **classes** of items. In this phase, the period of initial entry into morpho-syntax, usually around age 2, children reveal what Maratsos has termed "disjunct" behavior. For instance, they may attach the suffixes -*s, -ed,* and -*ing* to only, though not to all verbs in English, with some kinds of verbs taking one ending and others another. Such restriction of grammatical inflections to certain subsets of items is evident in children's use of verbs in other languages, too. There is evidence for a basically disjunct marking of punctual versus nonpunctual (or change-of-state vs. process) verbs in such disparate languages as English, French, Hebrew, Italian, and Polish (Berman, 1983, Bickerton, 1981; Weist, 1986). That is, children may use more than one type of grammatical marker, and they may do so in a semantically felicitous fashion, yet this behavior is not truly "grammatical", in the sense of productive application of structure-based rules. The very fact that preterite or perfective inflections are associated with one kind of predicate, while durative or imperfective marking is assigned to a different class of items means that the "classes" which may have been formed are spurious ones in terms of the grammar of these languages—since punctual verbs can take durative markers (as in English "the jar is falling") and process verbs can occur in the preterite ("he swam for hours").

Some of a child's early verbs will, however, exhibit formal alternations, almost from the start. That is, they pattern disjunctly across a single item. In Hebrew, for instance, such verbs may be inflected distinctly for present and past tense, sometimes also for future, as well as for imperative and infinitive mood (Berman, 1985a; Berman & Dromi, 1984). These verbs are typically basic, nonspecific, or "general-purpose" terms (Clark, 1978, 1983). They include the general activity verb *la'asot* 'to do, make'—for instance, a 2-year-old might say both past-tense *asiyti pipi* 'I-did/made wee-wee' and future-imperative *ta'ase li* 'do/make (it) for me'; general verbs of motion like *lavo* 'to come' and *lalexet* 'to go'—as in *aba halax la'avoda* 'Daddy went/has-gone to work' in the past and future-imperative *lex mikan* 'go from-here=away!'; as well as general terms for transfer of location and possession like *lasim* 'to put' and *latet* 'to give', which might early on alternate between imperative *ten li* 'give (it) to-me', infinitive *lo la-tet* 'not to-give = don't give', and past tense *ima natna li* 'Mommy gave (it) to-me'. But such alternations do not apply to more lexically specific terms—such as motion verbs meaning 'drive, travel', 'fly', or the verbs *lehikanes* 'go/come in' and *lacet* 'go/come out', although these are all common in early child speech. And this distinction cannot be attributed simply to input frequency, since there is some more principled reason why certain verbs—and other items—are relatively more or less common in both child input and output in the early years. Rather, it is the more typical or best exemplar terms (like basic verbs of motion, action, and transfer) which underpin children's eventual recognition of words as belonging to distinct classes. But this will only be achieved after they start to apply some morpho-syntactic alternations, as they move from rote to rule, from words to structures.

At the phase in question, the *step-b* transition from step-a, rote-knowledge of single items with no formal interconnection between them, to subsequent rule-formation in steps c and d, the child is beginning to work with certain types of elements—in the case noted here, activity verbs—as somehow related to one another, hence special or distinct. But these early modifications are very limited; there is no generalization across all and only members of that class of words as yet. These initial alternations thus form a basis for grammar-learning, and early rote-learned individual items together with items which first are alternated constitute the **content** to which grammatical rules will be applied. But the child's language is still pregrammatical: It lacks across-the-board productive applications of rules to structures, in the case under consideration here, to all and only verbs as a class distinct from all nouns and adjectives.

c. Subsequently, children will begin to apply nonnormative, often idiosyncratic, transitional strategies en route to endstate rules. These procedures are generalized beyond the individual items of step a, and they extend beyond the limited groups of items noted for step b. Rather, they are applied to classes of items on the basis of formal and/or semantic properties which they share. In this sense, then, these interim strategies or schemata are genuine "rules", as they are productively applied to linguistic forms in terms of their structural properties. They will often constitute quite feasible hypotheses about how a given subsystem might work in the target language, but they are not yet consistent with the rules of the endstate grammar.

One example of such an interim hypothesis is provided by Hebrew-speaking children's early construals of the form of present-tense verbs in their language. Thus, 2-year-olds often overextend prefixal *m-* when talking about ongoing events, even when this marker is not required by the grammar—e.g., they might say **misha'er* vs. normative *nish'ar* 'is-staying'; or **mesima* vs. required *sama* '(she)is- putting'. Such errors show that these young children are operating with a quite plausible hypothesis, with what is in a sense a viable rule, since a prefixal *m-* marker does in fact occur with many classes of Hebrew verbs to indicate an ongoing activity or present state—e.g., *me-saxek* 'plays, is-playing', *ma-rbit* 'hits, is-hitting', *me-vina* '(she) understands'. This marking, however, does not happen to apply to verbs like those asterisked above; they take rather different forms of marking to indicate present tense. Children overuse this tense/aspect marking only on verbs, never on nouns or adjectives, and this suggests that they are already working with **classes** of forms rather than with individual items. But their behavior in this connection still manifests some of the "disjunctness" noted for step-b above. Thus, overextensions of prefixal *m-* at this early phase of formal grammatical alternations are confined to verbs which semantically are most typically associated with activities currently in progress, rather than with punctual change-of-state events (for details, see Berman, 1983). In line, then, with our more general claims in the preceding section, prototypicality plays a role in determining the domain of the form-class boundaries within which children can be expected to apply their initial generalizations about linguistic structure.

Two other, rather later types of structurally motivated errors in children's use of Hebrew verbs also manifest recognition of classes of items as related within a given subset of the category defined by the endstate grammar as "a verb." Thus, children around age 3 and up may mark perfectivity by overextending a passive participial marking—with the same prefix *m-* and an associated vowel pattern with the passive marking *-u-*. For instance, instead of the word *ragil* 'used, accustomed', a child may say **merugal* (cf. *mesudar* 'tidy, arranged'), or **metufas* for *tafus* 'caught, taken'. Another transitional strategy applied to verbs, from around age 4, is use of causative prefixes and vowel-patterns with transitive verbs which do not take them in the conventional lexicon—e.g., **ma-dxif* 'make-be-pushed' for the regular verb *doxef* 'push' (cf. *markid* 'make-dance'); or **hi-srif* 'made-burn' in place of *saraf* 'burn' (cf. *hipil* 'made-fall' (Berman & Sagi, 1981). Such relatively late errors in the form of nonconventional use of word-formation devices are analogous to what has been observed for English-speaking children who overextend the *un-* prefix or particles like *off* to express a general category of separation or removal in relation to the class of process verbs (Bowerman, 1982). They are evidence that the child is attending to formal cues of word-class distribution in encoding regular form-meaning relations. But he or she does not yet have the details right, and still lacks knowledge of the specific constraints which make the rule in question either more confined or more general in terms of form-class assignment in the adult grammar.

d. The next step is that of endstate rule-acquisition. Here, learners go beyond manipulation of restricted groups of familiar instances to full productivity. This means that idiosyncratic, nonnormative interim schemata like those illustrated above as typifying step c give way to endstate rules of grammar. By age 4 to 5, children distinguish between words which pattern structurally one way rather than another—both in syntactic distribution and morphological marking. Here, rule-application is fully **structure-dependent,** in the sense characterized by Chomsky (1975). Rules, by their very nature, extend beyond words as instances to **classes** of items and to structural entities such as: Grammatical subject versus direct or oblique object, main versus embedded clause and, also, noun as against verb and, where applicable, adjective. Proof of this is supplied by children's ability not simply to keep the items distinct—as Maratsos has shown from the English data— but also to **cross** successfully from one class to another. From this point of view, strong evidence for the "grammaticization" of word-class distinctions is available once children are capable of forming denominal verbs and of constructing nouns out of verbs, or adjectives out of either nouns or verbs—in accordance with the structural constraints of their particular target language (Badry, 1983; Clark & Berman, 1984; Walden, 1982).

Levy (this volume) discusses extensively the lack of between-category crossing in the language of very young children. However, her interpretation of these data is different from the position that is argued for here.

    e. Finally, based on, but going beyond, rules of structure, discourse-oriented use of language manifests the ability to conform with the conventional norms of the established adult lexicon, on the one hand, and to deploy stylistic options both within and across word-class boundaries, on the other. Thus, for instance, an Israeli 4-year-old may have overextended the rule that the suffix *-ut* is used to form abstract-state nouns, leading her to coin the wellformed but nonconventional noun **tsemi-ut* to mean 'thirst(i)-ness' from the adjective *tsame* 'thirsty' (cf. such alternations as: *bari/bri-ut* 'healthy/healthiness' or *ayef-ut* 'tired-ness'). Knowledge of the established wordstock of her language will now lead her to abandon this form for conventional *tsima'on* as the accepted abstract noun for 'thirstiness'. In just the same way, a child who knows the Hebrew rule for deriving denominal adjectives by adding the ending *-i* and who has applied it in an innovative context such as *kova *kism-i* 'cap magic-al' = 'magic hat' from *kesem* 'magic' (cf. *tipsh-i* 'fool-ish'), will learn that the conventional form is a noun compound *kova ksamim* 'cap-of magics' = 'magic hat'.

    Another, related fact of this final phase is that now the grammatical, structure-bound rules first tried out in step c and then fully established by step d become flexibly deployed for a full range of discourse-sensitive stylistic functions. Here the speaker can select out of a full range of formal alternatives, those options best suited to his or her purposes in a particular discourse context and within a given register. Examples are the choice between such wordings as an adjective/noun complement in alternations like *she's beautiful/she's a beauty* or *he's mad/he's a madman* or between lexically incorporated versus periphrastic formulations such as *he's hopeful/he's full of hope, that's useless/that's no use*.

Research into the acquisition of noun compounds and genitive constructions in Hebrew (Berman, 1987, Clark & Berman, 1987) throws interesting light on the interrelations between knowledge of grammar and knowledge of usage. We found that by age 3 to 4, children quite freely use the genitive particle *shel* 'of' and other prepositionals to express relations between two nominals—both possessive as in *ha-kova shel rina* 'the-hat of Rina = Rina's hat' and others, e.g., *kova shel letsan* 'hat of (a) clown = clown('s) hat'; *kova im seret* 'hat with (a) ribbon'; or *kova mi kash* 'hat from straw = a straw hat'. On the other hand, it may take children up to as late as age 7 to acquire the full set of grammatical rules for forming bound genitives in Hebrew (so-called "construct-state" noun compounds) such as the earlier example of *kovaˆksamin* 'hat-of magics = magic hat', or *simlaˆrakdanit* 'dress-of ballerina = a ballerina dress'. Only much later, however, well beyond early school-age, are speakers able to deploy and also to **alternate** across an entire range of structural options: morphological affixation, bound genitives, free prepositionals, and also so-called double genitives (e.g., *kova-a shel rina* 'her-hat of Rina = Rina's hat', *sipur-av shel agnon* (stories-his of Agnon = 'Agnon's stories').

The point about such alternations is that the grammar qua grammar does not dictate to the speaker which is appropriate for what circumstances. Hence my claim that children need to go beyond knowledge of the structural options available to them in their native tongue to knowledge of how these options can be deployed interchangeably. In the case at issue here, once learners have mastered the formal and structural distinctions between nouns, verbs, and adjectives, they need to free themselves of grammatical rigidity which separates off the classes, so that they can choose items now from one and now from another formal class for different discourse purposes.

As noted, progression of learning can be summed up in terms of three main phases, observable across different domains of linguistic development and in different languages. The "pregrammatical" period of steps (a) and (b)—up until about age 2—represents an instance-bound phase of maximal specificity, when no generalizations are extracted to link items which display structural commonalities. Here, the child uses words as individual elements, without classing them together in terms of formal properties. Subsequently, in the intermediate phase of "grammar acquisition," children demonstrate that rule-learning is taking place by going beyond the individual elements of the previous phase and by being able to apply generalizations to new instances—in the shape of nonnormative step-c interim hypotheses, and then of normative grammatical constructions when they reach step-d. In making word-class distinctions, the grammar-learning child abstracts our broad superordinate categories—say of action versus state verbs, of agent and instrument nouns as a single class of words, or of statal versus denominal adjectives. The final "postgrammatical" phase is reached when speakers can vary the way they deploy rules of grammar in accordance with the requirements of discourse—as appropriate to different contexts or registers of usage. Such elaboration depends on increased exposure to numerous exemplars, and is affected by literacy and formal school studies. Here, speakers go beyond generalizations to finer distinctions of subclasses of items, to a more specific recognition of say, stative verbs as semantically differentiated in terms of perception, cognition, and affect (*see, know, like,* respectively); or of agent nouns being distinguished as occupations versus attributes (*lawyer* vs. *liar,* say). As these examples suggest, such differentiations need not have any grammatical correlates in terms of surface form or distributional properties. Nor as far as I know have such developments been the subject of psycholinguistic investigation with younger or with adult populations. There is, however, evidence, that other lexical subdivisions which have quite subtle and complex structural manifestations are typical of language use only in this latest, postgrammatical phase. In English, this is known to apply in the extension of basic word-class distinctions beyond the familiar Germanic wordstock to more learned, and morphophonolog-ically complex, items of the Latinate vocabulary. And in Hebrew, only older speakers will alternate across word-classes in a more formal register to use derived action nominals (corresponding to English words like *arrival* or *expecta-tion*) alongside of the more basic finite verbs, infinitives, and participials as verb-complement constructions; (Meroz, in preparation); similarly, in their deploy-ment of complex nominals, only more mature, step-e type speakers will modify nouns by means of Noun-Noun strings (as in the earlier example of *magic hat*) in addition to using basic and denominal adjectives or prepositional phrases for this purpose (Berman, 1987).

The question remains as to what motivates these phases, underlying the move from nonanalysis to structure-dependence and more felicitous, more varied de-ployment of grammatical devices. I would argue for an "integrative" explana-tion, in which pragmatic, semantic, and formal or distributional factors play a role. Initially, when the child is making entry into the system, communicative needs seem crucial, and learners rely on context-based, pragmatic cues both to assign semantic content to strings of sounds in their linguistic input, and to give shape to meanings in their own output. Structural factors which govern the morpho-syntax of natural languages do not seem to play a role at the very outset, and hence it is feasible that in very early language there is no categorization analogous to a noun/verb distinction at all. Yet the learning that goes on in this first, pregrammatical phase is very relevant to what follows, since it provides the child with the raw materials—from both input and output—for hypothesis con-struction and for rule-formation. What the child needs is linguistic content which will constitute the **substance** of verb/noun distinctions, with their innate under-pinning in the general argument/predicate divide. This substance is provided by the words, and combinations of words, available in the child's earliest experi-ence with language.

As children acquire a larger repertoire of sound-meaning units, and as the learners' linguistic (not merely realworld) experience is deepened and extended, word-class learning develops as a two-pronged process, motivated by generaliza-tions along both semantic and morpho-syntactic lines. Consider the following as an example of the lack of between-class confusion noted by Maratsos for En-glish: In place of the normative past-tense verb-form *shatiy-ti* 'drank-1st person'' = 'I drank', Israeli 2-year-olds often say **shata-ti* (cf. *nasa-ti* 'I went') manifest-ing the well-documented phenomenon of regularization to a familiar paradigm (Berman, 1981a). But these children will not come up with expressions like **bakbak-ti* or **bakbuk-ti* in the sense of, say, 'I-bottled' on the basis of the noun *bakbuk* '(a) bottle'.[5] The reason for this is twofold in my opinion: In morpho-

---

[5]Four to 5-year-old children may do precisely this kind of thing, but such an operation reveals deliberate class-switching, of the kind we noted as characteristic of the "grammaticization" phase of steps (c) and (d), when they have knowledge of the system as a whole even if not of all its lexical and other constraints.

syntactic terms, the child is familiar with such contexts as, say, *ani rotse li-shtot* 'I want to-drink' (cf. *li-knot* 'to buy') compared with *hine ha-bakbuk* 'here's the bottle' (cf. *ha-kos* 'the cup'). And semantically the child also knows that 'drink' describes something which people do, while 'bottle' refers to something which people see or use.[6] In principle, it does not seem to me that either grammatical processes (as argued in Hyams, 1986) or semantic generalizations (as argued by Schlesinger, 1982, and this volume) form the sole or even the major basis for children's extraction of a structural category in their language. Rather, at first they rely primarily on pragmatic, extralinguistic cues (as has been shown for early emergence of tense/aspect marking in a diary study by Sachs, 1982). In time they establish some conceptual commonality drawn from best exemplar instances of a class, and manifested in quite broad, nongrammatically motivated distinctions. This semantic categorization (of the kind currently termed "semantic bootstrapping" as characterized by Pinker, 1984) combines with observation of morpho-syntactic privileges of co-occurrence and word-internal modifications as the basis for extraction of abstract grammatical categories. This later phase entails a structure-dependent type of knowledge which incorporates a variety of formal properties of a given class: for instance, that while both verbs and some adjectives in English may end in *-ed*, only verbs are inflected for tense, and some but not all of these verbs can function as a past participle in passive constructions, while some but not all such adjectives will have syllabic endings (as in *kicked* vs. *wicked*.) Moreover, at an interim phase of the learning process, structural criteria may override other types of information necessary to constrain word-class distinctions in accordance with conventions and norms of usage—compare, say, *nice/niceness,* but *old/*oldness,* or the status of the suffixal *-en* in words like *listen, soften,* and *liken* respectively.

The child thus has a long path to follow until he or she will recognize that *a crayon, the moon,* and *thirstiness* are "all words of the same kind" by comparison with *draw, understand, necessitate,* on the one hand, and *cold, silent, complicated,* on the other. In considering the acquisition of word-class distinctions, then, similarly to a developing mastery of other categories and subsystems of the grammar,[7] there is no single leap from "no knowledge" to "full knowledge"; nor is there any single route by which children proceed from lack of command to endstate command of the systems, structures, and classes which constitute the grammar of their native language.

---

[6]Unlike in English, there is no noun with the same form as the verb *drink* (and see, further, section 4). And in Hebrew children will know the names for various kinds of drinks such as those meaning *milk, juice,* etc. long before they ever use the generic term *shtiya* from the same root as the verb, or more normative *mashke* for 'drink, beverage'.

[7]A very clear formulation of this kind of developmental approach is to be found in Karmiloff-Smith, 1979, especially pp. 234–236.

3. ARE VERBS LIKE NOUNS AND/OR ADJECTIVES IN ACQUISITION?

The question raised in this heading brings us back to an issue noted in Section 1. I will show that from the interim phase of "grammaticization"—steps c–d in the model outlined earlier—acquisition does not follow the same path for all of the three lexical classes which concern us here. Children construe the verbs they learn differently than nouns, while adjectives are treated as less autonomous as a structural class than are either verbs or nouns.

Consider verbs, to start with. The fact that verbs are learned (and, possibly, stored) differently than nouns seems very clear from Hebrew child language data. Note, first, that in **semantic** terms, Hebrew verbs incorporate a relatively large amount of information word-internally. For instance, motion verbs specify not only manner—as in English *limp* vs. *walk,* but also direction—Germanic *go up* or Romance *ascend* vs. *go,* as well as cause—*lift up* vs. *get up* (Talmy, 1985). Moreover, Hebrew verbs are **morphologically** distinct from nouns in a number of ways. By and large they take distinct forms of inflectional affixes; for instance, markers of 1st and 2nd person in past and future tense verbs have no analogue in nouns (e.g., *gamar-ti* 'finished-1st' = 'I (have) finished', *ti-gmor* '2nd-will-finish' = 'you'll finish'). Verbs do not have any clear unequivocal basic or citation form, to correspond with uninflected verbs like English *jump, enjoy,* and in this they contrast with the unmarked masculine singular form of nouns and adjectives in Hebrew. Moreover, and in this, too, they differ from nouns and adjectives, Hebrew verbs must be formed out of a consonantal root to which is affixed one of a restricted set of morphological patterns in the form of some half-dozen *binyan* conjugations.

These distributional facts are very relevant to the point made in Section 1, where verbs were noted as distinct from nouns because they constitute relational values, and serve as predicate-like functions rather than as autonomous argument-like terms. This suggests that children will learn verbs as interrelated with one another in different ways than nouns. Language-specific facts from Hebrew provide a good place for testing this hypothesis, since these distinctions are overtly manifested in its verb morphology. Thus, for any set of verbs constructed out of a given consonantal root, one can be construed as "basic" or nonderived, the others as supplementary in meaning (Berman, 1978b, 1980, 1982). Take, for instance, the root **g-d-l,** which carries the general sense of 'increasing in size': The intransitive verb *li-gdol* 'to grow, get bigger', transitive *le-gadel* 'to raise, make grow', and causative *le-hagdil* 'make bigger, enlarge' are clearly all versions of one another, in the sense that the two transitive verbs modify or add to the basic meaning of the intransitive verb 'grow' in specifiable ways. This cannot be said, however, of **nouns,** which are formed out of the same root. Which is most "basic," and what relationship can be specified between nouns that are also derived from the root g-d-l with the same core sense of 'increase in size'? Consider the following, for instance: *godel* 'size', *gdula* 'greatness', *gidul* 'growth, a tumor', *migdal* 'a tower'. Or take the root **k-t-v** meaning something like 'give graphic representation to linguistic entities'. The verb *li-xtov* 'to-write' is clearly semantically most basic and so can be analyzed as underlying other verbs constructed from the same root, e.g., *le-hikatev* 'to-be-written', *le-haxtiv* 'to dictate, cause to write', *le-hitkatev* 'to correspond, write to someone'. Yet nouns formed from the same root cannot be construed as derivable from one particular base-form or as semantically interrelated in any specifiable way; compare from this point of view the nouns *ktav* 'handwriting, script', *ktiv* 'spelling, orthography', on the one hand, or *mixtav* 'letter, missive', *katava* 'report, write-up', and *katvan* 'stenographer, typist', *katav* 'reporter, journalist', or *kotev* 'writer', on the other. These words share a common semantic core, but each is independently assigned to a distinct lexical class—of concrete product noun, process or result noun, agent or instrument noun, and so forth. One cannot be construed as more "basic" than another, nor can any semantic relationship be defined between them beyond the common meaning shared by their root consonants in the abstract.

We hypothesized that these structural differences between verbs and other classes of items would be reflected in their acquisition. Relevant evidence is provided by studies of children's innovative or otherwise nonconventional use of word-formation devices in Hebrew (see Berman, 1980, 1982; Berman & Sagi, 1981; Clark & Berman, 1984; Walden, 1982; and Badry, 1983 for children learning Moroccan Arabic). To start with, children neutralize across verb-forms, using one verb-pattern alone for a given root. This yields wellformed utterances in many cases, but also anomalies such as the equivalent of English 'I am-eating my dollie' in place of causative *feeding* [=Hebrew *oxel-et* vs. *ma-axila* from the root **?-x-l**] or transitive 'it *throwed* into the basket' instead of *dropped* [=Hebrew *zarak* vs. *ni-zrak* from the root **z-r-k**]. Later on, from around age 3, children learn to alternate verb-patterns appropriately along the axis of transitivity, but they still make numerous lexical errors in assigning a particular verb-pattern to a given verb-root—for instance, from the familiar transitive verb *pogesh* 'meet (someone)' they may form a nonnormative reciprocal in the intransitive form **mit-pagsh-im* 'meet one-another+Pl' in place of required *ni-fgash-im* in another intransitive verb-pattern; or they may form a causative verb from the adjective *tsafuf* 'crowded' by means of one transitive pattern to create unconventional **ma-tsfif* 'crowd = make-crowded' instead of the normative, established pattern *me-tsofef* for that same sense. Tests requiring children to interpret and produce verbs based on the same root but differing in morphological pattern (Berman, 1982) as well as research in progress on their ability to coin denominal verbs from familiar nouns and adjectives show that from age 3 to 4 years, Hebrew-learning children recognize verbs which share a common consonantal skeleton as being versions of the same general notion. That is, they will relate the two stem-final elements **x-l** in *axal-ti* 'ate+1st = I ate' and *he'exila* '(she) fed =

gave/caused to-eat', or the three elements **sh-b-r** in *ni-shbar* 'broke (Intrans.) = got-broken', *shabur* '(is-)broken' and *shabar-ti* 'I broke' to each other, as referring to the same kind of realworld event. And they may manifest this knowledge by trying to fill either real or assumed gaps in the conventional wordstock by using these consonantal skeletons in appropriate verb-pattern forms. What young children lack is detailed lexical knowledge of which version of a given verb-complex is required in a specific context.

Neutralizations and crossings like those we have observed within the lexical class of verbs are not, however, manifested for **nouns.** Children may start by using, say, the root **k-p-ts** both correctly, in the form *li-kpots* meaning 'to-jump' and also where the related iterative form *le-kapets* 'to hop', or causative *le-hakpits* 'to bounce' are required. But they will not use a noun such as *kapatsit* 'trampoline' or *kfitsa* 'a jump, leap' instead of *makpetsa* to refer to 'springboard'. They may mix up the causative verb *le-hadbik* 'to stick, paste in' with intransitive *nidbak* 'be/get stuck' and perfective *davuk* 'stuck'. Children will **not,** however, confuse these nouns with verbs; nor, moreover, will they interchange them with each other as they so often do with verbs—despite the fact that by as young as age 3, they may recognize that the nouns *madbeka* 'label, sticker' and also *devek* 'paste, glue' are from the same consonantal source.[8] Similar findings concerning differences between nouns & verbs in young Hebrew speakers are reported in Levy (this volume).

Instead, to start with, children acquire nouns as individual lexical items, without relating them to each other on formal bases of morphological structure. And this is true even in a language like Hebrew where this connectedness is quite typical of adult construals of word-class membership, in a way that is arguably rather different than for speakers of, say, English. Rather, as children add to their repertoire of nouns, they seem to relate them to other words belonging to the same semantic field. Take, for instance, instrument nouns familiar to Israeli 3-year-olds which share the same morphological pattern—e.g., *masrek* 'a comb', *mashpex* 'a funnel' or *mazleg* 'a fork'. By around age 4, children will, as noted, recognize them as being somehow connected to verbs with the same consonantal base. For instance, they will provide root-related verbs to explain the meanings or functions of such nouns—e.g., *le-histarek* 'to comb one's hair' or *li-shpox* 'to

---

[8]Evidence for this is provided by responses of 3- to 4-year-olds in a study which required them to interpret innovative agent and instrument nouns (Clark & Berman, 1984) as well as by another task in which children were required to give the meanings of innovative compound nouns in Hebrew (Clark & Berman, 1987). Thus, asked to explain the expression *maxberet madbekot* 'folder stickers' roughly equivalent to the English compound expression *sticker folder* in the sense of a folder for stickers, one child aged 3;0 responded with the morphologically and semantically related, though inappropriate noun *devek* 'paste, glue'; and another 3-year-old gave the response *madbik-im madbeka banyar* 'stick+Pl sticker in-paper' = 'we/people paste-in the sticker on paper'. By age 4–5, several of the children questioned on this item responded by combining the verb *le-hadbik* meaning 'to stick, paste in' with the noun from the same root, *madbeka* 'sticker, label'.

pour' (Clark & Berman, 1984). But that is not necessarily how they first learn such nouns. Rather, for children these nouns will be associated with the words for brush and mirror, for hammer and nails, and for spoon and knife respectively, rather than to each other. This is shown, for instance, in the fact that the younger children would so often give what we termed ''suppletive'' responses to such items: When asked to name an object that is used *le-hadlik* 'to-light (candles)', 3-year-olds would typically say something like *gafrur* 'a match', by contrast with older children, who would coin a noun based on the root **d-l-k** (Clark & Berman, 1984, and see, too, Walden, 1982). And even when children are able to coin nouns by means of formal word-formation devices they will do so on the basis of (relational-type) verbs and adjectives, and not on the basis of other nouns. That is, children will coin words by using affixes like *-an* to form agent nouns and *-ut* for abstract nouns, as in innovative **marbic-an* 'hits/is-hitting + Suffix' for 'hitt-er' in the sense of a kid who always hits, or they will say **ketsar-ut* '*short-itude' on the basis of the familiar adjective *katsar* 'short' in place of normative, but semantically restricted *kotser* 'short-ness'. But they will **not** form new nouns from others to yield, for instance, **xalom-an* 'dream-er' from the noun *xalom* '(a) dream' or **xom-ut* 'heat-ness' from the familiar noun *xom* 'heat' (cf. the related adjective *xam* 'hot').

All this suggests that nouns are learned initially on the basis of semantic field associations rather than in terms of form-class membership. Recognition of words such as the {maCCeC} examples given above as instrument nouns, or {CaCaC} forms as occupational agent nouns (e.g., *ganav* 'thief', *tayas* 'pilot', *sabal* 'porter') as identical in morphological structure as well as being members of a single semantic subcategory is knowledge that constitutes a later, structure-dependent kind of acquisition (often established as late as in school-age, see Berman, 1981b). That is, children start out by leaning nouns as individual items, and subsequently they relate them to given formal classes. In contrast, they acquire certain verbs right from the start as based on, and relating to, others which share a structural property in the form of a single consonantal skeleton. Once a Hebrew-speaking child uses both the transitive verb *shavar-ti* 'I-broke' and its intransitive counterpart *nishbar* '(it) broke', or both the action verb *nofel* 'fall' and its causative version *mapil* 'make-fall, drop'—he or she is using them as such, as versions of each other. The critical difference between such alternations and, say, the relationship we noted earlier between *devek* 'glue' and *mad-beka* 'sticker' is that in the case of verbs, the new ones are learnt as versions of, and based on, the verbs known from before. This is not the case in the way children learn nouns. Moreover, the form-meaning generalizations which learners eventually extract for nouns with a shared root will not be in any way as general, category rather than instance-based, as the knowledge they acquire with respect to root-sharing verbs in their lexicon and, subsequently, in their grammar.

These claims concerning children's learning of the basic categorial distinctions without exclusive regard for surface form are further attested to by the case of **adjectives**. Adjectives, too, are marked off by the morpho-syntax of Hebrew in a way which well suits their characterization as interim or halfway between N and V, sharing properties of both. The fact that adjectives can be semantically ranked as more nounlike or more verblike respectively will often be reflected in their surface shape in Hebrew. Compare, for the two roots noted above, the verblike participials *megudal* 'overgrown' (cf. *melumad* 'learned, erudite') and *katuv* 'written, nonoral' (cf. *sagur* 'closed, shut=nonopen')—all containing the *-u* vowel characteristic of passive verbs; less verblike in form and patterning, but nonetheless sharing a root with semantically cognate verbs are adjectives like *gadol* 'large, big' or *xam* 'hot' (cf. causative *le-xamem* 'to-warm-up, heat' or inchoative *le-hitxamem* 'to-get-hot'); and very nounlike in form and syntax are denominal adjectives based on a noun-stem plus adjectival suffix such as *tiv'-i* 'natur-al' from *teva* 'nature', *guf-ani* 'physical, bodily' from *guf* 'body'. Further evidence for the mixed-category status of Hebrew adjectives is the fact that while they may function syntactically as predicates, and hence resemble verbs, they are inflected like nouns for gender, number, and definiteness but not, like verbs, for person or tense.

It is feasible that children approach the task of adjective-learning rather differently than for nouns and verbs. One reason is that, since children use very few adjectives in their speech output before around age 3, their experience with this class of items is more restricted than with the distinct N/V categories. Moreover, data from Hebrew show that children do not treat adjectives in the same way as verbs—where immature intermixing of those constructed out of the same consonantal root shows that new verbs may be acquired as versions of an earlier-acquired familiar verb to which it is derivationally and semantically related. Nor are adjectives learned the same as nouns, with each treated as structurally self-contained and semantically related in quite idiosyncratic ways to other items within a given lexical field. Early adjectives, in contrast, seem to be learned in semantically **contrastive** terms—e.g., *big* not *small, red* as versus *blue* or *green*. Later on, when children start to be structurally innovative with respect to adjectives, they tend to mix between participial (passive or perfective) morphological patterns, particularly with the patterns {meCuCaC} and {CaCuC}— e.g., *metufas* for *tafus* 'taken, busy', and conversely also *takun* for *metukan* 'fixed, in order'. In such instances, children are clearly relating adjectives to verbs, to denote attributive states which result from an activity described by the verb. This makes good sense, since older preschool-age Hebrew-speakers will use verb-morphology to form inchoative process verbs from adjectives—e.g., innovative *hitrazeyt* '(you've) gotten thin' from *raza* 'thin' or *hitparati* 'I got untidy, messed-up' from the adjective *parua* 'wild, untidy'. This suggests that, as we would have predicted, at the point in development when verbs and nouns are already clearly set apart as distinct formal classes of elements, adjectives constitute a more fluid, less autonomous category. This is further demonstrated by the relative paucity of **denominal** adjectives in preschool Hebrew, even though there exists a straightforward and widely-used device for deriving such forms. Examples such as well-formed but nonoccurrent *kism-i* 'magic-al' or *sfina-ti* 'ship-like', *barzel-i* 'iron-ish' are few and far between in our corpora, and they are found only among children of advanced preschool or early school age.

In sum, findings from Hebrew child language are indicative of more general developmental patterns in the acquisition of word class distinctions. Similar data may not be so overtly accessible in a more analytic language like English, where the major source of evidence for those studying child language, as well as for its learner-users, lies in the domain of distributional facts of co-occurrence. This is especially true in the predominantly Germanic wordstock of preschool English. In Hebrew, by contrast, within-word modifications and contrasts are numerous in everyday preschool vocabulary. They are manifested both in a broad array of grammatical inflections which form part of early morphological acquisition and also in the slightly later acquisition of richly structured devices for derivational morphology characteristic of word-formation processes within and between the major lexical classes of the language.

Children start out by learning nouns as object-referring terms, and they will subsequently relate them to other items in the same semantic field, only much later to members of the same form-meaning subclass of morpho-lexical associates. Verbs from the start are construed as interrelated, with children early on encoding different perspectives on an event by means of different versions of the ''same'' word—cf. Hebrew *yored* 'go, get down' and its causative counterpart *morid* 'take, bring down', or transitive *raxats* 'wash (something)' and reflexive *hitraxets* 'wash (oneself)'. Adjectives enter the child's repertoire as a sizable class of items relatively later, once the other groups are already established, and they take a longer time to be recognized as distinct, both as predicating, hence verb-like, and also noun-related terms. This type of knowledge is not dependent solely on facts of surface form, even in the case of a Semitic language like Hebrew, where different word classes tend to be marked morphologically as distinct from one another, both with respect to the kind of inflections affixed to them and in the type of word-formation patterns into which they enter—by contrast to English, where conversion or zero derivation is a very common device—as in *to cook/a cook, a button/to button,* or *more purple/will purple.* Nonetheless, I argue in Section 4 that children perceive and learn word-class distinctions on far more general grounds, irrespective of the particular language they happen to be learning, and that the degree of isomorphism which their language manifests between surface morphological shape and lexical class membership is an ancillary rather than a central factor in the process.

4. EFFECTS OF LANGUAGE-TYPE ON WORD-CLASS DISTINCTIONS

Consider, finally, the nature of morpho-syntactic cues that might function in children's recognition of word-class categories, and how specific features of the mother-tongue may affect this process. How far do the cues which children seek, and the kind of information they treat as relevant to word-class distinctions (and to other kinds of grammatical generalizations, too, for that matter) in fact depend on the specific language being learned? I consider language-particular features to play an important role mainly from the intermediate phase of grammar-learning, by when children are freed from reliance on specific instances and prototypical exemplars, and when they have sufficient experience with different instances to make motivated comparisons and to extract structure-dependent generalizations.

Languages can probably be ranged along a scale from those where the surface shape of words provides children with only minimal cues as to possible grammatical category through to those where surface shape and class membership of words are largely isomorphic. Chinese would belong to the former class; some Germanic languages also show very few modifications of word-forms; Hebrew would be closer to the other extreme; and Latin (for which no child language data are likely to be available) is even more radically bound by the shape of words, since nouns are obligatorily marked for one set of inflections, verbs for another. From this point of view, English is more like Chinese, since it depends so largely on syntactic properties of co-occurrence and ordering of elements in a linear string—determiners and then adjectives before nouns, modals and then other auxiliaries before verbs, and so on. Yet English also displays considerable morphological variation—though this takes a rather different form in the basic Germanic vocabulary acquired in early childhood compared with Latinate or Greek-based words learned later on—compare, for instance, *child, children, childish, childhood* with *infant, infants, infantile,* and *infancy.*

I have argued elsewhere (Berman, 1986a, 1986b) that typological and language-particular factors will start to be particularly functional once children have moved into a phase where they are capable of making generalizations about the formal system confronting them—around steps c and d in the model outlined earlier. Thus, as Slobin (1985a, 1986) has argued cogently, not only the underlying "language-making capacity" can be seen as universal, but "basic child grammar," too, is shared across children and across languages. Subsequently, language-particular features of the native tongue become critical, and it is then that the English-speaking child, say, will pay attention to occurrences across words and also, perhaps centrally, to the endings of words, whereas Hebrew learners will realize that great importance attaches to word-internal modifications which devolve upon the consonantal skeleton in providing a central core of meaning to most of the verbs, nouns, and adjectives in the lexicon. In other words, concomitant with their early grammatical development in the 3rd year-of-life or so, children develop sensitivity to the structural cues which are relevant to the grammar of their particular native tongue.

Hebrew, as noted, affords a case where word-internal morphological cues rather than linear ordering of elements serve to specify word-class relations. Unlike in English or French, Hebrew **verbs** can be both sentence-initial and post-subject; compare *nafal li ha-kadur* 'fell to=from me the-ball' and *ha-kadur nafal li* 'the-ball fell from-me'—both meaning roughly 'I dropped the ball'; **adjectives** are like other noun modifiers in being postnominal—so that only the form of words distinguishes, say, Noun-Noun *bigdey kayits* 'clothes-of summer = summer clothes' from Noun-Adjective *bgadim keytsiyim* 'clothes summer-y = summery clothes; and inflectional marking of definiteness is needed to distinguish **attributive** from **predicative** Noun-Adjective strings—e.g., *kapit shvura* 'spoon broken = a broken spoon' vs. *ha-kapit shvura* 'the-spoon (is) broken'. It thus makes sense that from quite early on, Hebrew learners will pay attention to the internal shape of words at least as much as to what is happening across words.

On the other hand, the shape of words does not afford total isomorphism with class assignment. Inflectionally, the same plural markers are used for N, A, and [present tense] V—e.g., Masculine Plural *xaruz-im gdol-im nofl-im* 'bead-s big-Pl fall-Pl = big beads are-falling', Feminine *kubiy-ot gdol-ot nishar-ot* 'big blocks remain'; and the same gender marker may be used for N, A, and past-tense V—e.g., *rof'a tov-a azr-a* 'doctor-Fem good-Fem helped-Fem = a good lady-doctor was helping'. Such identity of surface markings may help children to learn syntactic rules of combination and agreement marking. But this is not the same as a one-to-one cue of the surface distinctness of a given word-class. Besides, the same surface forms may be used across different word-classes for different functions, too. For example, prefixal *ma-* is a present-tense inflection on many verbs, but it also occurs at the beginning of many nouns, including those which may denote instruments (cf. the verbs *ma-lbish* 'dresses', *ma-pil* 'falls'; the nouns *ma-srek* 'a comb', *ma-tos* 'airplane'; or the adjectives *matok* 'sweet', *marir* 'bitter'); and suffixal *-i* is an inflectional marker of first-person possessive on nouns and prepositions, but it is also a derivational marker of denominal adjectives, etc. Hence even a language with a rich bound morphology such as Hebrew, which affords numerous salient clues as to word-class membership in the surface shape of words, does require learners to achieve some greater level of abstract categorizing.

I argued earlier that children rely on varied sources of information for linguistic hypothesis-making, and that semantic, syntactic, and morphological cues interact in their developing grammars. Nouns are initially well-learned as referring to fairly constant objects and individuals; these same nouns can be grouped together as all taking plural markers; and they can be used with predicates to talk about people that do things—e.g., *baby cry*—and objects that things happen to—e.g., *bottle fell*. Verbs are used for talking about such events, though initially they may be used mainly to elicit actions (*give me, lookit*), and they can be made to refer to ongoing events or to things that have already taken place by addition of different formal markings. Adjectives are used initially to evaluate things as being big or nice or nasty, or to comment on perceptually salient properties of objects as dirty, round or red, and then they are made to agree in surface form with the number and gender of the nouns which they modify syntactically.

This all suggests a staggered kind of development where, irrespective of the particular language being learned, children do not proceed from nonknowledge of word-class distinctions to full mastery in a single jump. Instead, they start with a broad conceptual underpinning of constant-argument versus relational-predicate type categories; these are gradually related to the major noun/verb distinction as broad divisions of linguistic entities into different types—supported by converging evidence of best exemplars in morpho-syntactic and semantic terms; and as time proceeds, this knowledge is further refined and elaborated to include subclasses within and across these major categories. Further, the particular path taken by children will become increasingly attuned to the structural properties of their target language, as more experience is gained with a wider range of exemplars, and as more categorial knowledge is internalized. In English, nouns and verbs may initially be recognized by syntactic distribution and how they are linearly ordered with respect to other kinds of words, together with a few inflectional markers which apply across the board to all but a few common, rote-learned items (e.g., *sheep* or *put*); only later will this be extended to Latinate vocabulary and to the special morphophonological cues afforded by syllable-structure and word-endings (e.g., *electrical, electricity, electrician*). In Hebrew, by contrast, modifications in the forms of words will help children to recognize verbs as being marked for mood and tense as well as for transitivity and voice, and that these are categories which have no relevance to the shape of nouns in the language, but which will often depend on the particular noun-arguments with which such verbs co-occur in actual utterances.

This in turn suggests that the particular ways in which the target-language encodes word-class distinctions will not speed up or simplify the process in any crucial sense. True, the task might seem easiest for the language learner in cases where total distinctiveness is observed, inflectionally, derivationally, in linear ordering and in co-occurrence distribution of items. But I do not know of any such language. Besides, it seems to be the case that languages in which ordering of elements does not offer a good basis for word-class generalizations will make up for this by adpositions which get tacked on to words—as in Turkish, say—or by word-internal plus stem-external modifications of shape—as in Hebrew. In addition, crosslinguistic studies to date suggest that in production as well as comprehension, children cope quite adequately with the specific kinds of cues afforded them by their own language. Thus, the overall developmental path in different languages seems similar rather than different from the point of view of acquisition of different types of linguistic knowledge. This is shown by studies of sentence comprehension in typologically distinct languages (e.g., Slobin & Bever, 1982; Bates, McNew, MacWhinney, Devescovi, & Smith, 1982); of agent and instrument nouns in English (Clark & Hecht, 1982), Hebrew (Clark & Berman, 1984), and Icelandic (Mulford, 1983); as well as by studies which consider whether acquisition of grammatical relations is facilitated in languages with accusative compared with ergative or zero case-marking in the surface shape of words (Slobin, 1985a, 1985b). Since no crosslinguistic studies are available which address the particular question at issue here, there is no reason to believe that the overall developmental path pursued by children en route from nondistinction to full knowledge of word-class categories should in any way differ radically depending on a given input language.

In considering other aspects of language acquisition from a crosslinguistic perspective, I suggested that there might be a tradeoff kind of relation of relative difficulty in different parts of a grammar in different languages (1984, 1986b). Hebrew 2- to 3-year-olds may work hard on inflectional morphology, but English-learning children have the whole complex auxiliary system to cope with, those learning Turkish move into rich morphological regularities of their language early on but have a hard time with nominalized syntactic embeddings, while the Chinese child has to learn how to deploy discourse topics in what is likewise a lengthy process (Erbaugh, 1980, 1983). More important in my opinion is the fact that to start with, at the very early stages of their language development, children do not have either the conceptual or the linguistic wherewithal to attend to language-specific properties of word-class distinctions—and this is conceivably true, too, of other grammatical categorizations such as Subject vs. Object, Direct vs. Oblique vs. Indirect Object, etc. Once children do acquire the most rudimentary categorial distinctions, however, then they will also take notice of whatever is **relevant in their language** for the distinctions to be learned. And once typological expectations have been set up, once children know what kind of cues to attend to, the task as such will not be facilitated or hampered by the specific form those particular cues happen to adopt in a given target language. Although Hebrew and English appear so very different in how they distinguish verbs from nouns, and these in turn from adjectives. we have no reason to believe that they construe them as distinct in different ways or at an earlier developmental phase in Israel, than in the United States.

If, as was claimed in Section 1, the noun/verb distinction constitutes a linguistic universal, children as acquirers of endstate grammars must eventually come to conceptualize these categories in much the same way, irrespective of their mother tongue. This kind of knowledge will provide the basis for the semantics of predicate-argument relations, the pragmatics of topic-comment notions, the grammar of nouns as the heads of NPs and of verbs as the heads of VPs. This, at least, will be shared eventually. What will differ critically is the breakdown of form-meaning associations and specific lexical subcategorizations in the morphology and lexicon of different languages. Part of a knowledge of word-class distinctions in English, uniquely, say, is that the words *cook* and *drill* can function as either verb or noun; that *cooker* is an instrument but *driller* an agent; that while both *cooking* and *drilling* can refer to activities, the former alone can function attributively as an adjective; and, finally, that *cookery* represents a very special subclass of action-production nouns in English, that has no analogue derived from *drill*. This kind of knowledge is clearly highly specific to a given target language, going far beyond the broad prototypical convergences of properties first noted for an activity like cooking or an object like a drill. Such detailed knowledge is language-particular, it embodies a fullscaled, endstate knowledge of the native language, and it takes a long time to acquire.

ACKNOWLEDGMENT

This chapter is based on an earlier paper entitled ''Are Verbs like Nouns and/or Adjectives in Acquisition?'' written under the auspices of the Institute for Advanced Studies, Hebrew University, Jerusalem. The current revised version, prepared while the author was on leave at the Department of Psychology, University of California, Berkeley, has benefited greatly from detailed discussion with Martin Braine, and from helpful comments of Yonata Levy and Izchak Schlesinger—none of whom should be held responsible for its contents.

REFERENCES

Anderson, S. (1985). Inflectional morphology. In T. Shopen (Ed.), *Language, typology and syntactic description* (Vol. 2). Cambridge, England: Cambridge University Press.

Attias, T. (1981). *Adjective order in Israeli Hebrew*. Unpublished master's thesis. Tel Aviv University.

Badry, F. (1983). *Acquisition of lexical derivation rules in Moroccan Arabic*. Unpublished doctoral dissertation, University of California, Berkeley.

Bates, E., McNew, S., MacWhinney, B., Devescovi, A., & Smith, S. (1982). Functional constraints on sentence processing: A crosslinguistic study. *Cognition, 11*, 245–299.

Berman, R. A. (1978a). Early words: How a child acquires her first verbs. *International Journal of Psycholinguistics, 5*, 21–39.

Berman, R. A. (1978b). *Modern Hebrew structure*. Tel-Aviv: Universities Publishing.

Berman, R. A. (1980). Child language as evidence for grammatical description. Preschoolers' construal of transitivity in the Hebrew verb system. *Linguistics, 18*, 677–701.

Berman, R. A. (1981a). Language development and language knowledge: Evidence from the development of Hebrew morphophonology. *Journal of Child Language, 8*, 609–626.

Berman, R. A. (1981b). Children's regularizations of noun patterns. *Papers and Reports on Child Language Development, 20*, 33–44.

Berman, R. A. (1982). Verb-pattern alternation: The interface of morphology, syntax, and semantics in Hebrew child language. *Journal of Child Language, 9*, 169–191.

Berman, R. A. (1983). Establishing a schema: Children's construal of verb-tense marking. *Language Sciences, 5*, 61–78.

Berman, R. A. (1984). Cross-linguistic first language perspectives on second language acquisition research. In R. Andersen (Ed.), *Second languages: A Cross-Linguistic perspective* (pp. 13–38). Rowley, MA: Newbury House.

Berman, R. A. (1985a). *Acquisition of tense-aspect by Hebrew-speaking children.* Final report submitted to United States-Israel Binational Science Foundation (BSF), Jerusalem, Israel.

Berman, R. A. (1985b, October). *The place of grammar in language acquisition.* Universals symposium, 10th Annual Conference on Language Development, Boston University.

Berman, R. A. (1985c). Acquisition of Hebrew. In D. I. Slobin (Ed.), The *crosslinguistic study of language acquisition* (Vol. 1). Hillsdale, NJ: Lawrence Erlbaum Associates.

Berman, R. A. (1986a). A step-by-step model of language acquisition. In I. Levin (Ed.), *Stage and structure: Reopening the debate* (pp. 191–219). Norwood, NJ: Ablex.

Berman, R. A. (1986b). A crosslinguistic perspective: Morphology/syntax. In P. Fletcher & M. Graman (Eds.), *Language acquisition* (2nd Edition, pp. 429–447). Cambridge, England: Cambridge University Press.

Berman, R. A. (1987). A developmental route: Learning about the form and use of complex nominals. *Linguistics, 25*(5).

Berman, R. A., & Dromi, E. (1984). On marking time without aspect in child language. *Papers and Reports on Child Language Development, 23*, 23–32.

Berman, R., & Sagi, Y. (1981). Word-formation and lexical innovation of young children. *Hebrew Computational Linguistics, 18*, 31–62. (In Hebrew)

Bickerton, D. (1981). *Roots of language.* Ann Arbor, MI: Karoma Press.

Bowerman, M. (1982). Reorganizational processes in lexical and syntactic development. In E. Wanner & L. Gleitman (Eds.), *Language acquisition: The state of the art* (pp. 319–346). Cambridge, England: Cambridge University Press.

Braine, M. D. S. (1987). What is learned in acquiring word classes—a step toward an acquisition theory. In B. MacWhinney (Ed.), *Mechanisms of language acquisition.* Hillsdale, NJ: Lawrence Erlbaum Associates.

Bybee, J. L. (1985). *Morphology: A study of the relation between meaning and form.* Amsterdam, John Benjamins.

Chomsky, N. (1975). *Reflections on language.* New York: Pantheon.

Clark, E. V. (1978). Discovering what words can do. In D. Farkas et al. (Eds.), *Parasession on the lexicon.* Chicago Linguistic Society, pp. 34–57.

Clark, E. V. (1983). Meanings and concepts. In P. H. Mussen (Ed.), *Handbook of child psychology* (Vol. 3, pp. 787–840), 4th Edition. New York: Wiley.

Clark, E. V., & Berman, R. A. (1984) Structure and use in the acquisition of word-formation. *Language, 60*, 542–590.

Clark, E. V., & Berman, R. A. (1987). Types of linguistic knowledge: Interpreting and producing compound nouns. *Journal of Child Language, 14*, 547–567.

Clark, E. V., & Hecht, B. F. (1982). Learning to coin agent and instrument nouns. *Cognition, 12*, 1–24.

de Villiers, J. (1980). The process of rule learning in child speech: A new look. In K. Nelson (Ed.), *Children's Language* (Volume 2). New York: Gardner Press.

de Villiers, J. (1983). Patterns of verb use in mother and child. *Papers and Reports on Child Language Development, 22*, 43–48.

Dixon, R. M. W. (1977). Where have all the adjectives gone? *Studies in Language, 1*, 1–80.

Dromi, E. (1987). *Early lexical development.* Cambridge, England: Cambridge University Press.

Erbaugh, M. (1980). Why Chinese children's acquisition of Mandarin predicates should be "just like English." *Papers and Reports on Child Language Development, 22*, 49–57.

Erbaugh, M. (1983). Acquisition of Mandarin syntax: "Less" grammar isn't easier. *Journal of the Chinese Language Teacher's Association,* Vol. 18, No. 1.

Ferreiro, E. (1978). What is written in a written sentence: A developmental answer. *Journal of Education, 160,* 25–39.

Gentner, D. (1982a). Why nouns are learned before verbs: Linguistic relativity versus natural partitioning. In S. Kucjaz (Ed.), *Language development: Language, Cognition, and culture.* Hillsdale, NJ: Lawrence Erlbaum Associates.

Gentner, D. (1982b). Some interesting differences between nouns and verbs. *Cognition and Brain Theory, 4,* 2.

Griffiths, P., & Atkinson, M. (1978). A 'door' to verbs. In N. Waterson & C. Snow (Eds.), *The development of communication.* New York: Wiley.

Givon, T. (1979). *Understanding grammar.* New York: Academic Press.

Givon, T. (1984). *Syntax I.* Amsterdam: John Benjamins.

Gleitman, L. R., & Wanner, E. E. (1982). The state of the state of the art. In E. Wanner & L. R. Gleitman (Eds.), *Language acquisition.* Cambridge, England: Cambridge University Press.

Holden, S. H., & McGintie, W. H. (1972). Children's comprehension of word boundaries in speech and print. *Journal of Educational Psychology, 63,* 551–557.

Hopper, P. J., & Thompson, S. A. (1984). The discourse basis for lexical categorization in universal grammar. *Language, 60,* 703–752.

Hyams, N. M. (1986). *Language acquisition and the theory of parameters.* Dordrecht: D. Reidel.

Karmiloff-Smith, A. (1979). *A functional approach to child language.* Cambridge, England: Cambridge University Press.

Karmiloff-Smith, A. (1983). Language acquisition as a problem-solving process. *Papers and reports on Child Language Development, 22,* 1–22.

Karmiloff-Smith, A. (1986). Stage/structure versus phase/process in modelling linguistic and cognitive development. In I. Levin (Ed.), *Stage and structure: Reopening the debate* (pp. 164–190). Norwood, NJ: Albex.

Keenan, E. (1976). Towards a universal definition of subject. In C. Li (Ed.), *Subject and topic.* New York: Academic Press.

Keenan, E. (1979). On surface form and logical form. *Studies in Linguistic Sciences, 8,* 2.

Keil, F. C. (1986). On the structure-dependent nature of stages of cognitive development. In I. Levin (Ed.), *Stage and structure: Reopening the debate* (pp. 144–163). Norwood, NJ: Ablex.

Meroz, O. (in preparation). Acquisition of action nominals by Hebrew speaking children: Master's thesis, Tel Aviv University.

Mulford, R. (1979). Prototypicality and the development of categorization. *Papers and Reports on Child Language Development, 16,* Stanford University.

Mulford, R. (1983). On the acquisition of derivational morphology in Icelandic: Learning about *-ari. Iceland Journal of Linguistics, 5.*

Peters, A. (1983). *The units of acquisition.* Cambridge, England: Cambridge University Press.

Pinker, S. (1984). *Language learnability and language development.* Cambridge, MA: Harvard University Press.

Robins, R. H. (1966). The development of the word-class system of the European grammatical tradition. *Foundations of Language, 2,* 3–19.

Rosch, E. (1977). Human categorization. In N. Warren (Ed.), *Advances in cross-cultural psychology.* London: Academic Press.

Rosch, E., & Mervis, C. (1975). Family resemblances: Studies in the internal structure of categories. *Cognitive Psychology, 7,* 573–605.

Sachs, J. (1982). Talking about the there and then: The emergence of displaced reference. In E. E. Nelson (Ed.), *Children's language* (Vol. 4). New York: Gardner Press.

Schlesinger, I. D. (1982). *Steps to language.* Hillsdale, NJ: Lawrence Erlbaum Associates.

Slobin, D. I. (1985a). Crosslinguistic evidence for the language-making capacity. In D. I. Slobin (Ed.), *The crosslinguistic study of language acquisition* (Vol. 2). Hillsdale, NJ. Lawrence Erlbaum Associates.

Slobin, D. I. (Ed.). (1985b). *The crosslinguistic study of language acquisition* (Vols. 1 and 2). Hillsdale, NJ: Lawrence Erlbaum Associates.

Slobin, D. I. (1985c October). *Developmental paths between form and meaning: Crosslinguistic and diachronic perspectives.* Keynote address, Tenth Annual Boston University Conference on Child Language, Boston University.

Slobin, D. I. (1986, October). *The development from child speaker to native speaker.* Paper presented to the First Annual Chicago Symposium on Culture and Human Development.

Slobin, D. I. (1987, January). Frequency reflects function. Paper presented at conference on The Interaction of Form and Function in Language. University of California, Davis.

Slobin, D. I., & Bever, T. G. (1982). Children use canonic sentence structures: A crosslinguistic study of word order. *Cognition, 12,* 229–265.

Talmy, L. (1985). Lexicalization patterns: Semantic structure in lexical forms. In T. Shopen (Ed.), *Language typology and syntactic description* (Vol. 3). Cambridge, England: Cambridge University Press.

Thompson, S. A. (1986). *A discourse approach to the cross-linguistic category "adjective."* Paper presented at the 11th Annual Meeting, Berkeley Linguistics Society, Berkeley, CA, February.

Tolchinsky-Landsmann, L. (1986). *The development of written language among preschoolers and among first grade beginners.* Unpublished doctoral dissertation, Tel-Aviv University. (In Hebrew).

Walden, T. (1982). *The root of roots: Children's construction of word-formation processes in Hebrew.* Unpublished doctoral dissertation, Harvard University.

Weist, R. (1986). The development of tense-aspect systems. In P. Fletcher and M. Garman (Eds.), *Language acquisition* (2nd edition, pp. 356–374). Cambridge, England: Cambridge University Press.

4

The Nature of Early Language: Evidence from the Development of Hebrew Morphology

Yonata Levy
The Hebrew University

Chomsky's approach to the study of language, which has dominated linguistics in the last 2 decades, has pulled together theoretical linguistics and developmental psychology challenging both fields with the facts of language acquisition. Both linguists and psychologists have often shied away from this challenge— linguists have frequenty neglected issues that pertain to the learnability of their theories as well as to the psychological reality of their rules and constructs, while child psychologists have been only mildly disturbed by the fact that many of the proposed treatments of early linguistic abilities described children's language independent of existing grammatical descriptions of the target language. Many proposals were not clear on the issue of the development of more advanced, adult-type knowledge, nor were they specific enough on what the mechanisms of change should be.

The problem, which despite its centrality has received relatively little attention, can be put as follows: It has usually been agreed upon that adult linguistic knowledge makes use of abstract formal constructs and that mature cognition is freed from the here and now, has large memory spans, as well as the necessary computational power to generate natural language in all its complexies. But the nature of the observed early word combinations along with some accepted limitations upon children's thinking has led researchers to question the validity of attributing such qualities to children's early language and cognition.

Work that concerns the nature of early word-combinations has consistently shown that things children talk about are generally tied to the here and now (Snow & Ferguson, 1977), that they use unanalyzed speech-routines (Snow &

Ferguson, 1977), that they imitate parts of the input utterances (Snow, 1981), that their categories are semantic (Braine, this volume; Slobin, 1986), that their categories are pragmatic (Bruner, 1978, 1982), that the combinatorial rules are relational (Schlesinger, 1982), that there are form-function correspondence between the speech they produce and the speech-acts that they intend to perform (Ninio and Snow, this volume). In short, their language exhibits features that are not typically observed in adult language; in particular, it is asserted that child speech lacks abstract organizational principles.

Perhaps the most important contention, and the one that had the most serious implications for further work in the field, is the claim that the young child is inattentive to formal regularities in the system; specifically, when it requires the postulation of abstract categories and the understanding of correspondences that are not semantically or pragmatically motivated, but are constituents of the system qua system. A related conjecture has been that children do not regularize beyond specific situations, i.e., that language is acquired piecemeal and that throughout the beginning phases children do not consider language as a single coherent system but rather strive at solutions to local problems to satisfy the immediate needs of communication (Snow, 1981). In this chapter I show that these conjectures do not present an adequate characterization of early speech and that they suggest a rather impoverished view of the child as a language learner, a view which cannot be empirically supported.

Let us further spell out the argument: Two-year-olds' lives are organized around daily routines that repeat themselves with only very minor changes. In their lives the same people reappear every day and perform almost exactly the same functions. Children at this age are typically exposed to recurring speech styles, which relate to the same topics and address recurring needs. Language in these situations is likely to be highly repetitive and to abound in speech routines. Because the needs of communication are pressing, and the input data indeed offer routine locutions that are well suited for such specialized interactions, the child is wise to use these forms for communication. It is not surprising then, that *at one level of analysis* the language of the toddler can be described as imitative, routinized, and derivable to a large extent from the language that she is exposed to.

In other words, verbal skills that are restricted to a well specified situation, may be attained through ad hoc rote learning, which is done piecemeal. Furthermore, it may be achieved in a relatively short time and will undoubtedly prove communicatively useful in the context of the toddler's needs. So, it is probably true that successful verbal communication at age two can be achieved to a significant extent, through rote-learning, generalized examples and local rules, as recently restated by Berman (this volume) and Karmiloff-Smith (1979), which do not presuppose the existence of an underlying grammar in the linguistic sense of the term.[1] The question is: Is this an exhaustive picture or is there more going on in the early phases of language development? If one accepts the view of language as basically an internalized rule system which every mature speaker of the language is said to possess, and which he puts to use as a communicative and expressive tool, then a developmental approach must raise the issue of accounting for the acquisition of the language system, i.e., the grammar. alongside with the achievement of communicative skills. I believe that posing the question of language acquisition as involving these dual tasks: The learning of language as a complex system and the learning of its usage in communicatively adequate ways, can be fruitful, since it highlights the fact that these are indeed separate functions which can not be collapsed, despite their interactive nature.

The claim in this paper is that the child embarks upon both tasks from the early phases of her linguistic development, when word-combinations appear. The child, indeed, has to learn how to communicate, which sets an urgent task for her, but at the same time she is motivated to figure out regularities in the linguistic system that surround her, for the purpose of constructing a coherent, rule-governed structure. Such work may serve the sole purpose of rendering the system intrinsically coherent. This is a major driving force in and of itself, which compels the child to entertain hypotheses, such that a system can be seen to emerge. In other words, the drive to construct an orderly language system, which may be referred to as the drive to solve the "language puzzle," is in itself sufficient motivation that need not be subsumed under any other task. The "communication task" and the "puzzle task" both depend on the same data base and are clearly not independent of each other, although for the purpose of studying them, they can be looked at separately.

Summing up, the thesis of this chapter is that although the nature of children's early word combinations reflects the child's solution to the requirements of verbal communication, there is evidence that the child is also concerned with aspects of the system that do not contribute directly to the communicative power of the utterance. According to this view, the image that best characterizes the young language learner is that of a multilevel analyzer who is working with several types of analysis simultaneously, with different degrees of success, as learning progresses.

The data that are presented in this chapter concern the emergence of word

---

[1]To refer to this kind of "localized" knowledge Karmiloff-Smith (1986) uses the term 'procedural knowledge'. In her system this refers to the phase preceding the extraction of general rules in language, as well as in other cognitive areas. This notion is used differently by Anderson (1980) and others, in whose systems 'procedural knowledge' refers to the phase that follows earlier, often conscious and laborious learning. 'Procedural knowledge', in Anderson's sense, marks the achievement of automated, unconscious performance.

classes and morphological markings in children's language. The development of word classes is central to theorizing in the field of language acquisition because of the importance of grammatical categories to mature linguistic knowledge, as we conceive of it. Furthermore, since these categories are formally defined through a set of distributional interdependencies (Bloomfield, 1933; Maratsos, 1982; this volume), studying their emergence in child speech raises the issue of the child's abilities to cope with such categories, or, alternatively, his measures of avoiding the use of formally defined categories and rules in his early language.

The data in this paper are largely drawn from studies of the acquisition of Hebrew. Being a Semitic language, Hebrew has an elaborate morphological system which serves to express both semantic and syntactic distinctions. The data come primarily from a longitudinal study of two subjects, one boy and one girl (Levy, 1980; Rimor, unpublished), both native Israelis of middle class, educated families. The boy, Arnon, was studied longitudinally by the author who took daily notes and periodical recordings of his speech when he was 1;11–2;11. In this chapter we shall be mostly concerned with his speech between the ages 2;2–2;6. The speech of the little girl, Ruti, was recorded weekly by her father, typically in a book reading and play situation, between the age 2;0–2;4. Thus, both children were in the first months of their 3rd year, just past the one-word stage, in the beginning phases of grammatical development. Supplementary data come from group studies on 2-year-olds (Levy, 1980, 1983), as well as from published data by Bar-Adon (1957), Berman (1980, 1981, 1982, 1986), and Walden (1982) on the development of Hebrew. These data sometimes derive from older children at somewhat more advanced phases of their linguistic development. It can therefore only provide secondary support to our thesis.

In children learning Hebrew, the appearance of word-combinations is accompanied by the emergence of morphological markings—plurals, agreement, and verb inflections. The transcripts have been searched for evidence of productive usage of the inflectional and derivational system in Hebrew, with particular attention to the acquisition of portions of the system that are semantically arbitrary, the child's notion of a root and his grasp of the internal structure of words in Hebrew. Particular attention has been paid to evidence on the nature of early word classes. Throughout, I shall use the terms 'noun' and 'verb' for convenience, leaving aside the discussion concerning the partial overlap between adult categories and categories observed in children's language.

The following section offers a short description of the Hebrew verb and noun system with special emphasis on inflections, derivations, and root structure.

---

[2]Mean length of utterances (MLU) was not calculated because of the difficulties in applying this measure to inflectional languages, but see Dromi & Berman, (1982).

THE HEBREW DERIVATIONAL AND INFLECTIONAL SYSTEM

Hebrew is a Semitic language. Its vocabulary is built out of consonantal roots which are cast in vocalic word patterns. The roots are usually tri-consonantal and the patterns are in the form of vocalic infixes, as well as prefixes and suffixes. There are seven verb patterns—Binyaním—and about three dozen noun patterns—Miškalím.[3]

The Verb System—*Binyaním*

The following are examples of verb derivations. They are given in the past tense masculine, singular. Note that not all roots exist in all seven patterns. That is, the system has plenty of gaps. (See Table 4.1)

Notice the stop/spirant b/v, p/f, k/x, which regularly alternate in Hebrew as in B1 and B2 for the root D-B/V-K. Typically a root preserves its core meaning at least through parts of the derivation. Thus, derivatives of D-B/V-K have to do with 'sticking', and of B/V-Š-L have to do with 'cooking'. Historical developments have in some cases caused convergence among roots so that in modern Hebrew historically different roots have the same prononciation, e.g., *SiPéR* has the following meanings in modern Hebrew: 'counted, narrated, cut hair'.

Verbs in Hebrew are inflected for tense, number, gender, and person. The inflections typically effect the vowel pattern as well as attach prefixes, suffixes, and infixes to verbs. Table 4.2 gives examples—not the full paradigm—of inflected forms of the root D-B/V-K in the pattern B6—hiCCiC:

Verbs in the different *Binyamín* share inflectional prefixes, suffixes and infixes, and each paradigm is very systematic. Irregularities arise, however, in derivations that involve defective roots in which not all three elements appear in all the surface forms and thus result in root opacity. These are mainly roots that, as a result of phonological changes, have had an ancient consonant become a vowel, glide, or other form that alternates with zero. Compare the following forms:

1.	N-F-L	NaFáL	'fall-3rd,past,sing.'
vs.	R-U-C	RaC	'run-3rd,past,sing.'
2.	D-B-K	hiDBíK	'glue-3rd,past,sing.'
vs.	R-U-C	heRíC	'made run-3rd,past,sing.'

---

[3]Adjectives are constructed in the same way. The examples here, however, are confined to nouns and verbs. In preparing the following summary, I have greatly profited from similar expositions in Berman (1980, 1982) and Clark and Berman (1984).

TABLE 4.1
Binyaním and Their Associated Meanings

Binyan		Root	
(past tense singular, masculine)	B/V-S-L	G-D-L	D-B/V-K
B₁ CaCaC	----	GaDáL 'grew-stative'	DaváK 'adhered'
B₂ niCCaC	----	----	niDBáK 'glued-stative'
B₃ CiCeC	BiSel 'cooked-transitive'	GiDéL 'grew-transitive'	----
B₄ CuCaC	BuSál 'was cooked-passive'	GuDáL 'was grown-passive'	----
B₅ hitCaCeC	hitBaSéL 'cooked-reflexive'	----	----
B₆ hiCCiC	hiVSíL 'ripened-incohative'	hiGDíL 'enlarged-causative'	hiDBíK 'glued-transitive'
B₇ huCCaC	huVSáL 'was ripened passive'	huGDáL 'was enlarged-passive'	huDBaK 'was glued-passive'

3.	L-M-D	yiLMáD	'learn-3rd,fut,sing.'
vs.	N-S-ʕ	yiSá	'travel-3rd,fut,sing.'
4.	Y-R-D	yeRéD	'descend-3rd,fut,sing.'
vs.	K-N-S	yiKaNéS	'enter-3rd,fut,sing.'

The *Binyaním* serve to express a set of predicate relations. For each verb a "basic" sense can be established with all other forms being derivatives thereof (Berman, 1982). For example, B1 is basic (*hu YaŠáN* 'he slept'; *hi ŠaLXá mixtáv* 'she sent a letter'), B2 can be basic, or passive to B1 (*ha-yéled niXNáS* 'the boy entered'; *ha-mixtáv niŠLáX* 'the letter was sent'), B5 can be basic (*aní miŠtAéL* 'I cough') and reflexive or reciprocal to forms in the other Binyaním (*hem hitXaBKú* 'they embraced'; *hu hitLaBéŠ* 'he got dressed'), B6 can be basic or causative or incohative of forms in the other Binyaním (*Dan hiPíL otá* 'Dan made-fall her'; *ha-tapúax hiCHíV* 'the apple turned yellow').

This list, although not exhaustive, is fairly representative of the major functions of the *Binyaním*. Note that the system is only partially regular—the same

TABLE 4.2
Examples of Verb Inflections

	Present[a] Tense	Past Tense	Future Tense
1st sing. mas.	maDBíK	hiDBáKti	aDBíK
2nd sing. fem.	maDBiKá	hiDBáKt	taDBíKi
3rd pl. mas.	maDBiKím	hiDBíKu	yaDBíKu
3rd pl. fem.	maDBiKót	hiDBíKu	yaDBíKu

[a] Present tense forms are not inflected for person.

function may be expressed by more than one pattern and the same pattern clearly may have more than one function. B4 and B7 are the only fully systematic *Binyaním:* they serve as the derived passives of B3 and B6, respectively; they are also the least used.

The Noun System—*Miškalím*

Nouns in Hebrew are constructed, quite similarly to verbs, from roots that are cast in noun patterns. However, contrary to verbs, there are nouns for which this internal structure is not evident. As a rule, many more noun patterns exist than verb patterns, and the semantics of the patterns is less predictable, although it is functional in important segments of the noun vocabulary.

Table 4.3 presents examples of some noun derivatives from the roots B/V-Š-L, G-D-L and D-B/V-K.

TABLE 4.3
Examples of Miškalím and Their Associated Meaning

Root	B/V-Š-L	G-D-L	D-B/V-K
miškál			
CeCeC	--	--	DeVeK 'glue'
CiCuC	BiŠúl 'cooking	GiDúL 'growth'	DiBúK 'obsession'
MiCCaC	--	miGDáL 'tower'	--
miCCaCa	mivŠaLá 'brewery'	--	miDBaKá 'sticker'
CoCeC	--	GóDeL 'size'	--
haCCaCa	havŠaLá 'ripening'	haGDaLá 'enlargement'	haDBaKá 'glueing'
CCiCa	BŠíLa 'maturation'	GDiLá 'growth-abst.'	--
CCeCut	BŠéLut 'ripeness'	GaDLút 'greatness'	DVéKút 'adherence'

Some of the *Miškalím* are productive and carry specialized meanings and others are less specified semantically.

Nouns in Hebrew are either masculine or feminine and are inflected for plural according to their linguistic gender.[4] For example,

kadúr—kadurím	'ball—balls'	(masc.)
yéled—yeladím	'boy—boys'	(masc.)
agalá—agalót	'cart—carts'	(fem.)
tabáat—tabaót	'ring—rings'	(fem.)

---

[4]Many nouns may also be inflected for possession (*séfer-sifrí* 'book-my book') and may have a special form used when modified by a noun, e.g., *valdéi-kibútz* 'kibutz children'. Noun-noun modifications are not very productive in colloquial speech and appear mostly in lexicalized compounds, e.g., *beít-séfer* 'school'.

Many feminine forms are derived from the masculine by means of a feminine suffix:

par—pará 'bull— cow'
tarnegól—tarnególet 'cock—chicken'

Do nouns and verbs present similar opportunities for isolating roots and patterns? Compare:

meSaXéK	'he is playing'
leSaXéK	'to play'
SiXáKnu	'we played'
SiXáKti	'I played', etc.

with:

miSXáK	'game'
miSXaKím	'games'

Apparently many more comparisons exist in the verb paradigms that highlight the consonant structure than there are in the noun paradigms. In order to isolate roots and patterns in the nouns, one needs to compare across items, among nouns. For example,

miSXáK	'game'
SaXKán	'actor'
miSXaKía	'play-room'

Note that the roots express the semantic core of the lexical items. Nouns and verbs are created when roots are cast in specific vocalic patterns. In other words, it is the patterns that determine class membership, while a given root may be shared by words belonging to different word-classes, as the examples throughout this section illustrate. However, this is not without exceptions and for some inflected forms it may not be possible to determine class membership on the basis of their form alone.

Finally, it is important to note that the notion of a root is abstract and formal in both nouns and verbs. It may be inaccessible to native speakers without explicit tutoring, in cases of the defective roots which have typically less than three consonants in their surface forms, as the examples on pages 77–78 illustrate. Because of this, the notion of a root in the following sections has been restricted to the ''consonantal skeleton'' as it is realized in actual surface forms of words.

There is little doubt that, used in this sense, the crucial role of the root in Hebrew words is fully appreciated by mature speakers of the language and that the identification of the root consonants when they are overtly expressed in surface words, is part of Hebrew speakers' linguistic competencies (e.g., Clark & Berman, 1984; Walden, 1982).

In the next section data are presented that concern the early form of nouns and verbs in Hebrew learning children. It is argued that rudimentary word classes, which are distributionally defined, exist already in these early phases. Errors and overregularizations suggest that the children are attempting to systematize their knowledge on the basis of discerned formal regularities. The lack of category cross-overs of innovative lexical items in early language is discussed. This phenomenon should be construed as further evidence for the existence of word classes in early child language.

CHILD LANGUAGE DATA

Verb Inflections

Early in the two-word stage, children are surprisingly consistent in their use of person and number inflections (Levy, 1980). Although gender is the source of many errors, there are hardly any confusions in children's productions between singular and plural, or among persons. Both the longitudinal and the cross-sectional data show that once inflections come in and become productive, subjects do not find it difficult to correctly inflect nouns, whether animate or inanimate, as required by their numerosity, or by the person of the real-world referent.

In a study of the acquisition of agreement in inflected pronouns and verb forms (Levy, 1983a), it was found that gender agreement caused a few problems to children, when agreement depended on full nouns rather than on pronouns. Recall that nouns in Hebrew are phonologically marked as either masculine or feminine. However, in the case of pronouns, particularly second person pronouns which do not convey information about the gender of their referents through their phonological shape, performance was random long after agreement errors with nouns disappeared. This was the case for the acquisition of Hebrew as well as of a variety of other languages (Levy, 1983b). In other words, wherever correct marking of gender depended on identifying the sex of the referent in the real world rather than on some morphophonological cues, errors persisted. This finding is further discussed in the final section of this chapter.

In general, the correct marking of verbs for gender was dependent of the prior learning of the plural forms of nouns. Before achieving good mastery of noun plurals, agreement was randomly done (Levy, 1983a). But once plurals were learned, agreement fell into place without further effort.[5]

The most common errors were found in agreement between pronouns and their associated verb forms, and their referents in the real world. That is, gender

---

[5]Pinker, Stromswold, and Hochberg (in preparation) asked whether number agreement is applied by children differentially to noun phrases according to the different relations they are involved in, e.g. to agentive subject vs. experiencer subjects. Their findings are similar to ours: they show that once these rules are acquired, they function across the board for all nouns, regardless of thematic roles.

inflection was inappropriate for its intended referent in the animate world. I conclude that, in the case of gender agreement, systematizing the data on some formal nonsemantic basis was achieved by children earlier than their understanding of the semantic notion that this linguistic distinction carries when animate referents are intended.

Tense Forms

Our data had 1757 verb tokens for Arnon and 400 verb tokens for Ruti (ages 2;0–2;4). They were analyzed in terms of roots, tense and person inflections. Table 4.4 summarizes this data.

Tenses were counted on the basis of form alone. All tense forms were present in the children's repertoire at that time. Future forms often replaced imperative, as is the case in adult speech too (Berman, 1986). This accounts for the small number of future and imperative forms in the data. An analysis of the actual verbs used by the children showed that they had attained an across-the-board ability to inflect verbs, which was not restricted to individual items.

A telling piece of data come from the children's use of alternative forms for present tense feminine singulars: In Hebrew there are two forms for the feminine singular: Forms that end in /et/ and forms that end in /a/. These are only rarely in free variation: They are either fixed for a given verb as in *ŠoTá* and *RoCá*, where no other forms such as **ŠoTét* or **RoCét* exist, or they serve to indicate a difference in register, as between *OXéLet* and its extremely literary version, *OXLá*. Some common adjectives in the feminine are of a similar /a/ ending pattern, for example *GDoLá* 'big' (fem.); *YaFá* 'pretty' (fem.).

In the corpora of both Arnon and Ruti there were a number of errors, substituting what should be present tense verbs ending in /et/, by forms ending in /a/. By far the most striking example of this overgeneralization comes from one

TABLE 4.4
Inflected Verbs (%Tokens) in Arnon (Age 2;0-2;4) and Ruti (Age 2;0-2;3)

	Arnon (2;0-2;4)					Ruti (2;0-2;3)				
Verb tokens	1757					400				
Roots	100					81				
Tense	Pres.	Past	Fut.	Imp.	Inf.	Pres.	Past	Fut.	Imp.	Inf.
	25%	32%	20%	6%	16%	29%	32%	26%	5%	8%
	(456)	(562)	(351)	(105)	(283)	(116)	(128)	(104)	(20)	(32)
Person	Mas. Sg.	Fem. Sg.	Mas. Pl.	Fem. Pl.		Mas. Sg.	Fem. Sg.	Mas. Pl.	Fem. Pl.	
	36%	29%	28%	7%		32%	44%	21%	3%	
	(641)	(516)	(466)	(134)		(128)	(176)	(84)	(12)	

subject in the cross-sectional study (Levy, 1983a), age 2;2, who *consistently* gave these—sometimes nonexistent, sometimes highly literary—forms, instead of their rather familiar counterparts. Whether the children were generalizing on the basis of familiar adjectives or making the wrong choice of a present tense form, is impossible to tell. In other words, these may be either syntactic or morphological misuses, but there can be no semantic motivation for such a choice.

Arnon's infinitives were clearly differentiated from regular inflected verb forms—only rarely would he drop the initial /l/ which is the marker of infinitives in Hebrew. However, most of his infinitives could not have been reproduced from memory, since they were clearly nonstandard. As in the case of Berman's data (1980), the forms that Arnon produced were seldom simple analogies, but rather instances of more elaborate forms of combination, in the sense of Mac-Whinney (1978). So here again, form is attended to from very early on, aided by a working notion of a paradigm.

Binyaním

The most fascinating area of study of Hebrew grammar, one which raises many unresolved issues and allows for potentially interesting insights, is to be found in the study of the verb system—*Binyaním*. The *Binyaním* are a conjunction of semantic and morphophonological features which is sufficiently transparent to the eyes of the investigator to allow one to test rather specific hypotheses in a relatively straightforward manner. Data from the development of the *Binyán* system are also relevant to the discussion in this chapter.

The development of the *Binyaním* was studied extensively by Berman (1980, 1982), who paid particular attention to the development of the semantics of the *Binyán* system. Berman suggested that children start out *unaware* of the fact that these verb patterns can be used to express certain meanings as well as to mark syntactic relations. They then progress in a relatively predicted order, to discover expressions of transitivity, and finally other meaning components that are expressed through the *Binyaním*. During the period in which this semantic learning takes place, typically around age 4 to 5, the child attempts to overregularize the system by casting familiar roots in *Binyaním* in which they do not occur in adult language, so as to express specific meaning relations. For example, children may say **hiCLáLti oto* 'I made-dive him' which is presumably created on the basis of such verbs as *hiXTáVti* 'I made-write'; *hiXNáSti* 'I made-enter', assuming that this *Binyán* (B6) can be freely used to express the causative (Berman, 1982).

As was mentioned earlier, the most common verbs in 2-year-olds' language are not confined to a limited set of the *Binyaním*. For example, leSaXéK, leNaŠéK 'to play, to kiss, are in B3; *lehitRaXéC, lehitLaBéŠ* 'to wash, to dress' are in B5; *lehoRíD, lehaPíL* 'to put down, to drop' are in B6; *liGMóR, liXTóV* 'to finish, to write' are in B1; *lehiKaNéS, leheRaDéM* 'to enter, to fall asleep'

TABLE 4.5
The Distribution of Verb Tokens and Roots Among the
Different Binyanim in Ruti and Arnon

Binyan	Ruti				Arnon			
	Tokens 400		Roots 81		Tokens 1757		Roots 100	
B1	57.5%	(230)	53%	(43)	60.4%	(1062)	40%	(40)
B2	5%	(20)	5%	(4)	3.6%	(65)	7%	(7)
B3	13.75%	(55)	18.5%	(15)	16%	(283)	25%	(25)
B5	20%	(80)	18.5%	(15)	16%	(286)	22%	(22)
B7	3.75%	(15)	5%	(4)	3.4%	(61)	6%	(6)

are in B2.[6] These verbs are clearly in the lexicon of 2-year-olds. The rare *Binyaním* are the two strictly passive ones, B4 and B7, but those are not very common in adult language either. The distribution of the children's verbs among the various *Binyaním*, is presented in table 4.5. It is a fair approximation, although not an accurate replication, of the distribution of verbs in colloquial Hebrew.

Is there evidence for productive use of the various form patterns of the *Binyaním?* This issue is addressed in the following sections, through an examination of children's errors and lacunae in the use of the *Binyaním*.

Berman (1980, 1982) looked at children's productions of the *Binyaním*. She argues that very young children lack an understanding of the rationale behind moving between Binyaním. She observed that for a particular verb that exists in more than one *Binyán,* some children will settle on one form of the verb and will not alternate between *Binyaním* as required, thus creating some sort of neutralization of Binyaním differences. For example, some 2-year-olds use the transitive *SaGáR* 'closed' for both the transitive and the intransitive (*niSGáR*); or the transitive *LaVáŠ* 'wore', for the intransitive, the reflexive *hitLaBéŠ* and the causative *hiLBíŠ*. Similar examples were found in my data along with frequent instances of a variety of *Binyaním* for a given root. Typical examples are hit-NaŠKú–NiŠéK; CaXák–hiCXíK 'they kissed (each other)—he kissed; he laughed—he made laugh.'

Many instances in my data corroborate the description given in Berman (1980) of the three different types of analogies that young children resort to in their productive use of defective verbs;

1. Regularization to full paradigms—these are instances in which the defective verb is inflected like a nondefective verb.

2. Reference to partial paradigms—these are analogies based on other defective verbs, which constitute a different paradigm than the verb in question.

---

[6]Of course, there are differences in the frequency of verb types and tokens among verbs in the different patterns. Some *Binyaním* are distinctly more frequent than others in child speech, as well as in the adult language.

3. Reference to word-based paradigms—cases of verb forms produced on the basis of other words, not necessarily verbs that share the same consonant structure.

Furthermore, the kind of errors found in the data at this early stage suggest that the child is performing some analysis on the verbs. The errors suggest that the child realizes the special role of the consonant structure and the difference in status between consonants and vowel patterns, which permit one to vary the vowels but preserve the consonants without saying a *different* word. Table 4.6 presents typical examples of the above phenomena.

There is no need to go into the analysis of each example in Table 4.6. Suffice it to say that all the errors show the wrong choice of vowels or the absence of a prefix that identifies the *Binyán* pattern. The verbs are either in the wrong *Binyán* (e.g., nos. 2, 10, 13, 14, 15, 16), or show a failure to note that the forms are not in free variation (e.g., no. 3), or demonstrate the child's difficulties with defective roots which affect the vowel patterns (e.g., nos. 6, 8, 12). In general, difficulties in the vowel patterns involve both defective and nondefective roots.

Two important aspects of these examples should be noted: (a) The misformations almost always affect the vowels and prefixes, and only rarely the conso-

TABLE 4.6
Berb Forms in Arnon (2;0-2;4) and Ruti (2;0-2;3)

	Child's Form	Correct Form	Root	Gloss
1.	*gimár	nigmár	G-M-R	'was finished-mas.'
2.	*gimér	gamár	G-M-R	'finished-mas.'
3.	yošvá	yošévet	#Y-Š-V	'is sitting-fem.'
4.	*novéxet	nováxat	N-V-X	'is barking-fem.'
5.	*hifsák	hifsík	P-S-K	'stopped-mas.'
6.	*hocíti	hocéti	#Y-C-ʕ	'took out-1st.'
7.	*hicíti	hocéti	#Y-C-ʕ	'took out-1st.'
8.	*banáti	baníti	#B-N-	'constructed-1st.'
9.	*kibáti	kibíti	#K-B-	'turned off-1st.'
10.	*ritév	hirtív	R-T-V	'wet-mas. past'
11.	*ratáv	hirtív	R-T-V	'wet-mas. past'
12.	*racáti	racíti	#R-C-	'wanted-1st'
13.	*rigéz	hirgíz	R-G-Z	'made angry-mas.'
14.	*savár	hisbír	S-B-R	'explained-mas.'
15.	laváš	hilbíš	L-B-Š	'dressed-causat. mas.'
16.	raxác	hitraxéc	R-X-C	'washed-reflex. mas.'

* indicated illformed verbs.
\# indicated defective roots.

nants.[7] (b) Children's erroneous forms are almost always identifiable as verbs. This is due to the fact that in most cases the errors are drawn from the right stock of possible verb-forms so that the word *sounds* as a verb.

In sum, evidence from patterns of errors in children's early language reveal 2-year-olds' rudimentary understanding of the nature of the language they are acquiring. The data presented so far are at least suggestive of the child's having understood the fixed nature of the consonantal structure of Hebrew verbs. This is in contrast with the elusive nature of the vowels. This point is taken up again in the following sections when the learning of the noun system is discussed.

NOUNS IN THE LANGUAGE OF TWO-YEAR-OLDS

Plurals

Recall that nouns in Hebrew are either masculine or feminine and are marked for plurality. The linguistic gender of the noun determines the choice of the plural suffix. Nouns ending in /á/ or /t/ are feminine, with very few exceptions. All the others are masculine. Adjectives agree with the nouns they modify in gender and number, and verbs agree with their subjects in gender, number, and person. The system is syllabic and creates rhyming between words (e.g., *ha-yelad-ót ha-ktan-ót rac-ót*—'the-girls the-little are running (fem. pl.).

The development of gender and number inflections was studied longitudinally and cross-sectionally (Levy, 1980, 1983a). It was found that children started off by assigning masculine plural suffix /im/ to all nouns regardless of their linguistic gender. They then gradually became attentive to the relevant features of the noun's final syllable, which determine the correct plural suffix. Thus, the first step was to set apart all nouns that end in /a/ as requiring a feminine /ot/ suffix for plural, while the rest of the nouns—masculine as well as feminine

---

[7]There are two frequent types of errors in early language in which the consonant structure seems to be affected. Both reinforce the above generalization since they result from children's efforts to regularize nonregular verb forms: (a) In the case of defective roots that result in a surface form with only two pronounceable consonants, children as well as uneducated adults, may insert a third consonant. This is never done randomly. For example, in the case of roots with final /n/, e.g., N-T-N one may find *natánti 'I gave' instead of the nonregular natáti (Berman, 1982). Similarly, in the case of roots ending with the letter 'alef' which are defective, e.g., Y-C-ʔ, children sometimes say *yocétet instead of the two-consonant form yocét 'come out-fem. sing.'; that is, they reduplicate the suffix /et/ so that the surface form has three consonants (Bar-Adon, 1957). (b) The other source of confusion is found in the stop/spirant alternations such as those between p/f, b/v, k/x. My data (Levy, 1983a) suggest that the children do not yet understand the basis for these alternations, since they may occasionally use both forms of a word even within a single utterance. This point is further illustrated in the next section. Notice, however, that such instances, in combination with the absence of noticeable difficulties in comprehension, suggest that Hebrew learners know early that alternations between stops and spirants do not result in meaning differences, although it takes them a while to learn the principles, as well as the peculiarities, of these alternations.

nouns that do not end in /a/—still formed their plurals with a masculine /im/ suffix. The next development was to add an /ot/ to nouns that end in /et/, while still appending, mistakenly, an /im/ suffix to /it/ and /at/ ending nouns. Finally, all nouns ending in /t-t/ were assigned an /ot/ suffix for plural. By age 3, all the children in the study had excellent control of gender in nouns. Apart from nouns that are exceptions, the problem that remained concerned the internal vowel changes that typically occur in Hebrew nouns when plural suffixes are added. These were not mastered until the noun endings had been appropriately sorted out. However, once the children began to introduce vowel changes, it was not done haphazardly. Rather, they drew upon their knowledge of derived forms and tried them out as a possible basis for these changes.

Table 4.7 gives some examples of Arnon's plurals at various stages in the development of pluralization.

Of particular importance to the thesis of this chapter is the fact that whatever the child knew about plural formation was applied to *all* the nouns that he used at the time and not to a subsection thereof. There was no evidence for knowledge tied to any subportion of the vocabulary, and thus no piecemeal learning was evident.

Note that had the children been motivated to learn the system for the sole purpose of better communicating his intentions, the /im/ suffix would have probably done a good enough service of indicating plurality. Learning the correct plural marking of inanimate nouns would have been, at the very least, a protracted and tiresome process. The fact that children learn about noun gender with

TABLE 4.7
Stages in the Development of Noun Plurals in Hebrew [a]

Stage	Singular		Correct Plurals	Arnon's Plurals
A	simlá	(fem.)	smalót	*simláim 'dress'
	íma	(fem.)	imahót	*ímaim 'mommy'
1;10-2;0	ába	(mas.)	avót	*ábaim 'daddy'
	kcicá	(fem.)	kcicót	*kcicótim 'meatballs'
B	Ribá	(fem.)	ribót	ribót 'jam'
	mirpéşet	(fem.)	mirpaşót	*mirpéşetim 'balcony'
2;0-2;2	televísia	(fem.)	televísiot	televísiot 'TV'
	tabáat	(fem.)	tabaót	*tabáatim 'ring'
C	caláxat	(fem.)	calaxót	calaxót 'plate'
	máxat	(fem.)	mexatím	*máxot 'needle'
2;2-2;5	karít	(fem.)	kariót	*karítim 'pillow'
	magévet	(fem.)	magavót	*magévetim 'towel'
#D	toláat	(fem.)	tolaím	*tolím, *tolót 'worm'
	mexonít	(fem.)	mexoniyót	*mexonótim, *mexonítim 'car'
2;5-2;10	magévet	(fem.)	magavót	*magevím, *magevót 'towel'
	rakévet	(fem.)	rakavót	*raxevím, *raxevót 'train'

[a]Data from Arnon (Age 1;10-2;10).
#Stage D is beyond the age range that is biscussed in this paper.

remarkable ease in the early months of the 3rd year of life (at any rate, hardly ever beyond the 3rd year), is thus very informative. Early and effortless learning of gender was found not only in children learning Hebrew but for other languages as well (Clark, 1986; Mills, 1986; Smoczynska, 1986).

Noun Derivations

The brief description of Hebrew morphology (pp. 77–81) suggested that the Hebrew noun system is less flexible than the verb system. The citation forms of Hebrew nouns, especially in colloquial speech, undergo relatively little changes. Still, root and pattern analysis for nouns is probably less straightforward than it is for verbs. Most, although not all nouns are a blend of consonantal root and a vocalic pattern. To what extent can young 2-year-olds be credited with the knowledge of these facts which concern the typology of their language?

An examination of the longitudinal corpora of 2-year olds learning Hebrew reveals that they have some understanding of the derivational nature of nouns:

a. In a study of the acquisition of gender and number inflection (Levy, 1983a) children were confused about the internal vowel changes that are often introduced when the noun is pluralized. The subjects did not settle on one form for each noun but, rather, made use of the different possibilities. They seemed to know that stop/spirant alternations were required and the errors they made were nonarbitrary—they chose some existing derivative and used it with or without stop/spirant alternations. For example,

> Correct: *yaldá–yeladót* 'girl–girls'
> *kélev–klavím* 'dog–dogs'
> Children: **yaldót* = *yaldá*+/ot/ (no vowel change to the stem)
> **yéledot* = *yéled* 'boy'+/ot/ no movement of the stress.
> **kélebim* = *kélev*+spirant/stop alternation+/im/ no movement of the stress.
> **kalbím* = *kalbá* 'bitch'+/im/

Examples like these are extremely common in the speech of 2-year-olds (Berman, 1986).

b. The following are examples of children's misproductions which involved a choice of the wrong suffix or pattern. Note that these are not in free variation and will never be produced by adults:

1. **masayá* for the correct *masaít* 'truck'

2. **karyaná* for the correct *karyanít* 'woman announcer'

3. **xamiá* 'a stove' (*xam* 'hot'). This is a noun derived from an adjective.

However, in speech addressed to children 'hot' is often used referentially to indicate hot objects.

4. *'kaškéšet* for the correct *kiškúš* 'scribble'

c. Some examples of new coinages are found at this early stage as well. These are instances in which existing nouns or their stems are cast in different noun patterns to create new words:

5. *kukít* 'objects that one plays peek-a-boo with' (*kúku* in Hebrew)

6. *uganiá* 'a plate that is used to serve cake' (from *ugá* 'cake')

7. *bakbukiá* 'a bottle stand' (from *bakbúk* 'bottle')

8. *manelá* 'a key-hole' (from *manúl* 'lock' and *linól* 'to lock')

9. *maglexá* 'a shaver' (from *gilúax* 'shaving' and *lehitgaléax* 'to shave')

10. *nevoxút* 'the fact that the dog used to bark' (*linbóax* 'to bark' *nevixá* 'a bark'; /ut/ abstract noun suffix)

Nevoxút (Ex. 10) is a particularly interesting one: Abstract nouns ending in /ut/ are not very common in child speech. This little girl—age 2;3—produced this noun in talking about her dog and how disturbing his barking was to her. This is clearly an instance of an extension of an abstract nominal form to an action, and it speaks against a semantic basis for the productivity of this nominal pattern. *maNeLá* and *maGLeXá* are less clearly examples of an action word that is made into an object name. In these examples both the verbs and the nouns may be known to children (8,9) whereas in the previous example (ex. 10) the legitimate noun *NeViXá* is itself an action nominal. I shall refer to these examples later, when crossing over between word categories is discussed.

Note that similar means of coining new words—changing the suffix or casting the stem in a different pattern—are used by older children, as well as adults (Clark & Berman, 1984).

Examples of idiosyncratic forms are extremely rare. I have found two in my corpora:

kvasám for the correct *kvasím* 'sheep'.
makúmia, a self directed imperative meaning 'get up'. Possibly a blend of the noun *makóm* 'place' and the imperative *kúmi* 'get up—fem. sing.'

In sum, it is not surprising that nouns in the language of 2-year-olds do not show as much formal variations as the verbs do, since the language does not provide as many options for change in nouns as it does for verbs. However, young children do attempt some pattern manipulations with nouns as well, as shown by errors and innovations such as examples 1–10.

Summing up studies on early morphology in Hebrew, the following picture emerges: Two-year-old Hebrew learners have established inflectional and derivational paradigms the semantic underpinnings of which have often not been worked out. Thus, 2-year-olds have not worked out the semantics of the *Binyán* system (Berman, 1982) but they seem to be using the time-tense system correctly (Berman, Dromi, & Slobin, in preparation); they have difficulties with the semantics, but not with the morphology of the gender system (Levy, 1983b), but they distinguish numerosity and person (Levy, 1980). Their morphological paradigms are still very incomplete with respect to certain *Binyaním* which are less frequent in child language, and they are largely ignorant of the effects of defective roots as well as of other exceptions. But it seems that Hebrew learners appreciate already at these early stages, at least in some rudimentary sense, the central typological characteristics of the language; namely, that lexical items are derived from consonantal roots and patterns and that the consonantal structure of words is constant, while the vocalic patterns change. The errors that children produce suggest that they have some general notion of "permissible word forms" that constrain potential lapses. Furthermore, visibly missing from the productions of young children are instances of crossovers between the two major classes. Innovations involving verbs derived from nouns that keep the consonantal skeleton intact are missing from the corpora of young children. For example, *tešarvelí li* 'you-fem. roll up the sleeve to me' (*šarvúl* 'sleeve'); *tešaršér li* 'you-mas. put the necklace around my neck' (*šaršéret* 'necklace'). Those become frequent in the language of 4- to 5-year-olds (Berman, 1982). Younger children avoid such coinages despite the fact that Hebrew frequently uses the same roots to coin verbs. The finding that crossover between word classes. although quite natural for Hebrew, is not attempted by young 2-year-olds, is important in our attempt to understand the child's early notion of word classes.

The fact that young children avoid crossing class boundaries, first and foremost suggests that classes of some sort have been established. But then why are these toddlers so *conservative* in their errors? The data clearly rules out the possibility that the bulk of their vocabulary consists of rote learned forms of verbs and nouns. It is also most unlikely that while they attend to the consonants the vowel pattern is conceived of as some nonspecific *noise* around the consonantal skeleton. For, if this were the case, their errors would not be well differentiated between nouns and verbs. Another possibility is that young children do not comprehend meaning relationships that hold among nouns and verbs by virtue of their shared roots. If this is indeed the case, then they cannot see the relations that hold between nouns and verbs by virtue of their shared roots and have no reason to attempt crossovers between these two categories. But notice that even the relatively few changes and innovations in nouns, that were evidenced in our data, could not have been produced without an understanding of the nature of nouns in Hebrew.

Let us further examine young children's notion of a root in Hebrew words:

Experiments have presented evidence that 3-year-olds can tell roots from patterns in nouns as well as in verbs: In a study of word formation processed in 3- to 7-year-olds, Clark & Berman (1984) identified three types of errors in responses to questions requiring children to identify the action verb, given a noun that does not exist in Hebrew but uses a root that exists in forms familiar to the child.

1. Children use the root of the given noun, but put it in an inappropriate *Binyán*.

2. Children respond with an existing verb from a different, yet semantically related, root.

3. Children use the root of the innovative noun in a different <u>noun</u>, rather than in a verb.

The youngest subjects in this study were 3-year-olds and their errors were equally distributed among the three error types. It is of interest to our present discussion that the response patterns indicated that the subjects did identify the roots of the unfamiliar nouns they were presented with. However, let us not forget that the subjects in this study were in their 4th year. The question is: Do 2-year-olds have some notion of a root as well?

Unfortunately, similar experimental data is difficult to come by for 2-year-olds for obvious reasons, but some observations from corpora of natural speech can be brought to bear on this issue:

1. The instances of noun innovations that were found in the data presented in the previous sections could not occur without the child's understanding that nouns are, in a sense, "divisible wholes."

2. Parental input, as well as child speech at this age, are replete with examples such as the following:

teSaPéR li SiPúR   'you-masc. *tell me a story*'
bói le-hitNaDNéD ba-NaDNeDá   'you-fem. come to swing in the swing'
CiYáRt li CiYúR?   'you-fem. drew me a picture?'

In view of what is known of the salience of phonological patterning in speech perception, segmentation and storage (Peters, 1982; Slobin, 1986), it seems quite unlikely that for cases such as the above, consonant identity and the meaning correspondences that are established by virtue of the shared consonantal core will go unnoticed by children. Root similarities among the nouns of different *Miškalím* may be harder to discover than resemblances among verbs of different *Binyaním*. However, similarities *between* noun/verb pairs, as in the above examples, appear to be quite salient in many familiar instances in child speech.

3. As an illustration, consider a conversation between Ruti—age 2;3—and her father. The conversation took place within the first 20 minutes of the recording session. Parent and child were gluing pieces of paper together. During the exchange Ruti produced the following tokens, all derivatives of the root D-B/-K:

niyár DéVeK	'paper glue = tape'
*aDBéK	'I'll glue'
aDBíK	'I'll glue'
hiDBáKti	'I glued'
DéVEK	'glue'
niyár DéVeK	'paper glue = tape'
maDBiKá	'am gluing—fem. sing.'
taDBíK	'glue—you-masc.'
lehaDBíK	'to glue'
DéVeK	'glue'
niyár DéVeK	'paper glue = tape'
DaVúK	'glued', interpreted by the father to mean sticky
DaVíK	'sticky'
ADBíK	'I'll glue'

By the way, notice that the child moved from the stop to the spirant (B/V) as required.

The use of nouns and verbs that share the same root is indeed very common and most natural. It is difficult to imagine that children who regularly use this system will fail to notice the common consonantal core of these forms, as well as the fact that the topic of this conversation, namely 'glue' and its derivatives, is expressed by D-B/V-K. So, I do not claim to have demonstrated that 2-year-olds have a clear notion of a root, but I think that it is plausible that they do have at least a workable notion of the special role of the ''consonantal skeleton'' of words in their language.

Returning to our original query—the lack of category crossovers in early child speech—it seems that 2-year-olds define class membership by too stringent criteria. Productive innovations at this stage seem to be restricted to roots and patterns learned in the context of a particular class. In order to appreciate the full range of productivity that Hebrew allows and move to a more flexible system, the child needs to *relax* her definition of class membership to include all items that are cast in patterns typical of a given grammatical class, with no concern for the roots. The understanding that items can shift categories simply by assuming the right pattern, *Binyán* or *Miškál,* is a further developmental step. Although on the surface it looks as if it involves less concern for category boundaries, in fact it reveals a more abstract understanding of the structure of Hebrew.

Observations of the language of 4- to 6-year-olds support such a developmental picture: Children's innovations are this stage show plenty of instances of cross-categorization which are morphologically well-formed and immediately comprehensible to speakers of the language (Berman, 1980, 1982). Data from the development of other languages seem to present a similar picture. Clark (1981, 1982) studied children's word-formation processes. In her work on innovative denominal verbs in children's speech (1982), she notes the frequent occurrence of these new coinages in the language of 3- to 5-year-olds, and the relative rarity of coinage of new nouns from familiar verbs. Clark suggests a number of ways to account for these data; one is that children know about nouns more and earlier than they know about verbs (Gentner, 1982), and that, in English, no complex morphological manipulation is required to create denominal verbs (e.g., dream–dream; race–race). Notice, however, that this all too simple procedure results in homonyms for the English examples cited by Clark (1982) but not for the French and German examples.[8]

Clark's data suggest that denominal verbs are rather rare in younger children. Of 127 examples drawn from corpora of childen of different ages, only 18 (~14%) come from children comparable in age to the children we studied. Furthermore, 11 out of the 18 examples of innovative denominal verbs came from one German child, RN.

Children's tendency to overrestrict their rules and categories gains further support from Pinker's (1984) and Slobin's (1986) discussions of the learning of word order. The findings there suggest that "when a language has a fixed constituent order the child rarely utters ungrammatical orders, but when a language has free constituent order the child may well restrict himself or herself to a subset of the attested orders. This pattern suggests that the child records constituent orders from the start and relaxes it as the evidence warrants" (Pinker, 1984, p. 125).

Let me mention at this point that one of the major concerns of previous work on the formation of word classes has been the need to account for the learning of the distinctions between various predicate types, i.e., verbs and adjectives (e.g., Maratsos, 1981, 1982). However, early speech is remarkably devoid of adjectives (Feldman, Goldin-Meadow, & Gleitman, 1978; Gentner, 1982; Levy, 1980). As it is generally accepted that in order to make a case from the nonexistence of errors in a given corpus, there should be ample evidence for correct usage as well as plenty of opportunities to make mistakes, the problem does not really arise with regard to 2-year-olds whose repertoire of adjectives typically consists of *big, little, nice, yukky,* or some such very small set of adjectives.

---

[8]Macnamara (1982) reports that Brown's subject Sarah tended to use words to refer to either objects or actions and avoided the use of, e.g., *comb* in its double sense. He obtained similar findings in an informal experiment with his young son. Macnamara's interpretation of these findings as reflecting the existence of word classes, is problematic, though, since it may reflect the child's reluctance to deal with homonyms rather than some knowledge of categorization.

However, if in later stages, when adjectives do come in, the child is already equipped with the distinctions between nouns and verbs, and more importantly perhaps, with the analytic tools that enable him to discover distributional categories, the task of distinguishing between verbs and adjectives might become much simpler.

SUMMARY

In the preceding sections data has been presented to support the claim that children are engaged in work on formal properties of their language from the earliest phases of the development of grammar. Let me briefly summarize the findings and their theoretical import. The development of gender in Hebrew, as well as in other languages such as German (Mills, 1986) and Polish (Smoczynska, 1986), shows that 2-year-olds have no particular difficulty in acquiring gender inflections, despite the fact that it is largely semantically unmotivated and contributes very little to the content of the message. Of particular interest is the fact that these young children indeed acquire the system very early in their linguistic careers. For if one had to predict on the basis of existing models which linguistic subsystems will be late to develop, surely gender would have been one very prominent candidate for late acquisition. However, gender has an important role as an organizer of the linguistic material and as a means of establishing "linguistic cohesion" in the discourse (Karmiloff-Smith, 1985). The phonological marking of nouns as either masculine or feminine (or neuter, as in German) plus agreement marking of other parts of speech, are very helpful in discovering word boundaries and imposing order on units in the sentence (Peters, 1983). So, from the point of view of the systematization of the linguistic material, i.e., the "puzzle task" (p. 75), gender should be of considerable interest to the learner. Indeed, in languages in which gender is assigned regularly, 2-year-olds seem to acquire it readily, despite its minimal communicative value. Rote learning can explain very little of the observed learning. The important factors seem to be the degree to which gender marking in a language conforms to the child's expectations that some order can be imposed on the linguistic input, as well as the ease with which these organizing principles can be discovered.

Phonological dependencies among units in a sentence, in particular, among stressed elements, seem a very salient organizational feature for children (Peters, 1983; Wanner & Gleitman, 1982). Notice, however, that in Hebrew, these phonological similarities do not indicate any fixed feature of lexical items, except in the case of nouns, since all other parts of speech take endings according to the noun they agree with or modify. It is not clear yet whether gender is conceived by children as a categorical division of nouns which determines agreement, or as a more local dependency between related items in an utterance.

The development of verb and noun derivations in Hebrew, although different in many significant ways from the development of gender forms, is an example of a similar concern with organization of the linguistic material. The Hebrew data show that the children seize upon means of distinguishing between members of the major classes such as are available in the input. In Hebrew this will entail the discovery that it is consonant-vowel interchanges, in other words, phonological patterning, that do the work.

The process of discovering the details of noun and verb formation and modification in Hebrew is rather complex. Children indeed make many mistakes: They entertain some simplifying assumptions that eventually have to be given up, and they overgeneralize. Their efforts from very early on can be viewed as attempts to "spell out," so to speak, a major organizing principle, namely, that there are these two major word classes—nouns and verbs or some equivalent thereof. In the case of Hebrew the child will have to learn eventually that, although nouns and verbs are different morphological classes, they may share common consonantal roots. By preserving the root structure and adopting the appropriate pattern one can move both between and within word classes and produce modulations of meaning.[9]

In acquiring the verb system in Hebrew, children attend to the formal regularities and exceptions of the system long before they capture the semantic regularities of various patterns. Notice, that one could easily conceive of learning progressing along the semantic axis. For example, children might notice that a certain *Binyán* often serves to indicate reflexivity as in *hitRaXáCti, hitLaBáŠti, hitXaMáMti, hitRaGáZti* 'I washed (myself), I dressed (myself), I got-warmed-up, I became angry'. The semantic concept that is expressed here is probably known to children, as witnessed in their early use of combinations such as *KaTáVti levád* 'I wrote it "alone".'' The combinatorial nature of verbs and the semantic affinities that may hold between words sharing the same root are likewise familiar features of the system, as argued in the previous sections. So, theoretically, the child could have come up with a semantic hypothesis, namely, that particular patterns can be freely used to indicate certain semantic functions. However, the data show that this does not happen in the early stages. For example, children do not create innovative verbs by putting their roots in B5 to indicate reflexivity or reciprocity, or in B6 to indicate causation, until they are about 4 to 5 years of age (Berman, 1982), when they overgeneralize extensively in precisely these ways. However, they do distinguish between the forms, and use them even at a young age as candidates for phonological manipulations, and as indicators of class membership.

There may be a number of reasons for this. Some of these emerge from a

---

[9]In English, too, words can shift categories through derivational processes which often involve suffixation. It is perhaps significant that in English, too, the acquisition of derivational morphology which result in such cross over between categories is rather late (Clark & Hechet, 1983). However, the typological differences between the two languages call for caution in drawing conclusions from these findings.

comparison with the gender data, where the saliency of phonological determinants of similarity and the systematicity in the input data were the main predictors of ease of acquisition. Both in the case of the gender system and in the case of the Hebrew verb system, morphophonology seems to offer a more consistent clue to the organization of the system than semantics. The semantic basis of the *Binyaním* is probabilistic and, at best, offers good heuristic.[10] Of relevance to the present discussion is the fact that, in this case at least, children as young as 2 years can and will work with formal generalizations in the construction of an orderly system out of the language around them.

In sum, the data presented in this chapter argue for rich analytical abilities of the young language learner. The acquisition of inflectional languages provides evidence that the young child is indeed capable and motivated to work with the necessary nonsemantic generalizations and attends to phenomena pertaining both to the communicative function of the linguistic material and to its internal organization and coherence.

REFERENCES

Anderson, J. R. (1980). *Cognitive Psychology and its Implications*. San Francisco: W. H. Freeman.

Bar-Adon, A. (1957). *Lešonám hamedubéret šel yeladím beyisraél* [Children's Hebrew in Israel]. Unpublished dissertation, Hebrew University.

Berman, R. A. (1980). Child language as evidence for grammatical descriptions: Preschoolers construal of transitivity in the verb system of Hebrew. *Linguistics, 18*, 677–701.

Berman, R. A. (1981). Language development and language knowledge: Evidence from the acquisition of Hebrew morphophonology. *Journal of Child Language, 8*, 120–145.

Berman, R. A. (1982). Verb pattern alternation: The interface of morphology, syntax, and semantics in Hebrew child language. *Journal of Child Language, 9*, 169–191.

Berman, R. A. (1986). The acquisition of Hebrew. In D. I. Slobin (Ed.), The *cross linguistic study of language acquisition* (Vol. 1). Hillsdale, NJ: Lawrence Erlbaum Associates.

Berman, R. A., Dromi, E. & Slobin, D. I. (in preparation). The development of tense in Hebrew.

Bloomfield, L. (1933). *Language*. London: George Allen and Unwin.

Bowerman, M. (1982). Starting to talk worse: Clues to language acquisition from children's late speech errors. In S. Straus (Ed.), *U-Shaped Behavioral Growth*. New York: Academic Press.

Bruner, J. S. (1978). On prelinguistic prerequisites of speech. In R. M. Campbell & P. T. Smith (Eds.), *Recent advances in the psychology of language: Language development and mother-child interaction* (199–214). New York: Plenum Press.

Bruner, J. S. (1982). The formats of language acquisition. *American Journal of Semantics, 1*, 1–16.

---

[10]These phenomena may be caused by the difficulty of the semantic notions that are conveyed by the verb patterns *when seen as grammatical organizers*. In other words, these are cases in which the semantic strategies are not available to young children. Bowerman's data (1982) on the causative as a separate grammaticizable feature speaks to this issue. Her data show that children comprehend this notion as separable from individual lexical items only after they have been using verbs that convey causativeness for some time.

Clark, E. V. (1981). Lexical innovations: How children learn to create new words. In W. Deutsch (Ed.), *The child's construction of language* (299–328). London: Academic Press.

Clark, E. V. (1982). The young word maker: A case study of innovation in the child's lexicon. In E. Wanner & L. R. Gleitman (Eds.), *Language acquisition—The state of the art*. New York: Cambridge University Press.

Clark, E. V. (1986). The acquisition of French. In D. I. Slobin (Ed.), *The crosslinguistic study of language acquisition* (Vol. 1). Hillsdale, NJ: Lawrence Erlbaum Associates.

Clark, E. V., & Berman, R. A. (1984). Language structure and language use in the acquisition of word-formation. *Language, 6,* 542–590.

Dromi, E., & Berman, R. A. (1982). A morphemic measure of early language development data from modern Hebrew. *Journal of Child Language, 9,* 403–424.

Feldman, H., Goldin-Meadow, S., & Gleitman, L. (1978). Beyond Herodotus: The creation of language by linguistically deprived deaf children. In A. Lock (Ed.), *Action, symbol, and gesture: The emergence of language*. New York: Academic Press.

Gentner, D. (1982). Why nouns are learned before verbs: Linguistic relativity vs. natural partitioning. In S. Kuczaj (Ed.), *Language development: Language, culture and cognition*. Hillsdale, NJ: Lawrence Erlbaum Associates.

Gleitman, L. R., & Wanner, E. (1982). Language acquisition: The state of the state of the art. In E. Wanner & L. R. Gleitman (Eds.), *Language acquisition—The state of the art*. Cambridge, England: Cambridge University Press.

Karmiloff-Smith, A. (1979). *A functional approach to child language*. Cambridge, England: Cambridge University Press.

Karmiloff-Smith, A. (1986). *Structure versus process in comparing linguistics and cognitive development*. In: Levin, I. (ed.) *Stage & Structure Reopening the Debate* Norwood, NJ: Albex.

Levy, Y. (1980). *Gender in children's language—A study in first language acquisition*. Unpublished dissertation. The Hebrew University, Jerusalem.

Levy, Y. (1983a). The acquisition of Hebrew plurals—The case of the missing gender category. *Journal of Child Language, 10,* 107–121.

Levy, Y. (1983b). It's frogs all the way down. *Cognition, 12.* 75–93.

Macnamara, J. (1982). *Names for things*. Cambridge, MA: MIT Press.

MacWhinney, B. (1978). The acquisition of morphophonology. *Monographs of the Society for Research in Child Development, 43* (1–2, Serial No. 174).

Maratsos, M. (1981). Problems in categorial evolution: Can formal categories arise from semantic ones? In W. Deutsch (Ed.), *The child's construction of language*. London: Academic Press.

Maratsos, M. (1982). The child's construction of grammatical categories. In E. Wanner & L. R. Gleitman (Eds.), *Language acquisition—The state of the art*. Cambridge, England: Cambridge University Press.

Mills, A. (1986). The acquisition of German. In D. I. Slobin (Ed.), The *crosslinguistic study of language acquisition* (Vol. 1). Hillsdale, NJ: Lawrence Erlbaum Associates.

Mulford, R. (1983). Semantic and formal factors in the comprehension of Icelandic pronoun gender. *Papers and Reports on Child Language Development, 22,* 83–91.

Peters, A. (1983). *The units of acquisition*. Cambridge, England: Cambridge University Press.

Pinker, S. (1984). *Language learnability and language development*. Cambridge, MA: Harvard University Press.

Pinker, S., Stromsvold, K., & Hochberg, J. (in preparation). Children's number agreement: Syntactic, semantic or lexical?

Rimor, M. (unpublished). *Conversations with Ruti, age 2;0 to 2;4.*

Schlesinger, I. M. (1982). *Steps to Language*. Hillsdale, NJ: Lawrence Erlbaum Associates.

Slobin, D. I. (Ed.). (1986). The *crosslinguistic study of language acquisition* (Vol. 1). Hillsdale, NJ: Lawrence Erlbaum Associates.

Slobin, D. I. (1986). Cross-linguistic evidence for the language-making capacity. In D. I. Slobin,

(Ed.), *The crosslinguistic study of language acquisition* (Vol. 2). Hillsdale, NJ: Lawrence Erlbaum Associates.

Smoczynska, M. (1986). The acquisition of Polish. In D. I. Slobin (Ed.), The *crosslinguistic study of language acquisition* (Vol. 1). Hillsdale, NJ: Lawrence Erlbaum Associates.

Snow, C. E. (1972). Mother's speech to children learning language. *Child Development, 43,* 549–565.

Snow, C. E. (1981). The uses of imitation. *Journal of Child Language, 8,* 205–212.

Snow, C. E., & Ferguson, C. A. (Eds.). (1977). *Talking to children: Language input and acquisition.* Cambridge, England: Cambridge University Press.

Walden (Peres), Z. (1982). *The root of roots: Children's construction of word-formation processes in Hebrew.* Unpublished doctoral dissertation. Harvard School of Education.

5 On Formal Grammatical Categories in Early Child Language

Anat Ninio
The Hebrew University

One of the issues most debated in the field of developmental psycholinguistics has been the status of formal grammatical categories in child language. Two kinds of questions have been asked, the first being whether children can be credited with operating with formal categories at early stages of language development (cf. Bloom, 1970; Bowerman, 1973a, 1973b; Braine, 1963, 1976; Maratsos, 1983), the second concerning the nature of the process by which children come to possess or to acquire formal categories (cf. Chomsky, 1965; Maratsos & Chalkley, 1980; McNeill, 1966; Pinker, 1982).

In the following discussion of these issues I attempt to show that much of the controversy stems from the problematic nature of the transfer of concepts from linguistics to developmental psychology and that in some sense the developmental questions are half-way to being answered if the conceptual problems embedded in them are solved.

1. THE STATUS OF FORMAL GRAMMATICAL CATEGORIES IN EARLY CHILD LANGUAGE

The first question we discuss is whether children in the early stages of language acquisition can be credited as operating with endstate formal grammatical categories. The problem is methodological as well as theoretical. There seem to exist in children's language certain regularities which warrant the writing of grammatical rules on categories of terms rather than on individual lexical items. Thus, people attempting to write descriptive grammars of child language have to decide whether to use the adult grammatical categories of noun, verb, subject, etc., as primitive components of the grammar, or whether to posit different kinds of formal categories. Just to demonstrate the range of opinions, Bloom (1970) opted for endstate categories; Bowerman (1973a) decided to admit "lexical" categories such as noun but not major (or functional) categories such as subject; while Braine (1963) opted for more primitive structural categories such as the pivot and open classes, as elements of a descriptive grammar of child language.

At first glance, it seems obvious that it is not justified to use endstate category symbols like noun and subject in descriptions of child language. The use of category symbols such as noun, etc., is motivated in grammars written on adult language, not by some isolated feature of its rule system but by the complexly interrelated nature of the grammar as a whole.[1]

The organizational phenomena pertinent to "lexical" categories is the fact that whereas the lexicon contains a very large number of items, the grammatical rule system governing combinations of morphemes consists of a few sets of intercorrelated rules, each applying to a subgroup of morphemes. The existence of one-to-many mapping of rules to morphemes makes it possible to economize on the writing of rules in a grammar. Instead of item-specific combinatorial rules, rules can specify which group of morphemes they are written on, and it is possible to specify for each morpheme which group of rules applies to it. Such specification is carried out by means of (sub)category symbols such as noun or verb. Category symbols like these appear on the one hand in terminal strings of phrase-markers, so that an operation of lexical substitution may insert actual lexical items in place of these markers, turning an abstract structure into a concrete sentence. On the other hand, these symbols appear in every entry in the mental lexicon, specifying (together with some secondary selectional markers) the kind of syntactic contexts the relevant item may be inserted into. Thus, the subcategory symbols provide a bridge between the base component of the grammar and its lexical component; it is not only possible to substitute an actual lexical item for each symbol appearing in an abstract phrase-marker, but in principle it is also possible to substitute for each subcategory symbol in a lexical entry the list of all phrase structure rules applying to that term.

The motivation for major category symbols such as subject (or more precisely, the noun phrase directly dominated by the sentence node in deep structure), or predicate of a sentence, is a different organizational property of the linguistic system. This is the fact that whereas there are a very large number of possible different semantic relations among lexical items comprising sentences, these are syntactically marked by a limited number of structural devices. For

---

[1]The discussion of formal categories in descriptive linguistics is based on Chomsky (1965, 1975), Katz and Fodor (1963), and Katz and Postal (1964). Although other types of grammars have since been proposed, and although Chomsky's early model has been superceded (cf. 1981), most work in developmental psycholinguistics has been carried out within framework of his early phrase-structure grammar or one of its variants.

example, one logical-semantic argument of the verb in English sentences is mapped to a single structural role, that of the subject, and this regardless of the heterogenity of the meaning relations the relevant arguments have with the verb in the different cases. As with "lexical" subcategory symbols, the information mapping relational meaning to structural roles is provided in the lexicon: the lexical entry for each verb specifies which argument of that verb is mapped to which structural role (Bresnan, 1978; Chomsky, 1972). As is the case with subcategory markers, it is possible in principle to substitute for each major category marker in a lexical entry the list of all phrase structure rules applying to the relevant kind of grammatical role.

Thus, category symbols, whether in phrase structure rules or in the lexicon, are logically equivalent to the rules written on them, and as such are completely system-dependent: They are shorthand descriptions of the rule system as a whole. By anyone's theory, young children's linguistic system does not possess all the features of the endstate system. In other words their language cannot be described by the same grammar as the adult system. The use of category symbols N, V, NP or VP, etc., without any qualification is equivalent to using the whole of endstate grammar to describe child language; and that is unacceptable.

I believe that the argument in the literature around the question whether young children "have" syntactic categories such as noun or subject stems from a lack of recognition of the fact that grammatical category symbols are a kind of "package-deal." On both sides of the debate, people single out selected features of "nounhood" or "subjecthood," etc., and argue from their existence (or nonexistence) in child language to children's possessing (or not possessing) the relevant grammatical category in general. Not surprisingly, different authors seem to expect to find different sets of features of the syntactic categories in child language, while they pass over the obvious nonexistence of other features. Of special interest is the fact that some authors seem to see as basic, or minimally criterial of the possession of the categories, some of the syntactic features of these categories, while others seem to demand that their features as lexical category markers be established in the early stages of language acquisition. Thus, Maratsos (1983) argues that the *lexical* categories of noun, verb, etc., are not established in the early stages since there is no evidence that all the relevant items in the children's vocabulary are assigned the same set of syntactic rules. Similarly, Bowerman (1973b) points out that most early subjects are agents of actions, i.e., sentence subjects are not mapped to a variety of semantic relations as they are in the adult system. On the other hand, Brown (1973) uses structural arguments to demonstrate that the "verb phrase" constituent is established quite early: He points out that the privileges of occurrence of V+N combinations are similar to those of V alone, while Bowerman (e.g., 1973a) uses some different syntactic agruments to demonstrate that such a conclusion is unwarranted, e.g., that "children do not initially use phrases like 'do (so),' which make reference to a preceding VP" (p.179). Bowerman, in general, offers a variety of arguments as to the nonvalidity of descriptions of early child language in terms of subject-VP constituent structure. Interestingly, some of the latter are rejected by Bloom (1978) on the grounds that since it is illogical anyway to demand a perfect match between the features of a syntactic construct such as "subject" in child language and the endstate system, it is not necessary that a child's "subject" have precisely those features that Bowerman deems decisive.

In fact, the question whether young children operate with endstate grammatical categories is ill-defined. The system-dependent nature of these constructs does not allow a meaningful distinction between essential and inessential features, and it is logically impossible to point to a minimal set of features that has to be attained for a speaker to be credited with category knowledge. And finally, until children have mastered the whole of grammar, it will always be possible to find some feature or other of such category knowledge that children do not yet possess. In summary, it is only competent speakers of a language whose language can legitimately be described by the linguistic apparatus developed to this purpose.

2.   CAN CHILDREN BE CREDITED WITH KNOWLEDGE OF ABSTRACT GRAMMATICAL CATEGORIES? A REDEFINITION OF THE QUESTION AND SOME ANSWERS.

In section 1 we have concluded that it is not justified to use endstate category symbols like noun or subject in descriptions of child language, since the use of these symbols is motivated in grammars written on adult language by the complexly interrelated nature of the whole grammatical system. As long as child language does not follow the same rules, it cannot be said to possess the same organizational features as the adult language. It is possible that some kind of formal categories can be imputed to early language, but their character depends on the characteristics of the early rule system. It is more than expected that the early formal categories will be different in nature from the endstate categories, given the vast differences in the two rule systems.

However, we can still ask what sort of knowledge of the *endstate* formal categories do young children possess. As such categories are system-dependent entities, the right question about formal category knowledge is not whether at some point in development children have or have not formed such categories. As long as their rule system is different from that of adults, they cannot be said to have the same formal categories in any case. Rather, the question should be what kind of knowledge children have that can be considered a *subset* of adults' knowledge of formal categories. Here we need a definition of what to consider knowledge of formal categories. Because we cannot assume that young children's linguistic system is as well integrated as that of adults, we should make it possible to find evidence of fragmentary knowledge by treating the two aspects of category knowledge separately. On the one hand, category knowledge should be exhibited in the form of differential combinatorial privileges of different kinds of terms in children's lexicon; on the other hand, it should be evident by the range of applicability of different combinatorial rules in their repertoire, to the relevant items in their lexicon. That is, given that children use their words in combination, the question is whether they follow the same combinatorial rules as would govern the combination of the same items in endstate language. And, given that children apply some combinatorial rule to at least one item in their lexicon, the question is whether they apply the same rule to other items of the same subcategory in their lexicon.

Regarding differential combinatorial privileges, it is obvious that the implications of form class membership, even if some knowledge of this sort can be shown to be possessed by children, are severely restricted in the early stages of speech. Early language is notoriously lacking in structure: There is no morphology, and very little syntax. Keeping this basic fact in mind, it is still an important finding that children from the very first word combinations very rarely make form category errors. Thus, Brown (1973), summarizing the evidence on English-speaking children's early combinations from his own and from Bloom (1970), Leopold (1939–1949) and Schlesinger's (1971) data, concluded that such errors are very infrequent. Maratsos (1983), in a later review, reached a similar conclusion. Bowerman (1973a) found that most words in Finnish-speaking children's vocabularies that she classified to word classes according to adult syntactic privileges of occurrence, were classified similarly in adult Finnish. Category errors are also extremely rare in Hebrew (Berman, this volume; Levy, this volume). It seems that to the extent that children use some term in word combinations, they mostly do so in conformity with the combinatorial restrictions applying to such terms in the endstate grammar. Thus, syntactic markers like noun and verb seem to be justified in grammars of early child language, in the minimal sense that different kinds of terms fit into different, and mostly appropriate, syntactic environments.

As to the range of application of grammatical rules, it can be safely generalized that children do not apply every combinatorial rule to every term in their vocabulary to which such a rule could apply. The evidence is extensively reviewed in Maratsos (1983). Among the examples he mentions are the following. Bowerman's Eve (1976, p.157) started to produce combinations of want + [object wanted] when other verbs in her vocabulary still appeared only as single word utterances. Braine's subject David (1976) also had want + [object] combinations when other verbs such as hold or roll appeared only with "it" as object. Braine's Jonathan produced subject-verb combinations with sleep, sit, walk or work, but not with verbs like eat, drink, bite or drink, for which, however, he produced verb-object combinations. Expressions such as *don't* and *can't,* as well as inflections such as *-ed* and *-ing* are used with largely nonoverlapping sets of terms around Stage II (Bellugi, 1967; Bloom, Lightbown, & Hood, 1975; Bloom, Miller, & Hood, 1975; Bloom, Lifter, & Hafitz, 1980). Hebrew-speaking children first use verb + infinitive combinations exclusively with 'want', as in 'want to-go', and only quite later with other matrix verbs. They first produce sentence complements to only one of a whole range of perception, cognitive, and speech verbs, namely to 'say', as in 'he said that the baby is asleep.' Moreover, they first produce embedded (indirect) questions only with 'see' and 'look', as in 'see what happened' (R. Berman, personal communication).

These examples certainly show that children do not apply a given combinatorial rule to all the terms which could take such a rule according to adult usage. Although such production data does not prove conclusively that it is not within children's competence to produce the missing combinations, and although some of the examples are well explained on pragmatic rather than syntactic considerations (cf. Ninio & Snow, this volume), it seems quite well established that, in the early stages of language acquisition, syntactic subcategory symbols such as verb or noun in children's rule system do not seem to have the adult range of applicability to concrete terms.

The situation seems to be similar on both counts with regard to major (or relational) syntactic categories such as subject or VP. On the one hand, to the extent that children express the relation between some predicate and its arguments, the word order between the relevant constituents in most cases mirrors adult usage (Bloom et al., 1975a; Bowerman, 1973a; Braine, 1976; Brown, 1973; Brown & Fraser, 1963). It is evident that the mapping of predicate-argument relations into surface structure represents the internalization of a segment of the adult system. Thus, within the restrictions of children's undeveloped grammar, the use of major category markers is notationally justified for the relevant lexical entries. On the other hand, early syntactic constructions apparently involving major constituents do not have the same range of semantic mapping as in adult language. For instance, most early subjects are agents of actions (Bowerman, 1975; Pinker, 1982).

These two facts about the early status of grammatical categories have important implications for a decision about the terms in which a grammar of child language is to be written. On the one hand, the notational system should make prominent, rather than obscure, the basic continuity that exists between child language and the endstate system. In other words, it should explicitly make note of all structural knowledge that children seem to have accumulated about the differential combinatorial properties of different kind of terms and about the differential applicability of combinatorial rules, which is the true early form of endstate syntactic category knowledge. At the same time, the notational solution adopted should not mislead into implying that children's language has a higher degree of abstractness or generality than it actually possesses.

If the only objective of writing a grammar were the description of a child's current language, the terms in which a well-motivated grammar would be written would be derived from the child's own system. As is shown later, there are good reasons to believe that the best-motivated grammar of early child language would consist of specific combinatorial rules defined for individual "predicate" words and their arguments. Such a grammar would be neither syntactic, nor semantic, but lexical.

On the other hand, there are many considerations which would make it desirable to use endstate category symbols in a description of child language. It is a legitimate research strategy to plot the course of development in terms of its departure from its endstate. Such a move would make it easy to trace continuities between children's rule systems and endstate grammar as well as spot departures from it.

However, in section 1 we reached the conclusion that since category symbols are system-dependent entities, and since children cannot be credited with the same rule system as adults, it is unjustified to use the endstate category symbols in a description of child grammar. Let us now re-think this conclusion.

The reason we should not use endstate category symbols is because their use would misleadingly imply that children's language has the same organizational features as does adult language. Now, we have seen that although children's early grammar is different from adults', it is in fact similar to it in that whatever formal rules children possess, these are, with a few exceptions, correct segments of the endstate grammar. This was long ago pointed out by Brown (1973). Thus, the mistake in using endstate category symbols for the description of children's grammar would consist of imputing to children knowledge of a larger segment of adult grammar than they in fact possess but not in the very imputation of such knowledge. In particular, the mistake would be of attributing a wider range of applicability to any combinatorial rules in the system than these actually have, and the grammar would predict combinations which the children are actually unable to produce. This, however, is a mistake which can be averted. If endstate syntactic category symbols are used in grammars of child language, pains can be taken that their categories' restricted range is represented in the grammar as well. Such an effect could be achieved relatively simply and in accordance with the form of standard descriptive grammars if for each appearance of such symbols, a set of explicit mapping rules specified either the range of terms which can be substituted for the symbol, or the rules in which a given term may play the role of, e.g., the verb. Similarly, a set of explicit projection rules would take care of the fact that major category symbols such as subject or VP do not take all the argument relations which are admissible under adult grammar.

Thus, if a rule in a child's grammars's base component is

$$VP \rightarrow V + NP$$

and at a certain time the only verb which follows this rule is "want," this should be noted by a lexical insertion rule *attached* to the relevant phrase structure rule:

$$VP \rightarrow V + NP \qquad V \leftarrow want$$

The same information would also be as represented in the lexicon, where the lexical entry of "want" would include the potential syntactic environment of the VP whereas the entries of other verbs in the child's vocabulary would not.

There is no question in such a grammar whether the symbols VP or V are justified on any other grounds but the ones explicitly written into the grammar. The minimal and atheoretical claim is only that the syntactic category of VP has evolved in this child's language *to the extent* that he or she has mastered the formal devices of expressing the "direct object" relation with respect to the one term "want" or with respect to the semantic relation of wanting-to-the-object wanted. There is no ground on which such a description could be disputed as soon as it is realized that in this child's grammar it is useless to look for any other feature of the construct "VP," but that at the same time the child's knowledge of sentence-construction does definitely include the lawful combination of a verb with its argument class expressed as a direct object. This feature of explicitness of the proposed grammar could deal with most of the objections raised against the use of syntactic category symbols as overrepresenting structural knowledge, e.g., with Braine's (1976) argument that the introduction of the rule $S \rightarrow NP + VP$ to describe actor-action combinations would predict that the ordering of the constituents in a new combination such as expressing the relation of entity to location would already be known, and thus the combination would not have to undergo a phase of "groping" for order.

Another advantage of such a notational system would be that it could incorporate descriptions of any semantic categories the children might be operating with, in a manner concordant with the spirit of conventional descriptive grammars. The way to introduce such "semantic" rules might be to write categorical "projection rules." For example, if a child is thought to operate with the generalization that agents of action are mapped to the preverbal (i.e., pre-action-word) position in sentences, the corresponding base and projection rules would be

$$S \rightarrow NP + VP \qquad NP \leftarrow agents\ of\ action$$
$$VP \leftarrow actions.$$

This proposal is identical to Schlesinger's (1971), although neutral with respect to the claim that in child language, semantic categories fulfill the role of syntactic ones (cf. Schlesinger, 1971, 1974, 1977, 1981, 1982, this volume, and Bowerman, 1973a, 1973b).

Obviously, the restrictive annotations to phrase structure rules would be altered as children widen the scope of their rules. The problematic feature of this proposal is that it is extremely difficult to decide purely on distributional evidence when it is justified to stop enumerating the list of discrete terms or specific relations which make up a given category and assume that the adult range of organization has been achieved. I believe that this decision has to wait until children are mature enough to make grammaticity judgements.

Now, even if the proposed grammar would not be misleading, the very use of syntactic category symbols would violate a principle which is usually evoked against their use in child language. The principle is that even if it is possible to describe some linguistic phenomenon in endstate syntactic terms, such a usage is gratuitous as long as the same phenomenon can be described in other terms which are presumably closer to children's reality, for instance in terms of semantic categories (Bowerman, 1973a; Braine, 1976; Maratsos, 1982). For example, Maratsos (1982) says:

> Let us put the question this way: What can we mean by asking if categories such as noun or verb should be used to describe children's early constructions? I think what we would mean is something like this: Do any of their grammatical rules make reference to groups of terms that *cannot be united by semantic denotations* such as "object word" or "action word" or "word denoting a possessor," that is, to groups of terms that are semantically heterogeneous yet seem to approximate, somehow, the boundaries of the adult categories, with a somewhat similar organizational basis? . . . . . If we look at the available evidence for positive indications of adult form-class organizations, we see that not very much is presently known. What would constitute such evidence? Essentially, the child would have to show that he could predict new grammatical functions of a term on the basis of knowledge of some of its other functions, when this prediction *could not be made on the basis of the semantic nature of the term itself.* For example, children's making verb-operation overregularizations such as *breaked* and *runned* is not necessarily strong evidence: Because *break* and *run* are also actional terms, they might be employing the *-ed* past overregularization to apply to actional terms. (pp.248–251, italics mine)

Maratsos (1982), who uses this kind of argumentation throughout, nevertheless warns that "the conscientious use of sceptical arguments . . . could prevent the analysis of the beginnings of such grammatical unification in subsets of the system, or even prevent analysis of the completed system" (p.39). I want to add that the principle of deeming as gratuitous descriptions in terms of syntactic category symbols as long as they are not necessary or as long as other descriptions are equally valid is basically counterproductive as far as studying the course of grammatical development is concerned. The empirical findings reviewed above imply that the early development of category markers in the lexicon and category symbols in the syntactic rule system is best characterized as the gradual accumulation of *correct* information about, respectively, the syntactic environments in which a given term might appear, and the list of terms which might appear in a given environment.[2]

The fact that children seem to acquire formal rules in a piecemeal fashion for the expression of individual predicate-argument relations and at best generalize these formal rules to other semantically very similar predicate-argument relations (Bowerman, 1976; Brown, 1973; Braine, 1976; Francis, 1969; Macnamara, 1972; Maratsos, 1983; Roberts, 1983; Schlesinger, 1974), should not in fact be taken as evidence for their grammatical system being organized in ways alien to the organization of the endstate system. Indeed, children's combinatorial rules are expected to be tied to particular predicate terms and their argument relations, and they are expected to be individually learned. The reason is that their rules deal exclusively with the formal expression of predicate/argument relations between *words* rather than between *phrases,* and such rules are tied to particular predicate terms in endstate grammars as well. Both Chomsky's (1965) original transformational grammar and newer grammars like Bresnan's (1982) lexical functional grammar acknowledge the particular rather than general nature of projection and other mapping rules and register the relevant information about them in an individual fashion in the lexical entry of each word. In fact, in Bresnan's (1978) grammar some combinatorial rules are directly inserted in the lexicon: For example, for each verb the lexicon registers the immediate syntactic environments into which that verb might be inserted. As far as the immediate syntactic contexts of predicate words are concerned, endstate syntactic rules can be with justification described as concrete rather than abstract, as individually defined rather than applying to classes of words. As long as children's grammar is concerned exclusively with giving formal expression to predicate-argument relations among words, their syntactic categories are no less *unified* than those of adults. A similar point is made by Maratsos (1979) when he says:

> [L]earning individual or small groups of lexical distributional-meaning configurations, which can seem like a difficult way into adult structure, nevertheless comprises in many ways a natural one. For as already summarized, the distributional regularities and transfers of privileges that characterize the grammatical productivity of adult language must begin with the storage of individual lexical information and arise from abstraction of common distributional-meaning privileges in numbers of items. (pp.306–307)

---

[2]Although there are some interesting departures from adult rules, these can be given an adequate description in a completely explicit framework such as the one proposed here. For instance, a finding such as that Braine's (1976) Andrew produced "more fish," "more read," as well as "more hot," could be represented, for example, by the unusual semantic and syntactic features of the lexical entry of "more" for that child. Obviously, the final decision which lexical entry is divergent from the adult one should be made on the basis of the consideration of the child's total usage.

I want to go further than Maratsos and say that individual learning of predicate-argument configurations is not only a natural but a logically necessary way of learning the relevant facts of language. As far as this level of grammar is concerned (i.e., the level of rules for the formal expression of predicate-argument relations of individual predicate terms), the use of category symbols is no more than a notational convenience in adult grammar as well as in child language. It is only when specific predicate-argument relations are nested in higher-order constructions as phrases that their abstractness as constructional units is required in grammar or for that matter can be thought of as developmentally possible. These ideas are elaborated in the rest of this paper.

3. THE DEVELOPMENT OF ABSTRACT GRAMMATICAL CATEGORIES: A PROPOSAL

It is often assumed that the productivity of adult language as well as child language is a phenomenon of the lawful *generalization* of grammatical privileges. For example, Maratsos (1979) writes:

> [L]inguistic productivity can largely be formulated as a process of transfer of combinatorial privileges within classes of lexical items. (p.286)

Although this conception is quite widespread in developmental psycholinguistics, it is actually very different from the explanation of productivity derived from linguistic descriptions. Although it is true that the *manifestation* of productivity is the construction of new combinations on the basis of others which the speaker did hear uttered, in a linguistic framework the phenomenon underlying productivity is not generalization, but rather the *abstractness* of grammatical rules. The difference between the two is a matter of storage of rules. In talking of transfer or generalization, the assumption is made that combinatorial rules are in fact concrete, i.e., defined on specific concrete terms, and that they are transferred to other concrete terms according to some criterion of commonality, whether based on semantic similarity or on shared syntactic form-class membership. In any case, the rules are stored in terms of, and in contiguity with, some concrete lexical items. The notion of abstractness, on the other hand, implies that rules are written on abstract symbols or variable names, that they are stored independently of any concrete term, and that access to the right set of combinatorial rules is assured by a conceptually separate set of access rules, for example, by those that interpret subcategory symbols in the lexicon.

I propose that the linguistic notion of abstractness be taken seriously as the explanatory framework for the productivity of actual speakers. In particular, I suggest that all grammatical rules are indeed inherently abstract, that their abstractness stems from different principles at different levels of the rule system, and that there is a complicated interplay of abstract and concrete components at every level of the system.

Syntactic rules dealing with the lawful combination of two different terms, whether words or phrases, are inherently abstract as far as one of the components of the combination is concerned, and inherently concrete as far as the other term is concerned. The inherent abstractness of syntactic rules is due to the fact that the semantic relations, which are expressed by syntax, involve categories of entities rather than individual entities. That this is so is not due to any learned categorization but stems from the way meanings are encoded by words in a language. Every syntactic relation involves, at its core, one term which encodes as part of its meaning some logical-semantic relation defined on a class of entities. In formal terminology, such expressions have logical arguments (Reichenbach, 1947). Syntactic rules are without exception descriptions of the structural devices by which the relation between the different "predicate" terms and their arguments is expressed. It follows that basically a syntactic rule is defined on one fixed "predicate" term and one variable name standing for one of the argument classes of that term. It is important to point out that *all* the words and other morphemes in English, except for nouns, encode a relational meaning component and take logical arguments, and even nouns may do so (as shown by constructions like "baby carriage").

Hierarchical syntactic constructs represent the successive nesting of predicate-argument configurations in higher-order units, in which the lower-order predicate-argument pairs play the role of either the predicate or the argument. A logical calculus determines what the logical status of a given combination will be as a component of a higher-order unit: For example, if the configuration is of an adjective and a noun, the noun is the "head" of the phrase and the combination will play the argument role in higher combinations. Or, if the configuration is of a verb and a noun, the resultant combination will have the status of predicate if the noun fills the "object" role in relation to the verb. One function of syntactic "rewrite rules" is to regulate the logical status of phrases with respect to further combinations and, except for the case of full sentences, this is equivalent to the preservation of the logical status of the "head" term of the combination. This implies that part of the abstractness of the highest-order syntactic relations can be traced back to the abstractness of one of their component "predicate" terms. A similar point was made by Maratsos (1979) when he observed that "constituent structure arises from, in fact summarizes, generalizations about the combinatorial properties of individual lexical items" (p.300). Thus, part of the abstractness of the major constituent relation of subject to VP of a sentence can be traced to the fact that the heads of predicate phrases are verbs which have at least one logical argument. For instance, with respect to a main VP involving the verb "sit," the sentence subject role can be thought of as abstract because it is a variable slot that can accept any expression that is the sitter argument of "sit." That "sit" takes a "sitter" argument is a fact about the semantics of this word: The word sit is meaningless unless it is understood to entail that there is someone to do the sitting, and, moreover, the word is not understood correctly if it is not understood that many different persons may do the sitting.[3]

This implies that syntactic rules are, to some extent, abstract and productive from the very beginning of combinatorial speech: Their productive abstractness consists of the possibility of predicate words to combining with all terms in children's vocabularies that are arguments of the relevant propositional function (Bloom, 1970; Braine, 1976; Brown, 1973). The earliest combinations seem to consist of such formulae with one fixed element and one variable, such as this+[object noticed], when each element is soon accorded a fixed position in the string. I stress the point that not only the fixed element (i.e., "this") is mapped to a position in the sentence but the variable element (i.e., "[object noticed]") as well. Among "predicate" words observed in early speech are forms such as "no," "another," "up," "here"; determinatives such as "this"; adjectives; and verbs. In such combinations the semantic relation between the two items is an inherent component of the meaning of the fixed element. Once a certain relational term is chosen to express whatever semantic relation the child has in mind, it restricts the choice of the other terms in the combination to such items that are legitimate arguments of the predicate. Thus, there is good reason to believe that there is an intimate connection between the emergence of syntax and the acquisition of semantically complex vocabulary items.[4]

In producing their earliest word combinations, children demonstrate that they grasp the logical structure of words which encode inherent semantic relations and which therefore take logical-semantic arguments. Thus, the very ability of children to impose formal structure on their utterances follows from their ability to learn the meaning of lexical items that have a variable semantic component. Moreover, since the word-order between the "predicate" word and its argument(s) in most cases mirrors adult usage (Braine, 1976; Brown, 1973; Bowerman, 1973a; Brown & Fraser, 1963; Bloom et al, 1975a), it is evident that the mapping of each predicate-argument relation into surface structure represent the internalization of a segment of the adult rule system. Thus, children break into

---

[3]The preceding analysis can easily be extended to morphology. Grammatical morphemes are relational terms that take argument classes (Reichenbach, 1947). Their functional characteristics and manner of combination with other morphemes are to be individually learned, and for many grammatical morphemes this is fully equivalent to the formation of a lexical entry.

[4]See also Keenan's (1979) analysis of the semantics of function or predicate terms.

their language's syntax precisely because they are able to work with structural rules defined on variable names.[5]

4. THE EARLY ANTECEDENTS OF FORMAL CATEGORIES

The preceding analysis leads to the conclusion that the true antecedents of end-state formal categories in early child language are to be found in those grammatical entities which have reached the status of abstractness within the child's own system, namely in the argument classes of "predicate" expressions.

The earliest of these, appearing before the first two-word combinations, seem to be the reply-slots to certain well-comprehended questions such as "What is that?" or "Where is [entity]?" In the earliest word-combinations children produce, the relevant abstract entities are the argument classes of specific predicate words such as "this," "another," "no," "want," "eat," or "up," or of specific functional relations such as possession. At a slightly later stage, these are certain variable slots in simple sentence-frames, such as "This my+[entity]."

In order to account for this level of abstractness in the system, it is unnecessary to assume that any kind of categorization of lexical items occurs. Since words are inserted into the variable slots according to their meaning, i.e., accord-

---

[5]Another kind of combinations in early language are noun-noun combinations expressing semantic relations such as between possessor and possessed, actor and object of action, or an object and its location. Bloom (1970) termed such combinations "categorical" since she saw in them evidence of categorization by the child. Although the relationship expressed by noun-noun combinations is independent of the lexical meaning of either term in the combination, it is easy to see that fundamentally these combinations are very similar to the "pivotal" combinations discussed above. In all cases of noun-noun combinations, the two expressions are in an indirect logical relationship, namely, they represent two different arguments of an (unexpressed) "predicate." It is possible that the missing "predicate" word is actually known to the child and has been omitted due to some mistaken notion of ellipsis (as Brown, 1973, and Bowerman, 1973a suggest), or else it might not be known to the child as a lexical item but exist merely as a mediating concept linking the two arguments (as follows from Braine, 1974, 1976; see also Ervin-Tripp, 1970 on nominal answers to what-do questions). If we supply the missing "predicate," the terms participating in noun-noun combinations are shown to be restricted by their being legitimate arguments of a particular logical relationship the child had in mind, exactly as the argument terms are restricted by the "predicate" word in "pivotal" combinations. Thus, the combinatorial rules involving noun-noun combinations represent the mapping of particular argument-argument relations into surface structure, usually in accordance with adult word-order, just as the rules for "pivotal" combinations represented the realization of particular predicate-argument relations. In neither case is there any inherent categorization involved: just as we don't have to say that the word "another" is combined with a category consisting of its arguments, we don't have to say (as Bloom, 1970, and Schlesinger, 1971, say) that in the case of noun-noun combinations a semantic category of e.g., possessors is combined with a semantic category of possession.

ing to whether they fulfill the argument role specified by the relevant predicate, the scope and membership of an argument class is determined solely by the child's perception of the meaning of the "predicate" term and by the availability of appropriate argument terms in his or her vocabulary.

To a large extent, these argument classes are homogenous as to word class membership. Some terms, for example "this" or "give-me," have an argument class that consists of nouns, while others, e.g., "I-can't" or "don't," have argument classes consisting of verbs. This is explained on the convergence, on the level of individual predicate-argument relations, of semantic and syntactic selection restrictions on possible word-combinations. The only terms that fulfill the semantic-logical argument role in relation to a given predicate word are, in endstate grammar, of an identical form-class membership. To the extent that children have the right semantics, they will produce the right grammar as well. Thus, children do not say "my hot" or "get do" (Brown, 1973, p.126) as Braine's original pivot grammar would predict that they do, not because they observe formal restrictions on possible combinations but because they know that "my," for example, only takes entities as its argument and "hot" is not one. Some argument classes, e.g., those of "want," "more" or "no," are heterogenous as to word class membership. To some extent, this can attributed to the incorrect or fuzzy semantics, in young children, of the "predicate" words, or to insufficiencies of children's lexicon (see Ervin-Tripp, 1970). Another possibility is that because of the pragmatic centrality of "want," "more," and "no," children tend to use them when they are only approximately appropriate, in the lack of better alternatives at their command.

The argument classes of such discourse-slots, "predicate" terms and sentence-frames could be regarded as the forerunners of the adult formal grammatical categories. It is obvious that their scope is very narrow in comparison to the adult categories; but then the nature of formal categories changes in the course of development according to the nature of the rule system itself. When and to the extent that the rule system is discontinuous and fragmented, so are formal categories.

It could also be said that the argument classes we have been describing are the forerunners of adult "word classes". In effect, endstate argument classes are limited subsets of word classes. Shared membership of various items in many different argument classes is the phenomenon motivating the linguist's employment of the word class concept in the first place. However, the argument classes we have beed describing are best seen as the immature antecedents of such syntactic relational categories as subject or object and not of lexical categories such as noun or verb; early argument classes as well as endstate syntactic relational categories consist of terms that form a set only by virtue of standing in a common relationship with predicate terms.

At this level of grammar, the developmental process leading to closer approximation to the endstate category system is mainly the evolution of the semantics of different terms to the level where it will determine their participation in various predicate-argument combinations in accordance with endstate privileges and restrictions. Thus, it is expected that the argument classes of various predicate terms will undergo constant modification as the result of increased semantic learning and the expansion of the child's lexicon. Some evidence for such processes is provided by Ervin-Tripp's (1970) description of the gradual evolving of category-correct answers to product-questions. There is no need to describe these modifications as changes in the organization of the linguistic system, however. An argument class "existing" at a certain level of development does not have to be unlearned with further development as it only "existed" in the first place as a derivation of the semantics of the predicate and argument terms.

5. FURTHER DEVELOPMENT OF ABSTRACT CATEGORIES

Although the level of abstractness achieved by children goes a long way toward explaining the productivity of grammar, it is important to stress that the rules we have been discussing are predicate-specific, namely, abstract only with respect to the argument variables but concrete and tied to specific terms with respect to the predicate. I claim that this is as far as the inherent abstractness of low-level syntactic rules goes: There is no way to avoid the formulation of predicate-argument realization rules except in terms of each individual predicate term, and there is no way to avoid the storing of this information individually for each predicate term. In a real sense, the linguistic system is not generative on the level of individual predicates, and, regarding predicates, linguistic rules are concrete and item-bound rather than truly abstract.

However, the level of abstractness attributable to variable argument slots is insufficient by itself to account for the complete abstractness of the adult linguistic system. In the endstate system many different kind of abstract categories exist, and in particular, not only the argument slots of combinatorial rules are abstract symbols but the predicate slots are, too. The development of the full-blown abstract category system is however not an independent phenomenon but rather the byproduct of the development of the rule system itself. (See also, Schlesinger, 1982, pp.225–228 on this point.) Consequently, the nature of children's categories continuously and dynamically changes as their combinatorial rules change.

I argue that the evolution of abstract predicate categories, e.g., of adjectives or of verbs, is a phenomenon occurring later than two-term combinatorial speech, and that this development is intimately tied to children's gradually evolving ability to combine in a sentence the immediate syntactic environments of two

different predicate-argument relations, i.e., to the learning of rules for constructing hierarchical structures.

At the onset of combinatorial speech children typically have some two-word
combinations like

X + want   open + X
X + hit   want + X
X + give   hit + X
X + see   more + X
                                      no + X
                                      big + X
                                      this + X,

when X stands for any word that is an argument of the relevant predicate word
according to the child's current system. At some later point children realize that
there are formal means of expressing more than one predicate-argument relation
in the same string. In some cases children will express two different arguments of
the same predicate, e.g., subjects and objects of verbs. In one sense, such
constructions represent the knowledge that more than one of the arguments of a
single multiargument term can be realized at once, according to the relational
placement rules learned previously for each argument separately. However,
these constructions can also be seen as hierarchical ones, in which a [predicate +
argument] combination is embedded in the predicate slot of a higher-level
[argument] + [predicate] construct (Brown, 1973; Schlesinger, 1982), as in

X + [hit + Y]
X + [want + Y]
X + [give + Y].

There are the other complex constructions that appear in early child language
that clearly represent the nesting of one of the child's established functions as a
component in another such function, as in

this + [big + X]
no + [more + X]
no + [big + X]
I-can't + [open + X]
want + [this + X]
want + [another + X].

There are soon even more complex embedded constructions such as

no + [more + (big + X)]
want + [another + (big + X)]
X + [want + (another + Y)]

and so forth. In my opinion, such constructions are only possible due to the child's realizing that word-combinations inherit the logical combinatorial properties of one of their terms, and with it their formal (i.e., syntactic) combinatorial privileges. Although this sounds like a very complex idea for children to grasp, that is because we lack a simple vocabulary to talk about intuitions. Children understand the logics of their combinatorial rules. That means nothing more than that they understand the meaning of two-word combinations that they themselves produce; and it is the meaning expressed by these combinations that determines their logical status. E.g., a *big ball* is still a ball; and if you can say *another ball* you can also say *another big ball*. There is of course new learning involved in the transition to three- and four-term constructions but the kind of learning required is more in the character of an insight than a gradual accumulation of new rules. The insight is the realization that the combinations are also the predicates or the arguments of the same propositional functions as one of their components, and can therefore appear in the same kind of combinations as that component, and in the same position, too.

According to this analysis, the development of an abstract category of adjectives or of verbs is an outcome of the establishment of higher-order abstract units in three- or four-term word-combinations. These units can be filled by *phrases* as well as by single words. E.g., the argument slot of *"want"* can be filled by the phrases *"big X," "red X,"* or *"another X,"* as well as by single *X* s. In general, the argument slot of *"want"* can be filled by *any predicate-argument construction that is an argument of "want,"* and that means that *the phrase embedded in the "want" construct has a variable predicate slot as well as a variable argument slot.* All terms that can logically fill this embedded predicate slot form a common predicate class, in this case that of adjectives. Thus, the abstractness of the 'Adjective' slot in an immediate syntactic construct like Adjective+Noun derives from the abstractness of the *"predicate word"* slot *in this specific kind of noun phrase embedded in higher-order structures.* This *"embedded"* predicate class is simultaneously defined by its semantic, logical and syntactic properties.

Now what is shared by the class of all adjectives, or of all verbs, etc., is precisely their logical-semantic-syntactic common behaviour in higher-order word-combinations. We might say that part of the definition of an adjective is that it is a predicate word such that when it is combined with an argument in a [predicate word] + [argument word] construction, the combination functions as an argument. Similarly, a verb might be defined partly as a predicate word such that when it is combined with an argument in a [predicate word] + [argument word] construction, the combination functions as a predicate (as *"see a boat"* in *"I see a boat"*). The full definition of adjectives or of verbs is given by the total set of the different kind of combinations they can participate in and their logical status in these combinations. As children gradually learn to buid more and more complex hierarchical structures for constructing sentences, they gradually expand the abstract elements of the phrase structure and expand and refine their grammatical categories.

If this analysis is correct, it follows that it is not necessary to assume that any kind of categorizing or subsuming of different predicate terms occurs in the system; rather, the abstraction of predicate slots is a necessary outcome of the abstractness of phrases and, ultimately, of sentences. A possible prediction on this hypothesis could be that nonsyntactial grammatical combinations involving verbs and adjectives, e.g. verb morphology, would become productive only after the appearance of hierarchical syntax. This is borne out by the developmental literature: by the time morphological markers start to be produced, children's language has considerable structure (Brown, 1973).

In general, this model predicts that syntactic regularities of some kind are mastered before morphology. When, eventually, morphological markers and other closed-class items are acquired, they are probably learned as extensions and elaborations of existing sentence-frames rather than as a completely novel type of grammatical phenomenon. For instance, my corpora of Hebrew-speaking children shows that the definite article (a prefix in Hebrew) first appears *exclusively* as the extension of two or three simple sentence-frames, e.g., the extension of ''Here's X.'' to ''Here's the-X.'', where X stands for a noun. Other nouns in the same corpora that appeared in utterances basically lacking structure were never marked the same way. Thus, closed-class markers are incorporated into existing word-class-dependent syntactic frames, as endstate grammar determines they should be, rather than learned in isolation, as Maratsos and Chalkley (1980) have proposed. This explains why adjectives do not get inflected by verb inflections such as *-ed* for past tense (Maratsos, 1983) even if they have an ''actional'' character: They occupy a different structural slot than verbs (see also Schlesinger, this volume, on this issue). Ultimately, the way to the formation of formal grammatical categories or form classes is syntax, rather than morphology; and their evolution involves complex processes of semantic, logical, and structural learning, rather than the registering of purely surface distributional regularities.

The intimate relation we have been proposing to exist between the development of abstract constituents and the development of the ability to combine meanings into higher-order meaningful units follows directly from Chomsky's (1965, pp. 196–197) insight that sentence constituents are not only the units on which grammatical rules are defined, but that to be a constituent, a verbal string must be able to receive a semantic interpretation as well. Neither in linguistics nor in theories of language development can the two facets of structure be separated.

ACKNOWLEDGMENT

I would like to thank the editors and Ruth Berman for their thoughtful comments on a previous draft of this paper.

REFERENCES

Bellugi, U. (1967). *The acquisition of negation*. Unpublished doctoral dissertation, Harvard University.

Bloom, L. (1970). *Language development: Form and function in emerging grammars*. Cambridge, MA: MIT Press.

Bloom, L. (1978). The integration of form, content, and use in language development. In J. W. Kavanagh & W. Strange (Eds.), *Speech and language in the laboratory, school, and clinic.* Cambridge, MA: MIT Press.

Bloom, L., Lifter, K., & Hafitz, J. (1980). Semantics of verbs and the development of verb inflections in child language. *Language, 56,* 386–412.

Bloom, L., Lightbown, P., & Hood, L. (1975a). Structure and variation in child language. *Monographs of the Society for Research in Child Development, 40*(2, Serial No. 160).

Bloom, L., Miller, P., & Hood, L. (1975b). Variation and reduction as aspects of competence in language development. In A. Pick (Ed.), *Minnesota symposia on child psychology* (Vol. 9). Minneapolis: University of Minnesota Press.

Bowerman, M. (1973a). *Early syntactic development: A cross-linguistic study with special reference to Finnish.* Cambridge, England: Cambridge University Press.

Bowerman, M. (1973b). Structural relations in children's utterances: syntactic or semantic? In T. M. Moore (Ed.), *Cognitive development and the acquisition of language.* New York: Academic Press.

Bowerman, M. (1975). Commentary. In L. Bloom, P. Lightbown, & L. Hood, Structure and variation in child language. *Monographs of the Society for Research in Child Development, 40*(2, Serial No. 160), 80–90.

Bowerman, M. (1976). Semantic factors in the acquisition of rules for word use and sentence construction. In D. Morehead & A. Morehead (Eds.), *Directions in normal and deficient child language.* Baltimore, MD: University Park Press.

Braine, M. D. S. (1963). The ontogeny of English phrase structure: The first phase. *Language, 39,* 1–14.

Braine, M. D. S. (1974). Length constraints, reduction rules, and holophrastic pocesses in children's word combinations. *Journal of Verbal Learning and Verbal Behavior, 13,* 448–456.

Braine, M. D. S. (1976). Children's first word combinations. *Monographs of the Society for Research in Child Development, 41*(1, Serial No. 164).

Bresnan, J. (1978). A realistic transformational grammar. In M. Halle, J. Bresnan, & G. A. Miller (Eds.), *Linguistic theory and psychological reality.* Cambridge, MA: MIT Press.

Bresnan, J. (Ed.). (1982). *The mental representation of grammatical relations.* Cambridge, MA: Harvard University Press.

Brown, R. (1973). *A first language: The early stages.* Cambridge, MA: Harvard University Press.

Brown, R., & Fraser, C. (1963). The acquisition of syntax. In C. N. Cofer, & B. S. Musgrave (Eds.), *Verbal behavior and learning.* New York: McGraw-Hill.

Chomsky, N. (1965). *Aspects of the theory of syntax.* Cambridge, MA: MIT Press.

Chomsky, N. (1972). *Studies on semantics in generative grammar.* The Hague: Mouton.

Chomsky, N. (1975). *Reflections on language.* New York: Random House.

Chomsky, N. (1981). *Lectures on government and binding.* Dohrecht: Foris.

Ervin-Tripp, S. M. (1970). Discourse agreement: How children answer questions. In J. R. Hayes (Ed.), *New directions in the study of language.* New York: Wiley.

Francis, H. (1969). Structure in the speech of a two and a half year old child. *British Journal of Educational Psychology, 39,* 291–302.

Katz, J. J., & Fodor, J. A. (1963). The structure of a semantic theory. *Language, 39,* 170–210.

Katz, J. J., & Postal, P. M. (1964). *An integrated theory of linguistic descriptions.* Cambridge, MA: MIT Press.

Keenan, L. (1979). On surface form and logical form. In B. B. Kachru (Ed.), *Linguistics in the seventies: Directions and prospects.* Champaign-Urbana: University of Illinois.

Leopold, W. (1939–1949). *Speech development of a bilingual child.* Evanston, IL: Northwestern University Press.

Macnamara, J. (1972). Cognitive basis of language learning in infants. *Psychological Review, 79,* 1–14.

Maratsos, M. (1979). How to get from words to sentences. In D. Aaronson, & R. Rieber (Eds.), *Perspectives in psycholinguistics.* Hillsdale, NJ: Lawrence Erlbaum Associates.

Maratsos, M. (1982). The child's construction of grammatical categories. In E. Wanner, & L. R. Gleitman (Eds.), *Language acquisition: The state of the art.* Cambridge, England: Cambridge University Press.

Maratsos, M. (1983). Some current issues in the study of the acquistion of grammar. In P. H. Mussen (Ed.), *Handbook of child psychology: Formerly Carmichael's manual of child psychology* (4th ed.). New York: Wiley.

Maratsos, M., & Chalkley, M. A. (1980). The internal language of children's syntax: The ontogenesis and representation of syntactic categories. In K. Nelson (Ed.), *Children's language, Vol. 2.* New York: Gardner Press.

McNeill, D. (1966). Developmental psycholinguistics. In F. Smith, & G. Miller (Eds.), *The genesis of language: a psycholinguistic approach.* Cambridge, MA: MIT Press.

Pinker, S. (1982). A theory of the acquisition of lexical-interpretive grammars. In J. Bresnan (Ed.), *The mental representation of grammatical relations.* Cambridge, MA: MIT Press.

Reichenbach, H. (1947). *Elements of symbolic logic.* New York: Macmillian.

Roberts, K. (1983). Comprehension and production of world order in Stage I. *Child Dvelopment, 54,* 443–449.

Schlesinger, I. M. (1971). The production of utterances and language acquisition. In D. I. Slobin (Ed.), *The ontogenesis of grammar: A theoretical symposium.* New York: Academic Press.

Schlesinger, I. M. (1974). Relational concepts underlying language. In R. Schiefelbusch, & L. Lloyd (Eds.), *Language perspectives: Acquisition, retardation, and intervention.* Baltimore, MD: University Park Press.

Schlesinger, I. M. (1977). *Production and comprehension in utterances.* Hillsdale, NJ: Lawrence Erlbaum Associates.

Schlesinger, I. M. (1981). Semantic assimilation in the development of relational categories. In W. Deutsch (Ed.), *The child's construction of language.* London: Academic Press.

Schlesinger, I. M. (1982). *Steps to language.* Hillsdale, NJ: Lawrence Erlbaum Associates.

6 The Origin of Relational Categories

Izchak M. Schlesinger
The Hebrew University, Jerusalem

> *To speak of knowledge is futile.*
> *All is experiment and adventure.*
> —Virginia Woolf, *The Waves*

What knowledge does the child bring with him to the task of learning his language? Some writers insist that the categories of language belong largely to the child's innate linguistic equipment that enables him to acquire language. Language learning, according to this view, is much less a laborious assembling of bits of knowledge gleaned from the data than a recollection of what is already known, as a Platonist might phrase it.

The approach adopted in this chapter is quite different. The question posed here is how the categories of language might be acquired by the child either in the process of learning the grammatical rule system, or, alternatively, in the course of his prelinguistic development. For all we know, the nativist may be right, but at the present state of our ignorance there is no way of finding out. The theorist is therefore faced with two alternatives. He may either start from the assumption that the relevant categories are innate and let things rest at that, or he may try to show how their acquisition can be accounted for. I have opted for the latter alternative. I will try to show that there are good prospects of ultimately arriving at a learning account. The nativist alternative will as a consequence appear much less attractive.

The categories that are dealt with here are what we call relational categories, namely, those categories that the language realizes by grammatical constructions (word order, function words, or inflections). In the first section it is argued that in the child's early linguistic system these relational categories are semantic,

121

case-like categories (such as agent, patient, location) rather than syntactic ones. This raises the question of how the system of semantic categories develops into the adult system, since the latter is generally believed to be defined formally, rather than semantically. The solution I propose is that these categories are expanded through a process of semantic assimilation; and a large part of the paper is devoted to providing evidence for this proposal. Much of this treatment pertains to the adult system. After that (in Section 12) I return to the small child and consider the issue of how the early semantic categories may be arrived at.

This crab-like progression is not due to a penchant for eccentricity, but to the realization (arrived at through comments made by colleagues to earlier drafts) that without a full-scale presentation of the semantic assimilation hypothesis my treatment of early development would raise too many question marks in the reader's mind. I decided therefore to deal first with the problem of how the child's early grammar develops into the adult one, thus providing the theoretical underpinnings of my proposals for the attainment of early relational categories.

1. SEMANTIC AND SYNTACTIC APPROACHES

1.1 The Semantic Approach

According to a current view in the child language literature, grammatical relations in early child language are semantic in nature: they reflect the way the child interprets the world around him. It has been shown (Bowerman, 1973b; Braine, 1976) that semantic categories, like agent, patient, location, etc., are sufficient for describing the very young child's knowledge of language and that there is no evidence of more abstract, syntactic categories in early speech. The child interprets the environment in terms of such semantic relations and learns how these are expressed in his native language by means of word order, inflections, and function words (Schlesinger, 1971).

The semantic approach to child language was developed in response to difficulties in explaining acquisition of grammar that became apparent when the first attempts were made to explain language development along the lines suggested by Chomsky's transformational grammar. According to the latter, categories that are crucial in conveying the meaning of a sentence are not directly exhibited in its surface structure, and it is hard to see, therefore, how they could be learned by the child through an analysis of linguistic input. Chomsky (1965) in fact claimed that, in principle, they could not be learned, and that they must therefore be assumed to be innate. The alternative proposed by the semantic approach was that the child indeed does have access to the relational categories underlying sentences, since these are at first not abstract, formally defined categories, like subject or object (or, technically, the NP dominated by S or the NP dominated directly by VP, respectively), but categories that reflect the relations in the situations referred to by the sentences he hears: the agent of an action, the location of an entity, and so on. If anything, it is these cognitively based categories that must be assumed to be innate (Schlesinger, 1971).

1.2 Is Semantics Sufficient?

An important argument that has been advanced against this semantic approach is that it does not account for the end state of language development. The most parsimonious description of the mature linguistic system is couched in terms of syntactic categories, according to the currently most influential trends in linguistics. There is no simple correspondence between these syntactic categories and the semantic categories on which the child's linguistic system has been claimed to be based. For instance, while the agent is usually expressed by the subject of the sentence, there are many cases in which the subject (even the deep structure subject) is not an agent. A theory crediting children with semantic categories must show how they ultimately acquire the adult system.

1.3 And is Syntax?

This argument has led some writers to reject the semantic approach and return to the transformationalist view, predominant in the 1960s, that from the outset the child develops a grammar involving syntactic categories. What has not been sufficiently appreciated, however, is that the latter view raises a quite similar problem. As there is no simple correspondence between these syntactic categories and semantic ones, the child will have to learn how they map onto the meanings expressed by language. There seems to be no reason to prefer a theory according to which the child acquires a system based on syntactic categories, which he subsequently (or simultaneously) learns to map into semantic ones, to a theory that he first acquires a system based on semantic categories and later—perhaps only just prior to attaining full mastery of grammar—learns to map these onto syntactic ones. Whatever approach one espouses, a theory of language acquisition has to show how the link between semantic and syntactic categories are forged. The present chapter proposes a solution to this problem based on the claim that the child's early relational categories are semantic. The semantics-first approach, it is argued, can thus be vindicated.[1]

On the other hand, the syntax-first approach has still a long way to go in order to show how syntactic categories—assuming that the child starts out with them—are mapped onto semantic ones. A solution that seems to be favored by

---

[1]This should not be construed as a claim that early categories are *exclusively* semantic. There certainly are also pragmatic categories—see Ninio and Snow (this volume)—and even formal ones, as shown later on (Section 11).

some is that this mapping is attained in a piecemeal fashion, by successively learning a large number of narrow-range form-meaning correspondences. Specifically, these correspondences may be tied to the meanings of verbs: For each verb the child learns what semantic relationships hold between it and other categories in the syntactic deep structure (e.g., between it and its deep structure object).

Such a proposal is insufficient, however, for while it is true that much of what is learned resides in specific lexical entries (and these also play a major role in the proposal I present further on), we also can, and do, generalize from some of this knowledge. Suppose somebody has learned the meaning of the noun *sketch*. He now knows what a sketch is, but does not have as yet a lexical entry for the verb *to sketch* (which he has not heard yet), specifying its semantic relationships to its deep structure subject or object. Nevertheless, on hearing *John sketched Mary* he will immediately understand who sketches whom. He will generalize from his previous experience of what semantic relations are expressed by the subject and object of a sentence, and thus will attribute sketching to John and posing to Mary, rather than vice versa (see Pinker [1984, p.315] for experimental evidence). Now note that as soon as one invokes semantic relations, one has abandoned the idea that all learning is piecemeal, by way of lexical entries. Instead, one assumes that the child has to learn the mapping between semantic and syntactic relations, which, as stated, is not one-to-one. The problem to be solved by the syntax-first approach is, then, the same as that faced by the semantics-first approach: how does the child find out about semantic-syntactic correspondences?

A further consideration leading to the same conclusion pertains to the number of relations that would have to be registered in a lexical entry if lexical entries were to bear the brunt of learning the correspondence between syntax and semantics. Take languages where the inflection of the noun signals its case. Latin has, besides the nominative (i.e., roughly, the form of the noun that is the surface subject) and the vocative, four cases: accusative (the form of the direct object), genitive (possessive), dative, and ablative (for details consult your Latin grammar); Lithuanian has just as many; Finnish has 16 cases; Hungarian even more. Each case expresses a different semantic relation (some express more than one, and more than one case may express a given semantic relation). For lexical entries to take care of form-meaning correspondences, the information as to which form of the noun goes with each of these relations would have to be duplicated for each lexical entry (whether of verbs or of nouns—details of this utterly implausible suggestion need not concern us here). Clearly, if children are to learn Lithuanian, Finnish, and Hungarian at all—and it seems that many of them do—they must learn generalizations involving categories of semantic relations and not a myriad pieces of information.

A solution based entirely on lexical entries, then, is not feasible. For this reason, and for several others that become apparent in the following, I am very skeptic about the syntax-first approach in general. In the next section I return to my business of developing the semantics-first approach, and show how the child's early semantic relations can form the basis of the adult linguistic system. The solution of the problem, it is argued, lies with a process of gradual extension of semantic categories, a process called semantic assimilation.

2. SEMANTIC ASSIMILATION

The semantic assimilation hypothesis (Schlesinger 1974, 1977, 1981, 1982) states that the child's early semantic categories are gradually reorganized in accordance with the categorization adopted by the input language. In discussing semantic assimilation, all my examples are of a single semantic relation, the agent-action relation, and it is shown how this develops into the adult subject-predicate relation. The arguments advanced presumably hold, in general, also for other semantic relations and their syntactic counterparts, but the details have been worked out so far only for the agentive relation. Briefly, it is argued that the agentive relation starts out from a very circumscribed category, which serves as the basis of generalization and is gradually extended thereby. The notion of a prototypical agent that serves as the nucleus of a wider, more mature category has also been proposed by Slobin (1981). An account along similar lines of the acquisition of word classes is given by Berman (this volume).

It is widely agreed that the agent-action relation is one of the first to appear in child language. As is argued in Section 12.2, this relation is probably not a semantic primitive, but is itself the product of a learning process, but here we can safely sidestep this issue and take the agentive relation as given. Early two-word combinations apparently expressing this relation would be, for instance, *bunny jump, doggie run, Mummy wash* and *Bobbie kick*. The consistent use of word order—agent first, action last—may count as evidence that the child analyzes the situation in terms of this relation and has a grammatical rule for expressing it. The problem we now face is how this rule can eventually be made to apply to many other expressions involving subjects that are not agents. Here is a sample:

a. Billie found an empty bottle.   (1)
b. Doris sees the big dog.
c. Pamela remembers Uncle John.
d. This bottle contains arsenic.

Strictly speaking, finding, seeing, remembering, and containing are not actions. The subjects of these sentences do not refer therefore to instigators of actions, which is what agents, by definition, are.[2] So let us see now how semantic assimilation (SA) works.

But first, a comment is in order concerning the nature of many of the examples quoted in this and the following sections. Quite obviously, these are often not the kinds of utterances made by infants in the early stages of language acquisition, and one may even doubt whether the child is likely to hear such utterances addressed to him. This is immaterial to the present discussion, however, because what is at issue is the question of how the child eventually comes to master the relevant rules that account for sentences like those presented. Eventually, the child will be able to form sentences like those in (1), and the problem we are dealing with here is how that stage is arrived at.

To return to (1), suppose that the child has a rule for the primitive agent-action relation—one that enables her to deal with utterances about such prototypical actions as jumping, running, washing, and kicking—and hears (1)a. She will then note similarities between the relation described in (1)a and the primitive agent-action relation. Finding is usually embedded in a context of activity—one looks around, stops to examine, picks up, etc.—and although such activities do not always occur, and in fact are not part of the meaning of *find* (one may just stumble on something and then ignore it), they may serve to underline for the child the similarity between the event of finding and other prototypical action events. This similarity, together with the formal similarity (in word order, inflections) between (1)a and agent-action utterances, leads the child to analyze this sentence as an agent-action construction. This will entail a considerable saving in the rule system: rules acquired for prototypical actions will not have to be learned once again for *find*. Instead, finding will henceforward be regarded as a kind of action, and consequently sentences with *find* will be construed with any one of those rules that have been learned for agent-action constructions, e.g.,

a. It is Billie who found/took the bottle.   (2)
b. The one who found/took the bottle was Billie.
c. The empty bottle—Billie found/took it.
d. Billie—he found/took the bottle.
e. It is the empty bottle that Billie found/took.

The agent-action relation will continue in this manner to absorb various instances of similar relations. For example, Doris and Pamela in (1)b and c may be considered as *doing* something (seeing is not so different from looking, and the latter is action-like; remembering usually goes hand in hand with talking about what is remembered). Eventually, after some experience with metaphorical ex-

---

[2]It will be convenient to talk not only about relations but also about agents and actions; these terms should be taken as referring to the arguments of the agent-action relation. It is to the latter that linguistic rules apply.

tensions, a bottle may be conceived of as performing a sort of action when it contains something; see (1)d. (For suppose you hold a pile of books. Are you "doing" something? And how about the bookshelf that holds 30 volumes? But the shelf may also be said to contain the volumes!) This assimilation process continues until the boundaries of the child's semantic relational categories coincide more or less with those of the underlying categories in the adult system.

This explanation presupposes, of course, that subjects can, in general, be perceived to be similar to agents. That such similarities indeed exist is shown in detail in Sections 6 and 7.

Returning for a moment to the opposition between semantic and syntactic categories discussed in Section 1, we note that according to the SA hypothesis there is no longer any sharp contrast between the two. Relational categories are not either syntactic *or* semantic; they start out as semantic categories and gradually come to coincide with formally defined ones.[3] Whether one uses semantic or syntactic terms in dealing with child language will depend on a terminological decision, without any substantive issue being involved. I prefer to use semantic terms not only in talking about child language, but also in describing an adult production and comprehension model (Schlesinger, 1977), because these stress the semantic origin of relational categories. But one may be equally justified in using syntactic terms so as to focus on the end state towards which the child's categories develop. See also Ninio (this volume).

It is important to keep in mind what the SA hypothesis does **not** claim. It does not claim that there are similarities out there in the world which determine how our relational categories are to be organized, what is to be assimilated into what. True, there are correlations in the attributes of the environment, as Rosch (e.g., Rosch & Mervis, 1975) has shown, that predispose us to categorize our experience in a certain way. There is much similarity between some things and very little between others, and some possibilities of categorization therefore appear more "natural" than others. However, this **texture** of the experienced world (see Schlesinger, 1982, pp. 144–145, 177–178) merely suggests certain possibilities of categorization, and we are left some leeway in choosing between them. Consider the following analogy. Suppose we have a map of a part of a continent which we intend to divide up anew among states in a "natural" manner, i.e., in a way that respects the physical characteristics of the terrain. Clearly, the configurations of mountain ranges, rivers, etc. will constrain us in this task. But only somewhat: There will almost always be alternative possibilities, sometimes equally "natural" ones, of drawing in political boundaries.

The structure of the world does not impose itself upon our linguistic categorization; instead, the texture of experience merely suggests certain possibilities of

---

[3]Gleitman and Wanner (1982) argue that "if learning is a continuous process, the initial units must be grammatical ones" (p.31). The SA hypothesis describes a continuous learning process starting from semantic units.

categorization without deciding between them. (This is also the reason why languages may differ somewhat in the way they classify relations, as is shown in Section 12.5.). The child learning language is not free to choose among these possibilities; rather, she is constrained by the categorization of the particular language she learns. Formal similarities direct her attention to similarities in meaning between relations that might otherwise have gone unnoticed; and conversely, when semantic similarities are noticed, SA will be conditional on the existence of formal similarities.[4]

A schematic description of the SA process is given in Fig. 6.1. In the figure, R stands for a relational category for which the child has already learned a rule of linguistic realization—e.g., the agent-action category in the above example—and lower case r stands for a relation for which she has no such rule, and which is eventually to be assimilated into R—e.g., the relation between *Billie* and *found* in (1)a. The figure shows that the formal similarity between the utterances expressing r and those expressing R (Step 2) draws the child's attention to the semantic similarity (Step 3). Alternatively, when semantic similarity is especially salient, Step 3 may precede Step 2; the point is that formal and semantic similarity are mutually reinforcing. The result of this will be assimilation of r into R, which can take the two alternative forms indicated by steps 4a and 4b, and which are discussed in the following two sections.

3.   ASSIMILATION THROUGH LEXICAL ENTRIES

One possible outcome of SA, described in Step 4a in Fig. 6.1, may be illustrated by the following example. Suppose a child hears (1)a and notices the formal and semantic similarity of this sentence to agent-action constructions. What permits her to treat *find* henceforward as an action word is an addition she makes to the lexical entry for that word. This addition to the lexical entry must include not only the fact that *find* is an action word but also a specification as to which expression is the agent, i.e., the finder (see Schlesinger, 1982, Sections 9.2–9.3, for a fuller discussion of lexical entries). That this is necessary becomes clear on considering uses of *find* in sentences where the finder is not human or what is found is not a concrete object, as in:

a. Let's find something to do!   (3)
b. He found an excuse.
c. Winter found John in great distress.
d. John found the whole affair distasteful.

---

[4]The SA hypothesis can therefore not be refuted by cases where semantic similarity exists and the linguistic expression does not express this; that is, objections of the following form have no force: expression X_1 in Sentence S_1 is just as similar (or more so) to an agent as expression X_2 in S_2, and yet X_2 is the sentence subject whereas X_1 is not.

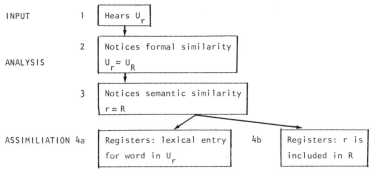

FIG. 6.1. Semantic assimilation · R is a relation for which child already has syntactic rules, and r is assimilated into it. U_R and U_r are utterances, in which these relations are expressed. Steps 2 and 3 may appear in reverse order.

(Obviously, such sentences do not occur in early speech, but as pointed out before, the SA hypothesis must account for the fact that the child will eventually have to be able to deal with sentences like these.) Why is *John* in object position in (3)c, but in subject position in d, rather than vice versa? The answer lies in the lexical entry for *find:* the entity that encounters something or experiences something functions as agent, and the entity encountered or experienced—as patient.

Not only *find,* but many other action verbs can be used figuratively. The child may hear expressions like

   a. Fear stopped him.   (4)
   b. The news hit him hard.
   c. She picked up a foreign accent.

and will often not have much difficulty in understanding such expressions. What makes this possible are (besides the general penchant for metaphor we humans seem to have) lexical entries for *stop, hit,* and *pick up,* that specify for each verb what can figure as agent term in a given situation. This information has been included in the entries already when the child learned to use these verbs in their more concrete meaning; already then she registered the fact that the agent was the one who caused the event (of stopping, hitting, and picking up).

But isn't the term agent misplaced here? After all, fear and the news are not conscious instigators of actions, and there are no actions going on in the first place. This is a common objection to the SA account: many sentence subjects are not agents, and often—as for instance in (3)—are not even similar to agents. Note, however, that the SA hypothesis does not claim that subjects are, from our adult vantage point, very much like agents, but rather that the subject category originates in the agent concept and does so on the basis of lexical entries which were made when similarity of meaning was perceived. The term *agent* should not be taken too literally.

One way SA proceeds, then, is through registering information in lexical entries. Now, it might be argued that if lexical entries have to be resorted to anyway, there is no longer any need for the SA process: The child just learns for each verb that does not describe an overt action—e.g., those in (1) and (4)— how it is to be used; and it would be gratuitous to hypothesize, in addition, an assimilation process based on semantic similarity. It will be remembered that there are arguments against the proposal that all of grammatical development is accounted for by the formation of lexical entries, but it might still be argued that lexical entries can take care of those cases for which SA has been invoked here, i.e., where a construction does not express the relation that it is typically used to express. However, it seems that even in these cases the hypothesized SA process is needed to avoid much undue reduplication of information in lexical entries:

1. Suppose a child hears (1)a and registers in the lexical entry of *find* how this word is used in the specific construction it appears in (e.g., that the expression preceding *find* refers to the person who sees something and gets hold of it, and the one following it—to that which is got hold of). This information would obviously be incomplete; for instance, it would be of no help in dealing with constructions like those in (2). On encountering one of the latter the child would have to register a new use of *find*. The various rules that give rise to these alternative constructions can obviously not be duplicated for every single verb in the language; they must operate on relational categories (according to the theory espoused here—on agent-action). Generalization to (2) can be achieved only by registering how *find* figures in this relational category, i.e., by semantic assimilation.

2. Another way in which SA affords a saving in learning effort is through generalization to other relations. Suppose one has registered in the lexical entries of *find, see, remember, contain,* etc., that these verbs can fulfill the function of action words. Then one has provided not only for constructions like those in (1), involving the agent-action relation, but also those involving other relations in which action terms figure: action-patient (*see the sea*), action-instrument (*see with glasses*), action-modifier (*see clearly*)—and a few more. If the child would merely register a specific use of a given word in its lexical entry, no such generalization would be possible.

In sum, it is argued that analysis of formal and semantic similarities of constructions leads to registering in the lexical entry of a verb not only how it is used in the particular construction in which it is encountered, but also how it functions in the rule system as a whole.

4. ASSIMILATION OF CATEGORIES AS A WHOLE

Figure 6.1 states that SA can either be lexically based (Step 4a), as discussed in the preceding section, or operate on a relation as a whole (Step 4b).

To illustrate the latter possibility, consider the following sentences:

a. The two documents were held together with a paper clip.　　　　(5)
b. Nail polish is removed with acetone.
c. You can exterminate bugs with this spray.

In each of these sentences, the noun in the *with*-phrase refers to the instrument with which the action was carried out. Now, the instrument can also be expressed by a different construction:

a. A paper clip held the two documents together.　　　　(6)
b. Acetone removes nail polish.
c. This spray exterminates bugs.

There are two ways to view constructions like (6). Case theorists, like Fillmore (1968) regard *a paper clip, acetone,* and *this spray* as Instruments in (6) as well as in (5), the difference between the two being a surface phenomenon: The Instrument is expressed as subject in (6), but not in (5). This seems logical, because an instrument is an instrument, whatever the way we talk about it. However, there is nothing in this truism to prevent us from viewing events in different ways, and the semantic assimilation approach claims just this: While the subjects in (6), objectively, denote instruments, the speaker of these sentences regards them **as if** they were agents. That is, the agent concept is metaphorically extended to include the instrument. The speaker is of course well aware that paper clips are not really agents (just as mountains do not really have feet), but he walks in the footsteps of language in talking about them as if they were agents (just as he may talk about *the foot of the mountain*). (The extent to which he is aware of speaking metaphorically may vary from instance to instance and need not concern us here.)

The same holds true for other relations that can be assimilated into the agent-action relation. The subjects of *find* in (3) are not really agents but treated like such for the purpose of linguistic expression; in (1), Pamela is ''really'' an experiencer of remembering, and the bottle the location of arsenic, but for all that we talk about them as of agents. There is no contradiction between knowing that an event instantiates relation X and speaking about it as if it instantiated a relation to which X is similar in some way. What we know about the relation in the event pertains to the cognitive level, whereas the way we talk about it pertains to the semantic one. The mapping between these levels is not one-to-one; see Schlesinger (1982, Section 9.5) for an elaboration of this point and further examples. In Section 7 evidence is presented that this approach is justified.

Case theorists, by contrast, go a long way toward collapsing the two levels, in that they determine case roles solely on the basis of the function fulfilled by the entities in question in the real world, as we know it. I propose that in assigning semantic relations much more attention should be paid to the linguistic realization, which shows us how events are viewed for the purpose of speaking. Where case theory takes its cue only from reality, the present approach takes its cue much more from the linguistic expression, which reflects the way reality is conceived of linguistically.

To return to (6), it is proposed that the subjects of these sentences, while they denote what are, objectively speaking, instruments, express the agents of the underlying semantic structure. The rule that instruments can be agents (see Schlesinger, 1985, for a detailed discussion) is productive in English, that is, any instrument can be an agent (subject to certain constraints to be discussed in a later section). The child who has learned to use this rule productively has assimilated the instrument category as a whole into the agent category. (The Japanese-speaking child does not arrive at this generalization: In Japanese the instrument cannot be subjectivized.) This, then, is an example of across-the-board assimilation.

Having described two forms of SA, we now examine the credentials of the hypothesis: Can the multifarious concepts expressed by sentence subjects really have originated from the agent category? To what extent are subjects similar to agents?

5.   EMBEDDEDNESS IN ACTION

Before dealing with the issue of similarity of subjects to agents, we must deal with a whole class of cases which seem, at first blush, to be counter-examples to our theory that subjects originate in agents, but actually can easily be accounted for without invoking similarity. Many verbs, among them some that are used by the child from early on, do not denote actions in adult use; for instance, *sleep, stand, see, miss,* etc. What permits us to view subjects of these verbs as agents?

The answer seems to be quite simple. The child presumably learns these words in contexts in which actions are involved, and therefore the fact that they are action words is registered in their lexical entries (see Step 4a of Fig. 6.1). Consider the verb *sleep:* Macnamara (1982, p.107) observes that for his son Kieran *sleep* meant to put his head on something and close his eyes. Likewise, we may assume that *see* will appear at first in contexts involving overt actions: turning one's head, pointing at what is seen, and often also walking up to it, and even doing something with it. Of course, for an adult these words do not *mean* all these actions, and the child will eventually have to learn this fact, by refining their lexical entries (cf. Schlesinger 1982, Chapters 5 and 6, on the development of word meaning), but initially they are for him action-like and are registered in the lexical entry accordingly.

This explanation seems to hold good for many verbs. Consider in what context one talks about missing a train (run, pant, wave your hands, throw them up in despair), failing an exam, or worrying about a person. When the meaning of the word *miss* or *fail* is learned, it will probably be in a context of an activity in which the one who misses or fails is engaged, and the same holds true for many other verbs.

Quite a few verbs have two uses: an active one and a stative one,[5] which suggests that the categories of active and stative verb are not very sharply delineated. Compare:

a. He stands up.   (7)
b. He stands on the ladder.

c. He lies down on the sofa.
d. He lies on the sofa.

e. He tasted the soup and refused to eat it.
f. He tasted the pepper in the soup.

g. He felt her hand.
h. He felt the dampness of her hand.

i. He bent down and smelled the violets.
j. He smelled the violets from afar.

The active use may lead to the verb being registered as an action verb, and this carries over to the stative use.

A frequent objection to semantic approaches of language acquisition is that the same situation can be referred to by two sentences in which the roles of the subjects and object are interchanged, so to speak. Compare (8)a with (8)b and (8)c with (8)d.

a. Sue received a book from Mary.   (8)
b. Mary gave a book to Sue.

c. Sue teaches Mary French.
d. Mary learns French from Sue.

Who is to be regarded as agent, so the objection runs, Sue or Mary? If it is Sue in (8)a, then the subject of (8)b cannot be an agent, and vice versa.

This objection loses its force once the claim made by the SA hypothesis is

---

[5]This was pointed out to me by Sidney Greenbaum.

clearly understood. The hypothesis does not state that all subjects **are** agents; such a claim would obviously be false. Rather, it is argued

(i) that subjects of certain words are often perceived as being **similar** to agents, and

(ii) that this fact will be registered in the lexical entry of the verb; and as a consequence, the verb and its subject will henceforward be used correctly even in those cases where no such similarity is perceived.

To return to (8), the child will analyze adult uses of *give,* and later of *receive,* and register this usage in his or her lexical entries for these words. Both words will presumably be learned in contexts involving overt activity, and will therefore be registered as actions. The lexical entry for *receive* will stipulate that the receiver functions as the agent, whereas the entry for *give* will indicate that the giver, rather than the receiver, functions as agent. As a result, the child will eventually be able to produce sentences like (8)a and (8)b correctly even in instances where he or she does not notice any agent-like qualities in the receiver (or giver). The same applies, mutatis mutandis, to *teach* and *learn.*

6. SEMANTIC SIMILARITY

In this section we examine in what ways subjects may be similar to prototypical agents (i.e., agents of overt actions, like jumping, running, kicking, and washing). Certain features of similarity are discussed, such that any given subject may be similar to agents in one or more of these features. This means that, while subjects are similar to agents, it is not the case that any two of these subjects will invariably be similar to each other: they may each be similar to agents in respect to different features.

It is proposed that prototypical agents have three features that are especially relevant to SA: the agent (a) is in **motion;** (b) is the **cause** of the action described by the verb and responsible for it; and (c) is in **control** of this action. Similarity in any one of these three features makes SA possible. However, presence of a feature does not guarantee SA; it is not a sufficient condition for it.

6.1 Motion

Each of the subjects in the following sentences refers to an entity that is in motion, the kind of motion involved being described by the verb:

a. The cat fell from the rooftop.   (9)
b. The building blew up.

   c. The gate closed behind him.

   d. The door opened.

Although no intention, no "instigation of action", can be ascribed to the cat, the building, the gate and the door, they are seen as similar to the prototypical agent in that they share with it the feature of Motion.[6]

As a result of hearing sentences like (9), *fall, blow up, close,* and *open* are registered as action words in their respective lexical entries. Henceforward the child will be able to deal also with sentences like the following, in which no physical movement is involved:

   a. Prices fell on the stock market.   (10)

   b. The quarrel blew up.

   c. The symphony closes with a crescendo.

   d. The affair opened with an announcement.

Note that presence of Motion is not a sufficient condition for SA: Not all entities that are in motion will figure as agents. Thus, when John pushes Paul, both are in motion, but only John will be expressed as agent of *push*. The lexical entry for *push* will stipulate that the one who pushes (i.e., moves in the direction of the other entity involved in the action, rather than away from it) is to be regarded as agent (cf. Section 3).

Motion, then, is a typical feature of agentivity which may give rise to semantic assimilation. One of the components of this feature—one might call it a feature of the feature Motion—is **Change of State.** The sentence subjects in (11) involve Change of State, and are similar in this respect to those in (9), just as the latter are similar to prototypical agents in respect to Motion.

   a. The pansies are growing fast.   (11)

   b. The ice cream has melted.

   c. The fog vanishes.

   d. Sugar dissolves in water.

In (11) we have therefore a second-order similarity to prototypical agents. These stages of SA are summarized in Fig. 6.2.

---

[6]But see Schlesinger (1982, Section 9.6) for an alternative treatment of (9)c and (9)d. In the case of *fall,* SA may be facilitated by the fact that *fall* can also be construed as referring to an intentional action. (Sidney Greenbaum, personal communication, 1980; cf. also Quirk, Greenbaum, Leech, & Svartvik, 1978, Section 7.15, note b).

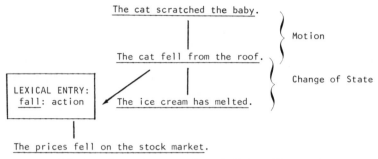

FIG. 6.2. Stages in semantic assimilation. (See text.)

6.2 Cause

In each of the following sentences the subject refers to the cause of the event described:

    a. Salt increases blood pressure.   (12)
    b. The hot weather wore him out.
    c. The pancreas produces insulin.

The feature of Cause is common to the subjects in these sentences and to prototypical agents. Note that this feature is inextricably bound up with that of Responsibility (not moral responsibility, of course), as shown by comparing (12) with the following:

    a. Salt is responsible for increasing blood pressure.   (13)
    b. The hot weather was responsible for his being worn out.
    c. The pancreas is responsible for producing insulin.

    Cause may also be a feature of abstract entities:

    a. The increase in tourism boosted sales.   (14)
    b. The news alarmed him.
    c. The experimental findings invalidate this claim.

As we have seen in Section 4, a whole relation can be assimilated into the agent-action relation: The instrument may be conceived of as agent; see (6), above. This is because the instrument may be viewed as the proximate cause, as what is responsible, in the absence of the "real" agent, for the event:

    a. The scarecrow keeps the birds away.   (15)
    b. The glue makes the planks stick together.
    c. The scaffolding supports the wall.

The instrument category, then, is assimilated wholesale into the action category (cf. Step 4b of Fig. 6.1). However, no such across-the-board assimilation occurs for all entities that have the feature of Cause, since there are cases where the causer does not figure as sentence subject, as will be seen further on. Nevertheless, there is probably a tendency to identify the subject with the cause. Suppose you have just learned the meaning of the noun *boost*, and then hear (14)a, without ever having heard the **verb** used before. Then, I expect, you would immediately interpret this sentence correctly. Or alternatively, if presented with *The increase in sales boosted tourism*, you would balk, and might (relying on your expertise in economics) correct the speaker.

It seems reasonable, therefore, to presume that, in sentences with direct objects, whenever the subject denotes an abstract entity, the latter shares the feature Cause with prototypical agents.

In discussing Motion (Section 6.1) we have noted that this feature itself has a sort of second-order feature on which SA can be based. Similarly, Cause has a second-order feature: the **Characteristic Responsible for an Event.** In the following sentences, the subject does not refer to the cause of the state of affairs described, but to an entity the characteristics of which are responsible for this state of affairs:

a. The hall seats 500 people.   (16)
b. This room sleeps two.
c. This box holds eight beer cans.

Some property of the hall (its size) is responsible for the fact that 500 people can be seated in it. By contrast, no characteristics of the hall, the room and the box are intimated in the following sentences, in which they do not figure as subjects:

a. Five hundred people sit in the hall.   (17)
b. Two people sleep in this room.
c. Eight beer cans are in this box.

For all we know, the hall may be crammed full, well above seating capacity, the room may be a huge one, in which more people might be accomodated, and the box may be half empty. Further evidence for our interpretation of (16) is presented in Section 7.

6.3 Control

This feature characterizes the subjects of experience verbs:

a. Joyce admires Bruce.   (18)
b. Joyce detests Bruce.

  c. Bill charms Joan.
  d. Bill shocks Joan.

In a series of studies I have shown that in sentences like these the subject is judged as being more in control than the object. Likewise, it was found that Control is assigned also to "experiencers" of less emotionally loaded experiences: to the subjects of verbs like *see, forget, recognize, notice,* and *know.*

Note that (18)c and (18)d differ from the first two sentences in that the subject, Bill, also has the feature of Cause, whereas in (18)a and (18)b, it is the object, Bruce, who has a characteristic that is responsible for making Joyce admire or detest him.[7] These examples illustrate the point made above, that Cause is not a feature that is conducive to across-the-board assimilation. SA here operates through the lexical entries of the specific verbs *admire, detest,* etc. (cf. Section 3).

The feature of Control together with that of Cause also characterizes the situation mentioned above, in which John pushes Paul. Both are in motion, but John is in control and is also the cause of pushing (at least, the immediate cause), and hence John, rather than Paul, is regarded as agent.

7. SEMANTIC CONSTRAINTS

We now examine a phenomenon that provides strong confirmation of our analysis in the preceding section of subjects as semantically similar to agents, and hence for the claim that the child's subject category develops out of the agent category.

If the subject develops out of the agent on the basis of semantic similarity, one may expect the degree of acceptability of a sentence to be influenced by the degree of similarity. This is in fact the case as far as the instrument is concerned.

Compare the following two sentences:

  a. This pen draws thin lines and that one thick lines.   (19)
  b. The pen was drawing lines.

---

[7]Brown and Fish (1983) presented subjects with sentences like those in (18) and asked them how likely it was that "this is because Joyce (Bruce) is the kind of person who admires people (who people admire)." More "responsibility" was attributed to the object of sentences like (18)a and (18)b and to the subject of those like (18)c. Assignment of responsibility to the object leaves open the question what caused the "less responsible" person to figure as subject. I therefore hypothesized that the feature of Control was operative here and designed a series of studies carried out with the help of Rina Shenitzer, Dorit Lutz, Jorge Vulej, and Alon Halter.

Anita Mittwoch has pointed out (personal communication) that constructions with experiencer verbs are more commonly encountered in the passive form (*I am surprised by the weather.*), and may be learned therefore as a variant derived from the passive.

Why does (19)b sound more awkward than (19)a? I suggest that this is because in (19)a the inherent characteristics of the pen are focused on, whereas in (19)b this is not the case. In both sentences the pen causes the action, but in (19)a it shares with prototypical agents also the feature Characteristic Responsible for the Event, and the greater similarity makes it more acceptable.

This explanation is similar to that given by Wierzbicka (1980) to account for the difference in acceptability between the following two sentences:

    a. Peter's key opened the door.   (20)
    b. Peter's stick beat up Harry.

There is nothing in the stick that makes it responsible for beating up Harry, but if Peter wouldn't have had the right key, the lock wouldn't have yielded.

Consider now some sentences in which the instrument has been assimilated into the agent:

    a. The axe cuts wood.   (21)
    b. The baton moved in circles.
    c. The spoon stirred the soup.

These sentences sound somewhat odd, except in special contexts. The reason is that we do not focus here on the characteristics of the instruments that make the action possible.

But why do the sentences in (15) sound better than those in (21)? There seems to be a difference in the degree to which Characteristic Responsible is involved, but this is not the whole story. Note that in (15) the "real" agent, the one who uses the scarecrow, the glue, and the scaffolding to achieve an effect, is imagined as not being on the scene. With the real agent gone, the instrument takes over, like the broom of the sorcerer's apprentice. On hearing (15)a we are not tempted to respond: "But it is not the scarecrow who keeps the birds away—it is the person who put it there!" As Fillmore (1977) puts it, the "manipulator [has been] left out of perspective" (p.76). On hearing (21), by contrast, we at once think of the one who wields the axe, the baton, or the spoon and tend to regard him as the real agent, who should be represented as such in the sentence.

Compare also (20) to

    a. Peter's letter of introduction paved the way for Mary.   (22)
    b. After being thrown into the air, Peter's stick fell down and hit Harry.

In (22)a Peter is no longer on the scene (he may even have passed away); his letter is on its own and achieves the effect. Hence, this sentence sounds better than (20)a. Likewise Peter's stick in (22)b is no longer attached to Peter and may therefore be conceived of as "acting" in its own right, which is not the case in (20)b (cf. Fillmore, 1977, pp.75–76).

While an instrument may play an agent-like role, this does not turn it into a full-scale agent wielding all the powers of an agent. For instance, it cannot be said to perform an action by using another object as an instrument. This has been called the Mediation Constraint by Schlesinger (1985), and is exemplified by:

a. The arrow killed the deer.   (23)
b. The bullet hit the deer.
c. * The bow killed the deer.
d. * The rifle shot the deer.

The bow's "action" is mediated by an arrow, the rifle's—by bullets, and just as (24), where mediating instruments are mentioned explicitly, is unacceptable, so are (23)c and d:

a. *The bow killed the deer with an arrow.   (24)
b. *The rifle wounded the deer with two bullets.
c. *The wind broke the window with a twig.
d. *The hammer made a hole in the wall with a chisel.

Another semantic constraint, the Deliberation Constraint (Schlesinger, 1974, 1985), states that the subjectivalization of the instrument will be blocked when the action requires deliberation. Compare the following sentence pairs:

a. The pen is scribbling fast.   (25)
b. *The pen is scribbling a poem.

c. The baton moved in circles.
d. *The baton conducted the symphony.

e. The chisel was carving sandalwood.
f. *The chisel was carving sandalwood into a statuette.

g. The pieces moved on the chessboard.
h. *The pieces played chess.

In the second sentence in each pair, the subject does not share the feature Cause with prototypical agents: The activities involved are such that Cause can be assigned only to a conscious and deliberately acting agent. These sentences are therefore totally unacceptable.

Note that in (25)b and f the verbs are the same as those in their acceptable counterparts. There seem to be no formal syntactic rules that might block the generation of these sentences. The interpretation must therefore be along semantic lines. The same holds true for all the other observations on relative acceptability discussed in this section: No explanation in terms of purely syntactic rules seems to be in sight. The explanations given here are all in terms of the features of the agent and the instrument and thus provide corroboration for our view of the role of semantic similarity. The subject, it appears, is not semantically neutral; it retains the flavor of the agent category from which it derives. Additional evidence for this analysis of the instrumental has been presented in Schlesinger (1985).

Our discussion so far has provided confirmation for, among others, the feature of Characteristic Responsible for the described state of affairs; cf. (19) and (20). Evidence for this feature has also been presented by Van Oosten (1977; see also Lakoff, 1977). Compare:

a. The tent puts up in about 2 minutes.   (26)
b. *The tent puts up in my back yard.

c. The wash-and-dry shirt washes with no trouble.
d. *The wash-and-dry shirt washes with no trouble, because I have plenty of energy.

There is nothing in the nature of the tent, argues Van Oosten, that makes it put up in the back yard, but the way the tent is constructed permits it to be put up in 2 minutes.

The data reviewed here support the thesis of the semantic origin of the subject. One objection that has been made to this interpretation of the data is that they do not demonstrate that semantic assimilation was operative in the development of the subject. If the subject is perceived as somewhat of an agent, this may be a later development: Many subjects refer to agents, and thus the subject concept acquires a flavor of agency.

This is a kind of last-ditch stand of those who believe that the child operates with a system of formal syntactic categories from the outset. That the agentivity of the subject is a later acquisition strikes one as utterly implausible. If the adult notices similarities between subject and the agent, why should the child studiously avoid taking account of those similarities? Why should the child doggedly pursue the road of purely formal analysis, disregarding meaning, and only become sensitive to semantic similarities when the system has been fully developed?

Besides, such an alternative to semantic assimilation would leave us without any clue to solving another problem, for which our hypothesis provides a solution, at least in outline. This issue is dealt with in the following section.

8.   WHAT IS EXPLAINED BY SEMANTIC ASSIMILATION?

So far we have discussed SA as a process of language learning. But such a process may operate not only in the child who sets out to master the adult system, as is seen presently.

It has often been said that the relational categories of a language (the subject, the object, etc.) are semantically heterogeneous. If this is so, one might well ask for the reason why languages came to be this way. Why did English, for instance, not develop into a more systematic language with semantically homogeneous categories? Such a language might be easier to operate with; in any case, there must be a reason why a language in the course of its development arrived at semantically arbitrary categories.

Now, as the previous analyses suggest, linguistic categories, though no doubt semantically heterogeneous, are not completely arbitrary. The subject category has a semantic nucleus, the prototypical agent, to which the members of the category bear some similarity. True, this similarity is not such that any two subjects are semantically similar to each other; as we have seen, there are several features of similarity, and it is possible for the subject of one sentence to resemble the prototypical agent in one of these features and that of another sentence to resemble it in a different feature. In other words, subject is a cluster concept, with family resemblances holding between the various instances.[8] This suggests that in the course of development of English something very similar occurred to what happens when a child learns English as her native language; that is, various relations were felt by speakers to be similar in some respects to the agent-action relation and hence the linguistic means were developed to deal with them in the way the latter is dealt with.

This is of course only a very schematic explanation, which does not account for the semantic composition of the subject in detail, that is, it does not explain why just these specific relations were assimilated to the agent-action relation and not some others which might resemble it just as much. Why does Japanese, for instance, treat the event of A seeing B differently from English, viz. refers to B as subject, rather than to A? Why is the experiencer of admiration referred to by the subject in (18)a, whereas the experiencer of the shock is the object in (18)d? We have no explanations for questions like these. But, while much of the arbitrariness remains, semantic assimilation provides at least a partial explanation for the problem of semantic composition of syntactic categories.[9]

The value of our notion of semantic assimilation thus lies in its applicability in two domains: the acquisition of language by the child and its historic development. So far only the assimilation of various relations into the agent-action relation has been worked out in detail, and it remains to be shown how SA

---

[8]Keenan (1976) also holds that the subject is a cluster concept, but he employs formal as well as semantic properties in its delimitation. Lakoff (1977) discusses prototypical agent-patient sentences, but he holds that there is one property, "primary responsibility", common to all subjects. DeLancey (1984) discusses the linguistic realization of non-prototypical agents in several languages. Wierzbicka (1980) holds that while each case has different but interrelated meanings, all the meanings of one case do not necessarily share the same meaning component.

[9]A question that comes to mind is why languages are not structured in a semantically more transparent way: one category for each semantic relation. This question is based on an ontological assumption, viz. that there is a small number of such relations, for each of which language might provide a different structure. I do not think this assumption is justified: there are indefinitely many relations, which language has to classify into a manageable number of categories so as to be able to provide them with distinct linguistic constructions. More about this in Section 12.2.

operates with other relational categories. Some relevant data are discussed in Schlesinger (1981, 1982, Sections 9.3, 9.4); cf. also Bowerman (1982) on some semantic notions expressed by the object.

Our claim, then, is that a subject is either similar to agents in one of the specified three features, or else it is subject of a verb that has been learned in a context where one of these features applies or in an action-embedded context. Now, while the preceding sections have substantiated this claim with a wide variety of sentences, this does not imply that it holds true for all sentences; in fact, I do expect counter-examples to crop up. Examples of verbs apparently resisting an interpretation along the lines proposed here are *owe, belong,* and *need.* It may turn out therefore that additional features of similarity will have to be hypothesized. Alternatively, it may be necessary to assume that for some verbs the child will have to learn on the basis of purely formal similarity how they function in sentences.[10]

The kinds of semantic similarity discussed so far do not seem to exist in subjects of adjectival and nominal predicates (e.g., of *is foolish* and *is a fool*). Elsewhere (Schlesinger, 1982, pp. 283–284) I have proposed that these have developed out of the attributive relation. Further, verbs with subject complements (see Quirk, Greenbaum, Leech, & Svartvik, 1978, Sections 2.4–2.5) do not seem to be amenable to a treatment similar to that in the preceding discussion. But the fact that the SA hypothesis does not explain every single instance hardly detracts from its value.

The semantic assimilation hypothesis does not pretend of course to explain everything that goes on in language learning; it only deals with the acquisition of a certain kind of categories. As seen in Section 11, there are other types of categories to which the hypothesis does not apply at all.

9. THE FUZZINESS OF RELATIONAL CATEGORIES

We have already noted that subject is a cluster concept. At its center is the prototypical agent, and around it there are instances of what are agents to a greater or lesser extent. A gradient of agentivity can also be observed in the following set of sentences:

a. She wrote the answer down.   (27)
b. She figured out the answer.

---

[10]As far as historical development is concerned, these verbs may originally have been more action-like. Anita Mittwoch has pointed out to me in conversation, that the subject category may be the result of assimilation to the topic. It would be worthwhile to pursue the possibility that assimilation to the topic and to the agent are complementary processes resulting in the mature subject category. Schachter (1976) shows that, while in most languages the subject is associated with both the topic and the actor, Philippine languages have a division of subject-like properties between topic and actor. Cf. also Chien (1985).

   c. She guessed the answer.
   d. She remembered the answer.
   e. She knew the answer.

As one moves down the line, the agent becomes less and less active, but even the subject of *know* is perceived as having some measure of control, as shown in the studies mentioned in Section 6.3.

Difference in degree of membership may have effects on the applicability of linguistic rules. The less action-like the verb, the less likely it is to take the progressive *-ing* ending and to enter into several other linguistic constructions; see de Villiers (1980) for some relevant data and discussion. However, it is not only the kind of verb that is crucial here, but also its use; see Quirk et al. (1978, Sections 3.40–3.41). The fact that, through semantic assimilation, a verb has been tagged as an action verb does not imply that it is always going to be regarded as denoting a full-blooded action.

It is instructive to examine the following examples of interchanges between two speakers (A and B), which illustrate the acceptability of pro-forms.

   a. A:The old man climbed the ladder.   (28)
      B:He always does it.
   b. A:The old man fell from the ladder.
      B:*He always does it.

The pro-form *do it* applies only to "real" activity. The response in (28)b would be acceptable only if the speaker's intention had been that the old man fell on purpose. By comparison, the pro-form *do that* is more tolerant, as shown in (29)b; but when the degree of agentivity declines still further, it too can be blocked:

   a. A:The old man climbed the ladder.   (29)
      B:I wonder why he did that.
   b. A:the old man fell from the ladder.
      B:I wonder why he did that.
   c. A:Bill shocks his wife.
      B:I wonder why he does that.
   d. A:Bill admires his wife.
      B:*I wonder why he does that.[11]
   e. A:Bill knows some Latin.
      B:*I wonder why he does that.

In (29)c the subject has both the feature of Control and of Cause, and it is

---

[11]Martin Braine has pointed out to me that *do* is more tolerant than *do that:* in (29)d, *I wonder why he does.* sounds all right.

therefore more similar to the prototypical agent than that of (29)d and of (29)e, which has only the feature of Control; cf. (18) in Section 6.3.

A much fuller treatment of these and additional pro-forms is to be found in Quirk et al. (1978, Section 10.55). Their treatment strongly suggests that verbs lie along a continuum of degree of membership in the action category.

10. SEMANTIC ASSIMILATION VERSUS "BOOTSTRAPPING"

A recent proposal concerning the acquisition of relational categories (Mac-namara, 1982; Pinker, 1982, 1984) is similar in certain respects to the SA hypothesis, but radically different in others. Macnamara and Pinker start from the assumption that there are innate grammatical categories. Saying that a category is innate, however, leaves us with problems of how an instantiation of it in the input language can be identified by the child. How, for instance, does the child know which word is a noun? Or which part of a given sentence is the innately known subject? Here semantic correspondences come to his aid. To each innate grammatical category corresponds a semantic one: three-dimensional objects correspond to the noun category, agent to the subject category, and so on. This correspondence, too, is innately known. The child assumes that the correspondence holds, and construes words denoting objects as nouns and the part of the sentence referring to an agent as the subject. In most cases he will not go wrong, because in talking to children, adults usually speak of objects, not of abstract concepts; of prototypical agents and not of experiencers, etc., that is, the correspondence is far greater than in adult language (cf. also Macnamara, 1982, pp.122–124, on correspondences in the child's productions). Once the child has identified grammatical categories through this correspondence, he begins to note their formal properties. It is such formal criteria that define the adult category, and once initial identification has taken place, the child begins to discover those and no longer relies on semantic correspondences. As Macnamara (1982) puts it: "Though semantics gets him off the ground, it cannot carry him all the way. Ultimately linguistic rules must take over the initial sortings" (p.104). Pinker calls this process of hooking on to semantic processes for identifying innate grammatical categories "semantic bootstrapping."

Both the SA hypothesis and the semantic bootstrapping hypothesis claim that the child capitalizes on semantic-syntactic correspondences in learning the grammatical system. But here the agreement between the two theories ends. According to the bootstrapping hypothesis, information about such correspondences is innate. It enables the child to take her first steps on the newly found terrain of language, but once she reaches the shore, she sinks the semantic boat that brought her there. The SA hypothesis does not postulate such innate knowledge and does not impute such volatility to the child. It claims that she retains the semantic boat, since it can still do good service in exploring other parts of the new territory. Macnamara's and Pinker's conclusion that the boat soon becomes useless is based on an all-or-none approach to the appraisal of semantics as a clue to linguistic categories: adult categories are not semantically defined, *ergo* semantics is of no use at all (beyond the initial bootstrapping) for the discovery of their extension. As the discussion in this chapter has shown, however, things are not as simple as that. While linguistic categories are not semantically homogeneous, various family resemblances hold between instances of the category, and these enable the child to stake out their boundaries. It would be extremely implausible to assume that the child is impervious to such similarities of meaning, considering that meaning is central to the child's concerns.

Besides considerations of plausibility, the two theories might be evaluated in terms of the range of the phenomena that they account for. Here the SA hypothesis has a distinct advantage on two counts:

1. Semantic constraint phenomena (see Section 7) show that the subject has the "flavor" of an agent. This can be explained as a consequence of the gradual extension of the agent through SA. The semantic bootstrapping hypothesis does not adress itself to these phenomena.

2. The phylogenesis of language. As shown earlier, the SA hypothesis at least adumbrates a solution of the problem of the semantically heterogeneous composition of linguistic categories. The semantic bootstrapping hypothesis, by contrast, offers no explanation.

11.   FORMAL CATEGORIES

Theory construction is a somewhat imperialistic enterprise. One tends to view a single construct, a single rule, a single process as providing the one, overall explanation of phenomena in a given area. As far as language acquisition and language functioning are concerned, this tendency should be resisted, in my opinion. Not that I intend to expostulate against the principle of parsimony, but it seems to me that if anything is certain in this field it is that the complexity of the processes involved is such as to rule out an explanation in terms of a single all-embracing principle. The heuristic strategy of seeing how far an explanation can be made to go should not be dispensed with, but one should not have any illusions as to the eventual outcome. To believe in simple explanations of language acquisition is to be simple-minded (see Schlesinger, 1977, pp.115–117, 123–124 for similar considerations regarding the comprehension process).

The fact that much of language acquisition involves discovering form-meaning correspondences should not lead us into the error of viewing semantics as the child's one-and-only clue to grammar. But this may often seem to be implied, though not explicitly stated, in the writings of proponents of the semantic approach (myself included). A forceful reminder that a semantics-only approach is not feasible is due to Yonata Levy's work on the acquisition of inflections (Levy, 1983, and this volume). She shows (convincingly, I think) that the acquisition of gender categories proceeds entirely on the basis of formal criteria, and argues that the fact that these categories are acquired early shows that the very young child must be assumed to engage in purely formal analysis.

That children are capable of forming categories based entirely on formal criteria hardly needs to be demonstrated by research; it becomes evident on considering languages that have different inflectional paradigms for nouns (i.e., the inflection for a given case—say the genitive—of one noun differs from that of another one), which do not have any semantic correlates. Learning the correct inflections for the various classes of nouns involves learning a purely formal categorization. The contribution of Levy's research, however, lies in that it shows (a) that such formal categories appear in children's speech from very early on, and (b) that in learning a classification that is not completely semantically arbitrary, like that of gender (which corresponds partly with the classification according to natural sex), the child does not adopt a semantic strategy: there is no evidence in the data reviewed by Levy that the child tries to assimilate masculine nouns into the category of male animate beings, for instance.[12]

Further, both Gordon (1985) and Gathercole (1985) have shown that the count-mass distinction is acquired through formal clues rather than via the semantic object-substance distinction. The reason seems to be that, in English, there is not a very consistent correlation between these two distinctions.

If children can thus be shown to engage in formal analysis in the early stages of language development, one might argue that there is no need to hypothesize an additional process of semantic assimilation. Perhaps **all** formation of relational categories is due to the child observing formal regularities (notice again the imperialistic streak!).

There is an important difference, however, between the formal categories of gender and of inflectional paradigms on the one hand, and the relational categories which we have been dealing with in the present chapter, on the other. The former are surface phenomena, for the acquisition of which distributional evidence seems particularly appropriate. Relational categories, by contrast, pertain to underlying structures whose often complex relationships with surface structures may be far from transparent to the child unless he resorts to meaning relationships in ferreting them out. The child's ability to handle surface phe-

---

[12]Note that such a process would be different from the semantic assimilation process as we have defined it here. Inanimate objects of masculine gender are no more similar to males, on the whole, than inanimate objects of feminine gender, and thus there is no semantic similarity that dovetails with the formal similarity. Levy's data are therefore not directly relevant to the SA hypothesis. Interestingly, children learning a language in which the formal properties of the gender categories are less systematic and hence less transparent to the child apparently learn these categories on the basis of semantic cues (Mulford, 1985; see, however, Gordon, 1985).

nomena by means of formal analysis therefore does not show that he is capable of discovering underlying categories by the same means. It should also be pointed out that rules for relational categories are presumably acquired first and those for gender, inflectional paradigms, and so on, are superimposed on them and modify them, as discussed in Levy and Schlesinger (this volume).

But let us disregard for a moment the lack of evidence and consider the proposal of a purely formal analysis on its own. The objections to such a proposal should by now be familiar. It does not have parsimony on its side, because the form-meaning correspondences would have to be learned in any case. Further, it has to make the totally gratuitous assumption that in performing formal analyses the child remains impervious to the semantic similarities, which, as we have seen, are ubiquitous. Finally, the SA hypothesis has the advantage of accounting for phenomena of semantic constraints discussed in Section 7, and to a certain extent also for the phylogeny of syntactic categories (Section 8).

Recently, Wolff (this volume) has shown that a computer program can be implemented that learns how to parse sentences. Distributional analysis employing a few simple principles is sufficient for discovering surface structures. Note, however, that the fact that they **can** be discovered in this manner does not imply that the child **does** so. The proposal that Wolff's computer program be taken as a model of the child acquiring language is open to the objections that have been made above: it does not solve the problem of learning form-meaning correspondences.[13] Nevertheless, Wolff's research is important for a theory of language acquisition, since the learning process described by him may reinforce other more semantically based processes. As is well known, redundancy in the system may be useful to combat noise.

To summarize, formal analyses have a part to play in the acquisition of semantically arbitrary categories and may also be ancillary to semantically based processes.

12.   THE PROBLEM OF PRELINGUISTIC RELATIONAL CATEGORIES

In our previous account of semantic assimilation we have shown how the child's early semantic categories gradually expand into the syntactic categories of the adult system. The existence of semantic categories was taken for granted: The child was assumed to start out with relations like agent-action, agent-location, action-patient, and the like, which he learns to realize in his native language. We now broach the question of whether this assumption is warranted. Are semantic

---

[13]Wolff (in press) has discussed applications of his model to the acquisition of semantic knowledge.

categories immediately given, or do they have to be formed by the child in the course of his development?

12.1 The Alternatives

The assumption that semantic categories are immediately given, i.e., that the child cannot help perceiving his environment in terms of agents performing actions on patients, seems to be a very plausible one. It is tempting for the theorist to make such an assumption, since it would provide him with a firm basis on which to erect his explanation of rule acquisition. I myself once succumbed to this temptation when I wrote that semantic relations were "part and parcel of our way of viewing the world—part of our intellectual outfit" (Schlesinger, 1971, p.98). But that a thesis is convenient for the theorist is not a very good reason to subscribe to it; rather, it is a reason to suspect it. And, on second thought, it seems that one might with just as much justification adopt a different thesis, namely, that the child "comes into a world that is a blooming and buzzing confusion, rather than one that is neatly parceled into Agents, Actions, and so on" (Schlesinger, 1982, p.71).

There are, then, two alternatives to be considered:

(i) Semantic categories are prelinguistic, that is, they are either part of an innate mental apparatus, or else are formed through the child's interaction with his or her environment.

(ii) Semantic categories are formed in the course of learning the native language.

These alternatives are explored more fully in the following. Here we only note that they are not necessarily mutually exclusive, since some semantic categories may be prelinguistic while others may be formed through learning the linguistic system.

Let us consider now several arguments that can be marshalled for and against these two possibilities.

12.2 Interpretation and Categorization

An argument for the existence of prelinguistic categories runs as folows. Once the child is called upon to use language meaningfully, he must already have at his disposal semantic categories, for it is notions such as agent, action, and patient, in terms of which he must interpret the world around him and relate to it. Learning the grammatical system cannot even get off the ground without the child having categories to start with.

I suspect these contentions stem from our proclivity to conceptualize cognitive activity in familiar terms; the only ones available seem to be those observed in the operation of language. Our linguistic way of handling thoughts is so deeply ingrained in us that we cannot imagine how one could manage without a language, or at least an unobservable "language of thought." At any rate, this argument for prelinguistic categories rests on a confusion. It fails to distinguish between interpretation of the environment and its categorization. Obviously, before the child begins to talk meaningfully about events and situations he must be capable of interpreting these events and situations, and he must do so basically in the same way adults interpret them: who does what to whom, what is situated where, and so on. This does not imply, however, that he **categorizes** the relations manifest in these events and relations.

This distinction is somewhat difficult to grasp because, when trying to describe how the child interprets the environment, we find ourselves impelled to use terms like agent, action, and patient. But note that it is **we** who conceptualize in these terms what goes on in the child's mind; it is not necessarily the case that the child, too, uses those categories. For consider what it would mean for the child to have a relational category, say, the agent category (i.e., the prototypical agent category, before it is expanded through semantic assimilation; see Sections 2–5, and cf. Note 2). It would mean that the child perceives the agent in one situation to have something in common with, or in some sense belong together with, the agent of a different situation. Intuitively this often seems to be extremely implausible. Consider the situation described in the following sentences:

  a. Polly puts the kettle on.   (30)
  b. Cindy hits Clara.
  c. Daddy climbs the ladder.
  d. The dog chases the rabbit.
  e. The cat jumps.

Situations like these can presumably be appropriately interpreted by the 2-year-old. But why should he regard the agents in all these situations as belonging to one category? On witnessing (30)b, what should make him lump Cindy together with Polly of (30)a? Why should it not be enough for Cindy to be regarded as the hitter and for Polly as the one who puts the kettle on, without their being perceived as having anything in common with each other? It is not even clear what could be meant by saying that the child views Polly, Cindy, Daddy, the dog, and the cat in these situations as belonging to one and the same category, for there could apparently be no direct consequence of such a categorization for the prelinguistic child's awareness of these events (see Schlesinger, 1982, p.94, for further discussion).

Things may begin to change when the child is exposed to language. Language treats Polly, Cindy, Daddy, the dog, and the cat alike in the above situations. The child will sooner or later notice this, and when that happens he may be said to "have" a category, which can then be employed in applying linguistic rules.

Thus language provides both the clue to the agent category and the motive for employing it. This possibility is discussed in detail in a later section. Before language starts, however, the child may manage without case-like relational categories. He presumably has categories of objects (e.g., food) and perhaps of events (e.g., play activities), but it is not at all clear that he categorizes relations between events or activities and places, between persons and activities, etc. Instead, in each case the child may perceive a relation that is unique, i.e., that is not perceived to be the same as the relation encountered in another, similar, situation. As the philosopher William Hamilton (1859) put it, ". . . a relation between particular objects is just as particular as the objects themselves" (p.318).

To avoid misunderstanding, it should be added that an absence of categories does not imply a lack of the ability to make distinctions and of the (obverse) ability to see similarities. Humans, and lower organisms as well, must have inborn similarity spaces if they are to be able to learn at all, since all generalization is based on perceived similarity. One boy running after another boy may seem to the child to be much more similar to (30)d than to (30)c. But having a similarity space is not tantamount to having a partitioning of this space, and attainment of categories requires such a partitioning. Put differently, seeing greater and lesser similarities is a precondition for categorization, but it does not entail it. Whether or not the prelinguistic child imposes such a categorization on the world is an empirical question that cannot be settled by "How else?" arguments. There is no *a priori* reason to rule out the following hypotheses:

H1: The child does not have relational categories prior to learning language.

If H1 is correct, the relational categories of the linguistic system will have to be formed in the course of learning this system; that is, the child will have to acquire grammatical rules and, simultaneously, the categories these rules operate on. That this is feasible is shown in Section 13. In the following, empirical findings relevant to H1 are discussed.

12.3   Experiments with Prelinguistic Infants

In an ingenious series of studies, Roberta Golinkoff investigated the prelinguistic categories of children who had not yet reached the two-word stage. The infants were exposed to a film showing two actors interacting—e.g., a man pushing a woman—and in which after a while the roles of the actors were reversed (the woman pushing the man). Role reversal resulted in greater increase of attention (as measured by cardiac deceleration and visual fixation) than change in a control condition in which the direction of action was reversed (Golinkoff & Kerr, 1978). However, there is no evidence that the categories of agent (actor) or patient (recipient) were operative in the experiment. The infants' attention may have increased because they noted that the one who at first did the pushing (i.e., moved in the direction of the other object) ceased to do so and was pushed instead; this change may have been more significant for the children than change of direction. In other words, the children may have interpreted the events correctly without having categorized them.

Aware of this possibility, Golinkoff (1981) conducted an additional experiment, similarly designed, in which the actor, puppet A, performed a variety of hitting, kissing and pushing actions on the recipient, puppet B. Then two new conditions were introduced: (i) a new action performed by the previous actor and recipient (puppet A hugs puppet B), (ii) a new action performed with role reversal (puppet B hugs puppet A). The finding that the latter type of change had a stronger effect on attention than the former, at least for some of her subjects, was interpreted by Golinkoff (1981) as "at least a hint that infants are functioning with generalized concepts and not action-specific rules" (pp.429–430).

But the hint is very faint indeed. To establish the existence of a general concept one would have to introduce not only different actions, as Golinkoff did, but also different agents or recipients (which is probably not feasible with this kind of experimental setup). As it is, her results merely show that children distinguish A-as-agent from A-as-recipient (and from B-as-agent), not that they consider all agents as belonging to the same category. Consider further that the child cannot even be claimed to have a general action category. The film showed actions of a specific kind—hitting, kissing, and pushing—that is, actions involving contact between the two puppets, and generalization was to hugging, which also involves such contact. If put to test, they might have failed to generalize to other types of action, e.g., to A throwing something to puppet B, or chasing puppet B, where there is no contact between puppets. We thus cannot credit Golinkoff's subjects with an action category, but only with a much narrower "contacting" category. Let us represent this by a formula:[14]

$$\text{puppet A}_{(contacter)} - [\text{contact}] - \text{puppetB}_{(contactee)} \tag{31}$$

This is still a long way off from the broad categories (agent, recipient, etc.) currently assumed to operate in child language. But it might be a preliminary stage in the formation of such categories, as discussed in a later section. On the other hand, there is nothing in Golinkoff's experiment to rule out the possibility that the child has, in addition, some broader relational categories.

There is, however, some indirect evidence that the child does not have such

---

[14]The following conventions will be adopted here: square brackets enclose variable terms, which can be substituted for by various words (unlike, e.g., "puppet A," which can refer only to this instance, since a different formula applies to "puppet B"). A dash is used to mark concatenation, whereas the plus sign indicates that the words that express the terms appear in a fixed sequence, according to a linguistic rule.

broad categories. The evidence is from three sources: (i) adults' judgment of the relations expressed in sentences, (ii) cross-linguistic comparisons of the linguistic expression of relations, and (iii) relational categories in early speech. In the following, each of these types of evidence is examined.

12.4 Judgements of Relations in Sentences

Indirect support for H1 comes from a categorization study (Schlesinger, 1979). It was argued that if relational categories precede language and are independent of it, they should lend themselves to the classification of events. Thus, adults should not have any difficulty distinguishing between events involving the instrumental and those involving what is called the comitative relation, i.e., between those exemplified in (32)a and (32)b, respectively.

a. Carol dug up the flower bed by means of a kitchen knife.   (32)
b. Carol dug up the flower bed together with her husband.

Cognitively, these two relations seem to be as far apart as any two relations could be. However, both may be expressed by the same construction in English (and many other languages), namely by a *with*-phrase: *with a kitchen knife, with her husband*. Already this fact should make us wonder what these two relations might have in common. The answer is that the instrumental and comitative, rather than being two discrete relations, lie on a continuum, with events like those in (32) lying close to the two poles of this continuum. This continuum is illustrated by the following set of sentences:

a. The pantomimist gave a show with the clown.   (33)
b. The engineer built the machine with an assistant.
c. The general captured the hill with a squad of paratroopers.
d. The acrobat performed an act with an elephant.
e. The blind man crossed the street with his dog.
f. The officer caught the smuggler with a police dog.
g. The prisoner won the appeal with a highly paid lawyer.
h. The Nobel Prize winner found the solution with a computer.
i. The sportsman hunted deer with a rifle.
j. The hoodlum broke the window with a stone.

Subjects were asked to rank these sentences (presented in a different sequence) from those expressing most clearly accompaniment to those expressing most clearly instrumentality, and they rather consistently ranked them in the above order. In a subsequent study (Schlesinger & Pat-Horenczyk, in preparation), subjects were asked to judge to which extent each of these sentences expressed the notion of accompaniment, and to which extent they expressed the notion of instrumentality. It turned out that in some instances one and the same sentence was judged to express both accompaniment and instrumentality; particularly (33)c-(33)e rated high on both these notions. A model of the mind as equipped with discrete relational categories does not fit in with this finding.

In general, the order of the sentences obtained in the ranking study, (33), was replicated in the rating study. That these results were not due to a possible ambiguity of the sentences was shown by still another study, in which the acceptability of paraphrase of these sentences was judged. When *with* in (33) was replaced by *together with* or by *and* (unequivocal comitative constructions), acceptability increased from a to j.

Schlesinger and Pat-Horenczyk (in preparation) obtained similar findings with an additional set of sentences that involved, besides the comitative and the instrumental, the notion of manner (e.g., . . . *with care*). Again, no pigeonholing of events into relational categories was found to be possible.

Now, if there are no discrete relational categories in the cognition of adults, there seems to be no reason to assume their existence in the minds of prelinguistic children. These studies thus support H1.

12.5 Crosslinguistic Evidence

In Section 12.2 we noted that events are interpreted in terms of relations (who does what to whom, where, when, and how, etc.), but that one cannot rule out the possibility that the latter are particular relations which are not classified as belonging to any relational categories. Suppose now that there are such relational categories and that these are taken over from the prelinguistic stage into the child's growing linguistic system. Then one would expect these categories to appear in all the languages of the world, because there are no grounds for assuming far-reaching differences in the innate mental apparatus of children the world over. Even environmental differences, great as these undoubtedly are, cannot be plausibly claimed to result in differences in the very early system of categories in terms of which the child apprehends the world verbally.

There is ample evidence, however, that the languages of the world differ in the extension of the relational categories they employ; they carve up reality in different ways. Here is an example. In English one says *I am cold* and *I am hungry;* in French one "has" cold or hunger: *J'ai froid, J'ai faim.* The variety of means employed by different languages to express the experiencer are quite impressive. A sample of ways of expressing just one kind of experience, being thirsty, is presented in Table 6.1.[15] The principle employed there in literal translation from these languages into English is quite simple: When a language

---

[15]These data were supplied by native speakers interviewed by the writer, except for the information on Moré, which appears in Nida (1964, p.214).

TABLE 6.1

Expression of Experiencer in THE MAN IS THIRSTY in Various Languages

Experiencer Expressed as	Languages	Literal Translation
attributee	English, Croation, Danish, Arabic	The man is thirsty.
possessor	French, Spanish, German, Estonian	The man has thirst.
possessed	Moré	Thirst has the man.
agent	Turkish, Tajiki, Mandarin	The man thirsts.
patient	Georgian, Efik, German	It thirsts the man.
recipient	Rumanian	It thirsts to the man.

expresses the relation between experiencer and experience by means of a construction used for expressing, e.g., *The man has a sister*, the translation *The man has thirst* is given; if it uses the construction employed for *The man walks* or *The man boils the water*, the translation is *The man thirsts;* and so on; and the relational categories given for *The man* are possessor and agent, respectively.

A similar picture emerges when the coding of other experiences—being happy, sad, ill, etc.—is looked at. Furthermore, the discrepancies appear not only across languages but also within one language. In English one *is thirsty* but *has a headache;* in German one has a headache, too, but can either be thirsty (*ist durstig*) or have thirst (*hat Durst*); and when a speaker of German is cold (note that, in English, the experiencer of cold is attributee!), he is regarded as a sort of recipient: *ihm ist (es) kalt* (*ihm*—dative). Most languages employ two or more relational categories for expressing the experiences studied.[16]

Suppose now that children categorize their experiences of reality before they begin to learn language. To which catgegories do they then assign such extremely common internal experiences as being cold, thirsty, hungry, etc.? Whatever the categorization adopted, it would fail to match the categorization of some of the languages of the world.[17]

The experiencer provides an especially striking example of interlinguistic divergencies of categorization. Similar phenomena can be observed in other domains as well. Take meteorological phenomena, like rain, snow, and hail. These are referred to by nouns. But in English (and several other languages) one may refer to them as actions or events: *it rains, snows, hails*. Not so in Polish,

---

[16]Some might prefer to interpret these phenomena (in line with Fillmore's [1968] case grammar) in terms of differences between surface realizations of a single underlying experiencer relation. However, the fact that these realizations are selected by the language stands in need of an explanation. According to the SA hypothesis, what is, logically, the experiencer has been assimilated into other categories.

[17]One might argue that while relational categories are innate and universal, there may be alternative ways in which events can be classified into those categories. Further, both broader and more narrow categories may be innate. This thesis differs from the one discussed here, and seems to be tantamount to the claim that our mental equipment enables us to discover the system of categories of our native language. Nobody would deny this.

which has *it rains,* but no verb for snow or hail; again, Russian has a verb referring to snow coming down but none for rain or hail. There may of course be purely formal linguistic factors at work here, but if a particular categorization went down with speakers of a language, this must have been because there was no previous language-independent system of relational categories which impelled them to categorize these natural phenomena in just one way rather than in another.

Another example. In English, sleeping can be expressed either as a sort of action, by means of the verb *to sleep* (with semantic assimilation obviously at work here), or as an attribute of the sleeper, a state he is in: *be asleep.* Polish and Russian are like English in this respect; French, German, and Hungarian, by contrast, offer no such choice: they provide their speakers only with verbs and not with adjectives to refer to sleeping. If there were an innate or acquired way of parcelling out events which decrees that being asleep is an attribute of the sleeper, one should expect all languages to conform and provide the linguistic means of describing sleeping as an attribute.

There are languages in which the boundaries of the agent category differ radically from those of this category in English and most European languages. So-called ergative language have the same case ending for the patient of transitive verbs and for the subject of intransitive verbs, while the subject of transitive verbs is accorded a different case. Thus, in ergative languages, *deer* would have the same form in (33)i as in *The deer escaped,* but a different form in *The deer tore up the grass.* For speakers of these languages, then, the agent of an action involving a patient is distinct from the agent of actions involving no patient.

12.6 Relational Categories in Early Speech

There is a growing body of evidence that the relational categories underlying children's two-word utterances are extremely narrow. Braine (1976) found patterns like

a. [ingesting]+[thing ingested]   (34)
b. [size]+[thing having size]

If the child had broad prelinguistic categories of the kind used in language, these would certainly come in handy in learning the grammatical system, and one would expect therefore these children to have exhibited these broader categories. Braine's finding suggests that, for the children observed, the categories in (34) were either in the process of being formed through language, or else that they were prelinguistic, while the corresponding broader categories, [action]—[patient] and [attribute]—[attributee] were not.

One might object that not too much store should be set by production data, since all corpora are selective and, besides, the child may fail to put to good use all that he really knows. But recently some evidence has been forthcoming for the restricted scope of early categories in comprehension as well. Roberts (1983) suspects that at early Stage I comprehension of verbs "may be learned initially within lexically specific formulas" (p.448). Another relevant study is by Huttenlocher, Smiley, and Charney (1983), who found that the child's first verbs are applied to her own actions and not to actions observed in others. In a comprehension study, these authors found that of verbs describing actions in others, verbs referring to what they call "motions" (e.g., *dance, sing*), were understood earlier than those referring to actions effecting a change in another entity (e.g., *bring, finish, hurt*). Parental input did not account for these findings. This study, then, suggests that among the child's earliest semantic relations is

$$\text{self}_{(\text{mover})}\text{—[moving]} \tag{35}$$

Only subsequently could others, and not only the child herself, figure as mover, i.e., (35) was generalized to

$$\text{[mover]—[moving]} \tag{36}$$

Now, these findings were obtained with children who were already using language. At the prelinguistc stage the child **may** have had (35), but not the later-appearing (36), and *a fortiori*, nothing like the agent-action relation.[18] It is possible of course that even (35) is formed only in the course of acquiring language, and that there are no prelinguistic categories at all.

12.7 An Alternative to H1

H1, it will be remembered, states that the child has no prelinguistic categories at all. The data reviewed in the preceding sections suggest an alternative hypothesis:

H2: Prior to learning language the child has only relational categories of very narrow scope.

Examples of such narrow categories might be (34) and (35). While the studies reviewed in the preceding sections do not provide evidence for such categories before the child approaches the language learning task, they at least make H2 seem plausible. The data on adults' judgments of relations in sentences and the crosslinguistic evidence cited above may perhaps be construed, with some diffi-

---

[18]Braine and Hardy (1982) report findings showing that before they have a comprehensive agentive category, children operate with a broad "Subject of Attribute" category. These findings, too, were obtained with older children (mainly 4–6 year-olds), and do not contradict the claim made here that the earliest categories are quite narrow.

culty, as compatible with the claim that there are some very narrow prelinguistic categories that are subsequently combined by language in different ways. The only positive evidence for H2, however, comes from a single experiment by Golinkoff, reviewed above, in which the effect of prelinguistic categories was observed only in "the younger girls (1 : 4) and the older boys (2 : 9)" (Golinkoff, 1981, p.429).

At the present state of our knowledge it seems best therefore to construe H2 as an upper bound: If there are any prelinguistic categories at all, they are of very narrow scope. The lower bound would then be represented by H1, which denies the existence of prelinguistic relational categories altogether.

H2 may afford some relief to those who have difficulty in accepting H1 on the grounds that it leaves the child without anything to hold on to in grappling intellectually with his environment and with language (an argument which has been found wanting in Section 12.2). By clinging to relational categories, however narrow, they may feel like being on firm theoretical ground, rather than in a vaguely conceived cognitive quagmire.

If H2 is true, then, as already remarked, certain relational categories must either be innate or acquired through interaction with the environment (or some may be innate while others are acquired). The possibility that they are acquired through nonlinguistic experience is further explored in Section 14. Whichever hypothesis is correct, H1 or H2, the relational categories in early language—like agent-action, action-location—cannot be taken for granted, but rather must be accounted for as a product of the acquisition process. One will have to show how narrow categories may be merged (in consonance with H2) into broader ones or how relational categories (if H1 is true) may crystallize out of particular relations (see Section 12.2 for an explanation of this notion). The following section proposes an account of the processes involved.

13.   FORMATION OF RELATIONAL CATEGORIES THROUGH LEARNING LANGUAGE

The child, we have argued, approaches the language learning task with either a very flimsy and inadequate system of case-like categories (according to H2) or none at all (according to H1). How, then, does he discover the categories employed by his language?

13.1   The Role of Formal and of Semantic Similarity

According to one proposal (Bowerman 1973a, pp.176–187, 1973b), the child notices that different situations and events are expressed linguistically in a similar manner, and as a consequence those elements of the situation that are treated similarly are assigned to the same category. For instance, "by hearing sentences in which all agents are treated in the same way, he acquires the agent concept with rules for realizing it in speech'' (Schlesinger, 1974, p.45).

But is such categorization according to purely formal similarities feasible at all? Consider what formal similarities there are to be picked up by the child learning English at the two-word stage (which is the stage at which knowledge of rules begins to be evident, and hence relational categories must be available). The agent word, for instance, appears in first position. Now, this is hardly a cue that singles out the agent; there are other relational categories expressed by first-position words, such as the attribute (cf. *big house*) and the possessor (*daddy's slippers*). True, such ambiguity of form need not be an insurmountable obstacle for the child. Conceivably, one category may initially be more frequent in the input, or more frequently attended to, and that category may be formed on the basis of its relative position well before another category characterized by the same relative position is tackled. But here the explanation becomes definitely labored.

A further difficulty with this proposal has to do with the insufficient saliency of formal cues in relatively noninflected languages, like English. In English, most of the cues for the principal relational categories available to the child in the earliest stages of language acquisition are positional cues. Now, position per se is not much to hold on to; that a given word appears, say, at the beginning of a short utterance is not something very likely to come to the child's mind when she encounters another utterance in which that word appears at the beginning. It seems, then, that formal similarities by themselves just do not suffice for the child who sets out to discover the relational categories operating in a language like English, which is poor in inflections and relies mainly on word order. The situation is different for the child learning an inflectional language, where relational categories are distinguished by case markings. (Inflection is presumably more salient than relative position, [Slobin, 1982]; that the child does not use inflections in his early utterances should not be taken to imply that he does not notice them.) At any rate a theory of the formation of relational categories cannot be based on formal similarity alone. We must look elsewhere for an explanation of how the child discovers the relational categories of a ''positional'' language like English.

Here we are reminded of the semantic assimilation hypothesis. Semantic assimilation, it will be remembered, rests on both formal similarity and similarity of content (cf. Section 2). The solution to be proposed in the following extends the explanation offered by the semantic assimilation hypothesis backward, to the earliest phases of acquiring relational categories. As argued before, one would have to assign a role to semantic similarity even if there were no good reason to doubt the sufficiency of formal similarity, because it seems quite implausible that the child should simply close his eyes to similarities of meaning when he is trying to find out how meanings are expressed. Semantic similarity by itself, however, often will not unequivocally determine how relations are to be assigned to relational categories (recall how the experiencer is expressed in different languages, Table 6.1). But formal cues and perceived similarities in the events referred to may be assumed to be mutually supportive. The formal system serves to categorize relational meanings, and conversely, the meanings actuate the categorization of forms. If formal similarity is weak and semantic similarity blind, the weak may lead the blind and be carried by it.

A handy example is the English plural. There are similarities in meaning between various pluralized words, but the similarity is not so large that the correct categorization forces itself upon the child. Consider that the plural form (_____s) is appropriate for, *inter alia,* heaps of things (apples), bunches (grapes, fingers), rows (books), pairs (eyes, hands) and extended patches (flowers in a flower bed). All these have to be lumped together as instances of plurality, being more than one of a kind. But "more than one of a kind" is a rather abstract notion with various concrete manifestations. Our linguistic habits may have already smoothed over the differences that have to be bridged here, which must have been more strident when, as children, we set out to form the notion of plurality. The plural form then clinched the matter.

Now note that "the plural form" is itself a category that has to be formed. The written form, _____s, masks the fact that there are different phonetic realizations of the plural: /s/, /z/, /Iz/. These will be assigned to a single category because of the similarity of the semantic notions referred to.

There remain problems to be solved, however. Not all categories the child acquires are semantically as coherent as the plural, and not all formal ones are as salient (in spite of the phonemic variants) as the plural _____s. The solution proposed in the following sections is based on the principle of gradual expansion of a relational category: the category will initially comprise instances between which formal and semantic similarity is greatest and will gradually attract those that are increasingly less similar. To develop this proposal, we have to look first at certain linguistic patterns that may serve as "stepping stones" to more mature constructions.

13.2   Pivot Patterns and Fixed Strings

The notion of **pivot pattern** (PP) has been introduced to account for the acquisition of relational categories (Schlesinger, 1982, pp.186–195). PPs are related to, but somewhat different from, Braine's (1963) notion of pivot grammar. The latter was discredited after examination of several corpora of child language had shown that the distributional patterns specified by Braine were not always present (Bowerman, 1973a; Brown, 1973, pp.97–104). Most of these distributional criteria are not included in the definition of a PP. A child is credited with a PP if his corpus includes two-word utterances in which (i) the same word appears in a fixed position, and (ii) the recurrent word stands in the same relation to the other

TABLE 6.2
Examples of Pivot Patterns

Relation	Language	Pivot Pattern	Examples
Agent-Action:	Swedish	Mamma + ____	mommy + <u>build</u>, <u>help</u>, ...
	Finnish	tipu + ____	chick + <u>sing</u>, <u>watch</u>, ...
	German	Mone + ____	Simone + <u>cry</u>, <u>ring</u>, ...
	English	____ + <u>walk</u>	<u>Andrew</u>, <u>daddy</u>, ... + walk
	German	____ + <u>schläft</u>	<u>teddy bear</u>, <u>doll</u>, ... + sleeps
Possessor- Possession:	English	daddy + ____	daddy + <u>shoe</u>, <u>car</u>, ...
	Swedish	Åså + ____	[name] + <u>diaper</u>, <u>hat</u>, ...
	German	Mone + ____	Simone + <u>spoon</u>, stick, ...
	Samoan	____ + <u>a'u</u>	<u>boat</u>, <u>candy</u>, ... + me

word in the utterance.[19] Condition (ii) did not figure in Braine's conception of a pivot grammar.

To illustrate, the following utterances have been reported for Eve at 25.5 months (Brown & Fraser, 1964, p.64):

a. carriage broken   (37)
b. chair broken
c. dolly broken
d. rocker broken
e. something broken

Here [attributee]+*broken* is a PP. The relation between *broken* and *carriage* is the same as that between *broken* and *chair, broken* and *dolly,* etc.

PPs are very widespread in child speech. Table 6.2 gives examples of PPs observed in different languages, involving what one might call (very roughly, as will become clear below) the agent-action relation and the possessor–possession relation. Further examples are given in Schlesinger (1982, pp.189–193; on the relationship between PPs and Braine's [1976] limited scope formulas, see ibid., p.207). The study by Roberts (1983) referred to in Section 12.6 also provides some evidence for patterns restricted to specific lexical items.

It is proposed that the PP is one of the stepping stones to mastery of what one may call **open relational patterns.** These are fully productive patterns in which any word in the two-word utterance can stand in a given relation to the other words. The PP [attributee]+*broken* develops into the open relational pattern [attributee]+[attribute] (where the attribute is predicative).

---

[19]This is not quite precise, for (as argued in Schlesinger, 1982, Section 7.2) the relations are almost never quite the same. But PPs involve very similar relations.

This open relational pattern might have the following instantiations, *inter alia:*

a. carriage broken   (38)
b. chair nice
c. dolly pretty
d. rocker big

Comparison of (37) with (38) shows that items in (37) are more similar to each other both in form (the same word appears in all utterances) and in relational meaning than those in (38). Because of the similarity in (37), the child who hears an utterance belonging to this PP may be reminded of other utterances belonging to it. Categories are formed by (explicit or implicit) comparisons of instances, and only when there is sufficient similarity between instances will such a comparison be performed spontaneously. It is a plausible conjecture that the similarity in cases like (37), where the same word occurs in the various utterances, will be noticed by the child, and thus a category will begin to emerge. By contrast, the similarity in a set of utterances like (38) is more abstract; it is based on such notions as object, attribute, etc., and the child will presumably fail to notice it. It is suggested, therefore, that a PP like (37) may serve as a nucleus around which a relational category begins to form. This process is discussed in Section 13.3.

Utterances that recur continuously will, on the whole, be better remembered than those that occur less often. Mother-child interactions are often replete with such recurring **formulas,** and one may surmise that these are remembered well. They may therefore be more available for the comparison leading to category formation than other utterances. These formulas may be understood by the child even though he has not yet analyzed them into their constituents.

Occasionally a corpus of child language contains evidence of a construction that the child apparently remembers well. Consider the following utterances:

a. want a drink of water.   (39)
b. I turn the light on.

The author of (39)a is a 15-month-old (Nelson, 1973), and at that age children do not have command of the rules required for the generation of such relatively complex constructions. Hence (39)a is most probably an utterance heard and remembered by the child without having been fully analyzed, i.e., a **rote learned string.** The same applies to (39)b, reported by Bloom, Lightbown, and Hood (1975, p.68) for a child at MLU 1.75. The examples in (39) are of fairly elaborate rote-learned patterns. In child language there are presumably many rote-learned patterns shorter than these, which go unreported because they are not as easily noticed by the investigator as those in (39). Rote-learned strings and the recurring formulas heard by the child are well-remembered patterns that will be available for comparison with subsequent utterances in the process of forming relational categories. We will use the term **fixed strings** (FS) for either one of these constructions. It is proposed that fixed strings are also one of the stepping stones to relational categories (Schlesinger, 1982). (Note that Berman [this volume] also believes that the child's categories—she writes primarily about word classes—are "instance-bound" at the beginning.)

13.3 Routes to Open Relational Patterns

In this section I flesh out the proposal that the child develops relational categories by taking note of both formal and semantic similarity. My objective is to show in general how the child who interprets his environment in terms of particular relations, i.e., who has as yet no relational categories, may form relational categories like [agent]—[action] by observing the regularities in the language he is exposed to. I illustrate the route taken by the child by showing how he may arrive at the [agent]+[action] pattern via certain patterns inolving relations of more narrow scope. My account here elaborates on the proposals made previously in Schlesinger (1982), and, as will be apparent, it has been heavily influenced by Braine (1976). The relations employed in the illustration are of course only examples, and for all I know, those actually occurring in children's speech may be different ones. For instance, as Ninio and Snow (this volume) show, the child's narrow relational categories include a pragmatic component.

Further, I hold no brief for the particular route charted in the following. In fact, I believe that one of the lessons that recent research on language acquisition teaches us is that there is no single route. Instead, my sights are merely set on showing that relational categories indeed **can** be formed even if the child starts "from scratch", so to speak, as H1 has it.

The child, as I am going to show, may proceed from a phase of no relational categories, through fixed strings and pivot patterns, to open relational patterns. It is important to keep in mind what is meant by saying that the child "has" a pivot pattern or an open relational pattern. On the one hand, it means that there is some regularity in the linguistic productions of the child, which can be formally represented by such a pattern, and on the other hand, it means that the child has formed the relational category appearing in this pattern. For instance, if the child is to be credited with the PP [attributee]+*broken*, he must be credited (i) with the relational category attributee of attribute, and (ii) with a rule that puts the word that refers to the attribute, *broken*, after the one referring to the attributee; the single formula states both (i) and (ii). The process by which he attains the pattern is one by which both (i) and (ii) are attained. Any rule that is learned applies to a relational category, and conversely, a relational category acquired in the course of learning a language is acquired through observing a regularity in the language, i.e., through learning a linguistic rule. Acquisition of rules and of relational categories are thus two sides of the same coin.

From FS to PP.   Suppose a child has acquired a fixed string, and let us see how this may serve as a stepping stone to the attainment of a PP. Take the FS *mummy run* (here we present the way the child utters the FS, not how he has heard it). Presumably, the child now knows what *mummy* refers to and what *run* refers to (she may have learned each word by itself, even if it was presented to her in the context of a sentence), and in what situations the whole string *mummy run* applies. Suppose now that she hears an utterance formally similar to this string, say, *daddy runs.* It is claimed that there will be a good chance that she will then be reminded of the FS *mummy run,* which is available to her as a rote-learned unit.

Now the formal similarity will draw her attention to the semantic similarity; since each of the latter utterances is analyzed by the child with reference to the situation it occurs in, she will notice the similarity of the relation involved in it to that in the situation referred to in the FS. Thus a generalization will be arrived at: the PP [runner]+*run.*

Here we are assuming priority of formal similarity: it is the physical resemblance of *daddy runs* to the well-established pattern *mummy run* which draws attention to the semantic similarity, and probably not vice versa. Because we are assuming now that the child does not yet have relational categories, the semantic similarity between these individual utterances will presumably not suffice by itself for their coalescing into a PP (considering that all utterances are semantically similar in some way to all other utterances). Hence formal similarity will have to act as a lever. Once a pattern based on a relational category has been formed, however, this pattern will be available for the analysis of further utterances, i.e., other utterances may be attracted to the pattern on the basis of semantic similarity. This is the principle underlying the subsequent steps discussed below.

The generalization leading to the PP may take place either by just hearing the relevant utterances and noting their formal and semantic similarity to the FS, or by the child modeling her utterances on the FS *mummy run.*

The attainment of an FS and of a PP are the first two steps presented in Table 6.3.

From PP to open relational pattern.   Suppose that after attaining the PP [runner]+*run* the child hears *Cindy jumps.* Although this utterance may not remind her of any other single utterance, since neither the formal nor the semantic similarity may be sufficient, it may remind her of the PP [runner]+*run.* Since this PP has already served in the analysis of various utterances, and is thus well-established, it will be available for the analysis of additional utterances. The relation in *Cindy jumps* is not the same as that in [runner]+*run.* Still, there is some similarity: both involve a movement of something animate. Once this semantic similarity is noticed by the child, the formal similarity may also be

TABLE 6.3
A Route to the Acquisition of Relational Patterns

Step	Pattern	Example of Pattern	Examples of Utterances Leading to Pattern
1	fixed string (FS)	mummy run	doggies run Cindy runs daddy runs
2	pivot pattern (PP)	[runner] + run	Cindy jumps baby kicks Bobbie waves
3	open relational pattern-restricted	[mover] + [moving]	baby cries daddy eats mummy hugs
4	open relational pattern	[agent] + [action]	

noticed: the word denoting the "mover" precedes the one denoting the movement.

Experience with several utterances involving movement will thus lead to the expansion of the PP. Utterances like *Cindy jumps, baby kicks, Bobby waves* may gradually generalize into a pattern [mover]+[moving]; cf. (36). (Here again, generalization may occur through analysis of heard utterances or through the child producing utterances modeled after the PP.) Now note that this is a relational pattern: a variety of words are eligible for first position and a variety of (different) words are eligible for second position in this pattern, provided, of course, that the relation between the words is appropriate. This relational pattern, presented as Step 3 in Table 6.3, is still very restricted, and it remains to be shown how the child can arrive at the more general [agent]+[action] pattern.

Extending the open relational pattern.   A restricted relational pattern is extended when semantic similarities are noticed between the pattern and utterances that are not instantiations of it. Hugging, crying, and eating, for instance, involve much more than movement; in fact, features other than movement may be more salient to the child than the movement itself. However, the movement component in these actions may make them sufficiently similar to the relation in the [mover]+[moving] pattern to be analyzed in terms of it. Thus, the child may say *mummy hug,* treating mummy as a kind of mover and putting the word denoting mummy before the one denoting the movement, hugging. Alternatively, she may hear *mummy hugs* and, capitalizing on the formal and semantic similarity to the [mover]+[moving] pattern, conceive of this utterance as an instance of this pattern. As a consequence, the pattern becomes extended and comprises more than just the prototypical movers performing prototypical movements. The extended pattern may now be described by the formula [agent]+[action]; see Table 6.3.

From that point on, semantic assimilation, as described in Sections 2-5, takes over: utterances involving events that can only marginally be regarded as actions are analyzed in terms of the [agent]+[action] pattern, due to formal and semantic similarities. Essentially, semantic assimilation is therefore the same process as the one hypothesized here for the formation of early semantic categories.

It is important to note that Steps 3 and 4 in Table 6.3 are presented as discrete steps merely for the purpose of exposition. In actual fact there will be a gradual process of expansion of the earliest restricted open relational pattern until it eventually assumes the scope of the fully mature pattern operating in adult language.[20] There is no "stage" at which one is entitled to talk of the agent category (or the [agent]+[action] pattern). What one child includes in its developing pattern—called by us for convenience [agent]+[action]—will differ from what another child includes in it. And for all children the boundaries of the categories involved will be continually shifting, until they correspond to those of the adult.

Alternative route.   In the foregoing the child was assumed, in accordance with H1, to approach language with no case-like relational categories whatsoever. The learnability of language under such conditions was established: Semantic and formal similarity, each insufficient in itself, may converge on the formation of gradually expanding categories. *A fortiori,* if H2 is correct and the child does have some narrow prelinguistic categories, the formation of relational categories like [agent]+[action] will be possible. The child would then start with restricted open relational patterns, Step 3 of Table 6.3, and expand these gradually.

If H2 is correct there are several alternatives to the route outlined in Table 6.3. First, not all steps need to be traversed. A PP may be attained directly, without FS serving as a basis, by noting recurring similarities of utterances having a word in common in a given position—cf. (37)—and the semantic similarities between these utterances. It is also conceivable that occasionally a restricted open relational pattern is attained directly from an FS, without an intervening PP, on the basis of semantic similarity alone. Whether or not such foreshortening occurs in the acquisitional history of a given child will presumably depend, *inter alia,* on the availability of the right kinds of utterances for the formation of the various patterns in Table 6.3. Individual differences between children may also deter-

---

[20]That the transition from Step 2 to Step 4 can also be rather abrupt is shown by Bowerman's (1976) report on Eva's course of acquisition.

mine the route that is chosen. As Ramer (1976) has shown, children differ in their tendency to take risks and try out new constructions; cf. also Bowerman (1976), on the differences in the acquisitional history of her two daughters.

Further, a pattern may derive from more than one earlier-appearing pattern. For instance, a restricted open relational pattern may be based on more than one PP, and there may be more than one restricted open relational pattern giving rise to the full [agent]+[action] pattern (for instance, [ingester]+[ingesting], besides [mover]+[moving] in Table 6.3).

By providing for alternative routes of acquisition, our theory becomes almost impervious to refutation. Suppose that it can be shown empirically that a particular child does not resort to one of the routes proposed here. Our theory will not be impugned thereby, because of the possibility that this particular child follows one of the other routes provided for in the theory. That the theory thus becomes difficult to refute is of course an undesirable consequence, which will have to be remedied in the future by adding more precise specifications as to which of the routes will be pursued under given circumstances. At the present state of our knowledge, however, it would be unwise to venture on such further specification.

Inflectional languages. Inflectional languages typically have relatively flexible word order, with pragmatic factors largely determining the sequence of words. In acquiring such languages, children obviously cannot deploy patterns based on fixed word order. But they may use, instead, patterns involving relational categories like those in Table 6.3 and characterized by inflections rather than by a fixed sequence. For instance, in a language marking the nominative (which in child language will usually go with the agent) by an inflection, there may be a pattern [runner]$_n$,*run,* where the subscript indicates the nominative inflection and the comma stands between members of an unordered pair.

It might be argued that, instead of resorting to semantic similarity, children learning inflectional languages rely on formal similarity in the creation of relational categories. Such a proposal has little to commend itself, however. In the first place it is implausible to assume that the child learning such languages would avoid making use of semantic similarity in forming categories, given that the latter provides a sufficient basis for such learning, as has been shown in the preceding.

Further, it should be noted that formal similarity will in any case not be sufficient for learning relational categories of languages that mark cases in a complex, apparently unsystematic manner. In Serbo-Croatian the accusative is marked by either one of the suffixes *-a, -o, -e,* or *-u* (or zero) for the singular, depending only in part on the gender of the noun. But the same suffixes (except *-u*) also mark the nominative, depending again only in part on gender, and for many nouns the marking does not distinguish between nominative and accusative. As Slobin (1982) remarks, "It is a challenge to all our theories of language development and cognition that such systems are learned in the first few years of life'' (p.157). The problem posed by such a language for the acquisition of the nominative and accusative categories can evidently not be met by formal similarity.

13.4   A Note on Linguistic Relativism

In the foregoing it has been shown how relational categories may be fashioned by language. Some readers may have become a bit uneasy about what they may think is an untoward implication of this theory, for it might seem that this account of acquisition implies linguistic relativism, i.e., that the categories we think with, or in, are determined by the language we speak (and linguistic relativism is no longer looked upon as quite respectable, in some circles).

Nothing like this follows from our account, however. The child may have learned merely the way experience is to be categorized for the purpose of using language, and for that purpose only. Apart from the use of language, cognition need not be cast into those categories. Consider a boy who says:

My pocket knife cuts anything.   (40)

English permits, in some cases, the expression of the instrument of an action as its agent, as in (40), whereas Japanese does not.[21] But one would hardly expect the English-speaking child to conceive of his pocket knife in a different way than the Japanese boy, for whom, linguistically, the pocket knife will not be an agent. Again, when John sees the mountain, John is expressed as agent in English and the mountain as patient. In Japanese, the mountain is expressed as the agent. Should one therefore ascribe to the Japanese a different conception of vision? (See also Section 12.5.) It appears, then, that we do not necessarily think in terms of the categories supplied by language. Whether cognition proceeds without any categorization (as suggested in Section 12.2; cf. also the more detailed discussion in Schlesinger, 1977, Ch.5) or employs its own system of categories is an issue that cannot be dealt with here.

Although our account does not imply an influence of language on thought, it does not preclude it either. It **may** be the case that the relational categories originating in language impose themselves on our thinking. The issue is an empirical one.

----

[21]The conventional way of putting this would be of course that the instrument, experiencer, etc., are expressed as subjects. But, as argued in Section 7, since the subject retains some of the flavor of the agent from which it derives, the present formulation seems to be justified.

13.5   The Formation of Word Classes

The chapters by Maratsos, Levy, Ninio, and Berman in this volume are all concerned with the acquisition of word classes. The present chapter, by contrast, deals not with categories of words but with relational categories. However, according to the theory outlined in Schlesinger (1982, pp. 225–228), these are two closely related issues: Word classes are defined in terms of the arguments of relational categories. A short presentation of this theory is therefore in order here.

It is proposed that as the child learns how to realize a given semantic relation she simultaneously learns which words may be employed to express each of the relational arguments. For instance, the child learning English must discover that the word denoting the attribute precedes the one denoting the attributee. She has to extract this rule from input utterances like *big doggie, nice baby, dirty hands*, and so on. Now, as the child analyzes *big doggie* and notes how the semantic relation is realized, she will also register the fact that *big* is a word that can express the first argument of the attribute–attributee relation, i.e., the attribute, and *doggie* the second argument. In the course of hearing various realizations of this relation she thus comes to form two categories of words: words that can express the attribute argument (*big, nice, dirty*, etc.) and those that may serve for the expression of the attributees (*doggie, baby, hands*, etc.).

In the same manner the child will learn which words may serve to express other relational arguments: agents, patients, possessors, actions, and so on. Thus, learning the rules for realizing a semantic relation and learning which words are eligible for the expression of arguments of this relation are, on this view, parts of one and the same process.

A caveat is in order regarding the action category. The term, as used here, does not refer to a semantic feature of a word, but to the argument of certain semantic relations, such as the agent-action relation and the patient-action relation. As has been shown in Sections 2–5, the latter are expanded in the course of language learning through the process of semantic assimilation. As a consequence, the class of action words will eventually also come to include words that denote what are not, strictly speaking, actions (*find, remember, receive, fall, hate*, etc.). Note that the present theory does not involve the claim, rightly criticized by Maratsos (this volume), that word classes originate in semantic notions, like objects, states, actions, but rather in **relational** notions (e.g., of an object standing in a certain relation to an action, say, as its patient).

What remains to be explained now is how these argument classes develop into the adult grammatical categories. The problem arises in particular with the noun class. Several relational arguments are expressed by nouns in the child's speech: agents, patients, possessors, instruments, and so on. As stated, for each of these the child forms a separate category. These categories must eventually merge into one broad class: the noun class. How does this merger come about? The answer is based on the fact that there is a large degree of overlap between some of the child's argument classes. Many of the words registered as agent words will also be registered as patient words, many of the latter will be found to function also as instrument words, and so on. The child will hear not only *The dog went out with daddy.*, but also *Daddy took the dog out.*, not only *the girl's ball*, but also *the pretty girl.* When several instances of a class are registered as having a certain property, there will be a tendency to generalize to other members of the class. Hence, when many of the members of the agent class are found to be eligible for the expression of patients, all other members will be regarded as thus eligible; and likewise for patients and instruments, possessors and attributees, and so on. As a result, these argument classes merge into one noun class.

A difficulty with this account of merging is that we do not know so far why it does occur in some cases and not in others. The noun class of English speakers does not merge with the verb class, although there is partial overlap between these categories: many English nouns can be verbs (cf. *find, cut, run, stand,* etc.).

Note, however, that the fact that the English noun class does not merge with the verb class is no evidence that no merging occurs in word categories at all. Our everyday experience with the generalization of properties indicates that categories can merge (we don't have to observe **all** monkeys filching things to keep a safe distance from all monkey cages). Further, experimental evidence for the merging of categories has been obtained by Ainat Guberman (with different materials; see Guberman & Schlesinger, 1985). The problem posed by English noun and verb classes is therefore not specific to the present theory; a theory according to which word classes are formed by distributional analysis (see Maratsos, this volume, and Wolff, this volume) also has to account for the fact that these classes do not merge. The solution will presumably have to be sought in the specific degree and kind of overlap required for merging.

14. POSSIBLE ORIGIN OF NONLINGUISTIC RELATIONAL CATEGORIES

We now approach a problem that we have shelved for some time. According to H2, there are prelinguistic relational categories. Where do these come from? How, for instance, did the children in Golinkoff's (1981) experiment (see Section 12.3) arrive at relational categories like (31)?

In trying to answer this question we must for the time being content ourselves with speculations to an even greater extent than has been the case in discussing the formation of categories in the course of learning language: We have no linguistic output of the child to fall back on.

14.1 Two Possible Elaborations of H2

If H2 is correct, there seem to be two possibilities: (i) there are innate pre-linguistic relational categories, or (ii) relational categories develop through experience. In the latter case, there seems to be no reason to assume that the process of forming categories occurs only prior to the acquisition of language and not also concurrent with it. The term **nonlinguistic relational categories,** rather than prelinguistic relational categories, will therefore be used in the following for the categories referred to in H2 (irrespective of whether they are innate or not).[22]

The plausibility of (i) depends on which relational categories are claimed to be innate. Thus it is very plausible to assume with Braine (this volume) an innate predicate-argument structure that molds the child's experience; it would be hard to imagine how the child can embark on the language learning task without it. Note, however, that this may be regarded as a relational category only if there is a linguistic rule defined over it; that is, if at some stage of language acquisition all predicates behave differently from all arguments. Otherwise, this is not a relational category in the sense the term is used here but a distinction the child applies in integrating his environment (see Section 12.2). At any rate, when it comes to specific case-like categories, like agent-action, action-patient, and so on, the need for innate categories becomes much less obvious, particularly in view of the considerations in Section 12. Would it not be reasonable to assume that (ii) applies to these categories?

Here one might raise an a priori objection against (ii): If, as has been argued, relational categories are not indispensable for cognitive development, there seems to be nothing that would impel the child to form categories (except for the purpose of using language, but here we consider nonlinguistic categories only). If, on the contrary, such categories are indeed a prerequisite for cognitive development, the child must be equipped with them from the outset; he cannot have learned them, because he cannot function at all without them. That is, they must be innate.

However, it may be the case that, although relational categories are not indispensable for getting cognitive development started, and while no immediate need is being met by them, they are formed spontaneously by way of analyzing experiences. Such spontaneous formation seems to be quite common in the case of nonrelational categories, i.e., in the case of concepts typically referred to by specific content words. Thus we may form the concept of a certain type of plant which we have often seen, without anybody defining it for us or telling us its name and without our making any specific response to it (which might have

---

[22]"Nonlinguistic **relational** categories" is used here to refer to categories that language expresses syntactically rather than by means of nouns, verbs, etc. Of course, there is no sharp boundary line between the two.

served in lieu of the name to tie the various instances of the concept together). How is such a concept formed? Presumably, on seeing one of those plants we are reminded of a previous instance due to the perceptual similarity between the instances. Eventually, we may not remember any specific instances, but on encountering such a plant we will just recognize it: "Here's _____ again!" (with no name supplied for the blank). Hardly any experimental studies of such spontaneous, seemingly unmotivated categorization have been carried out so far—the studies by Edmonds and Evans (1966) and Edmonds, Mueller, and Evans (1966) are the only ones I know of, which are even remotely relevant—but the phenomenon seems to be quite common, as the reader may attest from his own everyday experience. It seems plausible, therefore, that relational categories may be formed by a similar process. This proposal will be more fully developed in the next section.

14.2   Categorization through Similarity of Events

The foregoing discussion of spontaneous formation of categories suggests that perceived similarity may itself be sufficient for a category to be formed. However, in discussing the prelinguistic origin of relational categories (Section 12.2) it has been pointed out that many events the child experiences do not resemble each other sufficiently for the similarity to be noticed and a category to be formed accordingly. The example given was (30), reproduced here for convenience:

   a. Polly puts the kettle on.   (30)
   b. Cindy hits Clara.
   c. Daddy climbs the ladder.
   d. The dog chases the cat.
   e. The cat jumps.

But this example was presented as an argument against the claim that the agent category originates at one go by abstracting from a number of experiences. The categories originating nonlinguistically will presumably not be as broad as the agent category. Rather, they will be initially rather restricted in scope, and such core categories will gradually expand into wider ones on the basis of experience. (The parallel with our account, in Section 13, of the formation of categories through language should be obvious.)

It is proposed, therefore, that nonlinguistic relational categories may begin to crystallize around sets of events which have several elements in common, as for instance the events in (41).

   a. Mummy catches the ball.   (41)
   b. Mummy throws the ball.
   c. Mummy kicks the ball.
   d. Mummy rolls the ball.

Let us try to follow now a fictitious child who is just beginning to develop categories, one who is starting with a clean record, so to speak (for here we assume no innate categories). The child witnesses the events in (41). These events resemble each other; they have elements in common (mummy, ball). When she witnesses one of them the child will tend therefore to be reminded of the others. She may then have spontaneously formed a category of actions mummy performs on the ball; let us call them [impinge]. Mummy, of course, will not yet be viewed as an agent, nor will the ball be conceived of as a patient, for the simple reason that no such categories exist as yet in the child's mind. Instead, mummy is conceived of as the "impinger" and the ball as the "impingee." Strictly speaking, one should not even credit the child with the category [impinge] in isolation, but with a relational category, "impinge, where mummy is impinger and the ball impingee"; but we will just take this for granted in using the more compact formula [impinge]. In short, the relations the child now may be said to have are

$$\text{mummy}_{(impinger)}—[\text{impinge}]—\text{ball}_{(impingee)} \tag{42}$$

(There is no plus sign between the terms in (42) and words are not italicized, because we are not dealing with words and language, but with nonlinguistic categorization of events.[23]

Note that Golinkoff's (1981) experiment, discussed in Section 12.3, tapped conceptualizations that were (at least) at this stage; cf. (31). (They may of course have been more advanced, but the experiment provides no evidence for this.)

The category [impinge] provides the child with a tool for analyzing her experiences. It enables her to apply (42) not only to the events of (41) but to any event in which mummy does something to the ball. And some other events, too, as will become clear in a moment.

A further step will be taken when the child witnesses mummy performing actions on other objects: pushing the table, taking down toys, putting clothes in the dryer. These may now be analyzed in terms of [impinge], except that instead of the ball as "impingee" the child will now have formed a general category [impingee]:

$$\text{mummy}_{(impinger)}—[\text{impinge}]—[\text{impingee}] \tag{43}$$

Next, the child may generalize (43) to include not just mummy, but also daddy, other children, dogs and cats, performing actions involving physical contact with objects. The result may be that (43) is generalized to

---

[23]If the child has already formed a concept of ball (and not just a representation of a particular ball), '[ball]' will have to be substituted for 'ball' in (42); and if the child has the concept of a person—'[person]' for 'mummy'.

[impinger]—[impinge]—[impingee]   (44)

An obvious alternative route would be to form [impinger] first and [impingee] subsequently.

Where do we go from here? Could the child perhaps continue to expand (44), through observing other events, until she arrives at [agent]—[action]—[patient]? In answering this question we have nothing but our intuitions to go on, so any answer will have to be tentative. To me the suggestion that (44) could be gradually expanded **without** the aid of language does not seem plausible at all. For consider what might lead the child to notice such far-fetched similarities as evidenced in (30) (which seems to present a fair sample of juvenile agent-action relations). It seems, rather, that [impinger]—[impinge] is about as far as her nonlinguistic experience will lead. If this is correct, expansion to a broad agent concept can be actuated only by language, and this occurs presumably in the manner already summarized in Table 6.3. It will be noticed that with (44) the child has arrived approximately at the stage represented as Step 3 in the table. Once she notices that the word referring to the impinger precedes the one that refers to impinging, a restricted open relational pattern [impinger]+[impinge] has been attained. From then on, the route charted in Table 6.3 can be pursued.[24]

15. THE GROWTH OF CATEGORIES: A RECAPITULATION

By way of summary, let us restate the main strands of argument that pervaded this chapter:

1. Relational categories are intrinsic to the grammatical system of the language. The child who follows rules of grammar must be assumed to have relational categories on which these rules operate. Outside of grammar, these categories are not indispensable. That is, interpretation of the environment may be couched in terms of particular relations that are not categorized; see Section 1.2.

2. Relational categories are at first of very narrow scope, and each such category comprises relations that are similar to each other in meaning (i.e., that inhere in similar events). Gradually, these relations expand into the broad, formal categories of the mature linguistic system, which are no longer semantically homogeneous.

3. Relational categories are expanded on the basis of both formal and semantic similarity.

---

[24]Another possibility would be that the linguistically actuated expansion of relational categories begins already with (42).

4. Relational categories may originate (i) in the course of learning the grammatical system, (ii) through experience with the environment, or (iii) they may be part of our innate mental endowment. (It may be the case that some relational categories originate in (i), others in (ii), and still others in (iii), and there may also be individual differences, depending on the type of environmental and linguistic input, and the child's propensities.)

Let us expand a bit on the last point. In the course of the present chapter we have pursued the child's development backward, starting from the adult system, going on to early language, and ending up with the development of prelinguistic categories. Looking at relational categories in chronological order, the following picture emerges.

Conceivably, some relational categories of narrow scope may be innate—(iii) above. However, there are ways to account for relational categories without making assumptions about innateness. The child may observe similarities in experienced events and form narrow-scope relational categories, (ii). There is one experimental study of children before the two-word stage which suggests that children may have such prelinguistic categories (Section 12.3). These will have to be expanded in the course of learning grammar, i.e., of adjusting linguistic rules that apply to relational categories, and we have shown in outline how such expansion may take place on the basis of semantic and formal similarities. If there are any narrow relational categories that are innate, they will have to be expanded in the same manner.

To the extent that certain relational categories are not provided for by experience prior to learning language, they will have to be built up in the course of acquiring linguistic rules, and it has been shown how this may be achieved, using fixed strings and pivot patterns as "stepping stones." The resulting open relational patterns are gradually expanded—again on the basis of semantic and formal similarities—until they coincide with the formal categories of the adult linguistic system. We have discussed this semantic assimilation process at length in Sections 2–5 and have noted that it operates through lexical entries: Once the child registers in the lexical entry of a word how it is to be used as a term in a semantic relation, sentences involving this word can be understood and produced even where no semantic similarity to the relation in question is apparent.

The example of semantic assimilation that has been worked out in detail is that of the subject, which has been shown to derive from the agent category. Features of the agent were identified, and it was shown that subjects resemble agents in one or more of these (Sections 6–7). Evidence for this view of the subject comes from certain constraints on the acceptability of sentences, which do not seem to be amenable to an explanation along syntactic lines but are accounted for on the assumption that the subject shares semantic features with the agent and that their agentive connotations may block certain usages where these features do not apply.

These, then, are possible routes to the adult system of categories. They are characterized by gradual growth rather than saltatory changes. This approach has been developed here for the ontogeny of language. A plausible suggestion concerning the phylogeny of language is that similar processes have been at work there: relational categories developed gradually on the basis of perceived similarity.

ACKNOWLEDGMENTS

Part of the work on which this chapter is based was carried out while the author was a Fellow of The Institute for Advanced Studies, The Hebrew University, Jerusalem. Some of the reported studies and writing of this chapter were partially supported by the Human Development Center, Hebrew University. I am deeply indebted to the many people who read previous versions of this chapter. Among those whose comments lead to revisions and extensive reformulations I would like to mention Martin Braine, Yonata Levy, Mordechai Rimor and Catherine Snow. I have also benefitted very much from comments by Moshe Anisfeld, Sidney Greenbaum, Theo Herrman, John Lyons, Michael Maratsos, Anita Mittwoch and Ernst Moerk. I wish to express my gratitude to all of them.

REFERENCES

Bloom, L., Lightbown, P., & Hood, L. (1975). Structure and variation in child language. *Monographs of the Society for Research in Child Development, 40* (2, Serial No. 160).

Bowerman, M. (1973a). *Early syntactic development.* Cambridge, England: Cambridge University Press.

Bowerman, M. (1973b). Structural relationships in children's utterances: Syntactic or semantic? In T. E. Moore (Ed.), *Cognitive development and the acquisition of language.* New York: Academic Press.

Bowerman, M. (1976). Semantic factors in the acquisition of rules for word use and sentence construction. In D. Morehead & A. Morehead (Eds.), *Directions in normal and deficient child language.* Baltimore, MD: University Park Press.

Bowerman, M. (1982). Reorganizational processes in lexical and syntactic development. In E. Wanner & L. R. Gleitman (Eds.), *Language acquisition: The state of the art.* Cambridge, England: Cambridge University Press.

Braine, M. D. S. (1963). The ontogeny of English phrase structure: The first phase. *Language, 39,* 1–13.

Braine, M. D. S. (1976). Children's first word combinations. *Monographs of the Society for Research in Child Development, 41* (1, Serial No. 164).

Braine, M. D. S., & Hardy, J. A. (1982). On what cases there are, why they are, and how they develop: An amalgam of *a priori* considerations, speculation, and evidence from children. In E. Wanner & L. R. Gleitman (Eds.), *Language acquisition: The state of the art.* Cambridge, England: Cambridge University Press.

Brown, R. (1973). *A first language: The early stages.* Cambridge, MA: Harvard University Press.

Brown, R., & Fish, D. (1983). The psychological causality implicit in language. *Cognition, 14,* 237–273.

Brown, R., & Fraser, C. (1964). The acquisition of syntax. In U. Bellugi & R. Brown (Eds.), The acquisition of language. *Monographs of the Society for Research in Child Development, 29* (1, Serial No. 92).

Chien, Y-C. (1985). The concepts of topic and subject in first language acquisiton of Mandarin Chinese. *Child Development, 56,* 1359–1375.

Chomsky, N. C. (1965). *Aspects of the theory of syntax.* Cambridge, MA: MIT Press.

DeLancey, S. (1984). Notes on agentivity and causation. *Studies in Language, 8,* 181–213.

de Villiers, J. (1980). The process of rule learning in child speech: A new look. In K. E. Nelson (Ed.), *Children's language, Vol. 2,* New York: Gardner Press.

Edmonds, E. M., & Evans, S. H. (1966). Schema learning without a prototype. *Psychonomic Science, 5,* 247–248.

Edmonds, E. M., Mueller, M. R., & Evans, S. H. (1966). Effects of knowledge of results on mixed schema discrimination. *Psychonomic Science, 6,* 377–378.

Fillmore, C. J. (1968). The case for case. In E. Bach & R. T. Harms (Eds.), *Universals in linguistic theory.* New York: Holt, Rinehart & Winston.

Fillmore, C. J. (1977). The case for case reopened. In P. Cole & J. Saddock (Eds.), *Syntax and semantics, Vol. 8: Grammatical relations.* New York: Academic Press.

Gathercole, V. C. (1985). 'He has too much hard questions': The acquisition of the linguistic mass-count distinction in *much* and *many. Journal of Child Language, 12,* 395–415.

Gleitman, L. R., & Wanner, E. (1982). Language acquisition: The state of the state of the art. In E. Wanner & L. R. Gleitman (Eds.), *Language acquisition: The state of the art.* Cambridge, England: Cambridge University Press.

Golinkoff, R. M. (1981). The case for semantic relations: Evidence from the verbal and non-verbal domains. *Journal of Child Language, 8,* 413–438.

Golinkoff, R. M., & Kerr, J. L. (1978). Infants' perception of semantically defined action role changes in filmed events. *Merrill-Palmer Quarterly, 24,* 53–61.

Gordon, P. (1985). Evaluating the semantic categories hypothesis: The case of the count/mass distinction. *Cognition, 20,* 209–242.

Guberman, A., & Schlesinger, I. M. (1985). *Merging of categories.* Working Paper No. 16, The Goldie Rotman Center for Cognitive Science in Education, Hebrew University, Jerusalem.

Hamilton, W. (1859). *Lectures on Metaphysics and Logic* (Vol. 2). London: Blackwood.

Huttenlocher, J., Smiley, P., & Charney, R. (1983). Emergence of action categories in the child: Evidence from verb meanings. *Psychological Review, 90,* 72–93.

Keenan, E. O. (1976). Towards a universal definition of "subject." In C. Li (Ed.), *Subject and topic.* New York: Academic Press.

Lakoff, G. (1977). Linguistic Gestalts. *Papers from the thirteenth regional meeting, Chicago Linguistic Society,* Chicago.

Levy, Y. (1983). It's frogs all the way down. *Cognition, 15,* 75–93.

Macnamara, J. (1982). *Names for things.* Cambridge, MA: MIT Press.

Mulford, R. (1985). Comprehension of Icelandic pronoun gender: Semantic versus formal factors. *Journal of Child Language, 12,* 443–453.

Nelson, K. (1973). Structure and strategy in learning to talk. *Monographs of the Society for Research in Child Development, 38* (1–2, Serial No. 149).

Nida, E. (1964). *Toward a science of translating.* Leiden: Brill.

Pinker, S. (1982). A theory of the acquisition of lexical-interpretive grammars. In J. Bresnan (Ed.), *The mental representation of grammatical relations.* Cambridge, MA: MIT Press.

Pinker, S. (1984). *Language learnability and language development,* Cambridge, MA: Harvard University Press.

Quirk, R., Greenbaum, S., Leech, G., & Svartvik, J. (1978). *A grammar of contemporary English.* New York: Harcourt Brace, 7th printing.

Ramer, A. L. H. (1976). Syntactic styles in emerging language. *Journal of Child Language, 3,* 49–62.

Roberts, K. (1983). Comprehension and production of word order in Stage I. *Child Development,* *54,* 443–449.

Rosch, E., & Mervis, C. B. (1975). Family resemblances: Studies in the internal structure of categories. *Cognitive Psychology, 7,* 573–605.

Schachter, P. (1976). The subject in Philippine languages: Topic, actor, topic-actor, or none of the above. In C. N. Li (Ed.), *Subject and topic.* New York: Academic Press.

Schlesinger, I. M. (1971). Production of utterances and language acquisition. In D. I. Slobin (Ed.), *The Ontogenesis of Grammar.* New York: Academic Press.

Schlesinger, I. M. (1974). Relational concepts underlying language. In R. L. Schiefelbusch & L. L. Lloyd (Eds.), *Language perspectives—Acquisition, retardation and intervention.* Baltimore, MD: University Park Press.

Schlesinger, I. M. (1977). *Production and comprehension of utterances.* Hillsdale, NJ: Lawrence Erlbaum Associates.

Schlesinger, I. M. (1979). Cognitive and linguistic structures: The case of the instrumental. *Journal of Linguistics, 15,* 307–324.

Schlesinger, I. M. (1981). Semantic Assimilation in the acquisition of relational categories. In W. Deutsch (Ed.), *The child's construction of language.* New York: Academic Press.

Schlesinger, I. M. (1982). *Steps to language: Toward a theory of language acquisition.* Hillsdale, NJ: Lawrence Erlbaum Associates.

Schlesinger, I. M. (1985). *Instruments as agents.* Working Paper No. 15, The Goldie Rotman Center for Cognitive Science in Education, Hebrew University, Jerusalem.

Schlesinger, I. M., & Pat-Horenczyk, R. (in preparation). Cognitive notions and language.

Slobin, D. I. (1981). The origin of grammatical encoding of events. In W. Deutsch (Ed.), *The child's construction of language.* London: Academic Press.

Slobin, D. I. (1982). Universal and particular in the acquisition of language. In E. Wanner & L. R. Gleitman (Eds.), *Language acquisition: The state of the art.* Cambridge, England: Cambridge University Press.

Van Oosten, J. (1977). Subjects and agenthood in English. In W. A. Beach, C. E. Fox, & S. Philosoph (Eds.), *Papers from the thirteenth regional meeting, Chicago Linguistic Society,* Chicago, IL: University of Chicago.

Wierzbicka, A. (1980). *The case for surface case.* Ann Arbor, MI: Karoma.

Wolff, J. G. (in press). Cognitive development as optimisation. In L. Bolc (Ed.), *Knowledge based learning systems.* Heidelberg: Springer.

7

Learning Syntax and Meanings Through Optimization and Distributional Analysis

J. Gerard Wolff
Praxis Systems plc, Bath, England

INTRODUCTION

It is perhaps misleading to use the word *theory* to describe the view of language acquisition and cognitive development, which is the subject of this chapter. This word is used as a matter of convenience; it applies here to what is best characterized as a partially completed program of research—a jigsaw puzzle in which certain pieces have been positioned with reasonable confidence, while others have been placed tentatively and many have not been placed at all. The most recent exposition of these ideas is developed in two papers: Wolff (1982) and Wolff (1987). Earlier papers in this program of research include Wolff (1975, 1976, 1977, 1980).

Wolff (1982) describes a computer model of linguistic/cognitive development and some associated theory. Wolff (1987) describes extensions to the ideas in the first paper. These papers and previous publications are somewhat narrow in scope, concentrating on detailed discussion of aspects of the theory. The intention here is to provide a broader perspective on the set of ideas.

The chapter begins with a brief summary of the presuppositions of the theory. Then the theory is described in outline: first a brief description of the computer model which is the main subject of Wolff (1982) and then a more abstract account, including the developments described in Wolff (1987). The body of the chapter reviews the empirical support for the theory.

PRESUPPOSITIONS OF THE THEORY

There is space here only for a rather bald statement of theoretical and empirical assumptions on which the theory is based. I will make no attempt to justify these ideas.

1. The theory belongs in the *empiricist* rather than the *nativist* tradition: It seems that language acquisition may very well be a process of abstracting *structure* from linguistic and other sensory inputs where the innate knowledge which the child brings to the task is largely composed of perceptual primitives, structure-abstracting routines, and procedures for analysing and creating language. A *triggering*, nativist view cannot be ruled out *a priori* but the other view is plausible enough to deserve exploration.

2. It seems clear that, while children may be helped by explicit instruction in language forms, by reward for uttering correct forms, by correction of errors, and by other *training* features of their linguistic environment, including the grading of language samples, they probably do not need any of these aids. It seems prudent, as a matter of research strategy, to think in terms of learning processes which can operate without them but which can take advantage of them when they are available.

3. In a similar way it seems prudent to develop a theory in which learning does not depend on prelinguistic communicative interaction between mother and child but which is at the same time compatible with the fact that such interactions clearly do occur.

4. Although semantic knowledge may develop earlier than syntactic knowledge (or make itself apparent to the observer at an earlier age) it seems that the learning of both kinds of knowledge is integrated in a subtle way. One kind of knowledge is not a prerequisite for the learning of the other.

5. Mainly for reasons of parsimony in theorizing, it has been assumed that a uniform set of learning principles may be found to apply across all domains of knowledge—which is not to deny that differences may also exist. The mechanisms proposed in the theory appear to have a wide range of application.

6. It is assumed that there is a core of knowledge which serves both comprehension and production processes. The theory is framed so that the representation of this core knowledge and the posited processes for learning it are broadly compatible with current notions about processes of comprehension and production.

OUTLINE OF THE THEORY

As already indicated, the theory is based on the kinds of empiricist ideas of associationism and distributional analysis which were so heavily criticized by Chomsky (1965). Those earlier ideas have been extended and refined in two main ways:

- A series of computer models have been built and tested to provide detailed insights into the nature of the proposed mechanisms and their adequacy or otherwise to explain observed phenomena.

- The early ideas are now embedded within a broader theoretical perspective: learning may be seen as a process of optimization of cognitive structures for the several functions they must serve.

This section of the chapter will describe the theory in two stages:

1. a relatively concrete description in terms of the most recent of the computer models in which the theory is embodied: program SNPR.

2. a more abstract or "conceptual" view which includes ideas not yet incorporated in any computer model.

Program SNPR

Table 7.1 summarizes the processing performed by the SNPR model. The *sample of language* is a stream of letter symbols or phoneme symbols without any kind of segmentation markers (spaces between words, etc.). The main reason for leaving out all segmentation markers is to explore what can be achieved without them, given that they are not reliably present in natural language.

The letter or phoneme symbols represent *perceptual primitives* and should not be construed as letters or phonemes *per se*. If the model is seen as a model of

TABLE 7.1
Outline of Processing in the SNPR Model

---

1. Read in a <u>sample of language</u>.

2. Set up a data structure of <u>elements</u> (grammatical rules) containing, at this stage, only the <u>primitive</u> elements of the system.

3. WHILE there are not enough elements formed, do the following sequence of operations repeatedly:

BEGIN

    3.1 Using the current structure of elements, <u>parse</u> the language sample, <u>recording</u> the <u>frequencies</u> of all pairs of contiguous elements and the frequencies of individual elements.

       During the parsing, <u>monitor</u> the use of <u>PAR</u> elements to gather data for later use in rebuilding of elements.

    3.2 When the sample has been parsed, <u>rebuild</u> any elements that require it.

    3.3 Search amongst the current set of elements for <u>shared contexts</u> and <u>fold</u> the data structures in the way explained in the text.

    3.4 <u>Generalize</u> the grammatical rules.

    3.5 The most frequent pair of contiguous elements recorded under 3.1 is formed into a single new <u>SYN</u> element and added to the data structure. All frequency information is then discarded.

END

---

syntax learning then the symbols may be seen as perceptual primitives like formant ratios and transitions. If the model is seen as a model of the learning of nonsyntactic cognitive structures (discussed later) then the symbols may be seen as standing for analyzers for colors, lines, luminance levels, and the like.

Elements in the data structure are of three main types:

- Minimal (M) elements. These are primitives (ie letter or phoneme symbols).
- Syntagmatic (SYN) elements. These are sequences of elements (SYN, PAR, or M).
- Paradigmatic (PAR) elements. These represent a choice of one and only one amongst a set of two or more elements (SYN, PAR, or M).

The whole data structure has the form of a phrase-structure grammar; each element is a *rule* in the grammar. Although it starts as a set of simple rules corresponding to the set of primitives, it may grow to be an arbitrarily complex combination of primitives, sequencing rules (SYN elements), and selection rules (PAR elements). This grammar controls the parsing process.

The general effect of the repeated application of operations 3.1 (parsing and recording the frequencies of pairs) and 3.5 (concatenation of the most frequent pair of contiguous elements) is to build SYN elements of progressively increasing size. Early structures are typically fragments of words; word fragments are built into words, words into phrases and phrases into sentences.

The effect of operation 3.3 (sometimes called *folding*) is to create *complex* SYN elements, meaning SYN elements which contain PAR elements as constituents. For example, if the current set of elements contains $1 \rightarrow ABC$[1] and $2 \rightarrow ADC$, then a new PAR element is formed: $3 \rightarrow B \mid D$[2] and the two original SYN elements are replaced by a new SYN element: $4 \rightarrow A(3)C$. Notice that A, B, C, and D may be arbitrarily complex structures. Notice also how the context(s) of any element is defined by the SYN element(s) in which it appears as a constituent.

Operation 3.4 creates *generalizations* by using the newly formed PAR elements. For example, element 3, just described, would replace B or D in other contexts: $5 \rightarrow EB$ would become $6 \rightarrow E(3)$, and so on. Generalizations may also be produced by operation 3.5 as explained in Wolff (1982).

Operations 3.3 (folding) and 3.4 (generalization) do not come into play until

---

[1]The notation "$1 \rightarrow ABC$" means "the symbol '1' may be rewritten as ABC" or "the symbol '1' is a label for the structure ABC." To aid understanding in this and later examples, integer numbers have been used for references (labels) to structures ("nonterminal symbols" in grammatical jargon), while capital letters are used to represent the material described in the grammar ("terminal symbols").

[2]Read this as "the symbol '2' may be rewritten as B or D."

enough SYN elements have been built up for shared contexts to appear. Likewise, operation 3.2 (rebuilding) will not play a part in the learning process until some (over)generalizations have been formed.

Correction of Overgeneralizations

The *monitoring* and *rebuilding* processes shown in Table 7.1 are designed to solve the problem of *overgeneratizations:* If it is true that children can learn a first language *without explicit error correction* (and there is significant evidence that this is so), how can a child learn to distinguish erroneous overgeneralizations from the many *correct generalizations* that must be retained in his or her cognitive system?

Figure 7.1 illustrates the problem. The smallest envelope represents the finite, albeit large, sample of language on which a child's learning is based. The middle sized envelope represents the (infinite) set of utterances in the language being learned. The largest envelope represents the even larger infinite set of all possible utterances. The difference between the middle sized envelope and the largest one is the set of all utterances which are not in the language being learned.

To learn the language, the child must generalize from the sample to the language without overgeneralizing into the area of utterances which are not in the language. *What makes the problem tricky is that both kinds of generalization, by definition, have zero frequency in the child's experience.*

Notice in Fig. 7.1 that the sample from which the child learns actually overlaps the area of utterances not in the language. This area of overlap, marked

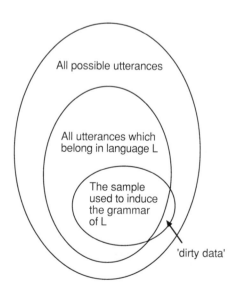

FIG. 7.1. Kinds of utterance in language learning.

'dirty data', and the associated problem for the learning system, is discussed later in the chapter.

To correct overgeneralizations, the monitoring process in SNPR keeps track of the usage of all constituents of all PAR elements in all the contexts in which they occur (remember that contexts are defined in terms of the elements built by SNPR). If any PAR element fails to use all its constituents in any context then it is *rebuilt* for that context (and only that context) so that the unused constituent(s) is removed. As a hypothetical example, a PAR element $1 \rightarrow P|Q|R$ may fail to use R in the context $2 \rightarrow A(1)B$. In such a case it becomes $3 \rightarrow P|Q$ and 2 is rebuilt as $2 \rightarrow A(3)B$. The structure $1 \rightarrow P|Q|R$ may still be used in other contexts.

This mechanism, in which structures are eliminated if they fail to occur in a given context within a finite sample of language, is an approximation to what one imagines is a more realistic mechanism which would allow the *strength* of structures to vary with their contextual probability.

This kind of mechanism will allow a child to observe that "mouses," for example, is vanishingly rare in adult speech and will cause the speech pattern for "mous" to be removed (or *weakened*) in the structure which generates "mouses," "houses," "roses," etc. The correct form ("mice") will be learned independently.

Preserving Correct Generalizations.   What is special about the mechanism in SNPR for correcting overgeneralizations is that certain kinds of generalization cannot be removed by it. The mechanism thus offers an explanation of how children can differentiate *correct* and *incorrect* generalizations without explicit error correction.

To see how it is that the rebuilding mechanism cannot touch some generalizations, consider the following example. From a text containing these three sentences:

John sings
Mary sings
John dances

it is possible to induce a fragment of grammar like this:

$1 \rightarrow (2)(3)$
$2 \rightarrow$ John|Mary
$3 \rightarrow$ sings|dances

Notice that there is a generalization: the grammar generates "Mary dances" even though this was not in the original sample.

Notice, in particular, that the monitoring and rebuilding mechanism cannot remove this generalization. The reason is that, in the sample from which the grammar was induced, "sings," "dances," "John," and "Mary" are *all* used in the context of the structure "1."

In running SNPR, many examples have been observed like this where generalizations are preserved and distinguished from other generalizations which are eliminated.

Other Mechanisms.   There is no space here for a full discussion of the problem of correcting overgeneralizations without external error correction. The mechanisms in SNPR are one of only a few proposals that have been put forward. Braine (1971) has proposed a mechanism but I have not been able to understand from the description how it can remove overgeneralizations without at the same time eliminating correct generalizations. The proposal by Coulon & Kayser (1978) apparently fails because, judging by the sample results they give, wrong generalizations are allowed through the net. The "discrimination" mechanism in Anderson (1981) seems to depend on the provision of explicit *negative* information to the model.

Other mechanisms that have been proposed (e.g., Langley, 1982) use covert error correction; to do this they need to make what I believe are unwarranted assumptions:

- that a child's knowledge of meanings may be used to correct overgeneralizations. If the learning process has to bootstrap semantic structures as well as syntactic structures (as children apparently do), then some other mechanism is needed for the correction of overgeneralizations.
- that there is a one-to-one relation between syntax and meanings. This is quite clearly false for natural language.

The process in SNPR depends on *relative contextual probabilities* of structures and does not employ any notion of falsification of hypotheses or the like.

The notion that a child may learn by creating hypotheses and observing whether they are confirmed or falsified is unsound for much the same reasons that scientific hypotheses cannot be either confirmed or falsified (Lakatos, 1978). A full discussion of this interesting issue is not possible here.

Summary

To summarise this outline of SNPR's functioning, the overall behaviour of the program is to build up cognitive structures by concatenation, using frequency as a heuristic to select appropriate structures. Interwoven with the building process are processes to form disjunctive groups, to form generalizations and to correct overgeneralizations. The structures built by the program have the form of unaugmented phrase structure grammars.

The Abstract View of the Theory

Program SNPR embodies most but not all of the ideas in the theory. This section describes the model in more abstract terms than in the previous section and incorporates ideas from the most recent phase of research (described in Wolff, 1987).

Taking the abstract view, the central idea in the theory is that language acquisition and other areas of cognitive development are, in large part, processes of building cognitive structures which are in some sense *optimal* for the several functions they have to perform. This view is a development of notions of "cognitive economy" which were in vogue in the 1950s and which have attracted intermittent attention subsequently.

This abstract view fits well with and in a sense grows from a recognition that human cognitive systems are products of natural selection and are therefore likely to be conditioned by principles of efficiency.

Compressing Cognitive Structures

One of the functions of a cognitive system is to be a store of knowledge. It seems clear that, *other things being equal,* storage demands of cognitive structures should be minimized. The brain's storage capacity is large, no doubt, but it is not infinite and it seems reasonable to suppose that natural selection would have favored compact storage.

There are at least six ways of reducing the storage demands of a body of data:

1. A pattern (a sequence of elements) which is repeated in a variety of contexts may be stored just once and then accessed via pointers from several contexts. A sequence like

ABCDPQRABCDABCDPQRABCDPQRPQR

may be reduced to 12112122, where $1 \rightarrow$ ABCD and $2 \rightarrow$ PQR.

This is *chunking.* It is also like the use of subroutines in computer programs.

2. Two or more patterns sharing the same context may be placed in a disjunctive group which is accessed via a reference or pointer from the given context. This saves repeated storage of the context pattern. For example, ABCPQRDEF and ABCXYZDEF may be reduced to ABC(1)DEF where $1 \rightarrow$ PQR | XYZ. This is *folding.*

3. *Frequent, large* patterns in 1 will clearly produce a bigger saving than rare small patterns. For reasons spelled out in Wolff (1982) it is best to concentrate on frequency in searching for repeating patterns. There is here a clear theoretical justification for regarding frequency as an important variable in learning. The importance of frequency was recognized in associationist psychology (e.g., Carr, 1931), mainly for intuitive reasons, but it fell out of favor when associationism went out of fashion.

186

4. Repeating contiguous instances of a pattern may be recorded just once and marked for repetition. For example, AAAAAAAAAA may be reduced to A* or A[11].[3]

This is *iteration*. A device with similar effect is *recursion*.

5. Storage space may be saved by simple *deletion* of information or *not recording it*. As discussed in Wolff (1982), there is a close connection between this mode of economy and the phenomenon of *generalization*. This point is amplified below in discussing the tradeoff between the size of a knowledge structure and its usefulness.

6. The last technique in this list is the principle of *schema-plus-correction;* this is described and discussed in Wolff (1987). The idea here, of course, is that a pattern may be recorded by reference to a class or schema of which it is an example, together with the details (corrections) that are specific to the given item. "Tibs" may be described as "cat[tabby, 5-years-old, one-leg-missing]."

Five of these techniques for reducing storage (or transmission) costs of data (items 1, 2, 3, 4, and 6) may be described as techniques for *data compression:* They exploit any *redundancy* that may exist in a body of data; in general, they do not result in a loss of information. The fifth principle is different because information is lost or never recorded.

Using Cognitive Structures as Codes

A second major function of a cognitive system is to provide a set of codes for patterns of information: afferent patterns coming from the senses, efferent patterns transmitted to the oganism's motor system, information patterns transmitted in the course of the brain's internal data manipulations (i.e., thinking), and also the patterns of information to be stored in the cognitive system itself.

An obvious and relatively simple example is the use of words as codes for perceptual/conceptual complexes; words certainly are not the only codes employed in the nervous system and need not, of course, be employed at all. As before, we are assuming that, *other things being equal,* codes that minimize the amount of information to be used for a given purpose will be preferred over other less efficient codes. Precisely the same compression principles may be applied to minimizing required storage space and maximizing the efficiency of codes.

Tradeoff

There is a tradeoff between the *size* of a knowledge structure and its *power* for encoding knowledge. At one extreme there is a very compact grammar like this:

$1 \rightarrow 2*$
$2 \rightarrow A|B|C|\ldots|Z$

---

[3] "*" means "repeat as many times as desired." "[11]" means "repeat 11 times."

This small grammar generates any (alphabetic) text of any size; but it achieves no compression because the text is encoded in the conventional way as a stream of characters.

At the other extreme is a "grammar" with one rule like this:

1 → "the complete sample of language observed to date"

This grammar is not at all compact but it provides a very efficient code: Given the existence of the grammar, one small reference ("1") may be used to represent the whole sample.

Between these two extremes lies a spectrum of grammars.

It is perhaps useful to remark in passing that there is a close connection between this spectrum and the phenomenon of *generalization*. The first grammar, above, is extremely general; the second is extremely specific. In between are grammars which, in varying degrees, are more general than any specific language sample.

The connection between generality in grammars and the size/power tradeoff is simple and direct when grammars are unambiguous (when any given pattern can be generated in only one way). The connection is less direct when, as is usually the case with natural languages, grammars are ambiguous.

Learning

In this theory of learning, it is assumed that a child starts with a small very general *grammar* like the first one above and gradually extends it. As the grammar is extended, it will become progressively more *powerful* as a means of encoding information. The term *grammar* in this context is shorthand for "syntactic/semantic structure."

Whether or not it becomes less general at the same time depends on whether the original general rules are retained in the grammar or discarded. They are almost certainly retained *in reserve,* so to speak, for occasions when generality is needed.

Additions to the set of rules should not be made indiscriminately. At every stage, it is likely that the child will choose the more *useful* rules in preference to less useful or powerful rules. According to the theory, the child should, at all times, try to maximize the effectiveness of each new rule as a means of encoding data economically: He or she should try to maximize the *compression capacity* (CC) or descriptive *power* of the grammar. At the same time, the child should try to minimize the *size* of the grammar which is being built; the size of the grammar is termed S_g.

The ratio between the descriptive power of the grammar and its size (i.e., CC/S_g—which is termed the *efficiency* of the grammar) should at all stages be maximized.

It is in the nature of the search process that the most powerful elements (those giving a large increase in CC for a relatively small increase in S_g) will be found early, and progressively less powerful elements will be found as learning proceeds. There is no reason to suppose that learning will cease when CC/S_g reaches a maximum. Rather, we may suppose that learning will cease when candidate elements that the child discovers or constructs do not add enough to the grammar's CC to justify the attendant increase in S_g. This point will depend on the relative value to a given child of CC and the information storage space corresponding to S_g. These values may depend on motivational factors and on the total available storage space among other things; they are likely to vary from one child to another.

The foregoing ideas are illustrated diagrammatically in Fig. 7.2. The graphs show the trade-off between the coding capacity or power of a grammar and its size. In general, big grammars are more powerful than little ones. Independent of this trade-off is the efficiency of a grammar, meaning the ratio of power to size. The most efficient grammars lie along the line marked "1"; the least efficient grammars lie along the line marked "4", and intermediate grammars lie in between these lines.

The learning process starts near the bottom left of the diagram in the region of small grammars which are not powerful. The learning process gradually builds the grammatical system keeping as close as possible to the highest of the lines ("1") in the diagram, thus maintaining as much efficiency in the grammar as possible at all times.

Other Factors.   Only the two functions mentioned have so far been considered in any detail but it is clear that at some stage others will need consideration. An obvious candidate is the facility with which information may be retrieved from a knowledge structure. As with information transmission, it seems that economy in storage may sometimes be bought at the cost of cumbersome retrieval. Likewise, reliability of cognitive operations may demand the preservation of some redundancy in knowledge structures. A point worth stressing here is

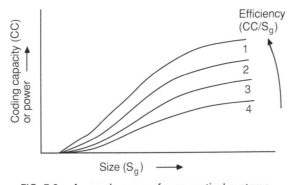

FIG. 7.2.   A search space of grammatical systems.

that concepts like *efficiency* and *optimization* are *functional* notions: It is meaningless to say that something is efficient unless one can say what ends are efficiently served. The theory thus offers a bridge between the cognitive and motivational aspects of mental life.

Realization of the Abstract Principles in SNPR

Program SNPR appears to be a realization of the first five of the optimization principles which have been described. No doubt, other realizations are possible. A model incorporating the sixth principle has not yet been attempted.

Constructs like CC and S_g are not employed explicitly by the procedures in SNPR. The effects to be described appear to be *emergent* properties of the SNPR algorithm.

The SNPR model builds its knowledge structures from an initial small base. The effect of the building operation is apparently to increase progressively the CC of the structures while maintaining a high efficiency. The key to this building process is the use of frequency as a heuristic to discriminate *good* structures from *bad* ones. The general tendency of the building mechanisms is to maximize the sum of the products of frequency and size of the structures being built; this promotes a high efficiency.

The generalization mechanisms usually have the effect of reducing S_g without a corresponding reduction in CC; the overall effect is thus usually an increase in efficiency. The rebuilding mechanism apparently has the effect of increasing CC for a given S_g and thus promotes a high efficiency. In general, the mechanisms which have been shown to succeed in discovering a grammar from a sample of its language appear also to be mechanisms that promote high descriptive efficiency in the knowledge structures.

Other Concepts

Before leaving this outline description of the theory and the computer model in which some aspects of it are embodied, we may note some general points about the character of the theory. It gives expression to a number of rather potent ideas, most of which have a fairly long history in psychology and cognitive science.

One of these ideas is the notion that the acquisition of one skill may be a *stepping stone* or foundation for the acquisition of another. This principle is exemplified in SNPR in the way that the program builds a heterarchy of elements, corresponding to a heterarchy of language skills, with complex elements constructed from simpler constituents.

Another useful principle, more recent in origin but now widely recognized, is the idea that knowledge structures may with advantage be constructed from *discrete modules* together with a *restriction on the range of module types* allowed. This feature, realized in the theory by the three types of element, has the advantage that it facilitates the processes of building or modifying a knowledge structure much in the same way that modularity facilitates construction and repair of buildings or electronic systems (or Lego models).

An idea in the theory which seems not to be widely recognized is the *separation of conjunctive groupings and disjunctive groupings* into distinct modules. The significance of this idea depends on a recognition of the significance of conjunction and disjunction in data compression and optimization. The conjoining of elements represents a reduction of *choice* in the knowledge system and thus an increase in its information content (*information* being used here in the Shannon-Weaver sense). Conversely, the disjunctive grouping of elements represents a preservation of choice and a corresponding reduction of information content. The quest for an optimum balance between S_g and CC is facilitated if the groupings which, so-to-speak, pull in one direction are kept separate from the groupings which have the opposite tendency. This design feature of a knowledge system facilitates the process of molding the structure to fit accurately the patterns of redundancy in the data base.

Mention may be made, finally, of a fourth idea, not new, which appears to have a broad significance in psychology and elsewhere. A modular knowledge structure can be optimized by processes akin to the processes of *natural selection* operating in the evolution of animals and plants. Those modules that are *useful* can be allowed to survive while the many rival modules that are less useful or, in some sense, less efficient may be progressively eliminated. This kind of *evolutionary principle* can be seen to operate in SNPR in the way that absolute and contextual frequency governs the retention or elimination of elements.

EMPIRICAL EVIDENCE

Although the theory is by no means fully developed, it is substantial enough for one to ask how well it fits with available data on people's mature knowledge of language and on the developmental processes leading to the mature system. Most of the evidence I review has been presented piecemeal in previous publications; the intention here is to summarize relevant evidence and to expand the discussion of certain points not previously considered in any detail.

Part of the empirical support for the theory lies in the presuppositions discussed above. To the extent that these presuppositions derive from observations (and in this they vary a good deal) the theory is likewise supported.

A second kind of empirical support is provided by the observed phenomena which the theory was designed to explain. To the extent that the theory does demonstrably succeed in providing explanations for these phenomena, they constitute validating data.

There is, lastly, a kind of empirical support, not always very distinct from the other two, which is phenomena not directly addressed by the theory which do nonetheless turn out to be explicable in terms of the theory; this kind of explanatory bonus can be quite persuasive. There are quite a few phenomena in this category that are considered after a review of those observations which the theory was originally designed to explain.

This section on empirical evidence ends with a discussion of certain observations that appear to be incompatible with the theory in its present form.

Phenomena Addressed by the Theory

The main phenomenon addressed by the theory is the observation that children can apparently discover a generative grammar from a sample of language, given only that sample as data. Insofar as SNPR does broadly the same thing, albeit with simpler grammars, it may be regarded as empirically valid. As an example, SNPR has successfully retrieved the grammar shown in Table 7.2, given only a sample of the corresponding language as input (Wolff, 1982).

In the following subsections, the components of this grammar-abstraction process are examined individually to see how well the theory fairs in each domain.

1. Segmentation

The first subproblem chosen for this project was to find a sufficient mechanism to explain how children could learn the segmental structure of language given the apparently insufficient and unreliable nature of clues like pause and stress.

The problem was artificially purified by assuming, contrary to probable fact, that such clues made no contribution to the segmentation process. The main alternative is some kind of distributional or cluster analysis designed to reveal statistical discontinuities at the boundaries of words and other segments. Ideas of this kind were, of course, central to distributional linguistics and had been explored by linguists (Gammon, 1969; Harris, 1961, 1970) developing tools for

TABLE 7.2
Artificial Grammar and Fragment of a Corresponding
language Sample

```
S → (1) (2) (3) | (4) (5) (6)
1 → DAVID  |   JOHN
2 → LOVES  |   HATED
3 → MARY   |   SUSAN
4 → WE   | YOU
5 → WALK  |  RUN
5 → FAST  | SLOWLY
```

Part of the sample used as input to SNPR:
    JOHNLOVESMARYDAVIDHATEDMARYYOURUNSLOWLY...

FIG. 7.3. Part of a 10,000 letter sample from book 8A of the Ladybird Reading Series showing a parsing developed by program MK10 at a late stage of processing (Wolff, 1977).

linguistic analysis and also by psychologists (e.g., Olivier, 1968) interested in psychological processes.

Word Structure. After a good deal of experimentation, a program was developed (a precursor of program SNPR called MK10) which produced good results in discovering word structure in artificial and natural language texts (Wolff, 1975, 1977).

A variety of search heuristics were tried, including transition probabilities between elements and measures derived from standard indices of correlation, but the best results by far were obtained with a simple measure of conjoint frequency of elements. In terms of the compression principles (which were recognized after MK10 was developed) this model may be seen as a fairly direct expression of principles 1 and 3.

Figure 7.3 shows part of a sample of an unsegmented text taken from book 8A of the Ladybird reading scheme; the tree markers show the parsing developed by the program at a late stage of processing.

There is an extremely good fit between these markers and the conventionally recognized word structure of the text, showing clearly that the program is sensitive to structures at this level. There is some evidence that the process is also sensitive to structures smaller than words. The performance of the program in identifying structures larger than words is considered in the next section.

Phrase Structure. If program MK10 is run on a text like the one just described, it will, given time, build up structures which are larger than words and which look like phrase-structure trees. The results obtained with the Ladybird text, and others, showed a rather poor correspondence between these trees and the trees which would be assigned to the texts in conventional surface structure analyses.

One possible reason for this poor performance is that the program was not designed to discover disjunctive groupings of elements. Program SNPR does seek disjunctive groupings but it is not yet efficient enough to be run far enough on natural language for its performance with phrase structures to be judged.

A stop-gap solution to the problem of disjunctive relations was to transcribe a text as a sequence of word classes and to use this transcribed text as data for MK10. This is not a wholly satisfactory procedure because it does not provide for disjunctive groupings above and below the level of words. Despite this shortcoming and the other clear shortcomings of MK10 (not taking account of semantics, for example) surprisingly good results were obtained (Wolff, 1980).

Figure 7.4 shows one sentence (and a bit) from a 7600 word sample from Margaret Drabble's novel *Jerusalem the Golden,* which was transcribed as a sequence of word class symbols and processed in that form by MK10. The dendrogram above the sentence shows a supposedly uncontroversial surface structure analysis assigned by a linguist and the author. The dendrograms beneath show the parsing developed by the program at a late stage or processing. There is quite a good correspondence between the two analyses in this and many other cases. Statistical tests have confirmed that the correspondence is very unlikely to be an artifact of chance coincidences.

As we have seen, these results on segmentation cannot be construed as proof that children actually do distributional analyses of this kind. They merely demonstrate that such processes are plausible candidates, perhaps sufficient by themselves to explain how children learn to segment language or perhaps working in conjunction with processes which use available prosodic and semantic cues. It is perhaps worth observing that the use of such cues as a guide to structure is, in a deep sense, also distributional. If redundancy and structure are in some sense

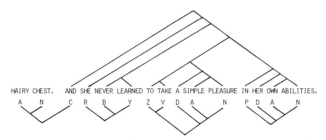

FIG. 7.4.   One sentence from a 7600 word sample from *Jerusalum the Golden* (Margaret Drabble) showing (above the text) a surface-structure analysis assigned intuitively and (below the text) the parsing developed by program MK10 at a late stage of processing (Wolff, 1980). This figure is reproduced by kind permission of Kingston Press Services Ltd.

equivalent (Garner, 1974) then all modes of discovering structure may ultimately be seen in terms of redundancy abstraction.

2. Parts of Speech and Other Disjunctive Categories

In the same way that the theory has developed ideas from taxonomic linguistics about the discovery of segmental structure, it has adopted and extended what is perhaps the most distinctive idea from this tradition: how part-of-speech and other disjunctive categories are established.

The basic idea of course is to look for groups of elements where the members of the group share one or more contexts (where *context* means either or both of syntactic and semantic context). If, for example, the child finds the two patterns AX and BX in the language that he hears then X may be treated as a *context* and a structure (1)X may be created where 1 is a pointer or reference to the disjunctive grouping (A | B).

The principle is quite simple but its proper realization in a fully specified working system has proved quite difficult. What has been achieved in SNPR is the precise specification of a process in which the searches for segmental and disjunctive groupings are *integrated* in such a way that elements of one type may be incorporated in elements of the other kind and this at any level. The discovery procedure produces a generative grammar rather than some less explicit description of the data.

The observations that languages contain disjunctive categories like nouns, verbs, and adjectives is, like any other observation, partly a product of one's theoretical preconceptions. There are, no doubt, other descriptive frameworks one could employ which do not use them. But categories like these seem to be so strongly determined by the linguistic data that it seems reasonable to characterize them as observed phenomena rather than theoretical constructs. Less well supported but still reasonably clear is the observation that categories like these are a (usually unconscious) part of every adult's unschooled knowledge of language structure. The main evidence for this derives from word association tests (e.g., Deese, 1965; but see the discussion below on the "S–P shift") and from speech errors (e.g., Fromkin, 1973).

If it is accepted that there is indeed something here requiring explanation we may ask how well the theory does in this respect. The performance of SNPR with artificial texts gives some indication of its ability to find disjunctive groups but, given that these groups have been artificially created, we cannot tell directly how it would do with natural categories.

Some attempt has been made to run SNPR on natural language but it requires impractically long program runs to get useful results. (This in itself should not be an objection to the model given that children, with much more computational power at their disposal, take several years to develop their linguistic knowledge.) Nevertheless, the program does develop some categories which correspond fairly well with recognized categories in English.

Validation of this general approach, though not the precise details of the current model, is provided in an interesting study by Kiss (1973). (Rosenfeld, Huang, & Schneider, 1969, obtained similar results although their theoretical interests were rather different.)

Using a rather simple definition of the *context* of a word (the word immediately preceding the given word and the word following), Kiss measured the extent to which each of a set of selected words in a sample of natural language shared contexts with other members of the set. He then applied a standard clustering algorithm to these data to determine the *strength* of association between words. The clusters of words identified in this way corresponded quite well with the categories conventionally recognized by linguists (nouns, verbs, etc.).

Mention may be made here of observations which provide some supporting evidence for the idea that children do do a systematic comparison of linguistic structures in an attempt to find elements shared by more than one structure, much as in SNPR. In Ruth Weir's classic study (1962) of her young son's presleep soliloquies one may find sequences of the child's utterances in which a word or a group of words recurs:

> . . . *which one; two; one; right one; now left one; this one.* . . (p.180)

and later,

> . . . *I'm taking the yellow blanket; too much; I have the yellow blanket; down; don't stop in the blanket.* . . (p.181)

and many similar examples.

One gets the impression (supported by direct evidence appearing elsewhere in Weir's protocols) that the child is repeating bits and pieces of language heard during the preceding day. The recurrence of words like "one" and "blanket" may simply reflect their recurrence in the original sequence of adult utterances but the overall impression one gets from Weir's records is that utterances are being brought together from disparate sources on the strength of shared constituents. We may here be witnessing part of the process of sorting and sifting required to establish disjunctive groupings of distributionally equivalent elements.

3. Generalization of Grammatical Rules and Correction of Overgeneralizations

The theory (in common with a number of other artificial intelligence theories of language acquisition) provides for the generalization of linguistic rules. Something like this is essential in any (empiricist) theory of language acquisition in order to explain how it is that both children and adults produce novel constructions which they are unlikely ever to have heard.

There is no great difficulty in creating generalizations. Almost any distortion in a grammar, including the deletion of rules, will lead it to generate constructions which it did not generate before. No strong claim is made about the particular generalization mechanisms in the present theory—it is a matter for future investigation to establish what mechanism or mechanisms children and adults actually use.

Correction of Overgeneralizations. The much more difficult problem, which has received relatively little attention from psychologists or other theorists, is to establish what theoretically well-motivated process can, without the aid of a teacher or informant, eliminate the wrong generalizations and retain the good ones as permanent fixtures in the grammar.

The monitoring and rebuilding mechanisms in SNPR offer a possible explanation. Other possibilities were briefly discussed in the section outlining the workings of SNPR. Here I review some evidence that the mechanisms in SNPR are empirically valid. The evidence is provided by the results of running the program on an artificial language sample (see Table 7.2); the details are described in Wolff (1982).

An artificial text with no segmentation markers was prepared from a simple grammar but all instances of two of the (64) sentences generated by the grammar were excluded from the text. When the program was run on this text it successfully retrieved the original grammar despite the fact that the generative range of the grammar was not fully represented in the sample. In the course of building up the grammar it produced many *wrong* generalizations all of which were corrected. Every one of the *correct* generalizations, including those required to predict the missing sentences, were retained as permanent fixtures in the grammar.

In this case, the criterion of *correct* and *incorrect* was the grammar used to create the text. But this use of an artificial grammar to validate the model, although it is justified as an aid to developing the model, is potentially very misleading. The grammar used to create the text is only one of many that could have produced the same text and without some independent criterion there is no guarantee that the one employed is the *best* one. It is a mistake to allow one's knowledge of English (say) to dictate what is right and wrong when one is dealing with a text which may look superficially like a subset of English but whose *true* structure may be significantly different from English.

A fully satisfactory validation of the generalization and correction mechanism in SNPR is likely to prove difficult. No proper judgment can be made until a model has been developed which can give results with natural language including a satisfactory semantic input. If the mechanism allows wrong generalizations through (*wrong* now in the sense that they are not acceptable to a native speaker of the language) this would be clear evidence against the mechanism. But the model may fail more subtly if it eliminates generalizations that native speakers would in fact accept. Errors like these may be very difficult to detect.

Apart from validating the model against the judgments of native speakers of a natural language it is also necessary to demonstrate that the model does in fact realize the optimization principles on which it is based. This is chiefly a matter of demonstrating that CC increases as learning proceeds and that CC/S_g is maintained at a high level. In order to validate the optimization principles themselves it will be necessary to show that improved performance on measures of optimization correlates with success in discovering satisfactory grammars as judged by native speakers of the language. These are matters for future research.

Explanatory Spin-off

The distinction between explanations considered in this section and those in previous sections is not very clear cut because the prominent facts of language acquisition have been born in mind at all times and they have affected the selection and rejection of hypothesized learning mechanisms. However, what follows was not a primary focus in developing the theory and may reasonably be counted as explanatory bonus, at least in part.

1.   The Rate of Acquisition of Words

Children typically produce their first word at about 12 months. In the following 6 months, new words are acquired rather slowly but then the pace quickens to produce a flood of words in the period of 18 months to 3 years. Because many of these new words are object names, this phenomenon is often called the ''naming explosion.'' The rate at which new words are learned continues to be high throughout most of the rest of childhood; this is not as noticeable as the first burst of activity because it is not quite as dramatic. It is also quite difficult, without special techniques, to assess the size of the person's vocabulary when it is anything but very small. From early adulthood the rate of acquisition of new words declines progressively into old age.

The picture of vocabulary growth just sketched derives mainly from observations of spoken words but it seems to be similar for receptive vocabulary.

This pattern of vocabulary growth can be explained quite well by the theory. We have supposed that children are, from birth, busy building up bits and pieces of language structure starting with very small primitives. Eventually, one of these pieces reaches word size or near word size and, particularly if it is meaningful, it will be identified by adults as the child's first word. The reason suggested by the theory for the initial slow growth of vocabulary is that the child is still engaged in constructing the elements from which new words are built. With only a restricted range available, vocabulary growth will be slow. When the range is bigger, the rate of acquisition of new words will increase because relatively little processing is required in the construction of each new word; the rate should remain high for some time.

We may expect an eventual decline because opportunities to observe new words will eventually become rare enough to put a damper on the learning of new words (but see later discussion of this question). There is some evidence that rare words are constructed from a greater variety of constituents than common words and this might also tend to limit the rate of vocabulary growth.

This kind of informal explanation of the way vocabularies grow is not entirely satisfactory because observed patterns of growth depend in a complex way on the processing characteristics of the child and the statistical structure of the language being learned. A better way of matching the theory with empirical data is to construct a working model and see what patterns of vocabulary growth emerge when it operates with natural language. This has been done and the patterns produced correspond quite well with the picture sketched above (Wolff, 1977).

2. The Order of Acquisition of Words and Morphemes

Except for an anomaly to be discussed, there is a clear tendency for children to learn common words before rare ones (Gilhooly & Gilhooly, 1979). Given that in most languages rare words tend to be longer than common words and the variety of rare words is greater than the variety of common words (Zipf, 1935) we would expect children to learn long words later than short ones and we would expect the increases in lengths of words at successive ages to become progressively smaller.

A clear implication of the theory is that common structures should be learned earlier than rare ones. The implication that long words should be acquired later than short ones depends purely on the known relationship between frequency and word length and is nothing to do with the fact that the program builds large structures from small ones: This feature of the program would be entirely compatible with zero or even negative correlation between word length and age of acquisition.

As in the previous section, a working model is needed to see in detail how well expected patterns of acquisition correspond with observed patterns. Program MK10 produces a very good match with available data (Wolff, 1977).

Figure 7.5 shows the relationship between the lengths of words acquired by a young child and the ages at which they were acquired (data from Grant, 1915). Figure 7.6 shows comparable data for program MK10 applied to three different samples of natural language. In both figures, the progressive increase in the lengths of words can be seen and also the progressive decrease in the rate at which lengths increase.

Over the age range covered in Fig. 7.5, the decreasing rate at which word lengths increase is not very obvious. But it is easy to establish that the curve will be less steep at later ages because a linear extrapolation of the curve in Fig. 7.5 would lead one to predict that children would be acquiring absurdly long words in their late childhood and teens.

The anomaly mentioned above is that, in the early stages of language acquisition, function words tend to appear later than content words (McCarthy, 1954)

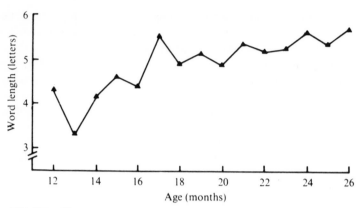

FIG. 7.5. The average lengths of words acquired by one child at differ-ent ages (Wolff, 1977; data from Grant, 1915). This figure is re-produced by kind permission of The British Psychological Society.

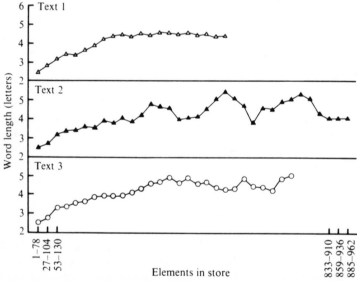

FIG. 7.6. The average lengths of words isolated by program MK10 from three natural language texts at different stages of processing (Wolff, 1977). This figure is reproduced by kind permission of The British Psychological Society.

although they are, typically, amongst the most frequent words in any language (Fries, 1952).

The best available explanation of this exception to the general pattern is that function words are largely meaningless until the larger syntactic patterns in which they function have been built up. A child may know the sound patterns of "and," "the," "into," etc., at an early age but have no cause to use them until they can be fitted into coordination constructions, noun phrases and prepositional phrases respectively. By contrast, words like "table," "Mummy," "more," etc., are quite useful by themselves and can sensibly be used as soon as they are learned. A clear prediction of the theory, then, which would be interesting but difficult to test, is that children do have a knowledge of function words at an age before they start to use them.

Brown's (1973) observation that there is no significant correlation between frequency of use by caretaking adults and order of acquisition of fourteen functional morphemes (e.g., present progressive "-ing," preposition "on," plural "-s" etc.) is completely at odds with the theory presented here. The argument used above (that the later acquisition of certain forms is more apparent than real) cannot be used here because all of the forms considered in this part of Brown's study are alike in that they are all functional morphemes, no one of which can sensibly be used as a meaningful utterance by itself. The criterion of acquisition was, in every case, correct use in 90% of obligatory contexts.

The conflict between the present theory and Brown's results is apparently resolved by the more recent conclusion (Forner, 1979; Moerk, 1980) that Brown's analyses of his data are in fact wrong. When defensible changes and refinements are made in the assumptions that go into the analyses then substantial and significant (negative) correlations are found between frequency of use and order of acquisition of these fourteen morphemes.

3. Brown's (1973) Law of Cumulative Complexity

Perhaps the most interesting general conclusion from Brown's (1973) classic study is that if one structure contains everything that another structure contains *and more* then it will be acquired later than that other structure. Given the variety of current linguistic theories there is some uncertainty about what the *content* of a structure might be but this "Law of Cumulative Complexity" seems to stand up almost regardless of the theoretical framework adopted.

The law is not as trivial as it may at first sight seem although it does correspond with untutored expectations about language acquisition. It is conceivable that children might, in a certain sense, *acquire* structures whose internal organization is, initially, quite unlike the mature form eventually attained. A pattern ABC might be acquired directly or built up as (A(BC)) and then, with the subsequent recognition of AB as a discrete entity, it might be restructured as ((AB)C).

It may at first be thought that Brown's Law follows directly from the way the SNPR model has been designed: the model may be thought to be less an explanation of the law than a restatement of it. It is true that SNPR builds its structures from previously established constituents but there is nothing in the model to prevent a structure being built up initially in one form and then reconstructed in another.

The suggested reason why children (and the model) do not generally do this is that (as with the building up of words) frequency is the guiding heuristic. As a matter of observation (Brown & Hanlon, 1970) complex structures are less frequent than their constituents. According to the theory, they should, therefore, be acquired later.

4. The S-P/Episodic-Semantic Shift

It has been recognized for some time that the way children respond in a word association task changes as they mature. Young children tend to give as their responses words which could follow the stimulus word in a sentence (syntagmatically related words) whereas older children and adults tend to respond with (paradigmatically related) words which can be substitued for the stimulus word in a sentence (see, for example, Entwisle, 1966).

More recently, Petrey (1977) has reexamined Entwisle's data and has argued, persuasively enough, that while the syntagmatic-paradigmatic (S–P) shift remains roughly true, changes in word association responses through childhood may be more accurately characterized as an "episodic-semantic" shift. What this means is that young children tend to give as responses either words which could follow the stimulus word in a sentence or words which signify objects or events which could have been experienced by the child at the same time and place as the object or event signified by the stimulus word, or both of these. A seeming example of a response based on physical contiguity is a child saying "cook" after the stimulus word "add." Petry points out that this superficially bizarre response makes good sense when you see that other responses to "add" include "flour," "milk," "water," "dinner," "cake," etc. *Adding* things is something which young children may well typically first experience in the context of cooking.

Older children and adults tend to give responses which are related to the stimulus word in some way more abstract than mere syntactic or temporal/spatial contiguity. This abstract relationship (sometimes called "semantic") is typically both a paradigmatic (part-of-speech) relationship and a meaning relationship as in "long-short," "wild-tame," "give-take," etc.

If we assume that word association norms at different ages reflect changing organization of stored knowledge then these phenomena make good sense in terms of our theory (see also Kiss, 1973). The theory postulates that children search for recurring clusters of spatially and/or temporally contiguous *events* both in their linguistic input and in their other experience. They also search for groups of elements in which members of the group share one or more temporal or spatial contexts. The disjunctive groups are incorporated in complex elements which represent clusters of similar patterns (see later).

The crucial point here is that the latter kind of search depends on the prior formation of clusters based on contiguity—it cannot get off the ground until there is a big enough set of simple clusters from which to derive common contexts and similarity groupings. If simple contiguity groups correspond to episodic knowledge and disjunctive/complex groupings correspond to semantic knowledge then the delay, just mentioned, in the construction of disjunctive/ complex structures provides an explanation of the episodic-semantic shift; we apparently have an answer to Petrey's (1977) question: ". . . by what process can episodic memories of words in context lead to the abstract semantic organisation of mature lexical storage?" (p.70).

There is other evidence supporting the present view of the S–P shift. This shift tends to occur earlier for high frequency stimulus words than for rare ones and it correlates with the variety of syntactic contexts in which a word appears (see Kiss, 1973). The second observation is probably equivalent to the first one given that words with a wide variety of contexts will tend also to be frequent. The late appearance of an S–P shift in rare words may be attributed firstly to the fact that such words are themselves learned late and secondly to the probable fact that they tend to fall in contextual patterns which are less frequent than the most frequent contexts of common words. There are details here that need quantification.

A seeming problem for the account just given is that, as Petrey points out, children are speaking more-or-less correctly by the age of 4 whereas the S–P shift is most dramatic between the ages of 6 and 8. If, as Petrey assumes, correct speech is evidence of a knowledge of part-of-speech categories then it is hard to understand why paradigmatic responding does not appear earlier.

It is plain that children are combining words in a creative way from a very early age and it is tempting to assume, therefore, that all their speech at all stages is produced by combining elements according to rule and guided by a knowledge of permissible substitutes in particular contexts. This is not necessarily so. As least some correct utterances may be produced as essentially direct replicas of utterances previously heard. Both the theory and the observation just mentioned would lead us to expect that young children would produce a relatively high proportion of utterances of this kind. It would be interesting although perhaps methodologically difficult to obtain evidence on this point.

5. Overgeneralizations

The idea that children, in forming linguistic generalizations, might, so to speak, overshoot their target and produce wrong overgeneralizations is not merely a byproduct of the theory. Clear examples of overgeneralization like "hitted," "mouses," etc., are very prominent in young children's speech and they are indeed one of the most salient pieces of evidence that children are abstracting general rules.

The theory not only provides a mechanism for correcting wrong generalizations but it seems to explain a quirk which has been observed in the way these generalizations arise. Children apparently produce irregular plurals and past tense verbs like "geese," "mice," "fought," etc., in their *correct* form initially. *Only later* do they substitute the overgeneralized "gooses," "mouses," "fighted," etc., and then revert eventually to the correct forms again (Slobin, 1971).

This pattern fits the theory well because, as explained in the section on the S–P shift, disjunctive groupings (and the generalizations that derive from them) can only be formed at a stage when there is a range of simple patterns to generalize from. The irregular nouns and verbs will be learned as they are observed and then displaced by generalizations when they are formed. The correction mechanism will restore them later.

6. The Slowing of Language Development in Later Years

The way in which vocabulary growth eventually slows down echoes the more pronounced way in which a child's learning of grammatical patterns is accomplished largely before the age of 5 and then tails off in later years (see Chomsky, 1969).

A commonsense explanation of these effects would be that the child cannot continue to build up his knowledge of language if he or she has extracted all the available patterns in the data. In order to account for a progressive slowing in language learning rather than a sharp cessation of learning one could refine this view by taking account of the way unlearned structures would become progressively rarer as the data becomes exhausted. The opportunities to observe new structures would become more and more sparse. Notice that this explanation does not depend on the observations that common structures are learned earlier than rare ones although it is entirely compatible with it.

Plausible as this *exhaustion* explanation may appear, it is very probably wrong or at least only partly true.

Although there are many uncertainties and methodological difficulties in estimating the total size of the person's vocabulary (Ellegard, 1960; Seashore & Eckerson, 1940), it is clear that most people in their lifetimes do not come anywhere near exhausting the word forms in their native language, certainly for a language like English with its exceptionally large vocabulary. While people may reach a stage in their learning where the frequency of any particular unlearned word is very low, the variety of as yet unlearned words is so great that the frequency of this class of words as a whole is relatively high.

There are considerable difficulties in determining the extent of a person's knowledge of grammatical patterns and there are uncertainties in what should or should not be regarded as a distinct pattern, but it seems reasonably clear that there are many esoteric patterns that people do not generally bother to learn.

"We found 9-year-olds and 10-year-olds who could not, even with prodding, respond with the correct answer: "What should I feed the doll?'' [in response to the instruction "Ask L what to feed the doll"]. The question that we wish to raise is whether these children are still in a process of acquisition with respect to this structure and will at some future time be able to interpret it correctly, or whether perhaps they may already have reached what for them consitutes adult competence. We have observed from informal questioning that this structure is a problematic one for many adults, and there are many adult speakers who persist in assigning the wrong subject to the complement verb. This seems to be a structure that is never properly learned by a substantial number of speakers" (Chomsky, 1969, p. 101).

Before we proceed to consider an alternative or supplementary explanation of the slowing down in the acquisition of new language patterns, one other commonsense explanation may be noted. Part of the cause of a slowing up in language learning may be a reduction in processing capacity because of physical deterioration in the brain. Barring disease, such an effect looks unimportant before old age. Even then it would seem to be only a minor factor because of the informal observation that people can pick up new words rapidly at almost any age if they are introduced to a new language.

The explanation suggested by the theory for why language learning slows up in later years has to do with the tradeoffs which are basic in the theory. The two that have been considered so far will serve the argument. Children are supposedly miserly in their use of storage space for long-term storage: New information will only be stored in a long-term form if it adds significantly to the usefulness of the knowledge structures for encoding information. In the early stages of learning, plenty of such patterns are observed and quickly incorporated in the child's long-term knowledge structures. Later on, patterns that are useful enough to warrant long-term storage will be encountered less and less often and acquisition will slow.

We might imagine that this gradual slowing in the growth of linguistic knowledge would have a sharp terminus when the child's database is finally exhausted of all structures that are useful enough to be worth storing. However, this expectation is based on the assumption of a fixed database. Given a continually expanding linguistic corpus and the resulting fluctuations in the observed frequencies of linguistic patterns, we have a second reason for expecting a gradual tailing off in language learning rather than an abrupt end to it.

The essential difference between this *tradeoff* explanation and the *exhaustion* explanation mentioned at the beginning of this section, is that it proposes optimization as a limiting factor rather than the availability of patterns in the data. Given uniform linguistic experiences and given variations in how miserly individuals need to be with storage (this in turn presumable depending in part on the total available storage), the preferred view predicts variations among individuals in how big their mature system will be while the other view does not. The two views differ also in that the preferred view does not require anyone to exhaust the data available to them whereas the other view does.

7. Nonlinguistic Cognitive Structures

As already stated, a working assumption in this project has been that a set of principles may be found to operate in all spheres of knowledge acquisition (which is not to say that differences may not also be found). Nonetheless, most work to date in this project has been done with input data and knowledge structures which are most clearly analogous to syntax. There has been a relatively unsuccessful attempt to develop ideas in the nonlinguistic sphere (Wolff, 1976), this at a stage before several important insights had been achieved. Wolff (1987) argues for a uniform system for encoding syntactic and semantic knowledge but relatively little is said about the latter. Only a little is said here. The topic really warrants a whole paper to itself.

The chief merit of my 1976 paper is to establish a set of target criteria of success for a theory of how classes of objects (*concepts* in this context) may be developed. Briefly, these are:

1. Natural classifications of objects differ from the artificial classes studied by, for example, Bruner, Goodnow, and Austin (1956), in that they are in some sense *salient:* They reflect structures inherent in the world which our concept learning systems can abstract without *explicit teaching.*

2. Our concepts are arranged in hierarchies and heterarchies.

3. There is overlap among conceptual groupings.

4. The boundaries of natural classes are in some sense *fuzzy.*

5. Natural classes are often *polythetic:* No single attribute or group of attributes need be shared by all members of the class. (This together with 3 and 4 above are the chief differences between natural classification systems and those developed by the majority of clustering algorithms.)

6. Attributes of objects carry varying *weights* in the process of recognizing new instances of a class.

The model described in Wolff (1976) was reasonably successful at meeting all the criteria, except the requirement of polythesis. Now it seems that program SNPR, although it was developed primarily as a model of syntax learning, meets all six criteria completely. This is not to say that it is a wholly satisfactory model of concept acquisition—there are other criteria that may be added to these six which it would not be able to model.

The reason that SNPR can be seen as a model of concept learning is that it develops disjunctive classes and it also develops complex elements that can be seen as intensional descriptions of classes of *similar* entities. For example, a complex element with the structure (A|B)X(C|D)Y (where | represents exclusive "OR") describes the extensional class of entities AXCY, BXCY, AXDY and BXDY. The members of this class are similar, obviously, because they share attributes X and Y and, less obviously, because there is some commonality among them in the attributes A, B, C, and D. Because X and Y are common to all members, this particular class is not polythetic. But SNPR is quite capable of developing intensional descriptions like (A|B)(C|D)(E|F) where the members of the corresponding extensional class (ACE, ACF, BCE, BCF, ADE, ADF, BDE, BDF) have no single attribute in common. This is a truly polythetic category.

The term *attribute* used here need not be confined to conventional perceptual attributes like shapes and colors. It may also cover functional attributes like the fact that a ball can roll (Nelson's, 1974 example). Contextual properties of concepts—fish are typically found in water, for example—are handled quite straightforwardly by the system because of the way it develops part-whole hierarchies: The concept of fish can be incorporated in a larger element representing fishy environments. Contextual or extrinsic attributes of concepts are arguably equal in importance to conventional intrinsic attributes in establishing the nature of a category.

SNPR also meets the other five criteria. The elements developed by the model are salient in the sense that they express redundancies in the input data and are discovered without explicit teaching. SNPR can develop part-whole hierarchies and it can also develop class-inclusion hierarchies in which overlap between classes can occur. Fuzziness of concepts and differential weighting of attributes can be dealt with by allowing the identification of new entities as belonging to one or other of preestablished categories to be a probabilistic matter (as in my 1976 model).

The relevance of the theory to the realm of nonlinguistic cognitions is underlined by the similarity between the complex elements developed by SNPR and the well-known notions of *schema* (Bartlett, 1932; Bobrow & Norman, 1975), *frame* (Minsky, 1975), and *script* (Schank & Abelson, 1977). Like these theoretical constructs, a complex element in the theory is a generalized pattern which reflects a commonly recurring set of entitites, be it a set of cultural expectations (Bartlett) or the things found inside a typical room (Minsky) or the typical pattern of events that occur when you eat a meal in a restaurant (Schank & Abelson). All these notions share the idea that there are *slots* in the framework where alternatives may be inserted, and they share the idea that one of the alternatives may function as a default—the assumed filler for the slot when there is no contrary evidence. In the syntagmatic elements developed by SNPR the disjunctive constituents are equivalent to slots. Since members of each disjunctive set typically vary in their contextual probability, the most probable one may be regarded as a default element.

The foregoing is intended to indicate how a theory largely developed with reference to syntactic phenomena may indeed generalize to semantic phenomena with little if any adjustment, in accordance with the working hypothesis of uniform structure-abstracting principles. The major gap in these ideas is some principled account of the origin and growth of *relational* concepts. This is a matter for future work (but see Wolff, 1987).

8. Nativist Arguments

Three planks of the nativist position have been that a knowledge of language structure must be largely known in advance because the available evidence contained in the language which a child hears is too much obscured by *performance* errors and distortions of various kinds; because the vagaries of individual experience of a given language and individual variations in ability do not square with the way everyone acquires essentially the same grammar; and because language acquisition apparently happens too fast to be explained by learning alone.

> A consideration of the character of the grammar that is acquired, the degenerate quality and narrowly limited extent of the available data, the striking uniformity of the resulting grammars, and their independence of intelligence, motivation, and emotional state, over wide ranges of variation, leave little hope that much of the structure of the language can be learned by an organism initially uninformed as to its general character. (Chomsky, 1965, p. 58)

And later:

> . . . there is surely no reason today for taking seriously a position that attributes a complex human achievement entirely to months (or at most years) of experience, rather than to millions of years of evolution or to principles of neural organization that may be even more deeply grounded in physical law . . . (Chomsky, 1965, p. 59)

That the data available to the child has a "narrowly limited extent" seems to be simply wrong. Anyone who has had any dealings with the recording of what adults say to children or in their presence will know that the quantities of data are enormous.

That the data are very often corrupted in terms of what native speakers with mature knowledge would judge to be correct, is clearly true; attempts to show otherwise seem to be misplaced. The 'dirty data' problem is illustrated in Fig. 7.1. A strength of the theory is that it neatly explains how children can learn from such data without being thrown off by errors: Any particular error is, by its nature, rare and so in the search for useful (common) structures, it is discarded along with many other candidate structures. (If an error is not rare it is likely to acquire the status of a dialect or idiolect variation and cease to be regarded as an error.)

In practice, the programs MK10 and SNPR have been found to be quite insensitive to errors (of omission, addition, or substitution) in their data. A good example with respect to omissions is the way SNPR was able to discover a grammar from data containing less than the complete range of terminal strings of that grammar.

It is probably true that the members of any given language community have grammatical systems which are quite similar, one to another. But they are not identical. There are many more-or-less subtle differences between individual systems (Broadbent, 1970). The uniformity of grammatical systems across a wide ability range seen by authors like Lenneberg (1967) may be attributed in part to unsophisticated methods of assessment. With more penetrating techniques like those pioneered by Chomsky (1969) many differences come to light which can otherwise easily be overlooked.

Even though there is wide variation in children's experience of any given language, we should not be surprised to find quite a lot of similarity between the grammatical systems that they develop. The reason is that, within one language community, children's experience of language can be varied at the level of particular sentences but quite uniform at the level of the grammatical patterns on which those sentences are modeled and uniform in terms of the words out of which they are constructed. (Without this uniformity it would not be reasonable to say that the children belonged to one single linguistic community.) Abstraction processes like those in SNPR which are guided by constancy (redundancy) are not distracted by idiosyncratic realizations of recurrent patterns.

The third argument, that language development is too fast to be explained by learning mechanisms, need not detain us. The computational power of a child's brain is clearly huge. The computational demands of current models are quite high but there is no reason to think they are unrealistically high. Given what has already been achieved with only a few hours of a conventional computer's time, there is every reason to think that with more computing power exercised over months and years this kind of process may discover the full complexity of language structure quite easily.

9.   The Word Frequency Effect

One of the most fully documented phenomena in psychology is the observation that a spoken or written word or other perceptual pattern is, in some sense, more easily perceived if it is frequent in the observer's experience than if it is rare. This effect is rather insensitive to varying modes of testing and to varying measures of perception.

There have been many attempts to explain the effect, all of which necessarily assume that people have a knowledge of the relative frequencies of these perceptual patterns. But none of them suggest any reason *why* people should have this knowledge. Now, in the theory, we have a natural explanation: A knowledge of the relative frequencies of perceptual patterns (linguistic or otherwise) is a byproduct of search processes which are, so to speak, *designed* to construct an optimal cognitive system.

Neutral and Disconfirming Evidence

Most of the empirical evidence presented so far is apparently explicable in terms of the theory and most of it provides support for the theory. There are of course many other observations of children's language development about which nothing has been said. This large residual set of observations may be divided into two parts: observations, which are in a sense neutral with respect to the theory, which will be considered briefly, and some that seem to be incompatible with the theory, which are discussed at more length.

An example of the kind of observation which is neutral with respect to the theory would be the particular utterances recorded by Braine (1963). It happened that the child, Andrew, said "all done," "all buttoned," "all clean," among other things, but he might just as well have said "all eaten," "all black," and "all found," etc.; no current theory can explain why Andrew said the particular things he did say. It would require an extraordinarily precise theory of motivation and the like to pin such things down.

There seems at present to be only one class of observations which conflicts directly with the theory. In its current form the theory makes a clear statement that children progress from small structures to larger ones by concatenating contiguous elements. What this means is that an utterance like "hit the ball" may only be built up as *((hit the)ball)* or (more likely) *(hit(the ball))* and children should never produce telegraphic utterances like "hit ball" as they have been observed to do (Brown, 1973). Likewise, at the level of word structure, it should be impossible for a child to learn a *schema* of salient features of a word with interstitial elements missing and then subsequently fill these details in (as claimed by Waterson, 1971). No child should ever say "[byʃ]" at an immature stage in the attainment of the adult word "brush," as Waterson's son was heard to do. In this example there is vowel substitution (which is explicable by the theory in terms of generalization) but the missing [r] represents a supposedly unbridgeable gap between the beginning and the end of the word.

CONCLUSION

A theory may suffer many ills. It may be a loose sketchy affair which does not allow one to make reliable inferences. It may be trivial in the sense that it does not do much more than redescribe the data it is meant to explain. Or it may be trivial because it is an overgeneral catch-all theory which cannot be falsified. Many theories in psychology are weak because they are applicable to only a narrow range of phenomena, often ones observed in a laboratory setting which may lack "ecological validity" (Neisser, 1976). "Micro theories" like these are usually weak also because they do not suggest any connections with a broader theoretical framework.

These points are made, of course, to introduce the claim that the theory described in this chapter is reasonably free from these defects. Certainly these pitfalls have been born in mind and considerable efforts have been made to avoid them.

As a theory of language development, the theory seems also to fair quite well against the useful criteria proposed by Pinker (1979) for evaluating such theories. It cannot yet meet the most stringent of these criteria: that it should propose mechanisms which are powerful enough to learn a natural language. But it does show promise in this direction.

The second criterion, that the theory should not propose mechanisms that are narrowly adapted to a particular language, seems to be met. It is almost axiomatic that a universal feature of languages is *structure* expressed as *redundancy*. Mechanisms designed to abstract redundancy will thus be quite general in their application. There is always the possibility, of course, that a language may be found containing a type of redundancy not yet brought within the scope of the theory.

Whether or not the kinds of mechanism proposed can learn a language within the same time span as a child cannot be decided with absolute confidence. But, as previously argued, there is no reason for supposing that they cannot. Pinker's fourth criterion—that the theory should not demand information in its database which is not reliably available to children—is certainly met by the theory. Stress has been laid in this chapter on the way only weak assumptions have been made about children's sensory input.

That a theory of language development should have something to say about the phenomena observed when children progress towards a mature knowledge of language is another criterion which the theory meets fairly well. We have seen how patterns of vocabulary growth, the Law of Cumulative Complexity, and other developmental phenomena may be explained by the theory.

The last criterion is that proposed mechanisms should not be wildly inconsistent with what is known about children's cognitive abilities. Again, the theory seems quite satisfactory in this regard. The child is seen as taking repeated samples of data and abstracting linguistic structures from them. No single sample needs to be very large and all potential problems of combinatorial explosion are met by the heuristic devices embodies in the theory. Quite a lot of computation is required but there is no reason to think that it is beyond the scope of the 10^{10} neurones which are available.

Future Work

Probably the most useful first step to take in future development of this theory would be to test and refine the ideas in Wolff (1987) by constructing a new computer model which embodies them. One aim would be to establish more clearly how parsing and production processes may be married to the proposed representational system. But the main goal would be to examine how well the proposed learning principles may operate with this system. At some stage a resolution must be found to the mismatch between the theory and the previously discussed observations on telegraphic speech.

An area that needs closer attention is the application of optimization principles to the acquisition of relational concepts. Also in need of fuller treatment is an examination in quantitative terms of how well different learning mechanisms can serve the optimization goal. Related to this is the need to test whether or not success in optimization correlates with success in discovering *correct* linguistic structures as judged by native speakers of a language.

Most of the empirical predictions of the theory have been tested against observations that are already recorded in the literature. There are however a few predictions from the theory that invite further empirical work. If a suitable testing method could be found, it would be interesting to see whether or not children really do have some kind of knowledge of function words at a stage before they use them. Likewise, it would be interesting to test whether babies do indeed have a developing receptive knowledge of word fragments at stages before they utter their first words as the theory predicts they should.

One other empirical question that deserves attention concerns children's developing knowledge of disjunctive grouping and the extent to which their utterances are constructed from smaller constituents or are direct readouts of stored patterns. The theory predicts, and the evidence from word-association tests confirms, that children's knowledge of distributional equivalences should lag behind their knowledge of acceptable strings of words. It would be useful if a method could be found of establishing, for any given utterance, exactly how it was produced. One might then be able to test the theory's prediction that the building of utterances from smaller constituents should become increasingly important as the child's linguistic knowledge matures.

The ideas discussed in this chapter are not intended to be a new dogma. As with any theory in this area there are too many points of uncertainty to warrant rigid views. The theory does, however, seem to have sufficient merit to serve as a framework for future theoretical and empirical work on linguistic and cognitive development.

SUMMARY

The chapter has provided a broad perspective on an *optimization* theory of language learning and cognitive development, details of which have been considered elsewhere.

The basic idea in the theory is that linguistic and cognitive development is, in large measure, a process of building cognitive structures towards a form which is optimally efficient for the several functions to be served.

The theory assumes among other things that language learning does not depend on overt speaking or gesturing by the child, it does not require any kind of reinforcement or error correction or other intervention by a "teacher" and it does not require graded sequences of language samples. But it may be helped by any of these things.

The theory provides or suggests explanations for a wide range of phenomena. These include the acquisition of segmental structures in language at word, phrase and sentence levels, the acquisition of part-of-speech and other disjunctive categories, generalization of grammatical rules (including recursive generalizations), correction of overgeneralizations (including some observed peculiarities of how overgeneralizations appear in children's speech), the varying rates at which words and other structures are acquired throughout childhood and beyond, the order of acquisition of words and more complex grammatical structures, the S–P or episodic-semantic shift, the development of semantic/conceptual structures, and some other observations. The theory fits well into a biological framework and is broadly consistent with current thinking about language comprehension and production.

There are some observations which are in conflict with the theory in its present form.

ACKNOWLEDGMENT

I am grateful to Alan Wilkes and Philip Quinlan of the University of Dundee for useful comments on an earlier draft of this chapter.

The chapter was first drafted while I was a lecturer at Dundee. I am grateful to the university for supporting this work and to my colleagues in the Department of Psychology for friendly criticism and stimulating discussion.

Some of the research described in the chapter was supported by a Personal Research Grant to me (HRP8240/1(A)) from the British Social Science Research Council.

REFERENCES

Anderson, J. R. (1981). A theory of language acquisition based on general learning principles. *Proceedings of the Seventh International Conference on Artificial Intelligence IJCAI-81*, 97–103.

Bartlett, F. C. (1932). *Remembering: An experimental and social study*. London: Cambridge University Press.

Bobrow, D. G., & Norman, D. A. (1975). Some principles of memory schemata. In D. G. Bobrow & A. Collins (Eds.), *Representation and understanding*. New York: Academic Press.

Braine, M. D. S. (1971). On two types of models of the internalization of grammars. In D. I. Slobin (Ed.), *The ontogenesis of grammar*. New York: Academic Press.

Braine, M. D. S. (1963). The ontogeny of English phrase structure: The first phrase. *Language, 39,* 1–13.

Broadbent, D. E. (1970). In defence of empirical psychology. *Bulletin of the British Psychological Society, 23,* 87–96.

Brown, R. (1973). *A first language: The early stages.* Harmondsworth, England: Penguin.

Brown, R., & Hanlon, C. (1970). Derivational complexity and order of acquisition in child speech. In J. R. Hayes (Ed.), *Cognition and the development of language.* New York: Wiley.

Bruner, J. S., Goodnow, J. J., & Austin, G. A. (1956). *A study of thinking.* New York: Wiley.

Carr, H. A. (1931). The laws of association. *Psychological Review, 38,* 212–228.

Chomsky, C. (1969). *The acquisition of syntax in children from 5 to 10.* Cambridge, MA: MIT Press.

Chomsky, N. (1965). *Aspects of the theory of syntax.* Cambridge, MA: MIT Press.

Coulon, D., & Kayser, D. (1978). Learning criterion and inductive behaviour. *Pattern Recognition, 10,* 19–25.

Deese, J. (1965). *The structure of association in language and thought.* Baltimore, MD: Johns Hopkins University Press.

Ellegard, A. (1960). Estimating vocabulary size. *Word, 16,* 219–244.

Entwisle, D. R. (1966). *Word associations of young children.* Baltimore, MD: Johns Hopkins University Press.

Forner, M. (1979). The mother as LAD: Interaction between order and frequency of parental input and child production. In F. R. Eckman & A. J. Hastings (Eds.), *Studies in first and second language acquisition.* Rowley, MA: Newberry House.

Fries, C. C. (1952). *The structure of English.* London: Longmans.

Fromkin, V. (Ed) (1973). *Speech errors as linguistic evidence.* The Hague: Mouton.

Gammon, E. (1969). Quantitative approximations to the word. *Tijdschrift van het Instituut voor Toegepaste Linguistiek (Leuven), 5,* 43–61.

Garner, W. R. (1974). *The processing of information and structure.* Hillsdale, NJ: Lawrence Erlbaum Associates.

Gilhooly, K. J., & Gilhooly, M. L. (1979). *The age of acquisition of words as a factor in verbal tasks.* Final Report to the British Social Science Research Council on Research Grant HR/5318.

Grant, J. R. (1915). A child's vocabulary and its growth. *Pedagogical Seminary, 22,* 183–203.

Harris, Z. S. (1961). *Structural linguistics.* Chicago: University of Chicago Press.

Harris, Z. S. (1970). *Papers in structural and transformational linguistics.* Dordrecht: Reidel.

Kiss, G. R. (1973). Grammatical word classes: A learning process and its simulation. *Psychology of Learning and Motivation, 7,* 1–41.

Lakatos, I. (1978). Falsification and the methodology of scientific research programmes. In J. Worral & G. Curry (Eds.), *The methodology of scientific research programmes.* Philosophical Papers, Vol. I. Cambridge, England: Cambridge University Press.

Langley, P. (1982). Language acquisition through error recovery. *Cognition & Brain Theory, 5,* 211–255.

Lenneberg, E. H. (1967). *Biological foundations of language.* New York: Wiley.

McCarthy, D. (1954). Language development in children. In L. Carmichael (Ed.), *Manual of child psychology.* New York: Wiley.

Minsky, M. (1975). A framework for representing knowledge. In P. H. Winston (Ed.), *The psychology of computer vision.* New York: McGraw-Hill.

Moerk, E. L. (1980). Relationships between parental frequency and input frequencies and children's language acquisition: A reanalysis of Brown's data. *Journal of Child Language, 7,* 105.

Neisser, U. (1976). *Cognition and reality.* San Francisco: W. H. Freeman.

Nelson, K. (1974). Concept, word and sentence: Inter-relations in acquisition and development. *Psychological Review, 81,* 267–285.

Olivier, D. C. (1968). Stochastic grammars and language acquisition mechanisms. Unpublished doctoral dissertation, Harvard University.

Petrey, S. (1977). Word association and the development of lexical memory. *Cognition, 5,* 57–71.

Pinker, S. (1979). Formal models of language learning. *Cognition, 7,* 217–283.

Rosenfeld, A., Huang, H. K., & Schneider, V. B. (1969). An application of cluster detection to text and picture processing. *IEEE Transactions on Information Theory, IT-15*(6), 672–681.

Schank, R. C., & Abelson, R. P. (1977). *Scripts, plans, goals and understanding: An inquiry into human knowledge structures.* New York: Wiley.

Seashore, R. H., & Eckerson, L. D. (1940). The measurement of individual differences in general English vocabulary. *Journal of Educational Psychology, 31,* 14–38.

Slobin, D. I. (1971). Data for the Symposium. In D. I. Slobin (Ed.), *The ontogenesis of grammar.* New York: Academic Press.

Waterson, N. (1971). Child phonology: A prosodic view. *Journal of Linguistics 7,* 179–211.

Weir, R. (1962). *Language in the crib.* The Hague: Mouton.

Wolff, J. G. (1975). An algorithm for the segmentation of an artificial language analogue. *British Journal of Psychology, 66,* 79–90.

Wolff, J. G. (1976). Frequency, conceptual structure and pattern recognition. *British Journal of Psychology, 67,* 377–390.

Wolff, J. G. (1977). The discovery of segments in natural language. *British Journal of Psychology, 68,* 97–106.

Wolff, J. G. (1980). Language acquisition and the discovery of phrase structure. *Language & Speech, 23,* 255–269.

Wolff, J. G. (1982). Language acquisition, data compression and generalization. *Language & Communication, 2,* 57–89.

Wolff, J. G. (1987). Cognitive development as optimization. In L. Bolc (Ed.), *Computational models of learning.* Heidelberg: Springer-Verlag.

Zipf, G. K. (1935). *The psycho-biology of language.* Boston: Houghton Mifflin.

8 Modeling the Acquisition of Linguistic Structure

Martin D. S. Braine
New York University

It has seemed to me for many years that child language research has desperately needed a model of the acquisition process that is good enough to be taken seriously, that is, a model that is worth improving by those who like its general lines, and worth criticizing by those who dislike it. Only in that way can we progressively improve our ideas about the acquisition process.

Quite recently, the field has seen a number of ambitious models of syntax acquisition (e.g., Anderson, 1983; Berwick, 1985; Pinker, 1984; Wexler & Culicover, 1980) which are either much broader in scope or more detailed in form (or both) than earlier ventures (e.g., Braine, 1971; MacWhinney, 1978). These new models undoubtedly mark a step up to a new level of scientific maturity in the study of first language acquisition. And they certainly satisfy at least one of the criteria of being taken seriously: They are evidently good enough to be worth criticizing.

However, it is not clear that they provide a satisfactory foundation on which to build. Opinions may well differ on that, of course, and the judgment need not be the same—and probably should not be the same—for all of these models. To introduce some of the issues, I begin by considering a prominent acquisition model that has been developed in mathematical work on language learnability (Wexler & Culicover, 1980), to which later models owe a certain debt. I ask whether it is empirically realistic as a conception of the way children acquire a native language.

Because it seems to be the wrong kind of model, I turn to the metascientific question of how best to set about constructing a language acquisition model. To try to set some constraints on possible models that would point to the general sort of model that is needed, I proceed, as in the game of twenty questions, by asking a series of general questions about language acquisition. Where appropriate, I compare the answers of different models, and propose a particular type of learning mechanism that seems to me to meet best the issues raised by the questions, and I show how the mechanism might be incorporated into an acquisition model.

I then offer three further proposals about issues relevant to language acquisition models.

THE LEARNABILITY MODEL

Surprisingly enough, it is possible to study language learnability mathematically, and there is a small continuing tradition of doing so. To do this, one specifies four things: First, the kind and perhaps the sequence of input data to which the learner is exposed; second, the class of grammars whose learnability is studied; third, the initial knowledge state of the learner; and fourth, a learning procedure.

The learning procedure processes each datum (item of input data) in turn. As a result of the processing, there may be a change in the current knowledge state of the learner. A language is said to be learnable if after a finite amount of input data has been processed, the learner reaches and remains in the final knowledge state that contains appropriate rules for the language. If every language of a given class is learnable, in this sense, then the class of languages is learnable.

In general then, a proof of learnability consists in showing that a learning procedure must arrive at an appropriate grammar within a finite time, given a specified kind of input and kind of grammar. It may also be possible to prove nonlearnability: that for a given kind of input and class of languages, there is no way a learner could discover the grammar. Some of the results in this field are in fact demonstrations of nonlearnability.

The field really began seriously with a provocative paper by Gold in 1967. However, Gold considered input data that contained no information about meaning, i.e., that consisted only of sentences of the language, or of a mixture of sentences and nonsentences. The grammars involved did not relate surface structures to deep structures or to meaning; the languages had no semantic component. But obviously, in a realistic learning model, the learner should not only learn rules for generating the sentences of the language but also rules which would enable him or her to understand the sentences generated.

An important step in this direction was taken in a series of papers by Hamburger, Wexler, and Culicover (Culicover & Wexler, 1976; Hamburger & Wexler, 1973, 1975; Wexler, 1978; Wexler, Culicover, & Hamburger, 1975), that had their point of departure in Hamburger's (1971) doctoral dissertation and culminated in the "degree-two" model (Wexler, 1982; Wexler & Culicover, 1980). According to the model, what is primarily learned are the transformations that map deep structures on to surface structures. In the most advanced form of the model, the input consists of sentences paired with their meanings. That is, it is posited that the situational context contains enough information for the child to diagnose the meanings of sentences heard. The strong assumption is made that the meaning of a sentence, as registered by the child, has the same hierarchical structure as its "deep" syntactic structure. That is, a "meaning" is basically an unordered deep structure, defined as in Chomsky's (1965, 1970) concept of deep structure except that the branches are not ordered. Thus, to convert a meaning into a deep structure, all that has to be learned is the ordering of the branches. The learner must first learn this ordering, which constitutes learning the base grammar; then the learner learns the transformations that map from base structures into surface structures.

It is not a difficult problem to write a procedure that will acquire an order. The difficult part is the learning of the transformations. In the early papers it was assumed that the input to the learner was the pair of a sentence and its deep structure, and what was to be learned was the mapping of deep structure onto surface structure. The later work extended this slightly by positing that it is possible to go from unordered deep structure to sentence in two steps, first the learning of the base order, and then the learning of the transformations. Assuming some restrictions on the applicability of transformations, it was proved that the language learning procedure converges on a correct transformational grammar after a finite amount of data has been presented. This constitutes the learnability proof.

The model coupled with the learnability proof are an intellectual tour de force. Also, from a psychological standpoint the model has some attractive features. Thus, in a general way it seems reasonable that the input to the child should consist of adult utterances paired with meanings that are derived from the situational context of the utterance. Another desirable feature, discussed in more detail later, is that the child is assumed to be able to learn from exposure only. That is, the input consists of sentences paired with their meanings, and corrections of the child's utterances are not assumed to play a crucial role in learning. In addition, two of the restrictions on transformations that are very important to the learnability proof—the so-called "freezing" and "binary" principles—may be independently motivated on linguistic grounds (Wexler & Culicover, 1980).

I should add that the authors' claims for the work are not modest. They claim to present "a *reasonable* (their italics) formal theory of language learning." It consists of "a complete formal characterization of the learning process and the language environment in which it operates. The assumptions are in general accord with psychological and linguistic principles" (Hamburger & Wexler, 1975, p. 137).

To some extent the model has been overtaken by changes in linguistic theory that have downplayed the role of transformations, as in the shift from the Standard Theory (Chomsky, 1965) to Government and Binding (Chomsky, 1981). Some current theories of grammar, like lexical-functional grammar (Bresnan, 1978; Kaplan & Bresnan, 1982), even contain no transformations and no distinction between "deep" and "surface" structure. However, they usually contain rules (in the lexicon, in the case of lexical-functional grammar) that do some of the work usually done by transformations, so that an acquisition mechanism for transformations may not be irrelevant. But in current systems the learner's learning task would encompass much more than the learning of transformations or transformation-like rules.

Despite these changes in linguistic thinking, it is important to assess the model's learning mechanism from a psychological standpoint, and it is from this point of view that I wish to discuss it. I comment only briefly on issues that are mainly linguistic, such as the plausibility of the restrictions on transformations and the appropriateness of the conception of the universal form of a human language.

The restrictions on transformations comprise the freezing and binary principles, a ban on optional transformations and several other assumptions (see Wexler & Culicover, 1980, pp. 419–422). It is important to note that these restrictions do little to restrict the *form* of transformations. As we shall see, the model has hardly any restrictions on the form of a transformation. Rather, they restrict how transformations can apply. In particular, the purpose of the freezing and binary principles is to guarantee that a language cannot have transformations that apply only to highly complex deep structures (i.e., structures with n embeddings where n may be large). Thus, they ensure that the evidence necessary to specify a transformation will always be manifest in some moderately simple sentences, specifically, sentences with not more than two levels of embedding. The restrictions, then, guarantee that evidence needed to discover errors in rule learning is available in relatively simple input.

Wexler and Culicover claim that the freezing and binary principles are innate, but it is not clear that innate linguistic principles are required in order to ensure that the evidence needed to discover errors is available in relatively simple input. Instead, suppose we assume, plausibly, that only sentences that are processed contribute to learning, and that the learner's working memory is limited so that the average complexity of the sentences that can be processed is less than two degrees of embedding. Then the rules whose learnability depends on processing of sentences with more than this complexity will not be learned, and languages that contain such rules will be filtered out from the set of human languages. Thus, no innate linguistic principles are needed just to guarantee learnability from simple input.

The ban on optional transformations is psychologically more problematic than the freezing and binary principles because it has a consequence that is pernicious for a realistic model: It means that transformations that one might want to regard as optional (e.g., the passive and some extrapositions) have to be formulated as obligatory. This requires that abstract elements triggering them have to be assumed to be present in deep structure. In the context of the total model, this means that the situational context of an adult utterance containing such a transformation must be assumed to contain cues indicating the presence of the transformation. For instance, suppose a child sees A punch B and simultaneously hears *B is being punched by A*, without perceiving a situational cue to passivity. Wexler et al.'s learner would construct from the situational context the deep structure underlying *A is punching B*. He or she could not then acquire the passive without unlearning the minimum transformations that underlie the active. Similarly, without a differentiating situational cue, learning *A called B up* entails unlearning *A called up B*. It seems counterintuitive to suppose that a child could determine from situational context alone that an utterance contains a passive or extraposition transformation.

From the point of view of psychological realism, the two aspects of the model that it seems most important to discuss are the assumptions made about the input, and the learning procedure for transformations. I think that it is intuitively obvious that the input assumption—that the situational context specifies the meaning of an utterance in sufficient detail to be tantamount to a deep structure—is unrealistically strong. So let us look first at the other aspect of the model, the mechanism for learning transformations, and see whether strong or weak assumptions are made about that.

The general nature of the procedure for learning transformations can best be indicated by describing what happens when the learner encounters a meaning (i.e., a base phrase marker) and a sentence that are not reconcilable, i.e., the transformations learned so far do not map the phrase marker into the sentence. The learning procedure then acts as follows: First, it computes the set of all the transformations which, if added to the existing grammar, would convert the base phrasemarker into the sentence given. This set defines the transformations that could be added to the grammar to make it consistent with the new piece of data. Then, either one transformation from this set is added to the existing grammar; or one transformation that could have applied to that input base phrase marker is eliminated from the grammar. Which of these possibilities happens, and which transformation is selected for addition or elimination, is a purely random matter. Once the new grammar is constituted, the model is ready for the next meaning— sentence pair.

Thus, the learning procedure works by either randomly dropping transformations that may be responsible for a wrong result, or by randomly adding transformations that give the right surface string. This is a very weak learning procedure: On each trial there is random sampling from a shifting pool of possibilities. How weak the procedure is will depend on the size of the pool of possibilities on each trial. It turns out that the number of possibilities is usually huge. It is huge because of the absence of restrictions on the form of a transformation. That is, even for very short and simple sentences, there are always very many ways that a transformation could be written that would map the deep structure into the surface string.

To illustrate this point, let us take a simple sentence and consider some of the

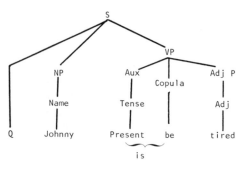

FIG. 8.1. Base phrase marker of *Is Johnny tired?* Note.— Many linguists would treat the Aux node as a constituent of S rather than of VP. Also in modern work, Q (or *wh-*) would hang from a Comp (i.e., Complementizer) node; Comp and S would then be co-constituents of a higher sentential node S̄. Neither of these changes materially affect the argument in the text; indeed, they would increase the variety of possible derived phrase markers.

ways the learning procedure might find for getting to it from its base structure. Suppose 2-year-old Johnny's mother says to him *Is Johnny tired?* and suppose little Johnny diagnoses what his mother means. Thus, according to the model, Johnny has received as input the deep structure shown in Fig. 8.1, paired with the surface string *Is Johnny tired?* How many ways of mapping the former into the latter will Johnny have to choose (randomly) from, in Wexler et al.'s conception? If my understanding of the model is correct, there are many hundreds of ways, at least.

I have worked out 426 different derived phrase markers that could be created.[1] The great majority of these are patently absurd. To enumerate them all would take more space than is warranted, but Fig. 8.2 provides a representative selection to show the variety and curious nature of the possibilities available in the model. For example, in Fig. 8.2a, the adjective *tired* becomes an auxiliary verb and is classified as a kind of tense. In Fig. 8.2b, the auxiliary *is* becomes part of a lengthened NP constituent *Is Johnny*. In Fig. 8.2c, *Johnny tired* becomes a new kind of auxiliary verb, and in 8.2d the whole sentence becomes an Adjective Phrase with *is* and *Johnny* as constituents. All these structures, and many others that could be hypothesized by the model, seem weirdly improbable. It is a serious defect of the model that it entertains them.

It should be added that the number of different transformations that could be hypothesized by the learning mechanism is considerably greater than the number of derived phrase markers: There is usually more than one transformation—often there are several—that will convert any given base phrase marker into a particular derived phrase marker. Thus, as shown in Fig. 8.2, there are four ways of mapping Fig. 8.1 into 8.2a, four ways of mapping it into 8.2b, and three of mapping it into 8.2c. Some of these ways are equivalent from the learner's point

---

[1]I could easily have made some mistakes of commission or omission, so 426 should be taken as approximate.

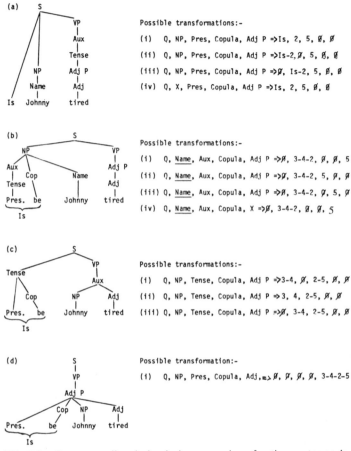

FIG. 8.2. Some peculiar derived phrase markers for the sentence *Is Johnny tired?* Each is associated with transformations that map the base marker of Fig. 8.1 into it.

of view since they would apply to exactly the same set of base phrase markers and transform them to exactly the same derived phrase marker. Thus, in each of 8.2a, 8.2b, and 8.2c, Transformations (i–iii) are equivalent, in this sense,[2] and Transformation (iv) in 8.2a and 8.2b is not equivalent to (i–iii).

In sum, then, the model of Wexler et al., given an input of base phrase markers paired with surface strings, would spend most of its learning time adopting and later discarding hordes of absurd transformations that would never

---

[2]It seems a severe defect of the formalism for writing transformations that it should allow such different ways of expressing the same structural change.

occur to a real child who was incapable of dreaming up sophisticated linguistic absurdities. Thus, the learner's "naivete" is not modeled.

The linguistic literature contains some proposals to restrict the form of transformations that would eliminate the possibility of deriving many of the absurd structures. However, there is no consensus among linguists about these proposals, and they are not embodied in the model's formalism for transformations. In part, the lack of agreement among linguists has been due to disagreements about how "deep" deep structure is. When the deep structures are taken as fairly close to the surface it is likely that very tight restrictions on the form of transformations would be possible; but if the deep structures are taken as very deep, as in the now largely defunct school of generative semantics, then hardly any restrictions are possible. But note that when the deep structure is taken as close to the surface structure it runs the danger of becoming quite far removed from the semantic representation—one of the motivations for "deep" deep structures was to render transparent the relation between deep structure and semantic representation. But, since it is only the semantic representation not the deep structure that could be specified by the situational context (and, usually, only a part of the semantic representation), the further removed the deep structure is from the semantic representation, the more implausible becomes the assumption that the situational context is capable of specifying something tantamount to a deep structure. So while one could simplify the model's task of learning transformations by tightly restricting the possible form of a transformation, such restrictions would render the acquisition of the base grammar itself problematic.

While the authors are aware of the problems raised here (e.g., Wexler & Culicover, 1980), they also contend (Hamburger & Wexler, 1975) that it is a strength of their model that it allows such a variety of transformations, because the learnability proof would go over a fortiori if the variety was reduced. However, it is a strength only within a very narrow mathematical perspective.

Let us consider their learning model from a broad psychological perspective. The model has a very weak learning procedure (i.e., with almost no constraints on the kinds of transformations it can hypothesize), and combines this with unrealistically strong assumptions about the input. These two properties go hand in hand. That is, if one wants to keep learnability, a weak learning procedure for transformations will force unrealistically strong assumptions about the input. Conversely, if one wishes to adopt more realistic assumptions about the input, it will be necesary to make the search for the right transformation much simpler. A realistic model would not make such strong assumptions about the input, i.e., it could not assume that situational context can specify meanings tantamount to deep structures. Without this assumption the acquisition of the base grammar itself would become a far from trivial problem, and in compensation, the model would need a learning procedure that saves the learner from sorting through enormous numbers of transformations. In a realistic model, the problem of finding transformations might be easier by a factor of many hundreds. Then one would have plenty of room for making more realistic assumptions about the input, without losing learnability.

To be fair, I should say that the problem of the lack of restrictions on the form of transformations has been a well-known problem of transformational grammar. Wexler et al. inherited the problem; it did not, of course, originate with them. Moreover, criticizing this aspect of the model makes it clear that we do need a theory of the kinds of changes or transformations to which children are sensitive, in order to reduce the pool of potential transformations drastically.

To sum up so far, a prime conclusion to be drawn from the work discussed is that a desirable model within the transformationist framework should keep transformation learning simple in order not to have to make unrealistic assumptions about the input.

A second conclusion to be drawn is that, with their input assumptions, the authors have succeeded in proving learnability for a wider class of languages (those in which the form of a transformation is not restricted) than the set of natural languages (whose transformations are, ex hypothesi, heavily restricted). There is no reason to believe that a human child could learn any language of the set they take as natural (e.g., that included "unnatural" languages with transformations like those of Fig. 8.2).

This conclusion points up a difficulty with a criterion for judging the adequacy of language acquisition models that Pinker (1979) calls the "learnability condition." To be adequate, an acquisition theory must, Pinker argues, posit mechanisms powerful enough to acquire any natural language. Thus stated, the condition appears at first sight unexceptional. However, it assumes that we have a suitable definition of "any natural language." The best approximations to a definition are to be found in linguistics, in theories of the general form of a human language. (There are no useful definitions outside of linguistics.) However, linguistic theories of generative grammars are generally too broad: They define classes of languages that are wider than the class of natural languages. Linguists know that the extant theories of universal grammar are insufficiently constrained. The research strategy in linguistics has been to posit rule forms that allow broader kinds of rules than occur in natural languages, and then to try out various constraints on the system, each constraint being a hypothesis about what is *natural* to human languages. This strategy necessarily results in a specification of the set of natural languages that is too broad, basically because all the constraints have not been discovered yet. Consequently, if one takes Pinker's learnability condition seriously, as Wexler et al. do, then one practically guarantees a model which will learn languages that no human child could ever learn. Something about it will be too powerful—in this case the unrealistic assumptions. In general, the learnability condition is nearly vacuous if we do not go to linguistics for a definition of "any natural language," but pernicious if we do.

PLAYING TWENTY-QUESTIONS WITH LANGUAGE-
ACQUISITION MODELS

Let us briefly consider the metascientific problem of how best to search for the most appropriate acquisition model. If my critique of the learnability model is valid, then the model is not a suitable starting point for further modeling efforts because it is not the right type of model to start with: It takes the acquisition of the base grammar and lexicon for granted, and it poses the learner's problem exclusively as one of finding transformations from large pools of possibilities.

But what is the *right type* of model? How can we discover that? Note that since we are looking for a model that is worth improving, we should not adopt as a primary goal to seek a model that is precise in every detail: A model that is vague in many important respects but which poses the problem of language acquisition perspicuously, and proposes the right kinds of mechanisms is more worth improving (i.e., developing) than one that is precise but of the wrong type.

But how is one to find the right type to start with? I believe that the method that will lead to the right type with least wasted effort is the procedure of the 20-questions game. That is, one poses a series of broad general questions about language acquisition to which answers can be found that will constraint the type of model that is appropriate. For each question, one does not attempt to provide any more precision about the model than is required by the answer to the question. As the questions proceed, the right type will become progressively clearer.

This strategy is adopted in the next part of the paper. A series of broad questions are proposed, and I discuss the implications of the answers for a model of human language acquisition, considering both ideas of my own and recent models in the literature. The first three questions have, implicitly, already been asked and answered. But let us briefly make them explicit.

Question 1: What is the Input to the Learner?

Along with the other recent models (Anderson, 1983; Berwick, 1985; Pinker, 1982, 1984), I agree with Wexler et al. that in some sense the input is a series of sentence-meaning pairs (although it is an important open question how much and what aspects of meaning may be inferred from context).

Question 2: Is There Memory for Past Input?

Unlike linguists, children are not in a position to survey a large corpus at once, comparing utterances with each other systematically. They have to acquire rules from utterances received seriatim. Existing evidence on short-term memory and comprehension (e.g., Sachs, 1967) indicates that memory for the surface form of an utterance tends to disappear as soon as subsequent utterances are processed. Thus, in a learning model's acquisition of rules, each input utterance should be processed and make its contribution to learning at the time of processing, and then be forgotten as the next input is received and processed. That is, the general answer to the question is "No."

This "no-memory" requirement need not be absolute. There is, of course, some rote learning by children of oft-repeated utterances. The literature also allows that the surface form of salient utterances is occasionally retained. And it is plausible that a child might compare two utterances similar in form or meaning that occur one immediately following the other in discourse. Also, of course, the no-memory requirement allows the possibility that the learner may compare an input utterance with an expected form, i.e., with the utterance that the learner's existing rule system would have generated in the same situation. However, these possibilities apart, it seems to me that a model should be suspect if it makes some aspect of learning depend on substantial specific memory for past input.

Wexler and Culicover (1980) accept—indeed argue for—the no-memory requirement. The only recent model that does not wholly accept it is Anderson's (1983); this is a problematic feature of his model to which I return when discussing Question 6.

Question 3: Can Children Acquire a Language Without Correction?

Along with Wexler and Culicover (1980) and other recent models (Anderson, 1983; Berwick, 1985; Pinker, 1984), I believe that the answer to this question is "yes." However, in considering this question, it is important to distinguish two claims—the strong claim that correction plays a trivial role (if any) in language acquisition, and the weaker claim that children can learn their language without benefit of correction (i.e., correction is not necessary for acquisition). The strong claim is controversial although I believe (along with many others, e.g., Baker, 1979; Bowerman, 1983; Pinker, 1982; Wexler & Culicover, 1980) that it is essentially correct—for detailed discussion, see, for instance, Braine (1971), Brown and Hanlon (1970), Moerk (1983), and Hirsh-Pasek, Treiman, and Schneiderman (1984). However, the weaker claim does not seem to be controversial, and is sufficient to dictate a model that is capable of learning without correction. It may be added that, while it is hard to prove conclusively that a child has learned all or part of their native language without ever being corrected for mistakes, it is the case that in the laboratory, acquisition of the syntax of miniature artificial languages without corrections has been repeatedly demonstrated (e.g., Braine, 1965, 1971; Moeser & Bregman, 1972; Morgan & Newport, 1981; Reber & Lewis, 1977; Smith 1969).

QUESTION 4: HOW DOES THE CHILD ARRIVE AT MEANINGS?

It seems apparent on commonsense grounds that when the child has no knowledge of the language the meaning must come entirely from the context. Once the child has learned a little of the language, the meaning will usually come in part from the context, and in part from a partial decoding of input sentences that uses the knowledge of the language that the child has acquired up to that point.

What this means is the following. At early stages of development, most of the learning is going to be based on relatively short, simple input sentences whose meaning is fairly obvious from the context. Longer input sentences and sentences whose meaning is complicated will be largely ignored by the child, because the meanings will not be diagnosable without the aid of some knowledge of the syntax of the language; there will not be a pair, meaning + sentence, and so such sentences will rarely be input data.[3] As the child becomes more competent in the language, the effective input (i.e., the input that is actually used by the child in acquiring structure) will increase in length and complexity. Context will serve primarily to flesh out meanings that could be only partially understood without its help.

What these commonsensical considerations indicate is that a realistic acquisition model must include a comprehension mechanism, as shown in Fig. 8.3. In order to understand each input string, the comprehension mechanism draws on existing knowledge of the language (Linguistic LTM), situational context, and Conceptual LTM (taken as including knowledge of the world). The output of the comprehension mechanism is the meaning of the input sentence. This meaning, paired with the input sentence itself, is the datum on which the learning mechanism operates. Essentially this scheme is followed in the most recent models (Anderson, 1983; Berwick, 1985; Pinker, 1984).

If the comprehension mechanism fails to arrive at a meaning, because existing knowledge together with situational cues are insufficient, or if the input string is too complex for the child's short-term memory, then there is simply no effective input pair established, and therefore no datum for the learning procedure to use.

Obviously, it follows from this conception that as knowledge of the language increases, the complexity of the input data will increase. Thus, an orderly sequence of presentation of input data is arranged naturally.

It should be noted that the answers to this and the prior questions above imply that the child's own productions play little or no role in learning. A child's own productions use the rules of the linguistic LTM. Changes in linguistic LTM are

---

[3]I say ''rarely'' because children do do some rote learning of strings they do not understand, if the strings are repeated often enough.

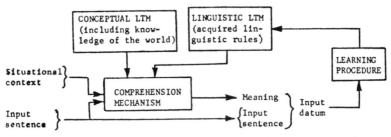

FIG. 8.3. ACQUISITION MODEL: The relation of components to the input.

brought about by the operations of the learning procedure on input data derived from comprehension. The learning procedure is not directly affected by the child's own productions.[4]

Now let us turn to the next question about the input.

QUESTION 5: IS THE INPUT FREE OF ERROR?

Ever since Chomsky (1965) claimed that the language sample that children were exposed to contained a nonnegligible fraction of odd and ill-formed sentences, and that children learned in spite of this, there has been controversy about whether there was error in the input to children. The empirical consensus is that children are exposed to relatively simple short sentences that are "markedly lacking in hesitations, false starts, and errors" (Ervin-Tripp. 1971, p. 192). However, while the incidence of ungrammatical sentences to children may be low, it is not at all clear that it is zero. It seems highly implausible that it should be zero, and I would strongly argue that a realistic learning model should be able

---

[4]However, there are two ways that are consistent with the answers to Questions 1–4 in which learning might be indirectly affected by the speaker's own productions. One way is more relevant to second-language acquisition than first, and especially to adult second-language acquisition. Adult learners may create internal monologues in L2 to practice it. Parts of these monologues may be generated by word-for-word translation from L1, often leading to L2 sentences that are not grammatical. When the resulting L2 sentence is not grammatical, the learner feeds him or herself with a wrong meaning-sentence pair, and the learning procedure would then work on the incorrect, self-given input and consequently learn some wrong rules.

The other way is proposed only in the model of Anderson (1983). Anderson argues, by way of analogy with other skills than speech, that the practice of speech production brings about an automatization of the production processes that is specific to production (i.e., does not affect comprehension—although an independent automatization occurs for comprehension). This is an interesting idea and could potentially account for differences between comprehension and production. However, Anderson has little specific to say about these automatization processes for language.

to tolerate at least a small amount of input error. There are three reasons to assume that the child's learning procedure is robust against errors in the input:

a. There is some experimental evidence that there is a mechanism for the acquisition of linguistic patterns despite some noise in the input. Some years ago, in an artificial-language experiment I compared learning from error-free input with learning from input containing a small percentage of error. Both groups of subjects learned the rules of the language, and learned them about equally rapidly (Braine, 1971).

b. The second reason comes from exceptions in natural language. For example, irregular forms of the past tense in English (for instance *brought* from *bring*) can be regarded as functionally equivalent to errors in the input from the point of view of the learner who is in the process of acquiring the regular past tense form. Children nevertheless learn the regular past tense form and overgeneralize it (e.g., Ervin, 1964). The literature is replete with evidence for the learning of rules despite exposure to exceptions.

c. In the scheme we have been discussing, there are two possible sources of input error. One is that the environment may provide some ungrammatical sentences. That is the only kind of input error that has been discussed so far in the literature. The other kind of error is that the child may hear a correct sentence but misdiagnose its meaning. Since the child's comprehension mechanism must rely heavily on situational plausibility, it follows that an incorrect meaning is quite likely to be guessed whenever somebody says something that is implausible. There are huge numbers of examples in the literature on the development of comprehension, of children arriving at incorrect meanings because their plausibility strategy has led to error. Now, people undoubtedly say implausible things to children less frequently in real life than they do in experiments, but, nevertheless, the claim that children never misdiagnose meaning in real life seems prima facie much too strong.

Thus, there are strong arguments supported by evidence that a realistic procedure must be robust against at least some input noise.

The model of Wexler et al. is not robust against input error. This follows immediately from the fact that after the correct grammar has been found, a wrong input would cause the model to reject some correct transformation or to introduce some incorrect transformation, and it might be some time before the model rediscovered the correct grammar. It might never do so if it encountered further errors.

The requirement that a language acquisition model be robust against input error constrains the possible form that a model can take. A guess-and-test model, for example, will not be robust against input error (Braine, 1971). To be robust against input error a model should have the property that no single datum can have drastic effects on the acquired rule system, for good or ill. An input datum can only have an effect cumulatively, that is, by adding slightly to the effects of prior inputs of the same type. Many years ago I described a model which had this property (Braine, 1971). To give it a name, I shall use the term "sieve memory" to refer to the kind of mechanism that was described there, a modified form of which is proposed again below. This type of mechanism has some family resemblances to models proposed by MacWhinney (1978, 1987), and to connectionist approaches (e.g., McClelland & Rumelhart, 1986). I believe that a sieve memory provides a type of learning procedure that is much more realistic than the kind proposed by Wexler et al.

The general nature of the mechanism proposed is as follows. The components of the model and their interrelations are shown in Fig. 8.4. Beginning on the left side of the diagram, an adult utterance and its situational context feed into a comprehension and scanning mechanism, referred to as the input processor. This seeks to understand the utterance using whatever the child already knows about the language (Linguistic Long-Term Memory [LTM]), and about the world (Conceptual LTM). I take the latter to include fairly broad categories like "Actor," "Action," "Location," etc. in addition to narrower categories of the kind normally encoded in word meanings, and to even more specific information. Once a resultant meaning has been determined, the sentence-meaning pair is scanned in order to detect pattern properties of the input sentence and, especially, of the relation between the input sentence and its meaning. The input processor causes these patterns to be registered in Linguistic LTM. The rules (i.e., features of pattern registered) can be at several levels of abstraction, from specific (rote learning of particular forms) to general (e.g., 'Actor + Action' is an utterance form); also they can be in terms of change from an expected form (e.g., *sang* = past + *sing;* fronting first auxiliary word = question).

Rules in linguistic LTM can vary in strength. Rule strength is governed by two principles concerned with consolidation and decay in memory, respectively. Thus, rules grow in strength with repetition (i.e., repeated detection by the scanner), and they decay in strength with nonrepetition. Only the rules that are above some criterion strength have access to the input processor, and to the child's speech output programmer.

Several consequences follow from the structure of the scanner and the linguistic LTM as described. First, learning occurs from positive instances only; no correction of the child's utterances is needed. Second, other things being equal, the rules acquired fastest will tend to be general rather than specific; this follows because broad and abstract properties are necessarily manifest in more sentences than specific properties, and therefore recur more often in the input. For instance, the property that Actors tend to occur in the first position vis-à-vis actions is a feature of many more English sentences than that *Daddy* tends to occur in first position vis-à-vis actions of his, like *eat* and *read*. Thus, the model predicts, correctly, that in any domain children will tend to learn common, moderately

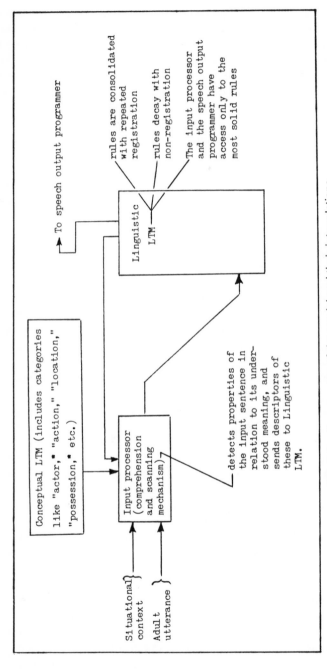

FIG. 8.4. Components of the model and their interrelations.

abstract patterns first, and exceptions and special cases later. Third, the learning mechanism can be tolerant of a certain amount of noise in the input: Unsystematic "errors" in the input (whether they come from ungrammatical adult utterances, wrong inferences by the child as to what an adult means, or irregularities in the language) will indeed be registered, but since they tend to recur rarely or not at all, the decay principle guarantees that they usually disappear from the memory system. On the other hand, irregular forms that recur frequently enough will eventually be learned. Thus, this kind of model can meet the twin desiderata of learning from positive instances only, while being tolerant of noisy input. It has other virtues too, I believe, some of which point out later.

The memory is referred to as a "sieve memory" because the consolidation and decay principles act to separate generative patterns from detail and noise. Thus, by "sieve memory" I mean a class of models in which several potentially competing features of an input element are usually registered, and in which ruels or patterns vary in strength as a function of input variables, notably frequency, so that there is selection from among the competing features.

Tolerance of input noise does not require a sieve memory per se; other models which allow rule strength to vary with input frequency are likely to have the property. But in general, much of a model's work of distributional learning has to be done by strength or strength-like mechanisms: How the input selects among possibilities depends on how rules gain or lose strength. However, not much thought has been given to this aspect of language acquisition in most recent models. For example, although Pinker (1984) allows rules to vary in strength, he provides hardly any discussion of how this strengthening mechanism might operate and how it might interact with other mechanisms in the model (Braine, in press).

I now take two examples to illustrate how a sieve memory might operate. The first example is the acquisition of the rules governing the first word combinations, the second the acquisition of a transformation. However, before we can consider examples, more definition must be given for the scanning mechanism of the input processor and for the information that it draws upon. That is, the model must be made more specific. While there are many ways in which a sieve-memory model might be developed, I illustrate the concept with the way I think most plausible.

The Input Processor and the Information It Has Access To

I make the following assumptions about the processing of the input. First, it seems an inescapable conclusion from the evidence of Ninio and Snow (this volume) that children are sensitive to the illocutionary force of utterances from the outset of language acquisition; I assume, therefore, that the comprehension process includes some assignment of illocutionary force or function to input sentences. Thus, input sentences are marked with an illocutionary function when they reach the scanning mechanism in the input processor.

Second, I assume that all concepts have, inherently, a predicate-argument structure, and that we do not demand that a language-acquisition model account for concepts having this structure. That is, the predicate-argument distinction is a primitive one that is used by the comprehension mechanism in understanding input sentences. Thus, the outcome of comprehension includes identification of the main predicate and its arguments, and noting of the components of the input sentence that indicate these.

In explanation and defense of this assumption, let us begin by noting that the distinction between predicate and argument merely brings together into one pair of terms the distinction between a concept and its instances and that between a relation and and the things it relates (a concept is a predicate with only one argument, and for concepts, "instance" is synonymous with "argument"; a relation is a predicate with more than one argument, and the things related are the arguments). There are strong reasons for thinking that the distinction is psychologically primitive. For instance, no student of learning seems to have envisaged the possibility of explaining how the distinction arises—note that although several theories of concept learning have been developed in the psychological literature, they all take the distinction between a concept and its instances for granted as available to subjects, and merely seek to explain how specific concepts are formed. Similarly, in linguistic semantics and philosophy of language, all semantic theories use a notation that systematically distinguishes predicate and argument (usually based on standard logic); there is no known way of doing semantics without taking the distinction as primitive. In the only philosophical debate that I know of that tries to put the distinction into question (Sellars, 1957; Strawson, 1957), both philosophers conclude that there is no avoiding taking it as given. In sum, the distinction has an excellent claim to being a fundamental category of thought (in the Kantian sense of "category").

For the child acquiring language, taking the distinction as primitive means that we take it for granted that children spontaneously encode scenes and events as consisting of objects that have properties and are related to each other by relations, e.g., a scene of a boy kicking a ball would be perceived as an action relation of kicking (predicate) between two objects, the boy and the ball (arguments). Language and conceptual learning may influence which properties and relations are noticed, but not the tendency to perceive within a predicate-argument framework.

I try to show elsewhere (Braine, 1987) that a parsimonious theory of word classes can be obtained if we take the predicate-argument distinction as primitively available, and combine that assumption with evidence on the abilities and limitations of language learners for performing distributional analyses. The parsimony comes from the fact that, unlike other theories (e.g., Grimshaw, 1981; Pinker 1984), the theory does not assume that the Noun and Verb categories are innate and that it is innately known that these are associated with the ontological categories of "object" and "action."

Third, in analyzing the meaning input, the scanner uses categories and relations established in the conceptual LTM. As noted earlier, these categories and relations are at various levels of abstraction. For instance, some are relatively narrow categories, at about the same level of generality as most ordinary word meanings. Some others are somewhat more abstract notions, like 'one' and 'more than one.' In the young child, I shall assume that the broadest categories include relations like 'action' and 'possession,' and proto-case categories like Actor and Location. The latter have about the same breadth as the meanings of words of seemingly greatest generality in young children's vocabularies, e.g., words like *do* for 'action,' *place* or *where* for Location.[5]

Fourth, when a predicate has more than one argument, the scanning mechanism uses the categories available to it (e.g., the proto-case categories) to distinguish the arguments. Thus, arguments are associated with case-like functions when a predicate has more than one argument.

In defense of this assumption, one may cite its evident efficiency, and the fact there there is evidence for it in young children (Braine & Hardy, 1982; Braine & Wells, 1978; Hardy & Braine, 1981).

Fifth, for these illustrations, I take the segmentation of input utterances into word-like units for granted.

Sixth, in analyzing a sentence, the scanner is inherently equipped to detect position, i.e., it can sense what occurs first and last, or perhaps, first, last, and middle. The position may be the absolute position within a phrase, or may be relative, i.e., position before or after some marker element; and the scanner can detect co-occurrence (a special case of relative position).

Finally, the well-consolidated part of the linguistic LTM (i.e., rules that are above some criterion strength) is available to the scanner. In fact, the operations of the scanner depend on the current state of the rule system. If there are some combinatorial rules in the linguistic LTM that would apply to the meaning input to yield a sentence, then these are applied. (Of course, they may well already have been applied during the comprehension process.) Let us call the resulting sentence the expected or self-generated sentence. The scanner compares the self-generated sentence with the input sentence, and detects differences. The dif-

---

[5]The question how cognitive properties and relations get into Conceptual LTM is beyond the purview of this paper. This paper aims toward a model of the acquisition of just linguistic structure, not a general learning model. Linguistic structure is enough of a problem already.

However, Schlesinger (1979, this volume) provides cogent arguments that the definitions of case categories—especially of the boundaries between certain categories—vary among languages, and that the formation of case categories must therefore be taken as part of the acquisition of linguistic structure. Some learning—at least of category boundaries—must eventually be handled within a language acquisition model.

ferences may take the form of changes in the positions of elements, or additions, or deletions. Descriptions of the differences are registered in the linguistic LTM together with descriptions of the meaning input, as illustrated and discussed below. If there is no difference between the self-generated and the input sentence, the scanner sends to linguistic LTM descriptors of the lexical items that instanced the rules used, and the lexical entries for these items are annotated for having been used in the rules they instanced. (This claim will be relevant to the discussion of Question 7, below.)

If there are no combinatorial rules in linguistic LTM that would apply to the meaning input to yield a sentence, then the scanner sends descriptions of the correspondences between the meaning and the sentence to linguistic LTM, as illustrated below.

Acquiring the First Productive Rules

At the time that the first word combinations begin to be acquired, the child has a small vocabulary and no syntax. That is, linguistic LTM consists of a small lexical memory in which words are mapped on to a subset of the concepts of the conceptual LTM, and the rule system contains no combinatorial rules. What are the first rules like? The data on children's first word combinations indicate that children acquire a collection of independent productive formulae of limited scope. Some of the rules are of fairly broad scope: These are formulae like "Actor + Action," "Located entity + Location," "Possessor + Possessed." Others are of narrower scope, e.g., "*More* + whatever there is more of," "*want* + what is wanted," and the like. There is no evidence for strictly syntactical categories like "noun" and "verb" or "subject" and "VP." This is the conclusion I arrived at a few years ago (Braine, 1976) and Schaerlaekens (1973) came to much the same conclusion from an independent collection of Dutch corpora.[6]

Thus, we have evidence for concepts at at least two levels of abstraction that are used in the emerging rule system. One level comprises the meanings of the words themselves. The other level comprises concepts like "Actor," "Action," "Possessor," "Location," etc. If one thinks in tree-diagram terms, these constitute node labels above the level of word meanings. Some of them, like Actor, Possessor, and Location, amount to proto-case categories. The combinatorial rules that are acquired at this stage consist in an ordering of the elements, that is in establishing the positions of the terms in a formula.

Now let us consider how such rules might be acquired. Suppose that Daddy is eating dinner, and that Mommy points to him and says *Daddy is eating*. Suppose further, that the words *Daddy* and *eat* are in the child's lexical memory, and that he or she guesses accurately what Mommy is trying to convey. That is, the

---

[6]Pinker (1984) has argued that the evidence in Braine (1976) is nevertheless consistent with a base phrase-structure grammar of the usual type with these categories. For comment on his arguments, see Braine (in press).

comprehension mechanism delivers the predicate 'eat' with Daddy as the argument that is doing the eating. We now have a paired input, *Daddy is eating* and its meaning.

Using the lexical memory, the scanner can associate the word *Daddy* with the argument, and the phonological string /ɪzitɪŋ/ with the predicate.[7] The scanner now analyses the sentence at various levels of abstraction, and it causes these analyses to be registered in linguistic LTM. One analysis is a word level analysis: that the string consists of *Daddy* + *is eating* (The ''+'' indicates registration of the element order) with the meaning EAT (Daddy). Another analysis is more abstract. The scanner uses the categories available in the conceptual LTM to categorize the elements. Among these are the categories Actor and Action—and of course to say that LTM contains these categories is to say that it has criteria for identifying instances of them. Thus, the scanner will detect that Daddy is Actor and that 'is eating' is an Action predicate, and that the Actor came first and the action second. So it will cause the linguistic LTM to register that a sequence Actor + Action predicate occurred. The scanner may also cause mixed levels of analysis to be registered, e.g., *Daddy* + action predicate, and Actor + *eat*.

The subsequent fate of these analyses depends on the subsequent input. A normal input will contain a fairly high density of Actor-action sequences, and the Actor + Action analysis will therefore increase in solidity or strength in linguistic LTM and eventually get learned (i.e., reach the criterion strength at which it becomes accessible to the input and speech output processors). Occurrences of utterances with the more specific analysis will have lesser density and fall through the holes of the sieve. However, if *Daddy is eating* has a high enough density in the input, it will be rote learned and the word-level analysis will become a trivial rule that generates one item.

One might wonder whether we have to assume that several levels of analysis are in fact made. I think we do have to. First, children do rote learn some expressions, which indicates that some word-level analyses are registered. Also, many of children's early rules—those that have a constant-plus-variable structure—seem to represent mixed levels. I return to the question of multiple levels of analysis when considering Question 6.

Acquiring a Question Transformation

Now let us consider the situation some months later when there are some syntactic rules in the linguistic LTM. First, let us note that the meaning delivered by the comprehension mechanism will then have more structure to it. For example, after the linguistic LTM contains a formula of Actor + Action, the meaning of a

---

[7]Since we are not dealing with phonological learning, I pass over the problem of how the child finds the word *eat* within the string /ɪzitɪŋ/; it also does not matter for our purposes whether the /z/ of *is* is seen as part of the argument or part of the predicate; it is a strength of the model that the same learning result will occur either way, at this stage.

sentence like *Daddy is eating* will no longer consist merely of a predicate 'eat' with an argument, Daddy. It will have more structure: *Daddy* will have a node label, Actor, and *is eating* will be labeled as an action predicate. An important consequence of this change is that *Daddy is eating* will now be interpretable without supporting situational context, whereas it was not before.

Now let us take a time point when the LTM has rules that generate *Daddy is eating,* but no question transformation. Suppose that the model receives the input sentence *Is Daddy eating?* and that the context is sufficiently clear that the comprehension mechanism perceives that this is a question. Thus, it has a meaning input that consists of a question cue + something that can be represented by its rules as 'Daddy present-be eating,' the latter corresponding to the self-generated *Daddy is eating.*

Thus, we have an analysis that comes jointly from context and existing rules that can be represented as

$$Q \ (Daddy \ + \ \underbrace{pres\text{-}be}_{is} \ + \ eating)$$

which is realized as

Is Daddy eating?

The scanner compares the two and registers that Q is associated with the change in the positions of *Daddy* and *is* (= pres-be). The scanner codes changes naively and directly. That is, it registers that *is* and *Daddy* have changed places; it does not have the ingenuity to think of such possibilities as recoding *Daddy* as an auxiliary verb.

The position change, and the fact that it is associated with Q, is registered with weak strength in the linguistic LTM. It is registered at various levels of abstraction. Thus, *is* may be coded as *is,* as pres-be, as first auxiliary word, as auxiliary, etc. *Daddy* is coded as *Daddy,* as Actor, and as subject (if that category is available at the time). One of these analyses is the one that is most frequent in the input, and this one will be the first to reach criterion strength, and will thus be the first systematic question transformation rule learned.

Note particularly that a very important question that the learning mechanism has to solve is the degree of abstractness at which the change is finally described. That is, in English, is it *is* that moves, or is it pres-be, or is it tense-be, or is it the first auxiliary word, or the entire auxiliary perhaps? And does it change places with *Daddy,* or with Actor, or with Subject. A sieve memory might solve this kind of problem in various ways, as might other models, a fact that leads to the next question.

QUESTION 6: THE DEGREE-OF-ABSTRACTNESS PROBLEM: HOW IS LEVEL OF ABSTRACTNESS DETERMINED FOR THE CATEGORIES USED IN RULES?

In principle, any word or phrase can be categorized in very many ways. Consider the possible input sentence *Mommy is singing* uttered in an appropriate context, and consider how *Mommy* might be categorized. Possible categories are 'Mommy,' 'woman,' 'female,' 'adult,' 'human,' 'animate,' 'concrete object,' 'singular,' 'ingestor of edibles,' 'singer,' 'agent,' 'subject,' 'topic,' 'argument of a predicate,' N, and NP, as well as a huge number of other categories. In English for the subject-verb agreement rule, 'singular' ends up as the category that is eventually selected; for the Question transformation, 'subject' is the eventual category found to be relevant. What is the child's method of selection?

Let us look at how selection is managed in some current models and the assumptions involved. Consider first Anderson (1983). If I understand the model correctly, for any particular kind of rule there is a specific level of abstractness at which the rule is always initially formulated. For instance (Anderson, 1983, p. 279), when *the boy* is marked as 'definite' in the meaning structure, the rule formulated is:

'Definite object' → *the* + object   (1)

That is, 'object' is the level of abstractness at which *boy* is automatically classified vis-à-vis definite and indefinite. (It's not clear to me how abstract 'object' is for Anderson's learner—whether, for instance, kisses, smells, earthquakes, etc., would be automatically classified as "objects.") To take another example (Anderson, 1983, p. 279), given *The boy shoots a lawyer*, the rule governing the main word order is formulated as:

'Relation agent object' → Agent + relation + Object,
if the relation is 'shoot'   (2)

Thus, *boy* and *lawyer* are automatically categorized by their case relation to *shoot*—i.e., quite abstractly—but the linearization rule itself is automatically sensitive to a context that is lexically specific—i.e., not at all abstract.

Since these initial levels of abstractness are often not the required final levels, Anderson's learner goes through a process of discrimination when the initial level is too broad, and through a process of generalization when it is too specific.

The discrimination process restricts a rule to a context or increases the restrictiveness of the context. It involves finding a feature true of the current context but not presented previously (Anderson, 1983, p. 280). The search posits a considerable amount of memory in the learner for previous utterances and their meanings. As discussed in relation to Question 2, a requirement of specific memory of this sort is an extremely implausible property of a language acquisition model.

Generalization among rules that are too specific is accomplished by a continuous process of editing for economy that collapses similar rules and creates word classes under specific (rather ad hoc) conditions. Although I cannot prove that it is wrong, it seems to me that a self-editing capability is an overly rich addition to a language acquisition model's innate structure: Other things being equal, parsimony should prefer a model without that capability.

Note that the discrimination and generalization procedures about which questions can be raised are forced into existence by the fact that the level of abstraction is fixed for the initial rules formed by Anderson's learner.

For Pinker (1984), the main phrase structure rules are also initially acquired at a specific level of abstraction—the abstract level at which such rules are formulated in standard adult grammars. This conveniently eliminates the need for generalization mechanisms for this kind of rule, but means that Pinker had to do battle with a lot of child data that argue for lower initial levels of abstraction (e.g., Bowerman, 1973; Braine, 1976).

Let us now consider the degree of abstractness problem from the point of view of a sieve memory. For a sieve memory, the problem breaks into two pieces: (1) How are the properties to which the child attends determined? (2) From among the properties attended to, how does the relevant property come to be selected? The answer to the second question is given jointly by the detailed structure of the sieve memory and the actual frequency of categories in the input. The answer to the first question, on which I now wish to focus, comes from aspects of an acquisition model external to the sieve memory mechanism itself. For the overall model to work, these external factors must reduce the number of categories submitted to the sieve to a manageable quantity.

One strategy might be to postulate that the external factor is an innate restriction on the properties the child attends to, e.g., following Pinker (1982), one might assume that the child knows innately the features that might be syntactically relevant—number, gender, animacy, etc., and not color, temperature, etc. However, as Pinker (1984) points out, given the large number of features used syntactically across languages, and the arbitrary nature of many word subclasses, this is not a promising way of limiting the number of properties attended to.

There is another way in which the properties a child attends to might be controlled. This is through biases in the comprehension and scanning mechanisms that process utterances prior to registration in memory. Two biases seem plausible. One bias is functional: The learner would attend to the semantic and syntactic properties and relations that were used by the comprehension mechanism in interpreting the input utterance. The other bias is towards registering features of surface structure.

The functional bias would guarantee that certain properties are fairly routinely attended to. These would include illocutionary force or function of an input utterance, and where appropriate (as in the case of a statement), identification of the main predicate and arguments, and assignment of case-like functions to the arguments when there is more than one argument. Other properties (e.g., number, tense) would be routinely attended to only after the form of the emerging linguistic system has progressed to the point that these features are routinely called up by the comprehension mechanism. Otherwise, features are called up by the comprehension mechanism and attended to only if something in the situational context causes them to be noticed. For instance, in the case of number, after the contrast Noun vs. Noun + /z/ has been associated with 'singular' vs. 'plural,' then 'singular' and 'plural' are routinely called up in the comprehension process and are available for submission to the sieve. Before that point, number is only registered when situational context clearly marks it (e.g., number would be clearly marked as relevant in the likely context of the maternal utterance *Just one cookie*). Like Pinker's abandoned proposal, a functional bias would guarantee that syntactically irrelevant properties like color and temperature are rarely noted (except, of course, in the case of utterances with color terms or predicates like *hot* in appropriate contexts).

The surface-structure bias would encourage registration of phrase positions, word order, and salient phonological properties, e.g., beginnings and ends of words, the character of stressed syllables, and the like. Registration of features of this sort leads to the formation of categories of words that are characterized phonologically, e.g., ending in -/a/, ending in [+ strident]; it also contributes to mixed characterizations, e.g., monosyllabic verbs ending in /ŋ/. Studies of the acquisition of morphology in inflected languages indicate the ready formation of such categories (e.g., Berman, 1982, 1986; Levy, 1983a, 1983b, this volume; MacWhinney, 1978).

QUESTION 7: HOW ARE OVERINCLUSIVE GRAMMARS DISCARDED?

An overinclusive grammar generates all the wellformed sentences of a language, but also generates sentences that are not wellformed. That is, it is possible to have two grammars both of which generate the wellformed sentences, but differ only in that one of them—the overinclusive grammar—also generates strings that are not grammatical to native speaker intuition. We face the following problem: Since every sentence the child hears is consistent with both grammars, and given the assumption that the child can learn without information about what is *not* a wellformed sentence, how does the child come to settle on the correct grammar and not on the overinclusive grammar? The problem is particularly acute since the overinclusive grammar will often be intuitively simpler than the correct one.

Three examples will serve to illustrate the problem.

1. The simplest case is provided by exceptions in morphology. For instance, in English the past of *throw* is *threw*. However, the overinclusive grammar allows *throwed* in addition to *threw*. It is known that English-speaking children pass through a phase in which regularized forms and exceptions seem to be in free variation, i.e., they use both the forms *threw* and *throwed*. They seem to have acquired the overinclusive grammar. How then do they learn that *throwed*, the form predicted by the past tense rule, is in fact not wellformed?

In the case of such morphological errors, many people will be tempted to consider it plausible that correction by adults may be responsible for the disappearance of *throwed*, despite our assumption. So let us consider a second example, taken from an earlier discussion of the problem of overinclusive grammars (Braine, 1971), in which correction provides a much less plausible explanation.

2. English presents the following verb phrase forms:

Make somebody do something	*Make somebody to do something
*Force/compel somebody do something	Force/compel somebody to do something
Let somebody do something	*Let somebody to do something
*Allow/permit somebody do something	Allow/permit somebody to do something
Help somebody do something	Help somebody to do something

That is, *to* obligatorily precedes the complement verb in the case of *force, compel, permit,* and *allow;* it is obligatorily absent for *make* and *let;* and optional following *help.* These details about English structure seem entirely unmotivated by any semantic or syntactic considerations. In the overinclusive grammar, all the forms listed are wellformed: *to* is optional in all cases, i.e., all these verbs are like *help.* Every sentence the child hears would be completely consistent with the overinclusive grammar, which by any ordinary intuitive criteria is simpler than the correct grammar. How do children discover, without being told, that in English one does not say *make (let) somebody to do something* nor *allow (permit/force/compel) somebody do something?*

3. The final example is from Baker (1979). English presents pairs of verb-phrase forms like the following:

Give the thing to somebody	Give somebody the thing
Tell the story to somebody	Tell somebody the story.

Many other verbs (e.g., *bring, take, deliver*) partake of both forms. However, there are verbs that have only one of these forms, e.g.,

Report the event to somebody	*Report somebody the event.

Most grammars for English contain a rule that generates the second form from the first:

[Subject] [verb] NP_1 to NP_2 $\Rightarrow$ [Subject] [verb] NP_2 NP_1.

Once a child has learned such a rule, they have an overinclusive grammar. The rules would generate all the correct forms but also incorrect forms like *Report somebody the event*. Again, the overinclusive grammar would be consistent with everything they hear. How then do they learn that forms like *Report somebody the event* are not wellformed?

The literature contains two kinds of answers to the question how overinclusive grammars are avoided or superceded. One answer (Braine, 1971) provides a method by which such grammars, once acquired, could be superceded. The other answer is exemplified by Baker (1979) and is more ambitious in that it aims to avoid overinclusive rules ever being acquired in the first place. I discuss Baker's approach first.

Baker proposes that there are innate restrictions in the child that control the kinds of rules and categories that will tend to be acquired, and that these restrictions are such that the right rules are learned initially: The overinclusive grammar is never acquired and thus never has to be discarded. The challenge of examples like 2 and 3 above is to find principles, which could be built in, which would prevent the child making the wrong (overgeneral) analysis.

Baker does not discuss Example 2 above, but in relation to Example 3 he proposes that there are restrictions on the kinds of transformational relations to which the child is sensitive, so that the transformational rule is not acquired. Instead, children learn the two base VP structures independently, i.e.,

[verb] NP_{obj} to NP_{rec}, and [verb] NP_{rec} NP_{obj}.

(obj = 'object' and rec = 'recipient.') Children register the environments possible for the verb, and thus register for each verb which structure it goes into. For *give* and *tell,* Baker's model would register both environments, and for *report* it would register only the environment: [_____] NP_{obj} to NP_{rec}.

The validity of this approach rests on the assumption that children never in fact pass through a stage where the overinclusive grammar is operative. That is, it predicts that children will never make errors like *report somebody the event*. Yet there is good evidence for such errors (Bowerman, 1983; Mazurkewich & White, 1984).

There is also some evidence for the overinclusive grammar in adult intuitions. For example, consider the new English verb, *to tavver;* it means 'to transfer something from one place or person to another with a zigzag motion of the hand.' Adults I have tested—readers can test themselves—accept both the following sentences as wellformed after being given just the definition of the verb:

Would you tavver the salt and pepper to your mother, please?
Would you tavver your mother the salt and pepper, please?

Similarly, consider the new verb *kithil,* which means 'to convey information telepathically,' Adults I have asked find both the following sentences acceptable:

I kithiled John the answers to the calculus test, but the silly fool wasn't paying attention.
I kithiled the answers to the calculus test to John, but the silly fool wasn't paying attention.

These observations indicate that the new verb can be available in both relevant contexts without actually having been heard in them. The judgments are incompatible with Baker's proposal that one only learns the grammatical frames that are specific for a verb. They suggest that the developmental sequence in acquiring a new verb (at least at late stages of development) must be to start with the more inclusive grammar and then narrow it (given that observed usage of the verb requires that it be narrowed).

The other proposal (Braine, 1971) assumes a sieve memory as the learning mechanism. However, it adds the following general operating principle governing the mode of operation of the scanner and memory system:

Whenever a newly acquired specific rule (i.e., a rule that mentions a specific lexical item, like *throw, make, allow, report* in the preceding examples) is in conflict with a previously learned general rule (i.e., a rule that would apply to that lexical item but also to many others of the same class), the specific rule eventually takes precedence.   (3)

Because of the frequency-based selector mechanism, in any domain of the grammar a sieve memory will typically begin by acquiring patterns or rules of at least moderate generality. However, learning does not stop with the acquisition of the general pattern; the learning mechanism continues to learn details. As noted earlier, when a sentence has been successfully parsed and understood through rules already acquired, lexical entries for the content words are annotated for the rules they instanced. (Thus, the linguistic environments of lexical items are continuously registered throughout life.) Like all registration in Linguistic LTM the annotation is initially weak and subject to decay, but it accumulates strength with repetition. This annotation process is important for the acquisition of the details of subcategorization frames (e.g., learning that *fall* is intransitive, that *knock down* is transitive, and that *drop* may be either). Thus, many lexically specific patterns within the domain of a general pattern are eventually acquired. Operating Principle 3 guarantees that when the specific patterns have finally been learned, they take precedence over the output of the more general rule. (Variations of this principle have been proposed by several people now; in fact, the idea goes back to the old notion of a bleeding order of rules. Note, however, that the sequence in which the rules are learned is important—a specific rule does *not* take precedence when it is learned *before* the general one.)[8]

Let us now consider the examples. The first is straightforward: *throwed* is eventually eliminated in favor of *threw* because Operating Principle 3 assures that specific forms like *threw,* once learned, will come to take precedence over the form generated by the general past tense rule.

Example 2 is discussed in some detail in Braine (1971), where it was proposed that the general rule has *to* optional before complement verbs. Children then go on to register patterns of cooccurrence for each verb (e.g., that *force* and *allow* occur with *to,* and *make* and *let* without it). As the specific patterns are learned they take precedence over the general rule. For *help,* both the specific patterns (*help* NP VP and *help* NP *to* VP) get registered; since there is no particular order of precedence among competitive lexically specific patterns, *to* ends up optional after *help.*

Turning to Baker's example, the general rule or rules would assign both environments

$$\text{(i.e., [---] NP}_{\text{obj}} \text{ } to \text{ NP}_{\text{rec}}, \text{ and [---] NP}_{\text{rec}} \text{ NP}_{\text{obj}})$$

to any verb of the appropriate type (i.e., verbs which indicate transfer of an entity to a recipient, with the agent as subject). (The precise nature of the rule(s) is irrelevant for our purposes. There could be two independent base structures, coupled with some semantic specification of the class of lexical items inserted in

---

[8]Of course, when a specific pattern is learned first, it cannot be annotated as a special case of the more general pattern. But in general, special circumstances must operate for a specific pattern to be acquired before a parallel general pattern. For instance, the categories of the general pattern may not be available to the scanner at the time the specific pattern is being learned, so that the specific pattern has a long lead through the memory filter. Another special case occurs when the specific patterns receive an analysis that is not parallel to that of the general pattern. For example, if *went, fell,* etc., are first analyzed as monomorphemic (i.e., not as *go* + past, *fall* + past, etc.) (Kuczaj, 1977), and if they are frequent in the input, then they may proceed through the memory filter faster than 'verb + past.'

Cases where a specific rule is learned before a more general one may be cases where the grammar becomes reorganized during the course of development. These cases are excluded from the purview of Operating Principle 3 because they may have special properties associated with them, inconsistent with the principle. For example, it is known that the very young child's first past tense forms may be exceptions like *went, did,* and *fell;* at a slightly later stage, the general past tense rule is learned and may prevail over the previously learned exceptions, e.g., the early *did, fell,* became *doed, falled* (Ervin, 1964). Later, the exceptions are relearned, and *then* they come to take precedence over the regularized forms. Thus, one can find developmental sequences like *fell > falled > fell ~ falled > fell.* The initial development (e.g., *fell > falled*) could be due to a substitution of a bi-morphemic for a monomorphemic analysis, coupled with the acquisition of the regular past tense rule. In any case, when a specific pattern is learned first, it does not take precedence over a later-acquired general pattern.

the verb slot; or the rules could state only one base structure and generate the other by transformation.) Once this general structure is acquired the grammar is overinclusive and generates *report somebody something*. At the next stage the child registers the frames specific to the individual items *give, tell, report,* etc. Both frames are learned for *give* and *tell*, but only one for *report*. These specific patterns, once learned, take precedence over the general rule and hence *report somebody something* disappears as a possible form. However, even after many lexically specific rules have been acquired, it will still be the case that a newly acquired verb will be subject to the general rule, until a specific frame has been associated with it. Thus, new verbs of the appropriate class, like *tavver* and *kithil,* will be acceptable in both environments, in conformity with the evidence cited earlier.[9]

Strictly speaking, Baker's proposal and mine are complementary, not competitive. That is, when the developmental facts indicate that the child acquires an overinclusive grammar and then narrows it, then my approach is needed to explain the development. But when the developmental facts indicate that an overgeneral grammar is not acquired where it might have been expected—i.e., the predicted errors do not occur—then Baker's approach is called for. However, children's common errors of overgeneralization indicate that narrowing an originally overinclusive grammar is a common developmental sequence, whereas Baker's proposal is still in need of an existence demonstration—that is, proof that there are cases where the developmental facts require his approach. But there are, of course, many areas of language development where the relevant facts are not yet known.

This is as far as I go in trying to play twenty-questions about language-acquisition models. In the remainder of the paper, I make a proposal and an argument, each about a specific issue in modeling language acquisition, and then

---

[9]Mazurkewich and White (1984) claim that verbs that occur in both environments are (a) of native rather than Latinate origin (which is correlated with being monosyllabic or disyllabic with stress on the first syllable), and also (b) the indirect object is the possessor or prospective possessor of the direct object. They propose that after children have learned the general alternation rule they learn these restrictions on its application. However, there are several problems with Mazurkewich and White's proposal. First, they provide no reason why children should regard the more general rule as false merely because they happened to perceive that native verbs with indirect-object possessors satisfied it; some principle favoring a newly-learned narrow rule over a previously-learned broader rule would be necessary. Second, there are many exceptions to both of the restrictions. Mazurkewich and White provide no evidence for the psychological reality of the restrictions, i.e., no evidence that children learn or that adults know either of these restrictions. For example, the fact that verbs that alternate tend on the whole to be of Germanic rather than Latin origin (and tend to have a certain phonological structure) could have a purely historical source, and need have no relation to what children now learn. By the same token, the many exceptions indicate that children must do a good deal of learning of the properties of individual lexical items anyway, so parsimony supports the assumption, until proved otherwise, that the learning that follows the acquisition of the general rule is lexically specific.

suggest an experimental methodology whereby language-acquisition models might be tested.

GENERALIZATION BY DEFAULT

Finding *tavver* and *kithil* suitable for both dative environments is an example of what might be called "generalization by default," i.e., it occurs because of ignorance of specific syntactic properties of these novel lexical items. I now argue that this kind of explanation of generalization may be relevant beyond *tavver* and *kithil*.

All generalizations depend on ignorance as well as rule knowledge, e.g., a child's saying *breaked* depends on not knowing that *broke* is the correct form as well as on knowledge of the regular past tense rule. Usually, we find errors interesting because of what they tell us about command of rules. However, sometimes it may be the ignorance rather than the rule knowledge that is the more critical or more interesting part of the explanation of the generalization or error.

Now I want to suggest that generalization by default may play a role in two interesting kinds of errors that have been discussed in the literature. The first kind are causative verb errors. For example, 26-month-old Stevie says *Tommy fall Stevie truck down* meaning that Tommy knocked it down; 27-month-old Kendall says *Kendall fall that toy* meaning that she dropped the toy; 24-month-old Rachel says *Don't eat it me* meaning 'don't feed it to me'; and 27-month-old Christie says *Full it up* meaning 'fill it up.' The now classic explanation for these errors is Bowerman's (1974, 1982). She argues that they reflect acquisition of a zero-derivation rule—either a transformation that maps noncausative into causative, or a productive lexical redundancy rule that creates causative out of noncausative lexical entries. The zero-derivation rule would come from a child having noted and generalized from the English speech they hear the regularity that the same lexical items that are used noncausatively are often used causatively with an Agent subject. That is, the errors come from an induction from English surface structure.

I was completely comfortable with this explanation until 4 years ago when I heard Ruth Berman say that the same kinds of errors occur early on in Hebrew (e.g., Berman, 1986). Now in Hebrew the errors cannot be due to a zero-derivation rule induced from sentences heard since Hebrew does not have verbs with the same form in both causative and noncausative meanings. So, for Hebrew at least, some other explanation is required. Let us consider what that might be.

The explanation I propose is that there is a particular kind of encoding bias in children that affects the way they attribute lexical structure to newly acquired words. They tend to encode words wholistically. For the words under discussion, they encode the action content more securely than formal features; in the case of a new verb this would mean preferentially encoding it as representing a kind of action, without restricting it to a particular set of arguments; in particular, the initial encoding might be vague about the presence or absence of an Agent argument. Thus, the initial encoding of *nafal* 'fall' might specify a falling action but be indifferent to the distinction between 'fall' and 'knock down' or 'drop.' I do not mean that the argument structure (i.e., the number of arguments, their roles, and the usual position relative to the verb of the argument playing each role) cannot be registered, merely that it is not preferentially registered, i.e., it takes more exposure to the verb to register its argument structure than to register the kind of action it represents. A verb for which only the action core has been encoded will be available for use both noncausatively, and causatively with an Agent subject; it will take on the meaning appropriate to the sentence frame in which it is inserted. This double availability occurs by default, i.e., because there is nothing in the lexical entry to restrict usage to one of these sentence frames. When the argument structure has been learned, then the usage will be restricted.

Note that this proposal requires that the child already have two different sentence schemas, one with a transitive verb and an Agent subject, and the other in which the subject is not marked as Agent. The onset of the errors should follow the acquisition of the causative sentence schema.

If this explanation of the early Hebrew errors is correct, then the same processes should apply in corresponding stages (i.e., early stages) of English. The reported English errors are completely consistent with this proposal. However, there are differences between the languages in the patterning of errors over time. In English the errors persist for years—indeed Bowerman (1982) contains examples of such errors from adult speech—whereas in Hebrew this kind of error occurs for only a short period of time and then drops out; some months later another kind of error begins to occur which reflects overuse of the main prefix-cum-infix which Hebrew adds to many verb roots to form causative verbs. So it is only for a brief early period that the errors in the two languages are similar.

The similarities between the two languages are accounted for by the same early stage of generalization by default in both languages. The differences are due to the subsequent learning of the language-specific patterns for forming causative verbs in each language—the zero-derivation rule for English and the prefix-cum-infix pattern for Hebrew. Since the zero-derivation English pattern is formally less complex than the Hebrew patterns, it may well be acquired somewhat faster. Of course, in English it is likely to be difficult to tell when generalization by default ceases and productive use of the zero-derivation rule begins (although it is possible that onset of the rule is marked by a sudden increase in the number of "invented" causative forms).

So much for causative verbs. Another interesting kind of error that may be due to generalization by default concerns children's frequent use of nouns as verbs. According to Clark's (1982) valuable collection of data for several languages, when a noun refers to an object that has a characteristic action, children often misuse it as a verb referring to that action (e.g., *make it bell* 'make the bell ring,' *I'm souping* 'I'm eating soup,' *The buzzer is buzzering, Don't hair me* 'don't brush my hair'). Clark calls these inventions "characteristic activity" verbs, which she defines as activities done by or to the entity named in the verb. She provides numerous examples from French and German as well as English, indicating that these forms are not a language-specific phenomenon. However, they are child not adult forms: Although adults often make denominal verbs, adult inventions are not of the characteristic-activity type. Adult inventions fall into other patterns, e.g., instrument (*he launderetted the clothes*), locatum (*she blanketed the bed*), location (*he stabled the horses*), and some other types.

Children's inventions often fall into the adult categories, but it seems to me that many of them are very similar to the characteristic-activity examples (e.g., instrument: *don't broom my mess* 'don't sweep . . .', *Mommy nippled Anna* 'Mommy nursed Anna,' *He's keying the door;* locatum: *Mommy trousers me* 'dressed me in trousers,' *I'm crackering my soup* 'putting crackers in'; location: *I'm going to basket those apples;* other: *when is she coming to governess us*). (All examples are from Clark [1982].)

In sum, adults form novel verbs from nouns that are instruments, locations, etc., but they do not form novel characteristic activity verbs. On the other hand, young children often form characteristic activity verbs, and their novel verbs formed from instruments, locations, etc., are readily interpreted as characteristic activity verbs.

Clark (1982) explains the children's forms as the result of a rule or pattern induced from hearing noun-verb pairs like *bicycle-bicycle, brush-brush, dress-dress,* etc. Children "make an over-broad generalization . . . to come up with a rule that might be characteristized as follows:

Any noun denoting a concrete entity can be used as a verb for talking about a state, process, or activity associated with that entity. (p. 417)

The alternative explanation would be that these errors are due to lack of information in the lexical entry that would restrict usage, and not to any induction of rules about how to make verbs from nouns. That is, they are cases of generalization by default. According to the wholistic encoding bias, a word for an object would be preferentially encoded for the kind of object referred to together with its function, e.g., its characteristic use or activity; these meaning elements would be encoded more securely than formal features, in this case grammatical status (verb, action noun, common noun, etc.). Then, in the absence of grammatical tags to restrict generalization, a word for an object with a characteristic activity is free to generalize across the noun-verb boundary. Changes with increasing age in the number and kind of inventions would reflect learning of patterns in the language and features of specific words.

I know of only one potential argument against the generalization-by-default explanation, and this would be relevant for both the causative and denominal verbs. Arguing against proposals that overlap somewhat with mine, both Bowerman and Clark point out that there is a directional asymmetry in children's inventions. There are more intransitive verbs used causatively than causative verbs used intransitively (Bowerman, 1982), and many more nouns used as verbs than verbs used as nouns (Clark, 1982), whereas one might expect generalization by default to occur in both directions. However, there certainly are cases of causative verbs used intransitively (Bowerman, 1982)—indeed a moderately large number of cases in some bodies of data (Lord, 1979)—and there are cases of verbs used as nouns (Clark, 1982), though apparently not very many. Thus, the asymmetry is relative, not absolute. A relative asymmetry could count against the generalization-by-default hypothesis only if the possible occasions for generalization were equal in both directions. Obviously, it is hard to count opportunities for generalization. However, for the causative verb case, a sampling in the dictionary indicates that English has many more intransitive verbs and adjectives without causative counterparts than it has causative verbs without lexically related intransitive counterparts, and that fact alone suggests that there is an asymmetry of possible occasions. In the case of the noun-to-verb and verb-to-noun asymmetry, we are dealing with a domain of activity and activity-related concepts, and it seems intuitively reasonable that reference to such concepts should more often be made with verbs than nouns. Moreover, where there are particular objects and activities that are closely associated with each other, it seems that the noun for the object is more likely to be familiar to the child than the verb for the activity; often there is no verb. Thus, there are nouns *soup, TV,* and *vacuumcleaner* but no verb specific to eating soup, watching TV, or cleaningwith a vacuumcleaner—in such cases the asymmetry of opportunity is absolute. In sum, the generalization-by-default hypothesis is consistent with the observed asymmetries in numbers of errors.

DOES A SEMANTIC BASIS FOR EARLY GRAMMARS IMPLY DISCONTINUOUS DEVELOPMENT?

There is now much evidence suggesting that the categories in children's early combinatorial structures are typically semantic in nature. Since the categories of the adult language are grammatical categories—i.e., categories that are not in one-to-one relation to a semantic category—it is often argued that we are faced with a dilemma: Either the initial categories are really grammatical despite the evidence, or else we have to posit a discontinuity in development, a shift from semantic to grammatical categories (e.g., Brown, 1973; Pinker, 1984)—the so-called tadpole-frog issue (Gleitman, 1981). I want to argue that this is a false dilemma. Development could start with semantic categories and end with grammatical ones without there being any discontinuity in development or change in the child's learning procedure.

First, there is often a probabilistic association of semantic categories with grammatical ones, e.g., 'actor' with Subject, 'patient' with Direct Object, 'property' (as opposed to 'activity') with Adjective, etc. Mechanisms have been proposed in the literature (e.g., Schlesinger, 1977, 1982, this volume) whereby initial semantic categories could gradually broaden until they become equivalent to the grammatical ones (cf. Schlesinger's [1977] notion of "generalized agent"). Regardless of the ultimate verdict on Schlesinger's proposals, they show the *possibility* of a transition from semantic to grammatical categories without discontinuity in the learning process.

Second, a recent miniature artificial language experiment (Braine, 1987) demonstrates the possibility of change from semantic to grammatical categories without a change in the learning procedure; it thus shows that a learning procedure must exist that will, in some circumstances at least, pass through the semantic category in discovering the grammatical one.

The experiment investigated the acquisition of semi-arbitrary noun gender categories. It compared the learning of two languages, an experimental and a control, both of which had a distinction between "masculine" and "feminine" nouns. Half the nouns designated objects and half kinds of people. In the experimental language, the male people were all in the masculine class and the female in the feminine class; in the control language, males and females appeared equally in both classes (i.e., there was no correlation between natural sex and noun gender). The objects were randomly assigned to the gender classes of both languages. The experimental language proved to be significantly easier to acquire than the control, as measured by the assignment of the correct gender to nouns designating objects in a generalization test. Only a few subjects discovered that the control language had two classes of noun.

The learning of the experimental language demonstrates a grammatical class being learned in two stages—formation of an initial semantic class followed by an expansion of this class to include items without the feature marking the semantic class. The subjects start with semantic categories ('male' and 'female') and end up with grammatical ones without any hint of discontinuity or change in the learning procedure. And, as in this experiment, so in nature, the proposition that children begin with semantic categories and end with grammatical ones in no ways implies any discontinuity in learning processes.

The use of the features 'male' and 'female' is almost certainly not crucial to the learning. We might well have obtained the same results if we had made half the items of one class striped, and of the other class spotted (or arranged that half the nouns of one class end with a certain vowel, and half those of the other class end with a different vowel). Thus, innate semantic markers of grammatical categories (Grimshaw, 1981; Pinker, 1984) are probably not required to avoid discontinuity.

It now appears that the oft-heard claim that the early categories are semantic has been somewhat overstated: As Levy (1983b; this volume) has forcefully argued, phonologically marked categories can also appear early. Moreover, the transition from phonological to grammatical categories is common, noun gender being a frequent case in point (Braine, 1987; Karmiloff-Smith, 1978; Levy, 1983a). The frequency of early semantic and phonological categories is, of course, consistent with the existence of functional and surface-structure biases in the input processor, as proposed above. In any case, given the common situation of a grammatical category probabilistically correlated with semantic or phonological features, it is hard to imagine a distributional learning mechanism that would not discover the semantic or phonological category before discovering the grammatical one.

HOW CAN ACQUISITION MODELS BE TESTED?

Many important questions about language acquisition either cannot be answered or are extremely difficult to answer with observational studies. Thus, one can often infer from observational study that a child has acquired a certain rule. However, one cannot tell from observational study whether the acquisition of the rule depends on particular properties of the language spoken to the child, or on particular properties of the interactional setting. Nor can one tell how far the acquisition depends on predispositions to acquire particular kinds of rules, or how input properties and predispositions interact. To answer such causal questions demands experimentation—controlled variation of the input and of the kind of rule to see how learning is affected. In fact, most hypotheses and proposals about language acquisition models are concerned with such causal questions and are not readily testable against field data.

Here I have a specific proposal. It seems to me that studies of the acquisition of miniature artificial languages offer the obvious methodology for investigating acquisition models. They allow control over both the input and the structure of the language, and the miniaturization of the language permits focusing on a single question at issue or a small set of questions at a time. I do not claim that all the hypotheses we would want to test can be conveniently explored with miniature languages. Nor, obviously, am I suggesting that we should stop observing children using their native language. But miniature languages seem admirably suited to the exploration of rule learning mechanisms. Moreover, being an experimental technique, miniature languages can explore causation, unlike observational studies.

For the present discussion, a miniature language comprises (1) a stimulus world consisting of a finite set of discrete objects or events that are presentable to subjects, and (2) a miniature grammar that defines a language whose sentences describe the events/objects of the stimulus world. The vocabulary items are English nonsense words. In miniature language experiments, subjects are exposed to a sample of sentence-event pairs under conditions that encourage attention. Subsequent tests determine what aspects of the rule system they acquired from the exposure.

I shall not review the literature on learning miniature artificial languages (see Braine, 1987, and Morgan & Newport, 1981, for brief selective reviews). Suffice it to say that although the miniature language methodology has been used, it has not been intensively exploited, probably because some potential problems in interpreting studies with artificial languages were raised early in the work (e.g., Bever, Fodor, & Weksel, 1965), and others have been raised subsequently. However, the problems seem far from insuperable. Let us survey them briefly.

The first two problems are that children may have special language-learning abilities not present in adults (e.g., Lenneberg, 1967), and that in learning miniature languages adults may use complex problem-solving strategies not available to children. These problems make it difficult in principle to generalize from adults learning artificial languages to children learning natural languages. However, both problems can largely be avoided by using preadolescent children as subjects. Using children as subjects avoids the first problem because the special language-learning abilities that children may possess are believed to last until adolescence (Lenneberg, 1967), and would therefore be possessed by the subjects. The second problem is also largely avoided by using children as subjects, although there may be some residual question whether there are important differences in language acquisition processes between the subject age group and younger children. However, the literature on second-language acquisition outside the formal classroom (e.g., McLaughlin, 1978) implicates similar acquisition processes at all ages, and certainly does not suggest important differences during the preadolescent years. Nevertheless, the question could be investigated if it were to become a major issue.

The third potential problem is that conditions of learning in experiments may not elicit processes of natural language acquisition. In its most general form this objection is too broad to be taken seriously—it invites the rebuttal that there is no reason to believe that ordinary language acquisition processes could be magically set aside at the laboratory door. However, the objection has mostly been raised with respect to the use of semantically empty languages (i.e., with a grammar and sentences, but no stimulus world). These can seem unnatural and it is easy to think that they might not elicit ordinary language acquisition processes. In this form the problem can be simply avoided by not using semantically empty systems.

The fourth potential problem is that learning artificial languages is a special case of second language acquisition, so that in interpreting results questions of transfer and interference between the first and the second language become relevant. This problem is a real one. However, recent work and thinking about second language acquisition (e.g., McLaughlin, 1978) indicates a very considerable communality in the processes of first- and second-language acquisition in children, so this problem is not a proper objection. When the question of transfer or interference from the first language arises most seriously, it can be studied by varying the native language of the subject while holding the artificial language constant.

In sum, the potential interpretive problems are less serious than they might at first sight appear and provide no reason for rejecting the methodology. Most of the problems can be avoided merely by using child subjects and by not using semantically empty languages. Other problems can be easily handled within the methodology itself.

There are a host of issues for which the methodology suggests itself. For instance, one can compare the learning of various kinds of rules with each other and with rote learning for their dependence on input frequency; one can ask whether there are preferred levels of abstractness at which rules tend to be formulated (i.e., whether rules at certain levels are learned with fewer trials than at other levels); one can find out whether rules at several different levels of abstractness tend to increment in strength simultaneously; one can explore how far forgetting on nonpresentation is an important factor in rule learning; and one can obtain answers to many other questions. Moreover, since the methodology allows clear definition of a learning trial, the dependence of learning on input frequency can be quantified and quantitative models of the learning mechanism developed and tested.

Some of the issues that can be explored (e.g., those just cited) are extremely important ones about a language acquisition model. Empirically based answers would enormously constrain our thinking about models and provide a foundation for extrapolating to issues hard to explore with miniature languages. For instance, given a well-founded type of model, we would be in a much better position than now to judge when we need to invoke innate constraints, and what kind.

SUMMARY AND CONCLUSIONS

The paper began by arguing, with respect to a well-known model developed from studies of learnability (Wexler & Culicover, 1980), that although it is an intellectually very impressive tour de force in theory construction, it is nevertheless not a useful starting point for developing a realistic theory of how human children acquire a native language. Basically, this is because the model's conception of the form of a transformation is so unrestricted that learning transformations becomes essentially a blind search among very many possibilities most of which are surely beyond a child's power to dream up. Learnability is achieved only because of assumptions about the input that are unrealistically strong.

It was also argued that, since linguists do not yet know all the constraints on human grammars, linguistic theories tend to define "human language" too broadly; hence, at this stage of theory development, the attempt to provide a learnability proof for any grammar allowed by a current linguistic theory could easily lead a learning model in seriously wrong directions and thus be counter-productive.

I then proposed that progress toward the goal of developing a psychologically realistic model of language acquisition is likely to be accomplished with least wasted effort if we keep in mind certain broad questions whose answers indicate a type of learning mechanism. Seven such questions were discussed, answers to which would constrain the type of learning mechanism that is plausible. From the first five questions, it was concluded that the effective input should be taken as consisting of utterances paired with meanings, the latter mediated through a comprehension process that uses plausibility based on situational knowledge and context; that one should assume minimal specific memory for past input (i.e., for sentences heard prior to the most recently processed one); that children are able to learn without correction (i.e., correction may be helpful but is not crucial); and that a model should be able to tolerate a certain amount of error in the input (adult mistakes, atypical exceptional forms, child mistakes of comprehension).

It was urged that a certain type of learning mechanism, called a "sieve memory," provides a natural and plausible way to satisfy these requirements. This type of mechanism causes features of the input to be registered in a memory in which rule consolidation is a function of frequency of registration, and in which rarely repeated features tend to be forgotten. It was shown how a sieve memory could operate to acquire the early productive patterns of word combination, and, later on, a transformational rule.

The next question asked how the degree of abstractness of categories used in rules was determined. The answers given by recent models in the literature and those available to the proposed sieve-memory model were discussed. This is a central question for a language acquisition model. It is one on which different models offer very different hypotheses, and for which a decision must somehow be found in empirical work.

The last of the questions is well known as a major conundrum of language acquisition—how overinclusive grammars become superceded in the course of development without requiring information about what is not well-formed. I argued that innate constraints do not solve the problem, at least for the cases discussed so far in the literature. On the other hand, the sieve-memory model provides a straightforward solution.

The remainder of the paper consisted of a proposal, an argument, and a suggested methodology. The proposal extended one source of overgeneral grammars into the concept of "generalization by default"—an error-producing mechanism resulting from lexical entries that lack formal features restricting generalization. I suggested that certain phenomena described in the literature were examples of it.

The argument was that a developmental shift from semantic to grammatical categories in no way entails any discontinuity in learning, as has been claimed. The shift has been demonstrated in an artificial language experiment without any hint of a discontinuity. Moreover, in the usual case where a grammatical category is probabilistically correlated with a semantic one, it is likely that almost any distributional learning mechanism that did not build in the grammatical categories would often yield this sequence of learning.

Finally, I urged the usefulness of the miniature artificial language methodology as a tool for investigating distributional learning mechanisms. The usual objections to this methodology are easily met by using children as subjects and by not using semantically empty languages (as in some previous research). The methodology seems particularly apt for researching the problem of how the degree of abstractness of categories used in rules is determined.

ACKNOWLEDGMENT

The first draft of this paper was written for the Conference on "Beyond Description in Child Language" organized by the Max Planck Institut fur Psycholinguistik in Nijmegen, Holland, in June, 1979. It was extensively revised and developed in 1983 at the Institute for Advanced Studies of the Hebrew University of Jerusalem, Israel. I am enormously grateful to my colleagues at the Institute for discussion of all the topics touched on. The paper has also benefitted from discussions with Brian MacWhinney, Melissa Bowerman, and Eve Clark. A final revision was made in 1986, supported by a grant (HD-20807) from the National Institute of Child Health and Human Development.

REFERENCES

Anderson, J. R. (1983). *The architecture of cognition.* Cambridge, MA: Harvard University Press.

Baker, C. L. (1979). Syntactic theory and the projection problem. *Linguistic Inquiry, 10,* 533–581.

Berman, R. A. (1982). Verb-pattern alternation: The interface of morphology, syntax, and semantics in Hebrew child language. *Journal of Child Language, 9,* 169–191.

Berman, R. A. (1986). Acquisition of Hebrew. In D. I. Slobin (Ed.), *The crosslinguistic study of language acquisition* (Vol. 1) Hillsdale, NJ: Lawrence Erlbaum Associates.

Berwick, R. C. (1985). *The acquisition of syntactic knowledge.* Cambridge, MA: MIT Press.

Bever, T. G., Fodor, J. A., & Weksel, W. (1965). On the acquisition of syntax: A critique of "contextual generalization." *Psychological Review, 72,* 467–482.

Bowerman, M. (1973). Structural relationships in children's utterances: Syntactic or semantic? In

T. E. Moore (Ed.), *Cognitive development and the acquisition of language*. New York: Academic Press.

Bowerman, M. (1974). Learning the structure of causative verbs: A study in the relationship of cognitive, semantic, and syntactic development. *Papers and Reports on Child Language Development* (Department of Linguistics, Stanford University). No. 8, 142–178.

Bowerman, M. (1982). Evaluating competitive linguistic models with language acquisition data: Implications of developmental errors with causative verbs. *Quaderni di Semantica, 3,* 5–66.

Bowerman, M. (1983). How do children avoid constructing an overly general grammar in the absence of feedback about what is not a sentence. *Papers and Reports on Child Language Development* (Department of Linguistics, Stanford University), 22,

Braine, M. D. S. (1965). The insufficiency of a finite state model for verbal reconstructive memory. *Psychonomic Science, 2,* 291–292.

Braine, M. D. S. (1971). On two types of models of the internalization of grammars. In D. I. Slobin (Ed.), *The ontogenesis of grammar: A theoretical symposium*. New York: Academic Press.

Braine, M. D. S. (1976). Children's first word combinations. *Monographs of the Society for Research in Child Development, 41,* No. 1.

Braine, M. D. S. (1987). What is learned in acquiring word classes–A step toward an acquisition theory. In B. MacWhinney (Ed.), *Mechanisms of language acquisition*. Hillsdale, NJ: Lawrence Erlbaum Associates.

Braine, M. D. S. (in press). Review of Pinker, S. (1984). *Language learnability and language development*. Cambridge, MA: MIT Press. *Journal of Child Language*.

Braine, M. D. S., & Hardy, J. A. (1982). On what case categories these are, why they are, and how they develop: An amalgam of a priori considerations, speculations, and evidence from children. In L. Gleitman & E. Wanner (Eds.), *Language acquisition: State of the art*. Cambridge, U.K.: The University Press.

Braine, M. D. S., & Wells, R. (1978). Case-like categories in children: The actor and its subcategories. *Cognitive Psychology, 10,* 100–122.

Bresnan, J. (1978). A realistic transformational grammar. In G. Miller, J. Bresnan, & M. Halle (Eds.), *Linguistic theory and psychological reality*. Cambridge, MA: MIT Press.

Brown, R. W. (1973). *A first language*. Cambridge, MA: Harvard University Press.

Brown, R. W., & Hanlon, C. (1970). Derivational complexity and order of acquisition in child speech. In J. R. Hayes (Ed.), *Cognition and the development of language*. New York: Wiley.

Chomsky, N. (1965). *Aspects of the theory of syntax*. Cambridge, MA: MIT Press.

Chomsky, N. (1970). Remarks on nominalizations. In R. Jacobs & P. Rosenbaum (Eds.), *Readings in transformational grammar*. Waltham, MA: Blaisdell.

Chomsky, N. (1981). *Lectures on government and binding*. Dordrecht: Foris.

Clark, E. V. (1982). The young work maker: A case study of innovation in the child's lexicon. In E. Wanner & L. R. Gleitman (Eds.), *Language acquisition: The state of the art*. Cambridge, England: The University Press.

Culicover, P. W., & Wexler, K. (1976). Some syntactic implications of a theory of language learnability. In P. W. Culicover, T. Wasow, & A. Akmajian (Eds.), *Studies in formal syntax*. New York: Academic Press.

Ervin, S. M. (1964). Imitation and structural change in children's language. In E. H. Lenneberg (Ed.), *New directions in the study of language*. Cambridge, MA: Harvard University Press.

Ervin-Tripp, S. (1971). An overview of theories of grammatical development. In D. I. Slobin (Ed.), *The ontogenesis of grammar: A theoretical symposium*. New York: Academic Press.

Gleitman, L. R. (1981). Maturational determinants of language growth. *Cognition, 10,* 103–114.

Gold, E. M. (1967). Language identification in the limit. *Information and Control, 10,* 447–474.

Grimshaw, J. (1981). Form, function, and the language-acquisition device. In C. L. Baker & J. J. McCarthy (Eds.), *The logical problem of language acquisition*. Cambridge, MA: MIT Press.

Hamburger, H. (1971). *On the learning of three classes of transformation components*. Unpublished doctoral dissertation, University of Michigan.

Hamburger, H., & Wexler, K. (1973). Identifiability of a class of transformational grammars. In K. J. J. Hintikka, J. M. E. Moravcsik, & P. Suppes (Eds.), *Approaches to natural language*. Dordrecht, Holland: Reidel.

Hamburger, H., & Wexler, K. (1975). A mathematical theory of learning transformational grammar. *Journal of Mathematical Psychology, 12,* 137–177.

Hardy, J., & Braine, M. D. S. (1981). Categories that bridge between meaning and syntax in five-year-olds. In W. Deutsch (Ed.), *The child's construction of language*. London: Academic Press.

Hirsh-Pasek, K., Treiman, R., & Schneiderman, M. (1984). Brown & Hanlon revisited: Mothers' sensitivity to ungrammatical forms. *Journal of Child Language, 11,* 81–88.

Kaplan, R. M., & Bresnan, J. (1982). Lexical-functional grammar: A formal system for grammatical representation. In J. Bresnan (Ed.), *The mental representation of grammatical relations*. Cambridge, MA: MIT Press.

Karmiloff-Smith, A. (1978). The interplay between syntax, semantics, and phonology in language acquisition processes. In R. Campbell & P. Smith (Eds.), *Recent advances in the psychology of language*. New York: Plenum.

Kuczaj, S. A., II. (1977). The acquisition of regular and irregular past tense forms. *Journal of Verbal Learning and Verbal Behavior, 16,* 589–600.

Lenneberg, E. H. (1967). *Biological foundations of language*. New York: Wiley.

Levy, Y. (1983a). The acquisition of Hebrew plurals: The case of the missing gender category. *Journal of Child Language, 10,* 107–121.

Levy, Y. (1983b). It's frogs all the way down. *Cognition, 15,* 73–93.

Lord, C. (1979). "Don't you fall me down": Children's generalizations regarding cause and transitivity. *Papers & Reports on Child Language Development* (Department of Linguistics, Stanford University), *17,* 81–89.

MacWhinney, B. (1978). The acquisition of morphophonology. *Monographs of the Society for Research in Child Development, 43,* Nos. 1–2, Serial No. 174.

MacWhinney, B. (1987). Competition. In B. MacWhinney (Ed.), *Mechanisms of language acquisition*. Hillsdale, NJ: Lawrence Erlbaum Associates.

Mazurkewich, I., & White, L. (1984). The acquisition of the dative alternation: Unlearning overgeneralizations. *Cognition, 16,* 261–283.

McClelland, J. L., & Rumelhart, D. E., (1986). On learning the past tenses of English verbs. In D. E. Rumelhart & J. L. McClelland (Eds.). *Parallel distributed processing: Explorations in the microstructure of cognition; Vol. II. Psychological and biological models*. Cambridge, MA: MIT Press.

McLaughlin, B. (1978). *Second language acquisition in children*. Hillsdale, NJ: Lawrence Erlbaum Associates.

Moerk, E. L. (1983). *The mother of Eve as a first language teacher*. Norwood, NJ: Ablex.

Moeser, S., & Bregman, A. (1972). The role of reference in the acquisition of a miniature artificial language. *Journal of Verbal Learning and Verbal Behavior, 11,* 759–769.

Morgan, J., & Newport, E. L. (1981). The role of constituent structure in the induction of an artificial language. *Journal of Verbal Learning and Verbal Behavior, 20,* 67–85.

Pinker, S. (1979). Formal models of language learning. *Cognition, 7,* 217–283.

Pinker, S. (1982). A theory of the acquisition of lexical-interpretive grammars. In J. Bresnan (Ed.), *The mental representation of grammatical relations*. Cambridge, MA: MIT Press.

Pinker, S. (1984). *Language learnability and language development*. Cambridge, MA: Harvard University Press.

Reber, A. S., & Lewis, S. (1977). Implicit learning: An analysis of the form and structure of a body of tacit knowledge. *Cognition, 5,* 333–361.

Sachs, J. S. (1967). Recognition memory for syntactic and semantic aspects of connected discourse. *Perception & Psychophysics, 2,* 437–442.

Schaerlaekens, A. M. (1973). *The two-word sentence in child language development*. The Hague: Mouton.

Schlesinger, I. M. (1977). *Production and comprehension of utterances.* Hillsdale, NJ: Lawrence Erlbaum Associates.

Schlesinger, I. M. (1979). Cognitive and linguistic structures: The case of the instrumental. *Journal of Linguistics, 15,* 307–324.

Schlesinger, I. M. (1982). *Steps to language: Toward a theory of language acquisition.* Hillsdale, NJ: Lawrence Erlbaum Associates.

Sellars, W. (1957). Symposium: Logical subjects and physical objects. *Philosophy & Phenomenological Research, 17,* 458–472.

Smith, K. H. (1969). Learning cooccurrence restrictions: Rule learning or rote learning. *Journal of Verbal Learning and Verbal Behavior, 8,* 319–321.

Strawson, P. F. (1957). Logical subjects and physical objects. *Philosophy & Phenomenological Research, 17,* 441–457, 473–477.

Wexler, K. (1978). Empirical questions about developmental psycholinguistics raised by a theory of language acquisition. In R. N. Campbell & P. T. Smith (Eds.), *Recent advances in the psychology of language.* New York: Plenum.

Wexler, K. (1982). A principle theory for language acquisition. In E. Wanner & L. R. Gleitman (Eds.). *Language acquisition: The state of the art.* Cambridge, England: Cambridge University Press.

Wexler, K., & Culicover, P. W. (1980). *Formal principles of language acquisition.* Cambridge, MA: MIT Press.

Wexler, K., Culicover, P. W., & Hamburger, H. (1975). Learning-theoretic foundations of linguistic universals. *Theoretical Linguistics, 2,* 215–253.

Concluding Chapter
The Child's Early Categories: Approaches to Language Acquisition Theory

Yonata Levy
Izchak M. Schlesinger
The Hebrew University

The nature and origin of categories that are operative in the beginning phases is a central issue in models of language acquisition. The contributors to this volume have all expressed their views on this issue either explicitly or implicitly in discussing their theories. In this concluding chapter we review the various theoretical approaches to the issue of categories and propose criteria for the evaluation of theories in the field of child language. We discuss the relevance of empirical data to contemporary models of acquisition, the issue of parsimony in theory construction, the appeal to continuity vs. discontinuity in language learning and the plausibility arguments that they involve.

From a historical perspective, it is interesting to note that the claims made by the protagonists of the various approaches represented in this volume are not as diametrically opposed to each other as those in a similar collection of papers might have been some years ago. The tendency to make radical, unqualified statements has given way to more moderate and reserved positions, which are more appreciative of the claims made by rival theoretical orientations.

The theoretical controversy in the present volume, however, is a real one. As shown below, underlying the authors' differences of opinions there are divergent conceptions of the child as a learner. There are those who credit the child with a powerful mechanism for analyzing the spoken input and extracting from it a system of purely linguistic categories and rules. Others regard it as unlikely that such abilities can be ascribed to a young mind. Language is considered as subservient to other interests of the learner, such as social communications and the expression of cognitively anchored notions that serve the child in his day-to-day dealings in the nonlinguistic environment. On this view, it is in some sense more natural, and therefore easier, to deal with those than with formal linguistic constructions.

It seems, then, that in the expositions in this volume, and in other similar statements, considerations of plausibility are at the heart of the dispute. Theoreticians bring with them their conception of the human mind, which functions as axiomatic in their theorizing. Such a priori notions have the status of plausibility arguments and should be explicitly discussed.

1.   TWO THEORETICAL APPROACHES

Before discussing the theoretical approaches represented in this volume, let us clarify our terminology.

The term **categories,** as used in the present chapter, pertains only to the surface string and not to the distinctions of meaning—cognitive and illocutionary notions—expressed in it. **Content categories** include both semantic and pragmatic categories, like Agent, Attribute, and Topic, while **formal categories** in the surface string include constructs like Noun phrase, Verb, surface Subject, and Auxiliary.[1] These two types of linguistic categories overlap to varying degrees with the meaning distinctions expressed in the language. For content categories, the overlap is usually large, whereas for formal categories, there is little or no correspondence with meaning distinctions. For instance, there is no semantic motivation for the fact that the preposition *to* comes after *owing,* whereas *of* is the correct choice after *because.* Nor does the particular realization of the plural /s/, as in *kids, kits,* or *kisses,* carry any semantic weight. How the plural ending is realized depends on the final phoneme of the pluralized noun, i.e., whether it is voiced, unvoiced, or sibilant.

As far as early categories are concerned, several basically different approaches can be distinguished in the current literature on language acquisition.

According to one widely established position, the child breaks into the linguistic system by observing how the distinctions in terms of which she conceives of the world around her are expressed by the categories of her language. Let us call the rules that capture these mappings **realization rules.** Realization rules, on this account, are the only rules learned by the child in the first stages of acquisition, and the only kind of categories operative in her language at that stage are therefore content categories.

This view is challenged by other theorists, who hold that the child analyzes the linguistic input and detects its underlying patterns and regularities regardless of whether the latter correspond to meaning distinctions or not. In other words,

---

[1]Deep structure categories are also formal. The process of their acquisition is not dealt with in this volume (but see Section 3).

he or she performs on the linguistic input a sort of **distributional analysis.**[2] On this view, then, the child acquires from the outset not only content categories but also formal categories.

A third view assumes the existence of innately specified linguistic categories which are available to the child at the beginning of language development. This view is not represented in this volume. Some comments on the ''bootstrapping'' process that is required by a nativist position are made in a later section. The following discussion focuses on the first two positions.

Within each of these approaches there exist certain variations, due to different emphases placed on content categories, on the one hand, and formal categories on the other. There are also further distinctions between theories. Thus, among those who credit the child in the first stages only with content categories, some accord primary importance to semantic categories, while others stress the role played by pragmatic categories. We return to these variations later, when we discuss the stands taken by contributors to this volume. But first we have to examine what options are open to a theorist in principle.

It cannot conceivably be argued that learning grammar is limited to the acquisition of content categories and realization rules. Likewise, language learning cannot be said to proceed wholly by means of distributional analyses. Such ''pure'' realizational and distributional approaches are out of the question, as will presently be shown.

That distributional analysis alone cannot account for all the knowledge the child has, even in the initial stages of language acquisition, can be easily shown. Suppose the child discovers through such an analysis that there are constructions of the form X's X, where X is a category of words corresponding (roughly) to what is usually called animate nouns. This permits, among others, the formation of both *Jessie's cat* and *cat's Jessie*. Provision will therefore have to be made for rules that map notions like Possessor and Possession (Possessed) into linguistic expressions and determine whether *Jessie's cat* or *cat's Jessie* is produced. As soon as the child says about a certain cat that it is *Jessie cat* rather than *cat Jessie,* about a certain book, *doggie book,* and not *book doggie,* and so on, she evinces a command of the appropriate mapping of the possessive relation, that is, she must have the relevant realization rule. Similarly, as soon as the child has acquired the opposition of, e.g., *hug mummy* and *mummy hug,* and uses each of these and similar expressions in the appropriate situations—and this means from very early on—she must be credited with realization rules that operate with content categories like Agent and Patient. For it is implausible that these alternative construc-

---

[2]Critics of this proposal (e.g., Pinker, 1984) have pointed out the enormous amount of computation required for such an analysis to achieve its objective. There exists a considerable body of evidence, however, for the human propensity to register frequency information automatically (Hasher & Zacks, 1984).

tions and their appropriate uses should have been learned ad hoc for each word, since there is some productivity of the relevant rules (as has been shown experimentally by Marantz, 1982, and by Wilson et al., quoted in Pinker, 1984, pp. 312, 315). Content categories, then, are among the child's earliest categories.

The acquisition of realization rules, then, is indispensable to the process of language learning. Proponents of a distributional approach can therefore argue only that in addition to learning realization rules, the child performs distributional analyses that introduce formal categories. By contrast, it is possible to claim that formal categories do not make their appearance in the child's linguistic repertoire till well after he or she has mastered the basic realization rules.

According to those advocating a realizational approach, then, these formal categories are acquired at a later stage. That the child sooner or later acquires formal categories does not imply, however, that she carries out a distributional analysis. There are several ways of forming such categories, as we see in the following.

The Acquisition of Formal Categories

We describe here several ways in which formal categories may, in principle, be acquired, using as an example the acquisition of the mass noun—count noun distinction.

Distributional analysis. Some theorists argue that the child may register formal regularities in the linguistic input without reference to the meaning distinctions that are encoded thereby. Thus, she may note that nouns preceded by *many* may, in other instances, be preceded by a number word and by *few*, and that these nouns can be suffixed with *-s* (in its various phonological realizations), whereas nouns preceded by *much* can only be preceded by (*a*) *little* and never receive such a suffix.

On this account acquiring the mass-count distinction is independent of the acquisition of any realization rule for the plural. In principle, the formal regularities could be acquired even prior to any such realization rule. That acquisition actually occurs in this sequence seems highly unlikely in view of the saliency of the notion of plurality, as documented by its early expression in child speech. A more plausible alternative would be simultaneous but independent acquisition of the realization rule, on the one hand, and formal regularities, on the other.

Semantic core. One might venture the hypothesis that learning linguistic distinctions which do not fully overlap with a semantic characterization proceeds in stages. Initially realization rules are formed for those cases only where there is a linguistic–semantic correspondence. For instance, the child might first acquire realization rules for nouns denoting individuated objects—*table, cat, lady,* etc.—and different rules for nonindividuated ones—*sugar, oil,* and *butter.* Each of these two notions constitutes a semantic core. This semantic core is then expanded as the child's experience with language grows. She notes, for instance, that *garlic* and *junk,* though referring to individuated objects, are treated linguistically like *sugar* and other mass nouns. The semantic core thus loses some of its semantic character as it grows into a formal category.

In the case of the mass-count distinction the semantic core hypothesis has failed to receive any support. Studies by both Gordon (1985) and Gathercole (1985) seem to indicate that these categories are not learned by the child via the semantic mass-count distinction. Likewise, it has been shown that gender agreement rules are not learned first for animate nouns in which grammatical gender corresponds to natural gender (Levy, this volume). Further, Maratsos (this volume) has shown that there is no support for a semantic core that functions in the acquisition of word classes. These negative findings, however, do not rule out the possibility that the acquisition of formal categories in other domains might be explained by the semantic core hypothesis.

Conditional realization rules. This proposal has not been discussed explicitly in the literature, to our knowledge, although similar ideas seem to have been assumed or hinted at previously. What is proposed here is that a realization rule may be made conditional on a linguistic category. To illustrate, the child might start out with a realization rule that results in adding *-s* to any noun to indicate Plurality—or "much of the same"—and using *many* for all nouns; alternatively, he or she might use *much* and *many* indiscriminately for all nouns. Subsequently, she learns for each noun individually whether it requires *much* or *many,* whether it takes the *-s* ending or not, and the rest of the relevant rules. That is, the original realization rule is bifurcated, and each of the two new realization rules is conditional on a category that has been assembled on an item-to-item basis.

The introduction of conditional realization rules may at times be somewhat more complicated than this. In the case of the present example, it is to be expected that the child will note the dependencies in the linguistic input and capitalize on them. Thus, she will note that those nouns that take *many,* but not those that take *much,* require the *-s* suffix, and will come to predict for any given noun one of these properties from the other. In other words, she will perform a distributional analysis on the data. But unlike the "straight" distributional analysis approach outlined above, the present proposal does not involve any analysis that goes on without regard to the meaning distinctions that are being realized; the process is always subservient to the learning of realization rules. In the above example these were the rules determining how the notions of Plurality (or "muchness") are to be expressed.

When a realization rule is refined and made conditional on other categories, as in the previous example, we propose to call the latter **conditioning catego-**

ries. Conditioning categories may be of various kinds. In the above example they are assembled on an item-by-item basis and thus are semantically and formally arbitrary.[3] Suppose now that the child eventually notices (as she is sure to do) that the conditioning category associated with *many* contains almost exclusively nouns referring to individuated entities, whereas the other conditioning category does not. Then these conditioning categories will be partially semantically defined.

An example of a semantic-pragmatic conditioning category is the notion of third-person-singular. After a child has acquired a rule for mapping the agentive relation into an utterance, she will have to make a differentiation within this rule and learn that the mapping for the third person singular is somewhat different (*s* is affixed to the verb). The rule will now be bifurcated, and which of the two variants applies to the subject-verb relation will become dependent on whether the action is predicated of the speaker or the addressee, or of more than one entity (in which case no -*s* is affixed) or not (in which case it is).[4]

Formal conditioning categories may be found in languages that have different inflectional paradigms for different, formally defined, nouns. Note that this is so only for a theory which claims that these paradigms are learned as realization rules; the notion of conditioning category has been proposed here not as a construct of linguistic theory, but as pertaining to language acquisition theory.

2.   EARLY CATEGORIES: SOME DIVERGENT VIEWS

In this section we review the contributions to the present volume, using the concepts and the framework developed in the previous section. Among the various theoretical options discussed above, there are some on which not all authors take a stand. But the two basic theoretical approaches outlined in section 1 can be clearly identified in their writings: the approach based exclusively on realization rules and the one that emphasizes, in addition, distributional analysis and the early appearance of formal categories.

Examples of theories emphasizing content categories introduced by realization rules can be found in the chapters by Ninio and Snow and by Schlesinger. These authors differ on the question of what kind of content categories the child

---

[3]Note that although they are formally arbitrary, the categories mass noun and count noun delimited by them are formal ones. This is because of the realization rules that are conditional on these conditioning categories specify a different linguistic environment for each of the two noun categories. A similar proposal has been made for word class categories in Schlesinger's chapter. These are claimed to be introduced through the realization rules. Since it is discussed in that chapter, this possibility of acquiring formal categories, which applies only to word classes, will not be dealt with here.

[4]This is so only if the sentence is present tense. "Present" here is an additional conditioning category.

starts out with. While Schlesinger holds that the child's first categories are semantic, **Ninio** and **Snow** propose that they are pragmatic. They argue that semantic categories like Agent and Patient are too abstract and lie beyond the child's concerns. What the child is interested in is to communicate, and accordingly she approaches the language-learning task with a set of communicative intentions. The child's categories are at first pragmatic—e.g., Force of Request, Object under Consideration, and (later on) Location of Object. These predate the acquisition of language. The language-learning child analyzes the conversational situation and matches pragmatic functions with linguistic expressions.

The rationale behind this view seems to be that since pragmatic categories are not specific to language—that is, they can be realized also in other, nonlinguistic ways (through gestures, for instance)—the child may be assumed to continue attending to those distinctions that preoccupied her before she embarked on the language learning task. Ninio and Snow, then, view pragmatic distinctions as particularly salient for the very young child, and it is therefore these categories for which he or she first finds a systematic mapping into the linguistic output.

The child's system, at this stage, is a communicative one, according to Ninio and Snow. Her early word combinations do not reveal a grammar, properly speaking, since there is no formal rule system. Grammar, in this sense, is a later development which is relatively more independent of communicative categories. As the authors recognize, this means that the child's system of rules must undergo a qualitative change, involving categories that were previously not functional.

Schlesinger holds that the child's first categories are not pragmatic, as in Ninio and Snow's model, but semantic. He conceives of the child as initially dependent on meaning in analyzing the incoming speech stream, and holds that semantic categories are cognitively the most salient ones. They are based on the cognitive notions in terms of which the child organizes her perception of the world. But as shown presently, they are not necessarily identical with the latter.

The child's earliest semantic categories are not taken to be the full-fledged case-like categories functioning in adult language (which, as we have just seen, Ninio and Snow believe to be too abstract for the child to attend to), but are of much narrower scope. Two alternatives are explored. One is that through perceiving similarities in the events occurring in her environment the child spontaneously forms rudimentary semantic concepts of restricted scope, which are subsequently developed in the course of acquiring the grammatical rule system. The other possibility is that when language learning begins, the child has not yet any semantic concepts in terms of which realization rules are later defined (such as Agent-Action). The formation of semantic categories is dependent on the learning of linguistic rules and is part and parcel of the same process.

The semantic relational categories of the child's early rule system form semantic cores, which are gradually expanded into formal categories. The specific process achieving this, according to Schlesinger, is semantic assimilation: Semantic categories are continuously redefined on the basis of linguistic input data, but while formal factors now assume a decisive role, semantic similarity continues to be attended to. Furthermore, some formal categories may be introduced through conditional realization rules in the manner outlined in the previous section.

The question may now be raised of how a pragmatic theory, like Ninio and Snow's, accounts for the acquisition of semantic categories and the rules defined on them, and conversely, how a semantic theory like Schlesinger's accounts for the acquisition of pragmatic categories and rules. One possibility would be that these are subsequently acquired as conditional realization rules. Thus, Ninio and Snow might argue that the early pragmatic rules are refined and made conditional on semantic categories. Similarly, a semantic theory might propose that after the child has acquired rules for realizing semantic relational categories, subrules are learned for realizing the same categories in questions, negations, and so on.

So far we have discussed theories that accord some sort of priority to one sort of categories—pragmatic or semantic ones. That neither of these need be accorded priority can be seen from Braine's contribution, which we discuss next.

Braine holds that the initial acquisition process consists in a mapping of previously existing meaning distinctions onto those parts of the linguistic input which the child is able to construe. Certain semantic distinctions are already available to the child when she embarks on the language learning task (though these are not the full-fledged adult categories, but rather "proto-cases"). In particular, Braine believes the predicate-argument distinction to be a basic one, which has to be available to the child before learning of grammatical rules can begin. This distinction also plays a central role in Ninio's model, discussed below, and its importance is also recognized by Berman and by Levy in their chapters.

A central component of Braine's model is the "scanner," which analyzes the input in terms of the previously available semantic distinctions. Linguistic regularities are recorded and stored when they are exemplified in the input with sufficient frequency. The scanner is sensitive not only to semantic categories but also to the illocutionary force of the utterance, and thus learns pragmatic rules. Furthermore, provision is made in Braine's model for rules defined entirely in terms of formal categories by positing that the scanner is sensitive to surface regularities.

Braine, then, does not accord a privileged status to either semantic, pragmatic or formal categories: These can all be acquired at an early stage if they are salient enough and appear with sufficient frequency and regularity in the input. However, while Braine's scanner is not limited in principle to any one type of category, it is held to have the tendency to attend to meanings. Semantics thus provides the child with a point of entry into language.

It should be noted that there are far-reaching similarities between Braine's model and Slobin's (1986) Language Making Capacity (LMC), which is the mechanism by which a child learns language. In Slobin's theory, LMC cannot proceed without "knowing" how to assign words to elements of "scenes" in a linguistically relevant sense. The prototypical scenes include a manipulating agent, a manipulation, and an object to be manipulated. These are the sources of the child's pristine grammatical markings and distinctions. The major task of the child is to map various aspects of the Manipulative Scene onto their linguistic expressions.

Much like Braine, Slobin accepts as a basic prerequisite for language learning, children's attention to and storage of meaningful utterances. He proposes a mechanism that selects content words and major structural distinctions which are already understood, but at the same time stores for future work bits and pieces of the utterance that it cannot yet comprehend. For example, Slobin (1986) assumes that LMC will encounter in storage segments that have not been mapped as content words. These will be "the opening wedge for the discovery of grammatical morphemes."

One of the issues dealt with in Braine's chapter is that of the changing scope of the child's rules, a concern he shares with **Berman.** In her chapter, Berman develops a model in which the earliest phases of acquisition are lacking structure in any linguistically interesting sense, since the child's rules are then still "instance bound," i.e., defined on prototypical exemplars. The application of a rule (any rule) implies generalization. A grammatical rule will become operative only when the child begins to generalize from these exemplars.

Berman holds that in her attempts to bring order into the system the child's attention is not occupied by one type of category to the exclusion of others. Early categories, conditioning categories included, may be of various kinds: semantic, pragmatic, or formal. They develop out of a confluence of cues, which become unified into a system of classes on which the rules of grammar operate.

Reliance on very restricted early constructions is also a central feature of **Ninio's** theory. Like Braine and Berman, Ninio recognizes the special role of the predicate-argument distinction and proposes that it underlies the child's early two-word utterances. Her account of the child's earliest linguistic constructions is in the lexicalist tradition. She holds that the child starts out with constructions in which the predicate is typically a constant, i.e., a specific word rather than a set of words, whereas the argument is variable (a proposal akin in spirit to Braine's [1976] "limited scope formulae"; see also Schlesinger, this volume). These greatly restricted structures are only given up, on her account, when the child begins to learn hierarchical structures, that is, when she starts operating with constructions of more than two words.

One of the questions discussed at length by Ninio is whether it is admissible to credit the child with the formal categories of adult grammar. She observes that infantile categories do not fit the definitions of categories in the mature system. On the one hand, therefore, the use of the same terms for the child's early and mature categories is potentially misleading. On the other hand, a description of child language should make it apparent that many of the categories deployed stand in a part–whole relationship to the corresponding adult categories and, Ninio feels, this fact ought to be captured in their notation. She accordingly makes a novel notational proposal to deal with this dilemma.

For an example of a theory based on distributional analysis we now turn to **Wolff**'s chapter. Wolff holds that the child brings to the learning task "perceptual primitives"—the propensity to register sensory impressions—structure abstracting routines, and parsing procedures. The child's first categories, attained through distributional analysis of the linguistic input, are already formal in nature and include collocations of sounds and of words, and of classes of the same. For learning to get under way, she does not need to have any "preconceptions" as to what kinds of notions are expressed by language. In other words, acquisition is not dependent on her coming to the learning task equipped with semantic or pragmatic concepts. The child does not need to rely on meaning distinctions as a sort of crutch, as theorists like Ninio and Snow and Schlesinger have argued. Distributional analysis is a powerful enough tool for forging the first categories, proposes Wolff. He has shown by means of computer simulation that distributional analysis unaided by considerations of content may in fact be sufficient to account for the acquisition of at least sizable portions of the grammatical rule system.

Since formal categories appear in this model from the outset, one of the problems a theory based entirely on the acquisition of realizational rules (like Ninio and Snow's or Schlesinger's) has to deal with does not arise here. The problem is: How is the system reorganized so that it corresponds with that of the adult speaker? (It will be remembered from the previous section that other solutions of this problem are the expansion of a semantic core and the formation of conditional realization rules.) In a theory like Wolff's, acquisition is conceived of as a continuous process of refining the formal categories with which learning starts out.

Levy is basically in agreement with Wolff in respect to the role played by distributional analysis and regarding the early appearance of formal categories. She does not accept the reasoning that underlies the theories of those who argue that semantic and pragmatic notions are in some way easier for the child to operate with and thus provide her with a lever for breaking into the language system. Such a priori arguments for a sort of cognitive primacy of content categories carry little weight, according to Levy. Instead, she holds that the issue is a strictly empirical one and will have to be settled by a thorough examination of the data.

While Wolff supports his model through computer simulation (which may be regarded as a kind of feasibility proof), Levy marshals evidence from the acquisition of Hebrew arguing that the child masters from early on certain formal categories: word-classes as well as certain morphological categories. In acquiring these, the child does not capitalize on meaning distinctions with which these formal categories partially overlap. This establishes that the young child is perfectly capable of operating with formal categories, and will actually acquire them when they are frequently and systematically represented in the language.

Maratsos deals in his chapter with the acquisition of word classes. Grammatical categories, like noun, verb, and adjective are formally defined in adult grammar. There are certain semantic correlates (e.g., many nouns denote solid objects, many verbs refer to actions or states,), but Maratsos presents evidence that already at the earliest stages of child language word classes are not semantically homogeneous, and this implies that the semantic core hypothesis does not account for the acquisition of word classes. He maintains that these can be learned only through distributional analysis.

Although Maratsos adopts a distributional approach, as far as the acquisition of word classes is concerned, he believes that the presently available evidence bears out the claim of those theorists who hold that children's earliest categories are semantic. However, he argues that early semantic categories, like Action, do not seem to be operative in the formation of word classes.

3. AGREEMENT AMONG DISAGREEMENTS

Despite their divergent views of language acquisition, the contributors to this volume share some basic assumptions. They have in common the belief that language learning is essentially similar to other learning and involves the same kinds of cognitive mechanisms. The problem of language acquisition must be solved, on this view, within a general theory of learning. The contributors share a conception of the human mind that differs radically from the one implicated by nativist theories of language acquisition. Let us explain.

The formal categories discussed by Wolff, Levy, and Maratsos pertain to the surface string, and thus are relatively accessible to the child. For nativist theorists, the child's formal categories are largely deep structure categories, like underlying noun phrase, verb phrase, and so on. These are motivated by certain grammatical phenomena that are more complex than those typically encountered in early child language. The acquisition of rules pertinent to these is not dealt with by the contributors to the present volume and it remains to be seen to which extent their models will eventually prove capable of dealing with those phenomena. Nativists, at any rate, argue that theories like those of these authors are incapable in principle of accounting for the child's attaining the adult system. For this to be accomplished, they believe, a rich innate component is required. They therefore postulate specifically linguistic innate categories—such as noun, verb, and subject—by dint of which the child acquires the language.

Presupposing such a rich innate component, however, does not rid one of the following problem. It is not sufficient for the child to be endowed with linguistic categories unless he or she also has a way of identifying them in the input. To account for the ability to correctly identify the components of the utterance, Pinker (1984), following Grimshaw (1981) and Macnamara (1982), hypothesizes a **semantic bootstrapping** process. Pinker proposes that in analyzing input utterances, the infant assumes, so to speak, certain correspondences between perceptual and cognitive notions, on the one hand, and formal syntactic ones, on the other, and these presuppositions are also innate.

The innate formal categories are "flagged": Nouns correspond to objects, verbs to actions, the subject to the agent, and so on. When the child hears a word he or she knows to refer to an object, the noun category is triggered; on hearing a word referring to an action, the verb category is triggered; a phrase referring to the agent triggers the subject category, and so on, until the full set of formal categories needed for the construction of grammar have been bootstrapped. In the earliest stages of development these correspondences actually hold, in the majority of instances, in the adults' input to the child, and as a consequence the child will succeed in identifying the innate formal categories correctly.

It seems to us, that nativist theories like Pinker's (1984) may be viable without resorting to such an extensive bootstrapping process. Unlike Schlesinger, Ninio and Snow, and Braine, in Pinker's model a formal category that has been bootstrapped, continues to develop on the basis of its distributional features; in this sense his theory is similar to those of Levy, Maratsos and Wolff. Yet, the latter have shown that at least some linguistic distinctions for which Pinker invokes an innate bootstrapping process, can *arise* through distributional analysis.

Semantic bootstrapping, however, might still be needed for making the primary analysis of the surface string into predicate and argument(s) (see Braine). The postulation of an innate basis for this distinction would be quite in line with the positions of Berman, Braine, Levy and Maratsos.

4.   CRITERIA FOR EVALUATING THEORIES

Having presented the various theories espoused by the contributors to this volume, the question may be raised: How are these to be evaluated? Strictly speaking, such an evaluation is possible only in the case of a fully developed theory which makes specific predictions regarding the course of language learning. The theories presented in the present volume have not yet attained this stage. What we therefore do in this final section is propose a number of considerations that are relevant to theories even at this stage of development.

The first criterion for evaluation that comes to mind is the fit of the theory to the available data. It seems to us, however, that in the field of language acquisition the applicability of this criterion is severely limited. The kind of observational data presently available cannot be expected to decide between theories.

As a case in point let us look at the theoretical implications that have been claimed to hold for the very extensive collections of child language data now available. Several investigators (e.g., Braine, 1976) have noted that the linguistic input to children and the child's own linguistic productions preserve a close correspondence between semantic relations and grammatical functions, and have interpreted this as providing support for a semantic approach to early language. The same data, however, have been interpreted by other investigators—for instance by Ninio and Snow (this volume) as supporting a pragmatic approach. Again, Pinker (1984) views these data as consistent with his theory, according to which there are syntactic categories from early on. Rather than providing evidence for a semantically based grammar, the correspondence between semantic and syntactic categories in early word combinations attest, in his view, to a stage at which semantic bootstrapping is still going on. The observational findings, then, can be accommodated by widely differing theories.

Now, a similar state of affairs holds, of course, in many other fields: Theories, as is well known, are underdetermined by the data. But in the case of language acquisition theories, it seems to us to be in the nature of the available data that they do not permit one to arbitrate between theories. Observational data pertaining to child language can tell us, at best, what the child knows about her language at a given point of time, whereas a theory of language acquisition purports to tell how this knowledge is attained. Child language data and the theories built on them thus involve two logically distinct domains: the former pertain to a state and the latter to a process. The process normally eludes our observation. Significantly, there is hardly any study in the field that purports to show us the learning process in action.

As for experimental research, few experimental techniques are applicable to children at the age at which acquisition of grammar begins, and in any case, these can give us, at most, a glimpse of the child's knowledge, not of the process by which it is attained. And results of experiments with older children do not have unequivocal implications for processes operative at an earlier age.

Our data may show what knowledge there is; our theories then try to explain how this knowledge is arrived at. Now, a theory may make predictions about what the child knows at a certain stage of linguistic development and this prediction can obviously be disconfirmed. If, for instance, it could be shown that no rules based on formal distinctions appear in early language, this would provide support for the realizational approach, and the distributional approach would be in deep trouble. In fact, it has been shown that at least some formal distinctions are mastered by the child at a very early age. This is sufficient for retaining the distributional approach as a whole as a viable alternative. (That certain other formal distinctions appear only later may be due to their greater formal complexity.)

The point we wish to make is that the theoretical approaches reviewed in this chapter are all at a stage at which they can not be disconfirmed empirically, when one considers the approach as a whole. The theory developed within a given approach may make specific predictions, and the latter can of course be tested against the data. When a prediction is not borne out, this will require a revision of the theory in respect to certain details, and will not count against the theoretical approach as a whole.

Being buffeted by the data is what develops and refines a theory. It is with this aim in mind that we should obtain empirical findings, and not in order to show the untenability of a rival approach. To this end our theoretical formulations will have to be tightened up so that specific predictions emerge from them.

To illustrate, at their present stage of development no such predictions are yielded by those theories reviewed here that claim that the child starts out with content categories and develops formal categories only much later. This is because these theories postulate a process of change by which formal categories are acquired, i.e., the expansion of a semantic core or the acquisition of conditional realization rules. As long as the theory is stated in general terms and does not make some rather specific statements about the timing of these changes, it will be able to accommodate practically any finding about the nature of the child's categories. Suppose one comes up with the finding that, at a given developmental stage, the child's categories are formal. Then this will be accounted for by the theory as reflecting a stage at which the originally semantic or pragmatic categories have already developed into formal ones. The hypothesized process of change itself can of course still less readily be verified or refuted, since, as pointed out earlier, data on child language are only indirectly relevant to the process by which the child arrives at linguistic knowledge. To provide for falsifiability, such theories will therefore have to be spelled out in much greater detail.

Empirical findings, then, will not provide a sufficient basis for choosing between theoretical approaches. Instead, such a choice will be influenced largely by some very general and often not quite unequivocal criteria, such as parsimony and plausibility.

The methodological issue of parsimony has been prominent in some recent discussions in the literature in the form of claims about what have been called continuity theories being preferable to theories positing discontinuity in acquisition. In the following, we take a closer look at the issues involved here.

There is a consensus among linguists that the grammar of a language is defined in terms of formal categories. Constructs like subject, object, noun phrase, and prepositional phrase, which are the warp and woof of grammar, have no semantic definition. It follows that at some point of time the child must have acquired a set of formal categories.

Theories according to which the child's initial categories are semantic or pragmatic have to explain how these eventually change into formal ones. They therefore assume a discontinuity in development, as pointed out by Gleitman and Wanner (1982) and Pinker (1984), in contrast to nativist theories and theories that start out with formal categories, for which linguistic development is continuous. Gleitman and Wanner (1982) argue that continuity theories are preferable to discontinuity theories, other things being equal. They accede, however, that an account of early semantic categories is better supported by the available data and more commonsensical than one crediting the child with formal syntactic categories from early on. But the child must eventually learn a formal system. Hence, they observe, we are confronted with "a mismatch of plausibilities." We can opt for a discontinuity theory, which, besides having greater empirical support, is more plausible in that it starts out with semantic categories, but is less plausible in that it has to assume discontinuity. Alternatively, we can adopt a continuity theory, which posits formal syntactic categories from the outset, and is thus not so well supported by the data and less commonsensical. We cannot have it both ways.

The concept of continuity invoked by these authors stands in need of closer examination.

A theory may be discontinuous in that it makes claims about a qualitative change in the mechanisms implicated in development. Discontinuity of this type is involved, for instance, in the proposal that there are maturational changes due to which the child moves from an analysis of language in semantic terms to one based on formal syntactic notions (Gleitman, 1981).[5]

Note, however, that a theory claiming that the child starts out only with content categories is not necessarily committed to this invidious kind of discontinuity. The change from content categories to the formal ones of the adult system may be a gradual one and may occur without the introduction of any additional, qualitatively different process (cf. explanations based on the assumption of a semantic core, e.g., the semantic assimilation process proposed by Schlesinger; see also Braine, this volume, on this point). Theories of this kind are discontinuous only in the sense that the mature system of categories is claimed to be different from the child's early system. Therefore considerations of parsimony do not apply here.

*   *   *

The issue of the nature of early categories remains a controversial one and is likely to remain so for a long time. By marshalling arguments for their various conflicting views, the contributors to this volume will have helped to clarify the issues involved.

---

[5]Martin Braine has pointed out to us that theories which postulate a change from surface structure to deep structure categories also involve a qualitative change, and thus are open to the charge of discontinuity.

ACKNOWLEDGMENT

We are grateful to Moshe Anisfeld and to Martin Braine for many helpful comments on earlier versions of this chapter.

REFERENCES

Braine, M. D. S. (1976). Children's first word combinations. *Monographs of the Society for Research in Child Development, 41* (1, Serial No. 164).

Gathercole, V. C. (1985). 'He has too much hard questions': The acquisition of the linguistic mass-count distinction in *much* and *many*. *Journal of Child Language, 12,* 395–415.

Gleitman, L. R. (1981). Maturational determinants of language growth. *Cognition, 10,* 103–114.

Gleitman, L. R., & Wanner, E. (1982). Language acquisition: The state of the state of the art. In E. Wanner & L. R. Gleitman (Eds.), *Language acquisition: The state of the art.* Cambridge, England: Cambridge University Press.

Gordon, P. (1985). Evaluating the semantic categories hypothesis: The case of count/mass distinction. *Cognition, 20,* 209–242.

Grimshaw, J. (1981). Form, and function, and the language acquisition device. In C. L. Baker & J. J. McCarthy (Eds.), *The logical problem of language acquisition.* Cambridge, MA: MIT Press.

Hasher, L., & Zacks, R. T. (1984). Automatic processing of fundamental information. *American Psychologist, 39,* 1372–1388.

Macnamara, J. (1982). *Names for things: A study of child language.* Cambridge, MA: MIT Press.

Marantz, A. (1982). On the acquisition of grammatical relations. *Linguistische Berichte: Linguistik als kognitive Wissenschaft,* 80–82, 32–69.

Pinker, S. (1984). *Language learnability and language development,* Cambridge, MA: Harvard University Press.

Slobin, D. I. (1986). Crosslinguistic evidence for the language making capacity. In D. I. Slobin (Ed.), *The crosslinguistic study of language acquisition* (Vol. 2). Hillsdale, NJ: Lawrence Erlbaum Associates.

Author Index

Subject Index

281